T0252347

FUZZY EXPERT SYSTEMS AND FUZZY REASONING

FUZZY EXPERT SYSTEMS AND FUZZY REASONING

William Siler
Kemp-Carraway Heart Institute,
Birmingham, AL 35234

James J. Buckley
Mathematics Dept., University of Alabama at Birmingham,
Birmingham, AL 35294

WILEY-
INTERSCIENCE

JOHN WILEY & SONS, INC.

Library of Congress Cataloging-in-Publication Data:

Siler, William.
 Fuzzy expert systems and fuzzy reasoning / by William Siler, James J. Buckley.
  p. cm.
 Includes bibliographical references and index.
 ISBN 0-471-38859-9
  1. Expert systems (Computer science) 2. Fuzzy systems. I. Buckley, James J., 1936-II.
 Title

 QA76.76.E95S557 2005
 006.3'3–dc22

10 9 8 7 6 5 4 3 2 1

CONTENTS

PREFACE

In this book, we will explore the emulation of human thought, capable of dealing with uncertainties, ambiguities, and contradictions.

We agree with Anderson (1993) that much human thought can be expressed in rules (Anderson, 1993). To handle uncertainties, ambiguities, and contradictions, we will use fuzzy systems techniques, implemented by a fuzzy expert system. We supply the fuzzy expert system language FLOPS with this book, so that the readers can actually use our supplied example programs and write their own programs.

An overwhelmingly important fact about human reasoning is that it is not a static process. Data are gathered; some preliminary hypotheses are advanced and tested; some of these may be rejected, and new hypotheses advanced; more data may be required, until finally some conclusion is reached. A computer program to emulate reasoning must proceed similarly. Unfortunately, in much mathematical description of the thought process the dynamic nature is lost. We cannot afford to make this error.

Expert systems are computer programs, designed to make available some of the skills of an expert to nonexperts. Since such programs attempt to emulate in some way an expert's thinking patterns, it is natural that the first work here was done in Artificial Intelligence (AI) circles. Among the first expert systems were the 1965 Dendral programs (Feigenbaum and Buchanan, 1993), which determined molecular structure from mass spectrometer data; R1 (McDermott, 1980) used to configure computer systems; and MYCIN (Shortliffe, 1976) for medical diagnosis. Since the middle 1960s there have been many expert systems created for fields ranging from space shuttle operations through intensive-care-unit patient alarm systems to financial decision making.

There is a variety of ways in which the problem of creating computer programs to act like an expert has been approached; a valuable reference is Jackson (1999). One of the earliest methods employs *rule-based systems*, which use "If ... Then ... " rules to represent the expert's reasoning process (*if* the data meet certain specified conditions, *then* take appropriate actions). Other approaches include *semantic or associative nets* (Quillian, 1968), *frames* (Minsky, 1975) and *neural nets* (Haykin, 1994), currently very popular in a wide variety of fields. Of these, clearly dominant are the complementary rule-based systems and neural net approaches.

Neural nets do not require that the thinking patterns of an expert be explicitly specified. Instead, two sets of data are required from the real world. These data include all the inputs to the system, and the correct outputs corresponding to these input values. The first data set or *training set* is used to train the neural network so that, as nearly as possible, the correct outputs are produced for each set of input values. The second data set or *validation set* is used after the neural net has been trained to make sure that correct answers are produced on different input data. An advantage of neural nets is that it is not necessary to extract the thinking patterns of the expert and to render these explicit. Disadvantages are that a substantial training set is required, and that while the neural net may produce reasonably correct answers, in general, we have little or no idea how it does this. Considerable work has been done on extracting rules from a trained neural net, but this work is not yet advanced to a very satisfactory state.

Rule-based systems require that the expert's knowledge and thinking patterns be explicitly specified. Usually two persons (or groups) develop a system. These are the *domain expert*, who knows how to solve the problem at hand but who is seldom acquainted with computer programming; and the *knowledge engineer*, who is thoroughly familiar with the computer technology involved and expert systems but who has little or no knowledge of the problem at hand. Obtaining this knowledge and writing proper rules is called the *knowledge acquisition* phase (Scott et al., 1991). After the system has been written, it must be tuned for accuracy using a tuning data set similar to the training set of a neural net, but usually much smaller. After tuning, a rule-based system must be validated in the same way as a neural net. Rule-based systems have two advantages. A large training set is usually not required, and since the expert's thinking is explicitly spelled out we now know how he thinks about the problem. They have the disadvantage that the knowledge acquisition phase may be difficult. A great advantage of fuzzy expert systems is that most rules can be written in language that the expert can directly understand, rather than in computer jargon; communication between domain expert and knowledge engineer is greatly eased.

Another advantage of rule-based expert systems is the potential ability of rule-based expert systems to learn by creation of new rules and addition of new data to the expert knowledge data base. Probably the first example of a rule-based expert system to rival human experts was DENDRAL, which deduced the molecular structure of organic compounds from knowledge about fragments into which the compound had been broken (Jackson, 1999, pp. 383 ff). One set of DENDRAL's programs worked directly with the data to produce candidate structures. An additional program, Meta-DENDRAL, worked directly with the DENDRAL rules to improve them and discover new rules, thus discovering new concepts about the data. Meta-DENDRAL was not itself written as a rule-based expert system, but the ability of a rule to generate new rules and new expert factual knowledge opens the possibility for writing expert systems that can create new rules and store new expert factual knowledge. This exciting possibility has not as yet been well explored, perhaps due to the common (and, we think, quite incorrect) assumption among conventional AI practitioners that expert systems are no longer to be considered as artificial intelligence.

Rules, called *production rules* or simply *productions* have a long history in computer science, ranging from the simple "if ... then ..." statements employed in such computer languages as BASIC, FORTRAN, and C to complex systems especially designed for processing rules such as the OPS family of languages by Charles Forgy (Brownston et al., 1985) and the AI language Prolog and its fuzzy version Fril (Baldwin et al., 1995). Their use in AI for psychological modeling was pioneered by Newell and Simon (1972), and in expert systems by a number of AI pioneers (Buchanan and Shortliffe, 1984). Certainly rule-based expert systems are capable of emulating human thought patterns that are well defined; they are also capable of emulating human learning, as we shall show. An appreciable body of thought, especially among cognitive psychologists, agrees (Anderson, 1993). Since the authors are deeply interested in the emulation of human thought, this book is concerned with rule-based expert systems.

The systems we describe require that the knowledge engineer/programmer learn three important new concepts: non-procedural data-driven languages; fuzzy systems theory (fuzzy logic, fuzzy sets, and fuzzy numbers); and a parallel language, rather than the conventional one-statement-at-a-time languages that dominate programming at the present.

Most of the systems we shall describe are *data-driven* and *nonprocedural*. Common computer languages (C, Fortran, Basic) are *procedural*; that is, program statements are executed in the order in which they appear, unless explicit transfers of control are executed. In data-driven rule-based programs, rules may be fired (executed), whenever the data permit and the rules are enabled; the sequence in which the rules appear in the program has little or nothing to do with the order in which they are executed.

The systems are based on fuzzy systems theory, and include data types new to most programmers: *fuzzy sets*, *fuzzy numbers*, and *truth values*. The use of discrete fuzzy sets permits convenient handling of ambiguities and contradictions. All data and rules are associated with *truth values* or *confidences*.

Finally, rules may be fired either *sequentially*, one rule at a time, or may be fired effectively in *parallel*. (Few programmers have any experience with parallel languages.)

The effect of these new concepts is a considerable increase in both power and speed of conventional expert systems, at the expense of some mind stretching.

The FTP site that accompanies this book has a complete demonstration version of a fuzzy expert system Integrated Development Environment (IDE) and run-time package, and a number of example programs. Whenever possible, we use extremely simple examples to illustrate the techniques involved. We hope the reader will not confuse *simple* with *trivial*. For example, in illustrating a blackboard system example programs will exchange one word of information; if we can exchange one word, we can exchange a dozen or a thousand. Our examples of programs that learn are equally simple.

Most books written for academic use concentrate on presenting didactic knowledge. This book, while presenting a fair amount of didactic knowledge, concentrates on teaching a *skill*: actually writing and debugging a fuzzy expert system. This is by no means an easy task. Learning how to construct a fuzzy expert system by reading a book is much like learning how to play tennis by reading a book; you have to play the game, hit keys, write and debug programs on the computer. The theory of fuzzy mathematics is highly advanced; with the exception of fuzzy control systems, the theory behind fuzzy expert systems for other than numeric outputs is quite ill developed. Much of the fuzzy expert systems theory in this book is original, and sometimes differs substantially from existing theory. For fuzzy reasoning, as distinct from fuzzy control (in which there are several excellent books), there is little literature to which we can refer, except for the work of William Combs, Earl Cox, James Baldwin and his colleagues and Nikola Kasabov; consequently, there are far fewer references listed than is usual in a technical book. We hope that the theory in this book will stimulate others to develop the theory of multistep fuzzy reasoning further.

The debt that those of us in the fuzzy field owe to Professor Lotfi Zadeh is incalculable; see Klir and Yuan (1996) for a selection of his most important papers, and Klir and Yuan (1995) for an exposition of the most important concepts in fuzzy systems theory. Not only did he originate the entire field and define its basic concepts many years ago, but also he continues through the years to challenge and inspire us with new ideas. We can only thank him and wish him many more productive years.

WILLIAM SILER
JAMES J. BUCKLEY

A hair perhaps divides the false from true.
—The Rubaiyat of Omar Khayam, translated by Edward Fitzgerald.

1 Introduction

The objective of this book is simple: to enable the reader to construct successful real-world fuzzy expert systems for problem solving. Accomplishing this objective, however, is not simple. We must not only transmit a good deal of knowledge in several different fields, but must also transmit the skills necessary to use this diverse knowledge fruitfully. To do this, we have concentrated on techniques that are simple in themselves, and that embody considerable power in problem solving. The examples we have chosen to illustrate these techniques are also must often quite simple. But do not be misled; there is a vast difference between "simple" and "trivial".

Our scope will be, of necessity, somewhat larger than the preceding paragraph might indicate. In real life, we solve problems by thinking about them; we must therefore deal with the emulation of human thought by a computer program. In real life, we do not often think about problems as conventional computers do; we deal constantly with uncertainties, ambiguities, and contradictions. We sometimes use deductive logic, but more often we think intuitively, assembling information relevant to a problem, scanning it and coming to a conclusion. Besides this, we can often learn from our experience.

Expert systems tend to be viewed as retarded children by conventional artificial intelligence practitioners. Indeed, a conventional expert system may not have sufficient capabilities for meaningful emulation of thought. There may be two reasons for this: insufficient capability for emulating complex thought patterns; and lack of capability for understanding natural language. FLOPS addresses the first of these problems; it does not address the second, and still relies on a formal language. The FLOPS language does, however, permit emulating thought patterns of considerable complexity, including two different types of learning.

This book will have far fewer references than would normally be expected in a book of this type. There is a reason for this. Fuzzy systems theory has had a major impact on the field of process control, and in this field there are many references to be found. But this book reports theory and methods for general purpose reasoning, a much more difficult task than process control, and a field in which there has been very little research and very few meaningful papers published. There are books by Kandel (1991) and Kasabov (1998) that deal with fuzzy expert systems, but not in the detail necessary to actually construct one other than

Fuzzy Expert Systems and Fuzzy Reasoning, By William Siler and James J. Buckley
ISBN 0-471-38859-9 Copyright © 2005 John Wiley & Sons, Inc.

for control, nor in the requirements that the emulation of though places on general-purpose fuzzy reasoning systems.

Computer programming of rule-based fuzzy expert systems can be difficult for those trained in Western dichotomous thinking. There are three novel concepts involved: *fuzzy systems theory*; *nonprocedural data-driven programming*; *and parallel programming*. Fuzzy systems theory permits handling uncertainties, ambiguities, and contradictions. Nonprocedural data-driven programming means that when FLOPS is in run mode and firing (executing) rules, the order in which rules are fired has nothing to do with the order in which they appear in the program, but only on the available data and on which rules or blocks of rules are enabled or disabled for firing. (Conventional procedural languages execute their statements *sequentially* in the order in which they are written, except for explicit transfers of control.) *Parallel programming* language means that all fireable rules are executed effectively at once instead of some predefined order.

In Chapters 1 and 2, we treat the basic programming problems. Chapters 3–5 deal with the requisite fuzzy mathematics involved; Chapters 6 and 7 treat methods of fuzzy reasoning, that is, inferring new truths. Chapter 8 deals with fuzzy expert system shells, the integrated development environments for constructing fuzzy expert systems. Chapters 9–12 handle increasingly sophisticated problem-solving techniques. Finally, Chapter 13 considers real-time on-line expert systems in which the data are automatically acquired from an external source. Because of the number of concepts and techniques that are unfamiliar to many readers, we have occasionally covered a topic more than once in different contexts to avoid flipping back and forth in the book.

1.1 CHARACTERISTICS OF EXPERT SYSTEMS

Expert systems are computer programs, designed to make available some of the skills of an expert to nonexperts. Since such programs attempt to emulate the thinking patterns of an expert, it is natural that the first work was done in Artificial Intelligence (AI) circles. Among the first expert systems were the 1965 Dendral programs (Feigenbaum and Buchanan, 1993), which determined molecular structure from mass spectrometer data; R1 (McDermott, 1980) used to configure computer systems; and MYCIN (Shortliffe, 1976) for medical diagnosis. Since the mid-1960s there have been many, many expert systems created for fields ranging from space shuttle operations through hospital intensive-care-unit patient monitoring to financial decision making. To create expert systems, it is usual to supply a development environment and possibly a run-time module; these are called expert system shells, of which a number are available. We can view human knowledge as *declarative* (facts we have in stored in memory), and *procedural*, skills in utilizing declarative knowledge to some purpose.

Most AI practitioners do not consider expert systems as deserving the name of Artificial Intelligence. For example, Schank (1984, p. 34) states: "Real intelligence demands the ability to learn, to reason from experience, to *shoot from the hip*, to use general knowledge, to make inferences using gut-level intuition. Expert systems can do none of these. They do not improve as a result of experience. They just move on to the next if/then rule". The Random House unabridged dictionary gives one definition of learning as "the act or process of acquiring knowledge or skill"; certainly an expert system, by adding to its database of facts, acquires knowledge, and by adding new rules acquires skill. *FLOPS permits both of the learning techniques.* While we agree with Schank's categorization of "Real intelligence", we cannot agree that "Expert systems can do none of these". FLOPS can construct new rules and add to its existing database of factual knowledge, and in parallel mode can scan a database quickly without the inordinate systems overhead required by sequential systems. These capabilities deny Schank's blanket statement that expert systems are incapable of any of the characteristics of real intelligence.

There is a variety of ways in which the problem of creating computer programs to act like an expert has been approached (Jackson, 1999). The earliest employs *rule-based systems*, which use If-Then rules to represent the expert's reasoning process (*if* the data meet certain specified conditions, *then* take appropriate actions). There is a respectable body of opinion among cognitive scientists that a very significant part of human reasoning can be expressed by rules (Anderson, 1993); this view lends additional interest to rule-based systems. Other approaches include *semantic or associative nets* (Quillian, 1968), *frames* (Minsky, 1975) and *neural nets*, currently very popular in a wide variety of fields. Of these, clearly dominant are the complementary rule-based systems and neural net approaches.

We are concerned in this book with representing procedural knowledge by rules; *IF* the available facts meet certain criteria *THEN* do whatever the rule specifies. Declarative (factual) knowledge may be represented by stored data.

Whatever type of expert system is employed, we must consider what the prerequisites are for constructing a successful system. The two primary sources of knowledge are the skills of an expert in the field, and available historical data. Rule-based expert systems rely considerably on incorporating the skills of an expert in the problem domain, but relatively little on historical data; neural networks rely heavily on an extensive historical database, and relatively little on a domain expert.

1.1.1 Production Systems

We distinguish between two types of expert systems; *procedural* systems, written in conventional procedural languages such as C++, and *production systems*, that employ rules of the type "IF (the data meet certain specified conditions) THEN (perform the specified actions)". The "IF" part of the rule is called the *antecedent*; the "THEN" part is the *consequent*.

The "Tower of Hanoi" is a typical AI toy problem. We have three vertical spindles; on one spindle we have a number of disks of decreasing diameter from the bottom up. The problem is to move the disks from one spindle to another, one disk at a time, never placing a disk on top of one of smaller diameter. A production rule from this problem might be

```
rule (goal Fires if only one disk to move)
IF (in Spindles n = 1 AND source = <S> AND destination = <D>)
THEN
    write "*** move <S> to <D> ***\n",
    delete 1;
```

In the antecedent of this rule, Spindles is a data structure containing items n (number of disks on the spindle), source (name of the spindle from which we are moving a disk) and destination (name of the spindle to which we are moving a disk). If there exists an instance of Spindles in which n is 1, source has some value <S> (whatever it is) and destination has some value <D>, then we write a message to the screen and delete the instance of Spindles. A production system may contain dozens, hundreds, or even thousands of rules.

1.1.2   Data-Driven Systems

Of especial interest are *data-driven production systems*. Such languages are quite different from the common procedural languages like C, Pascal, Fortran, or Basic. In a procedural language, the statements that comprise a major part of the language are executed in the order in which they appear (unless a specific transfer of control is encountered); in a data-driven language, the rules that comprise a major part of the language are candidates for execution whenever the data satisfy the data specifications in the "IF" part of the rule.

If the data satisfy more than one rule at once, common rule-based languages such as the well-known OPS languages fire their rules *sequentially*, one at a time. First, we determine which rules are made fireable by the data. Next, a *rule-conflict algorithm* decides which of these should be executed (*fired*). The fireable rules that were *not* picked for firing are usually placed on a stack for firing later on in case no rules are newly fireable (backtracking). The selected rule is fired, that is the THEN part of the rule is executed, and we go back to looking for newly fireable rules.

1.1.3   Special Features of Fuzzy Systems

Most fuzzy expert systems provide for *parallel* firing of concurrently fireable rules; that is, all fireable rules are fired effectively at one time, emulating a parallel computer. Parallel operation has several advantages for fuzzy systems. A parallel language is especially appropriate when working with fuzzy sets: It makes programming easier and runs considerably faster than an equivalent sequential system. But sequential programming has advantages too in some cases; it is appropriate for eliciting information from a user when each question to be asked depends on the answer to the previous question. Accordingly, a fuzzy expert system language should provide both sequential and parallel rule-firing mode. These features of a fuzzy expert system language, unfamiliar to most programmers, creates a steep learning curve. The budding fuzzy expert system builder has to learn:

- Working with IF-THEN rules as the primary element of the language.
- Learning the basics of fuzzy systems theory: fuzzy sets, fuzzy logic, and fuzzy numbers.
- Learning a data-driven non-procedural language.
- Working with both sequential and parallel language execution.

To ease the entry into such novel languages, it is extremely important that the integrated program development environment (IDE) provide a solid base of help files to the user, as well as a variety of both simple tutorial and simplified real-world programs.

1.1.4 Expert Systems for Fuzzy Control and for Fuzzy Reasoning

There are two general types of fuzzy expert systems: fuzzy control and fuzzy reasoning. Although both make use of fuzzy sets, they differ qualitatively in methodology.

Fuzzy process control was first successfully achieved by Mamdani (1976) with a fuzzy system for controlling a cement plant. Since then, fuzzy control has been widely accepted, first in Japan and then throughout the world. A basic simple fuzzy control system is simply characterized. It accepts numbers as input, then translates the input numbers into linguistic terms such as Slow, Medium, and Fast (*fuzzification*). Rules then map the input linguistic terms onto similar linguistic terms describing the output. Finally, the output linguistic terms are translated into an output number (*defuzzification*). The syntax of the rules is convenient for control purposes, but much too restrictive for fuzzy reasoning; defuzzification and defuzzification are automatic and inescapable. There are several development environments available for constructing fuzzy control systems. A typical fuzzy control rule might be

- IF input1 is High AND input2 is Low THEN output is Zero.

Rules for fuzzy reasoning cannot be described so compactly. The application domain of fuzzy control systems is well defined; they work very satisfactorily with input and output restricted to numbers. But the domain of fuzzy reasoning systems is not well defined; by definition, fuzzy reasoning systems attempt to emulate human thought, with no *a priori* restrictions on that thought. Fuzzy control systems deal with numbers; fuzzy reasoning systems can deal with both numeric and non-numeric data. Inputs might be temperature and pulse, where temperature might 38.5°C and pulse might be 110 and "thready", where "thready" is clearly non-numeric. Output might be "CBC" and "Admit" and "transfer MICU" (not very realistic, but illustrates non-numeric data input and output). Accordingly, rules for fuzzy reasoning do not make fuzzification and defuzzification automatic and inescapable; they may be broken out as separate operations that may or may not be performed as the problem requires.

The syntax of fuzzy reasoning rules accepts a wide variety of rule types. Here are two.

1. IF symptom is Depressive and duration is $\sim>$ about 6) THEN diagnosis is Major_depression;

   This rule resembles a fuzzy control rule, but it is actually quite different. In a fuzzy control rule, "symptom" would be a scalar number; in the fuzzy reasoning rule, "symptom is a (fuzzy) set of linguistic terms of which "depressive" is a member. Similarly, in a fuzzy control rule "diagnosis" would be a scalar number; in the fuzzy reasoning rules, "diagnosis" is a (fuzzy) set of diagnoses of which "depressive" is a member.

2. Rule block 8 (goal Generates rule for response to conditioned stimuli)

```
IF (in Count id1 = <ID2> AND id2 = <ID1> AND N > 2)
   (in Wired-in id = <ID2> AND response = <R>)
THEN
    rule block 3 (goal Conditions stimulus <ID1> to
    stimulus <ID2>)
    IF (in NewStimulus id = "<ID2>")
    THEN
      message '<ID1> - LOOK OUT - <ID2> coming\, <R>!\n';
```

A rule for learning, this rule has no counterpart at all in fuzzy control. Under specified circumstances, a new rule is created associating previously unassociated stimulus so that (e.g.) the burnt child learns to dread the fire.

1.2 NEURAL NETS

Neural nets (Haykin, 1994) do not require that the thinking patterns of an expert be explicitly specified. Instead, two sets of data are required from the real world. These data include all the inputs to the system, and the correct outputs corresponding to these input values. The first data set or *training set* is used to train the neural network so that, as nearly as possible, the correct outputs are produced for each set of input values. The second data set or *validation set* is used after the neural net has been trained to make sure that correct answers are produced on different input data. An advantage of neural nets is that it is not necessary to extract the thinking patterns of an expert and to render these explicit. Disadvantages are that a substantial training set is required, and that while the neural net may produce reasonably correct answers, in general we have little or no idea how it does this. Considerable work has been done on extracting rules from a trained neural net, but this work is not yet advanced to a very satisfactory state. A rough comparison between neural nets and expert systems is shown in Table 1.1.

TABLE 1.1 Comparison of Fuzzy Rule-Based Systems and Neural Nets

Property	Fuzzy Expert System	Neural Net
Data required to construct system	Minimal	Considerable
Expert knowledge required to construct system	Considerable	Minimal

Conditions under which neural nets may be the best approach include the following:

- There are ample data to form a training set of actual inputs and correct outputs corresponding to the inputs.
- No one has a good idea how outputs are related to inputs.
- We are not particularly interested in how inputs and outputs are related, so long as the system works.

The first of these conditions must be met; the second militates strongly in favor of a neural net; and the third helps incline us toward a neural net.

Conditions under which a fuzzy expert system is likely to be better than a neural net:

- We have a domain expert who knows fairly well how inputs and outputs are related.
- We do not have sufficient data to form a training set, possibly because the possible combinations of inputs and outputs are too numerous, or because collecting a training set would be prohibitively expensive.
- We are quite interested in the way in which outputs can be derived from inputs.

The first condition is almost essential, although a very skilled knowledge engineer may be able to become a domain expert with the dedicated help of persons less than fully expert in the understanding the task to be performed.

1.3 SYMBOLIC REASONING

Key to expert systems (and to AI generally, for that matter) is the concept of *reasoning with symbols*. (Ordinary procedural computer languages such as C and Fortran use symbols, but in a more restricted context.) In procedural languages such as C, symbols can represent numerical or character string data, or a collection of such data in data structures. Symbols can also represent logical propositions (simple Boolean comparisons between simple data items), program flow control by such constructs as "if ...", "for ...", and "while ...", and smaller subprograms (functions). In object-oriented programs, symbols can represent *objects*, collections of both data items and functions. However, for the *symbolic reasoning* required by AI, symbols can represent almost anything, and languages more appropriate than

C or FORTRAN for symbol manipulation are used, such as LISP and PROLOG. For expert systems, specialized AI-based languages for rule-based reasoning such as the OPS family, Prolog, and CLIPS can be used.

For fuzzy expert systems, using familiar words as symbols to represent such concepts as fuzzy sets, fuzzy numbers, uncertainties, and modifying words (adjectives and adverbs) called *hedges*, special languages are available such as METUS (Cox, 1999); FLOPS, a fuzzy superset of OPS5, described in this book; and FRIL, a fuzzy superset of PROLOG (Baldwin et al., 1995). There are also special languages for fuzzy process control, but while very good for that purpose they lack the generality usually expected of an expert system language.

The buzz-word phrase "Computing with Words" has been very popular with fuzzy systems people for some years now. However, their use of words has been largely confined to words that describe numbers. This severe and very unfortunate limitation has greatly handicapped developing the enormous potential power of fuzzy systems theory. FLOPS is intended to permit emulation of human thought, although it has a long way to go to complete its objective; consequently, we must be concerned with words in a much more general sense than fuzzy control programs. At a minimum, we must think of words as parts of speech: nouns (e.g., age), simple verbs (equals), adverbs (approximately), conjunctions ("and") and adjectives (about), and define these appropriately (in the semantic sense) and precisely (say in Backus-Nauer Form) for our computer language.

1.4   DEVELOPING A RULE-BASED EXPERT SYSTEM

Rule-based systems require that the expert's knowledge and thinking patterns be explicitly specified. Usually, two persons (or groups) develop a system together. These are the *domain expert*, who knows how to solve the problem at hand but who is seldom acquainted with computer programming; and the *knowledge engineer*, who is thoroughly familiar with the computer technology involved and expert systems, but who usually has little or no knowledge of the problem at hand. Obtaining this knowledge and writing proper rules is called the *knowledge acquisition* phase (Scott et al., 1991). After the system has been written, it must be tuned for accuracy using a tuning data set similar to the training set of a neural net, but usually much smaller. After tuning, a rule-based system must be validated in the same way as a neural net. Rule-based systems have two advantages. A large training set is usually not required, and since the expert's thinking is explicitly spelled out, we now know how he thinks about the problem. They have the disadvantage that the knowledge acquisition phase may be difficult. A great advantage of fuzzy expert systems is that the rules can be written in language that the expert can directly understand, such as "if age is about 40" or "if patient is very old", rather than in computer jargon. Communication between domain expert and knowledge engineer is thus greatly eased.

Another advantage of rule-based expert systems is their ability to learn by creation of new rules. Probably the first example of a rule-based expert system to rival human experts was DENDRAL, which deduced the molecular structure of organic compounds from knowledge about fragments into which the compound had been broken (Jackson, 1999, pp. 383 ff). One set of DENDRAL's programs worked directly with the data to produce candidate structures. An additional program, Meta-DENDRAL, worked directly with the DENDRAL rules to improve them and discover new rules, thus discovering new concepts about the data. Meta-DENDRAL was not itself written as a rule-based expert system, but the ability of a rule to generate new rules and new expert factual knowledge opens the possibility for writing an expert system that can create new rules and store new expert factual knowledge. This exciting possibility has not as yet been well explored, perhaps due to the general (and, we think, incorrect) assumption that expert systems are no longer to be considered as artificial intelligence.

Many years ago the British scientist Alan Turing proposed a test for machine intelligence. In one room, we have a computer terminal with a human operator. This master terminal is linked to two other rooms. In one of these rooms we have a computer; in the other, a terminal with a human operator. If the operator at the master terminal cannot detect which of the other two rooms has the computer, then the computer's program can be called intelligent. There is no restriction on how the computer program does what it does; its performance is all the Turing test considers.

Our interest is not in passing the Turing test. Instead, we are interested in the nature of a computer program; we would like it to be constructed so as to emulate the thought processes of a human and particularly those thought patterns that can be verbally expressed. If a computer program *acts* as if it were intelligent, but does so through symbol manipulations that have little or no connection to normal thought, we are not especially interested.

As we have mentioned, a substantial body of thought, stemming largely from the work of Artificial Intelligence pioneer Allen Newell, contends that much verbal reasoning can be successfully expressed in *production rules*, called here simply *rules* (Anderson, 1993). We subscribe to this line of thought. Rules take the form "IF the data available meet certain specified conditions THEN take these specified actions", in which "actions" should be viewed in a very broad context, including drawing conclusions, firm or tentative. A sample simple rule might be "IF the car engine will not turn over when attempting to start THEN check if the battery is discharged". A more complex fuzzy rule might be "IF the pulmonary artery systolic pressure is considerably reduced AND the diastolic pressure is at least normal THEN the pressure reading might be damped".

1.5 FUZZY RULE-BASED SYSTEMS

Fuzzy rule-based systems, in addition to providing convenient handling of uncertainties of values (which can be done in other ways), furnish several additional capabilities. Approximate numerical values can be specified as fuzzy numbers. Numerical input values can be easily translated into descriptive words such as

"Fast" or "Large". Ambiguities and contradictions are easily handled by discrete fuzzy sets. Modifying words such as "very" and "slightly" are easily incorporated into the rule syntax. The approximate versions of the full range of Boolean numerical comparisons such as "$\sim<=$" or "approximately less than or equal to" are easily implemented. Most of our experience with fuzzy rule-based systems has been gained over the past 15 years using the fuzzy expert system shell FLOPS (Siler et al., 1987), and this book will rely heavily on that language. We have shared experiences and ideas with Earl Cox (1999, 2000), who developed the fuzzy expert system shell Metus, and who has deployed many expert systems using that language. We are also aware of the important PROLOG-based shell FRIL by Baldwin et al. (1995). The FLOPS language is still under development, but it does provide most of the features discussed here.

Fuzzy rule-based systems capable of both sequential and parallel rule processing add additional features to conventional expert system languages: convenient handling of uncertainties, ambiguities and contradictions, and modifying words such as "very" and "somewhat". Thus fuzzy systems increase our ability to emulate the non-rigid thinking patterns of (say) physicians and biologists as well as the relatively rigid patterns of (say) computer scientists. It is very unfortunate that most fuzzy expert systems have been devoted to control applications, and hence have concentrated almost exclusively on symbols that represent numerical quantities. While the enormous success of fuzzy control systems makes this understandable, it means that the ability of fuzzy rule-based systems to emulate reasoning with both numeric and non-numeric quantities remains to a large extent unexplored. We hope that this book will help illustrate the capabilities and potentialities of fuzzy rule-based systems for the emulation of thought in a much more general sense.

Most if not all human thinking is initially nonverbal. However, we have become reasonably successful in translating some thought into words (How can I say this?); knowledge engineers spend a great deal of time with domain experts converting their thought patterns into words, an hence to rules. Some nonverbal thought can be expressed in mathematical terms (e.g., feature extraction from images). A decent expert system language should enable writing a computer program using both words and mathematical transformations.

1.6 PROBLEMS IN LEARNING HOW TO CONSTRUCT FUZZY EXPERT SYSTEMS

The first problem for the knowledge engineer is to become adept at a different kind of computer language. Next is the problem of acquiring relevant knowledge from the domain expert. Finally, there are the problems of writing, debugging, calibrating, and validating the expert system itself.

Rule-based expert systems, and especially fuzzy expert systems, pose some learning problems for the programmer used to procedural languages such as C, Fortran, or Basic. Rules are basically IF statements: IF (this is true) THEN (execute the following instructions.) The IF part of a rule is called the *antecedent*, and the

THEN part is called the consequent. At this level, there does not seem to be any substantial difference between a rule-based expert system and a conventional C or Fortran program. However, the most powerful expert systems are not executed in a step-by-step procedural fashion, in which statements are executed in the order in which they appear, unless a specific transfer-of-control instruction is encountered. Instead, many expert system programs are *data-driven*; that is, rule are executed (fired) whenever the data sufficiently satisfy the antecedent, regardless of the sequence in which the rules appear in the program. This immediately creates the first problem—what do we do if the data satisfy the antecedents of two or more rules simultaneously? If we select one of these rules for firing next, what do we do with the fireable but unfired rules? Alternatively, we might elect to fire all the concurrently fireable rules effectively in parallel. Very few programmers have any experience with parallel languages—most of us have experience only with languages in which the instructions are executed sequentially. Another problem involves running time—if we change a piece of data, must we then examine all the rules over again to see which ones are now newly fireable? Charles Forgy's RETE algorithm goes a long way to solving that problem, but running time for a data-driven expert system is still long compared to procedural language programs, a price paid for the flexibility of data-driven systems and their inherent similarity to human thought patterns.

Another learning problem involves the use of multivalued logic. In a fuzzy expert system, things may be completely true, completely false, or anything in between. Ambiguities abound in fuzzy systems, and contradictions are frequently encountered; fuzzy systems provide structured ways of handling uncertainties, ambiguities, and contradictions, none of which are ordinarily encountered in conventional computer programming. Fuzzy systems also employ some special terms and concepts: fuzzy sets, fuzzy numbers, and membership functions. Monotonic and non-monotonic reasoning become routine concepts and acquire special meaning.

All this means that a fair amount of effort is required to become fluent in a fuzzy expert system language. There are, however, some bright points. You will be able to write rules using common words such as "very slow", "somewhat", and "roughly 60", making communication between knowledge engineer and domain expert much easier.

1.7 TOOLS FOR LEARNING HOW TO CONSTRUCT FUZZY EXPERT SYSTEMS

While this book aims to provide the reader with some theoretical and practical knowledge about fuzzy expert systems (which might be useful in passing an examination), we also aim to teach the reader a *skill* in constructing these systems in the real world. It is impossible to teach a skill without practice; if the reader does not actually run and write programs, he will no more learn this skill than a person who tries to learn to play tennis by reading books and listening to classroom lectures.

The CD Rom that accompanies this book has important tools to aid the reader. First, there are the two major programs: FLOPS itself, the inference engine and run-time

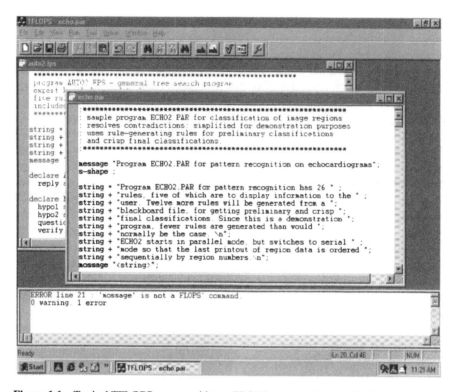

Figure 1.1   Typical TFLOPS screen, with two FLOPS programs being edited and an... error log from a FLOPS run.

environment for executing and debugging FLOPS programs; and TFLOPS, the IDE for writing and testing FLOPS programs. Extensive help files are available in both FLOPS and TFLOPS, including an on-line manual and basic fuzzy math tutorial. Second, there is a fairly large number of example FLOPS programs, both tutorial and simplified versions of working expert systems. Third, there are simple specialized programs to illustrate some theoretical points made in this book. The reader is urged to make full use of these tools, especially TFLOPS for editing and running FLOPS programs. A typical TFLOPS screen is shown in Figure 1.1.

1.8   AUXILIARY READING

While this book is designed to be self-sufficient for our major purpose, we also recommend some auxiliary reading for readers with special interests. Jackson (1999) gives excellent coverage of non-fuzzy expert systems, although his treatment of fuzzy expert systems leaves very much to be desired. Klir and Yuan (1996) give in-depth coverage of modern fuzzy mathematics. Scott et al. (1991) cover issues of knowledge acquisition by the knowledge engineer. Anderson (1993) discusses rules from the viewpoint of a cognitive scientist interested in how the mind functions.

Finally, Cox (1999) presents much information on fuzzy expert systems from the viewpoint of finance and management; his discussion of modifying words used in rules, such as "somewhat", "very", and so on (called *hedges*) is unsurpassed, and his experience in constructing real-world fuzzy expert systems is extensive.

1.9 SUMMARY

Expert systems are computer programs designed to bring an expert's skill to solving a particular problem. The most common types of expert systems are rule-based programs and neural networks. These differ considerably in the availability of expert knowledge and data required to construct the system, although there is little difference in the data required to validate the system once constructed.

Production systems are rule-based systems whose rule syntax is "IF (the data satisfy these specified conditions) THEN (perform these specified actions". The "IF" part of the rule is the antecedent; the "THEN" part is the consequent. Production systems are most often data driven; that is, the eligibility of a rule for firing depends solely on the data, and is independent of the rule's placement in the program. During a program run, the truth value of a rule's antecedent is calculated; if the antecedent is sufficiently true, the rule is eligible for firing. If sequential rule-firing has been chosen, one of the rules whose antecedents are sufficiently true is chosen for firing by a rule-conflict algorithm; if parallel rule-firing has been chosen, all fireable rules are fired, effectively in parallel. Because of the features of a fuzzy expert system language which are unfamiliar to most programmers, it is especially important to have a good IDE, which makes available good help files on a number of topics. Special debugging tools should be available.

Two types of persons usually develop rule-based expert systems: domain expert and knowledge engineer. Ideally, the domain expert is thoroughly familiar with the problem domain and how to solve problems that arise in that domain, but who may be completely ignorant of computer programming and expert systems. The knowledge engineer, in contrast, is thoroughly familiar with expert system tools and with the construction of expert systems, but may be completely ignorant of the problem domain. These two work together on the expert system's construction, sharing knowledge and skills.

1.10 QUESTIONS

1.1 In what three respects does FLOPS differ from conventional programming languages?

1.2 How does a data-driven non-procedural language differ from conventional procedural languages?

1.3 What can a language using fuzzy mathematics do that conventional programming languages cannot?

1.4   What is the difference between a parallel and a sequential program?

1.5   In what major respect can FLOPS programs conform to Roger Schank's definition of intelligence?

1.6   In what fundamental respects do expert systems differ from neural networks?

1.7   How do expert systems for fuzzy control differ from those for fuzzy reasoning?

1.8   What two kinds of people are usually involved in the construction of an expert system?

1.9   In what major respects do fuzzy expert systems differ from nonfuzzy systems?

1.10   What problems are encountered when first constructing a fuzzy expert system?

1.11   What important tool should be available for constructing a fuzzy expert system?

2 Rule-Based Systems: Overview

Throughout this and other chapters of this book, we will make extensive use of the demonstration programs supplied on the CD ROM, which accompanies this book. Remember that since FLOPS is a fuzzy system, truth values (certainty factors) are attached to all data values and, if we wish, to rules themselves. In FLOPS, crisp truth values (true or false, 0 or 1) are a special case; in general, truth-values may range anywhere from false to true and anything in between.

2.1 EXPERT KNOWLEDGE: RULES AND DATA

It is common in books about AI to equate a "knowledge base" to a set of rules. We disagree emphatically with that viewpoint. We view a knowledge base in a light commensurate with the definition of learning given in Chapter 1: the acquisition of knowledge or skill. The factual knowledge that we have acquired is part of our knowledge base; the skill with which we use that knowledge to accomplish tasks, acquire new facts and new skills, and even invalidate cherished beliefs, incorporated in rules, is an indispensable other part. We then divide a knowledge base into two parts. Factual knowledge relevant to the problem at hand is realized as data or perhaps (more organized) as a database or bases. The skills needed to use the knowledge available to us to solve a problem, and perhaps guide us in acquiring new facts and learning new skills, are realized as rules. In the course of this book, we will have simple examples of both of these kinds of learning.

It would be very nice if all skills could be efficiently represented as rules, and in fact a great number of skills can be so represented, notably those that involve verbal human thought. However, some skills, such as the recognition of what is represented in an image, can be only partly represented by rules. Other skills, such as that of a ballplayer in throwing or catching a ball, really defy efficient representation by rules. Skills like these usually require programs written in a procedural language. Consequently, the expert system should be able to use rules that will call procedural language programs and interpret their results. (Rule-based systems are notoriously bad at number crunching!)

Fuzzy Expert Systems and Fuzzy Reasoning, By William Siler and James J. Buckley
ISBN 0-471-38859-9 Copyright © 2005 John Wiley & Sons, Inc.

We will represent a knowledge base of skills as a set of rules. Our rules will be of the form

$$\text{if (this is true) then (do that)} \qquad (2.1)$$

A very simple example of an everyday rule might be

$$\text{"if the light is green then cross the street"}. \qquad (2.2)$$

We will now examine this rule structure more closely.

2.2 RULE ANTECEDENT AND CONSEQUENT

In (2.1) the clause ("the light is green", or more generally "this is true") is called the *antecedent*; the clause ("cross the street", or more generally "do that") is called the *consequent*. In applying this rule, we first evaluate the truth of the antecedent. If the antecedent is sufficiently true, we execute the consequent instructions.

We suppose that we have previously learned that the rule is valid. Assuming we wish to cross the street, we first see if the antecedent is true by comparing the observed data (the color of the traffic light) to the value given in the rule (red). If the comparison in the antecedent holds, then we execute the consequent instruction and cross the street. (Our rule here is not very good; it neglects to check for a car, which might be turning right directly in front of us.)

2.2.1 Antecedents

In formal terms, the antecedent is a logical proposition whose truth can be determined. The antecedent may be complex, made up of several simple propositions whose individual truths are combined by AND, OR, and NOT connectives, such as

"IF (speed is fast) AND (it is raining) AND NOT (windshield wipers on)

THEN turn on windshield wipers, reduce speed   (2.3)

Most antecedent clauses will be comparisons between a data value for the case at hand and a value specified for a particular rule. Clearly, the range of circumstances, which a rule could cover, will depend on the types of data admissible in the syntax of our rules. In a conventional non-fuzzy expert system, data types commonly provided include numbers (if x is 35) and character strings (if name is "John"). Fuzzy expert systems provide additional data types: fuzzy numbers (if age is about 30) and fuzzy sets (if speed is fast) where speed could be slow, medium, or fast; the degree of truth value we have in a specific value (if we are only 0.9 sure that name is "John", then the truth value in that value is 0.9 and can be tested in a rule antecedent. Other words that can be used in a rule antecedent are modifiers called *hedges*, and are used to modify truth values. For example, if we have a fuzzy set called age that could take on values of young, middle-aged, or old, we can ask "if age is young", but can also ask "if age is somewhat young" or "if age is very young". In this way, fuzzy expert systems provide a very flexible syntax for rules compared to non-fuzzy expert systems.

2.2.2   Admissible Data Types

Like most modern computer languages, FLOPS data are typed, and must be declared. Data are stored in simple structures, like those in C programs, called data elements; the individual structure elements are called *attributes.* Following is a declaration of a data element name "MyData". (Complete definition of fuzzy sets and fuzzy numbers must await Chapter 3 on fuzzy mathematics.)

```
declare MyData
   X int      :integer
   Y flt      :floating point
   Z str      :character string
   area fznum :fuzzy number
   size fzset (Small Medium Large); :fuzzy set
```

In this data, declaration MyData is a memory element; X, Y, Z, area and size are attributes.

In addition to the types above, FLOPS generates two other data types. Each attribute of type int, flt, and str has an associated truth value, a measure of how sure we are that the value of the attribute is valid. Truth values are system-furnished attributes, accessed by appending. cf to the attribute name. Thus Y.cf is an attribute whose value is the truth value level of attribute Y. In addition, each instance of a data element has an identifying time tag, assigned in sequence as instances are created or modified; the time tag is accessed as system-furnished attribute tt. Members of the fuzzy set fsS, Small, Medium, and Large, are also attributes whose value is the truth value that the member (e.g., Small) is a valid descriptor of something in the real world. (Fuzzy data types and their use will be more fully described in Chapter 3.)

Although FLOPS does not at present implement them, arrays of the basic integer, float and strings data types can also be useful.

"Membership functions" are a special type of data that will be discussed later in this book.

2.2.3   Consequents

There is a great variety of consequent instructions available in fuzzy expert systems. There are instructions for input of data and output of data and conclusions; for modifying old data and creation of new data; and instructions to control the rule-firing process itself. The most controversial instructions in a fuzzy expert system are those that modify data and the truth values in data. The whole process of deriving new data and conclusions from given data is the *inference* process in logic; since fuzzy logic is quite a new branch of mathematics, some of the inference methods presented in this book are controversial. (However, they have all been tested in practice over the past 15 years.) Rules with consequent instructions that control the rule firing process are called *metarules* in AI parlance, and are of great importance in an inference process that involves several steps. (Most real-world problems require multistep inference.)

FLOPS has about 70 different instructions, called *commands*. (We have just met one FLOPS command, *declare*, which identifies a data declaration.) Any of these instructions can be used in the consequent of a rule. One important command is *rule*, which identifies the definition of a FLOPS rule. Since any FLOPS command is legal in the consequent of a rule, a rule can generate other rules. FLOPS rules can also generate data declarations.

Some typical FLOPS commands follow:

:output to screen:
```
write "Hello, World!\n";
message "Turn on ignition switch";
```

:creation of a data element:
```
make MyData ix = 3 fy = 3.1416 sz = "Check gasoline tank";
```

:input of data from a data file in FLOPS format:
```
transfer MyData from datafile.dat;
```

:transferring control to a different FLOPS program module;
```
open Program2.par;
```

:copying screen output to a disk file:
```
outfile MyOutput.out;
```

:Setting program trace level when debugging a FLOPS program:
```
debug 2;
```

The complete set of FLOPS commands is described in the help file manual.hlp, available under the HELP menu when running FLOPS or the integrated development environment TFLOPS.

2.3   DATA-DRIVEN SYSTEMS

It is perfectly obvious that rule (2.2), "if the light is green then cross the street", and rule (2.3), "IF speed is fast AND it is raining AND NOT windshield wipers on THEN turn on windshield wipers, reduce speed" are not likely to be applicable in the same situation. If one piece of data is that our subject is a pedestrian then rule (2.2) might be applicable, and if the data is that our subject is NOT a pedestrian, then rule (2.3) might be applicable. This idea was extended more than 20 years ago with the formulation of *data-driven* rules. If rules are data-driven, then they are called into action whenever the rule antecedents are satisfied; the order in which the rules are written has nothing to do with the order in which they are fired (consequent commands executed). Data-driven languages are *non-procedural.* Years ago, when computer programs were written on punched cards, we used to worry about dropping a deck of cards and totally messing up the program. This was, of course, because almost all common computer languages are not data-driven, but are *procedural*; the order in which statements are executed depends on the order in which they appear in the program. If we had had data driven languages, it would not matter if we dropped the deck; the program would run OK anyhow. Adapting to a non-procedural data-driven language requires a little work for computer programmers experienced in procedural languages.

2.4 RUN AND COMMAND MODES

FLOPS has two types of operational modes; *command*, in which FLOPS commands are directly executed in the order in which they are encountered; and *run*, in which FLOPS rules are fired.

FLOPS always starts out in command mode, reading its commands either from a FLOPS program disk file or from the keyboard. *Command mode is procedural; commands are executed in the order in which they are encountered.* FLOPS remains in command mode until a *run* command is executed, placing FLOPS into run mode, or until a *stop* or *exit* command terminates the FLOPS run.

In *run* mode, FLOPS rules are fired. *Run mode is data-driven and non-procedural*; the order in which rules are written has nothing to do with the order in which they are executed. FLOPS remains in run mode until no more rules are fireable; a *halt* command is executed; a specified number of rule-firing steps has been carried out; or until the FLOPS run is terminated by a *stop* or *exit* command. On leaving run mode, FLOPS reverts to command mode unless the program has been terminated.

Exercise Hello1.fps. For years the most popular introductory program for a language has been one that prints out "Hello, World!" to the monitor screen. We will use two versions of a FLOPS Hello program. The first of these is executed entirely in command mode. The program itself follows:

```
:Hello1.fps - simplest "Hello, World!" program.

message "Hello, World!";
exit;
```

FLOPS always starts in command mode. When we tell FLOPS to open a program, it reads the program line by line, ignoring comments and executing commands. FLOPS will remain in command mode until a run command is encountered.

We first open TFLOPS, then open file Hello1.fps in subfolder examples. Note that the first line, a comment, uses a gray font. In the next line, "message" uses a blue font since it is a FLOPS command, and the string "Hello, World!" uses a red font, the FLOPS color code for a character string. Finally, "exit", another FLOPS command, is also color-coded in blue.

To run Hello1, we click on "run" on the menu bar, then "run hello1.fps". FLOPS is now invoked, and opens the Hello1.fps file in command mode. The comment line is ignored, as is the null line that follows, and the "message" command is read and executed. Immediately a dialog box with the message "Hello, World!" is displayed. We click the "OK" button, and FLOPS reads and executes the "exit" command. A termination dialog box is displayed, FLOPS terminates and we return to TFLOPS with an error log "0 warnings, 0 errors" displayed at the bottom of the screen.

If you wish, you can display other messages by adding or changing FLOPS commands. If you intend to modify the program, it is important to save it under another name, such as "temp.fps" before any modifications are made. Click on the "Help" menu bar item, then click on "Manual", then select "Input/Output commands". Your two output options are "write", which writes a message to the screen without pausing, and "message", which puts up a dialog box displaying the selected text with "OK" and "Cancel" buttons.

It is easy to see that command mode is limited in its power, especially since there are no program loops. Command mode is essential when setting up a FLOPS program to run; in command mode a FLOPS program may be read, the data declarations are implemented, rules are compiled, and initial data are set up. For the FLOPS programmer, command mode is very important in program debugging, since FLOPS has a number of commands especially for debugging. But the real work of an expert system is done in run mode, illustrated by Hello2.fps.

Exercise Hello2.fps. Although very tiny, Hello2 has the elements of a non-trivial FLOPS program: a data declaration, a rule, a command to create initial data, and a "run" command to switch from command mode to run mode. Unlike Hello1, Hello2 does its work in run mode.

```
:Rule-based "Hello, World!" program.

message "Compiling Hello2.fps;

declare Data output str;

:rule r0
rule (goal Write message to screen)
IF (in Data output = <Str>)
THEN message "<Str>";

make Data output = "Hello, World!";
message "Hello2 ready to run";
run;
exit;
```

As before, we invoke TFLOPS and open hello2.fps in the examples folder. After hello2.fps is loaded, we run it in the same way as we ran hello1.fps in the previous exercise.

Flops starts running Hello2 in command mode, just as in running Hello1. As before, the initial comment is ignored. The message command is executed, displaying the "Compiling Hello2.fps" message. Next, the data declaration is executed, and the single rule is compiled. The initial instance of data element Data is created; this instance of Data makes rule r0 fireable. After another message to the user, FLOPS executes the "run" command and switches to run mode. The rule fires and executes the consequent "message" command, displaying "Hello, World!" in a dialog box.

After rule r0 has fired, no more rules are newly fireable; rule r0 will not fire again on the same data. We return to command mode, read and execute the "exit" command, and return to TFLOPS.

2.4.1 Run Mode: Serial and Parallel Rule Firing

In data-driven expert systems, it often (even usually) happens that the data make two or more rules concurrently fireable. In that case, the computer has two options. The first option is taken by almost all non-fuzzy expert systems; a *rule-conflict algorithm* decides which rule will be fired, and the rest of the fireable (but unfired) rules are placed on a *backtracking stack*. After firing the selected rule, we look to see if any rules are newly fireable. If so, the process is repeated, and again any fireable but unfired rules are placed on top of the backtracking stack. If at some point no rules are newly fireable, a rule is popped off the backtracking stack and fired; this is called *backtracking*. This option is called *sequential* or *serial rule firing* mode. mode or terminates the program.

The second option is used by most fuzzy systems. If the data make several rules concurrently fireable, they are *all* fired, effectively in parallel. However, a new problem can arise; if two or more rules attempt to modify the same data item in different ways, a *memory* conflict occurs, and must be resolved by a *memory conflict algorithm*. In expert systems that work with fuzzy sets, parallel rule firing is considerably more efficient than serial rule firing, permitting faster speed, greater clarity, and economy in the number of rules needed.

The choice between serial and parallel rule-firing modes can depend on the nature of data input. If information must be elicited from the user in a context-dependent fashion, so that each question to be asked depends on the answer to the previous question, serial rule firing is indicated. (It may also be useful in the depth-first search of a decision tree, or in the emulation of deductive reasoning, although one should first make sure that a parallel program will not work better.) A serial program can be much slower than an equivalent parallel program, since systems overhead is very much higher. Parallel programming is indicated if data are supplied to the program without user input from the keyboard, as in real-time on-line operation, or when the data are input from a disk file. In general, parallel programming is to be preferred to serial programming, unless there is a specific reason why serial programming is indicated. Parallel FLOPS programs have a .par suffix; serial programs have a .fps suffix. For example, programs badger.fps and auto2.fps ask a series of questions of the user, and the next question to be asked cannot be chosen until the previous question has been answered, and serial rule firing is employed. Program echo.par takes its input from a disk file prepared by a previous C program; program schizo.par asks a fixed sequence of questions; and program pac.par takes its input on-line in real-time from a patient physiologic monitor; all these programs use parallel rule firing.

The situation may arise when a combination of these modes is desirable; perhaps serial mode to obtain necessary information, and parallel mode to draw conclusions from these data. The FLOPS commands *serial* and *parallel* permit switching from one mode to the other.

2.4.2   Checking which Rules Are Fireable: The RETE Algorithm

In both serial and parallel rule-firing modes, we first check to see which rules the data make fireable. In serial mode only, we select a rule for firing using a rule-conflict algorithm. Next, we fire our rule(s) and place any other fireable rules on the backtracking stack. We use a memory-conflict algorithm to decide whether memory-modifications are permitted. This process is then repeated.

Data-driven systems spend most of their time finding out which rules are fireable. An obvious way to check for rule fireability is to set up a loop over all rules, then inside this loop set up another loop over the data too see if a rule is fireable. This can be terribly time-consuming. To reduce this time and speed up programs, Charles Forgy devised the RETE algorithm, which speeds up this process considerably (Forgy, 1982). Since in parallel programs the rules have to be scanned for fireability less often, *parallel rule firing* tends to run considerably faster than *serial rule firing*. No rule conflict algorithm is needed.

2.4.3   Serial Rule Firing

Serial rule firing amounts to a depth-first search of a decision tree. Figure 2.1 illustrates the dynamics of rule firing in serial mode. At the start of the program, rules R1, R2, and R3 are concurrently fireable; R10 through R15 represent goal states, and will fire when we have reached a conclusion.

At the start of the program, rules R1, R2, and R3 are concurrently fireable. Our rule conflict algorithm selects R1 for firing, and R2 and R3 are placed on the backtracking stack with R2 on top. R1 is fired, making R4 and R5 fireable. R4 is selected for firing, and R5 placed on top of the backtracking stack, which now holds R5, R2, and R3. R4 is fired, but does not make any rules newly fireable; R5 is popped off the backtracking stack and fired. The backtrack stack now holds R2 and R3. R5 is fired, but does not make any rules newly fireable; R2 is popped off the backtracking stack, which now holds only R3; R2 is now fired. R2 makes R6 and R7 newly fireable; R6 is selected, and R7 added to the backtrack stack that now holds R7 and R3. R6 makes R12 newly fireable; we select R12, and fire it. No rules are newly fireable; our goal

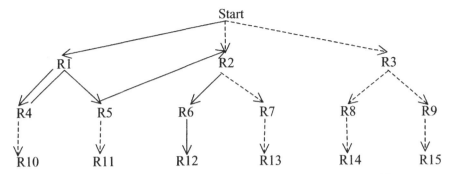

Figure 2.1   Rule firing sequence in serial mode, illustrating backtracking.

state has been reached, and we return to command mode. The important feature that serial rule firing requires is the rule conflict algorithm (Jackson, 1999), to decide which of two or more newly fireable rules will be selected for firing. We first consider rule-conflict algorithms designed for crisp 0-1 logic. There are several points to be considered when selecting a rule for firing. These include *refractoriness*, which includes the obvious requirement that a rule should not be permitted to fire twice on the same data; *recency*, which considers how recent they are in the rule antecedent; and *specificity*, which considers the complexity of the antecedent. All commonly used strategies use refractoriness first. The LEX strategy then sorts by recency; and the MEA (Means-End Analysis) strategy is a development of the LEX strategy (Jackson (1999), p. 87) to include specificity.

FLOPS rule-conflict strategy first ranks the rules for firing by the truth value that the rule antecedent is true combined with the truth value that the rule itself is valid, the posterior confidence <pconf>. If there is a tie among the first-ranked rules after this step, FLOPS then employs the MEA algorithm. If there is still a tie for first, one of the tied rule is randomly selected. The backtracking stack is maintained, with fireable but unfired rules being placed on top of the stack and, if no rules are newly fireable, rules are popped off the top of the stack and fired.

2.4.4   Parallel Rule-Firing

Parallel mode amounts to a breadth-first search of a decision tree, and is a bit simpler than the serial mode. If several rules are concurrently fireable, we fire them all. Since all fireable rules are fired, there is no backtracking. Parallel programs are organized by rule blocks, and these blocks are turned on or off for firing by *metarules*. In AI parlance, metarules are rules whose purpose is to control the sequence in which program sections are invoked. Metarules may enable or disable individual rules, blocks of rules, or entire programs, and are essential in parallel programs. Within those blocks of rules that are enabled, rule firing is data-driven and non-procedural. Metarules furnish procedural organization of enabled rule blocks and programs. Rule firing in a parallel FLOPS program then consists of a procedurally organized sequence of non-procedural steps.

Parallel rule-firing is shown in Figure 2.2.

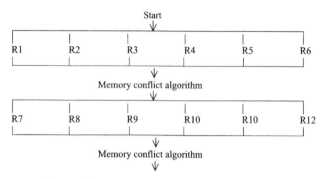

Figure 2.2   Rule-firing sequence in parallel mode.

2.5   FORWARD AND BACKWARD CHAINING

An expert system rule may be formulated as

$$\text{if A then B} \tag{2.4}$$

where A is a set of conditions on data and B is a set of instructions to be carried out if the rule is fired. In *forward chaining*, that sequence is followed. The rules are examined to see which rules are made fireable by the data, that is, A is satisfied, and a rule or rules selected for firing. When the rule is fired, the set of instructions B is executed. This is the way most rule-based expert systems work, including FLOPS.

In *backward chaining*, a different sequence is followed. In backward chaining, we specify what conclusion we would like to reach, that is, we specify B. We find a rule or rules that have the desired consequent, and look at the antecedent A to see what the data must be to satisfy A. Now we find out how those data can be established, and look for rules that have those data as a consequent, or input data from a user to see if the antecedent can be satisfied. In backward chaining we work backward from goals to data; in forward chaining we work forward from data to goals.

Some systems permit both forward and backward chaining. Forward-chaining systems can emulate backward chaining, but it is hard for backward-chaining systems to emulate forward chaining. FLOPS, like CLIPS, Fuzzy CLIPS, and OPS5, is a forward chaining system. (Sample program badger.fps illustrates the emulation of backward chaining in FLOPS.)

2.6   PROGRAM MODULARIZATION AND BLACKBOARD SYSTEMS

It has been many years since anyone attempted to write an expert system that was not broken into modules. A most important step in structuring modularization of expert system was taken at Carnegie-Mellon University in 1980 with the construction of the HEARSAY programs, designed to recognize and understand speech (Jackson, 1999, Chapter 18).

The HEARSAY project was modularized into a number of individual programs, each performing different tasks. The programs communicated with each other by writing and reading data to a *blackboard*; in modern PCs the blackboard is a hard or RAM disk, and each program writes or reads files (usually in relational data base format) to the blackboard. A special *blackboard monitor* program watches what is on the blackboard and schedules the individual programs so that the task proceeds according to plan.

The elements of a blackboard system are then individual programs; the blackboard itself, with a common general format for the data files; and provision for scheduling the various programs to reach the desired goal. The individual programs may be expert subsystems, but since there are some tasks for which expert systems are ill-suited, provision should be made to incorporate programs written in any language. The scheduling task may be done by a special blackboard monitor, or may be accomplished by metarules in the individual expert systems.

FLOPS employs a very simple basic blackboard system, with the hard disk serving as the physical blackboard. Data are normally written to the blackboard in a simple flat-file relational format, in which the first field in each record identifies the data element whose attribute values the record holds. Program sequencing is accomplished by metarules; provision is made for a FLOPS program to call another FLOPS program, or to call programs written in any language and stored on disk as executable program files.

2.7 HANDLING UNCERTAINTIES IN AN EXPERT SYSTEM

There are many sources of uncertainty in data. There is, of course, imprecision in numerical measurements (we might report a speed as 60 miles/h when it is actually 62.345. . . . There is also uncertainty as to facts (I think her name is Joan, but I'm not sure), and ambiguous terms (He was going fast). There are several ways of handling uncertainties in an expert system, and of combining uncertainties (He is heavy, short, and middleaged). In FLOPS, we represent uncertainties as *truth values*, how sure we are that a datum or a rule is valid. Ways of expressing and combining uncertainties include probability; fuzzy logic; Bayes' theorem; and Dempster–Shafer theory, each with their own advantages, disadvantages and problems.

There are two simple ways of representing uncertainties. In the first, a single number (usually, but not always, between 0 and 1), called variously *certainty factor*, *confidence*, or *truth value* represents how sure we are that the data to which the factor is attached is indeed valid. In the second, two numbers are attached to a value, one representing a lower limit of certainty (called *belief* in Dempster–Shafer theory and *necessity* in fuzzy mathematics) and the second representing an upper limit (called *plausibility* in Dempster–Shafer theory and *possibility* in fuzzy mathematics). The lower limit can represent the extent to which the data support a value, and the upper limit can represent the extent to which the data refute a value.

When a single number is used to represent uncertainty it represents the extent to which the data support a value; if we believe the value to be invalid, its truth value would be 0; if we believe a value to be true, its truth value would be one. It is not immediately clear how complete ignorance should be represented. FLOPS is pessimistic; if it does not know anything about a value, FLOPS assumes it to be false.

When two numbers are used to represent uncertainty, we have a clear way of unambiguously representing complete ignorance. If we do not know anything about the truth of a value, its lower limit (say belief) is 0, since at this point no data have supported the value; its upper limit (say plausibility) is 1, since no data have refuted the value. As we continue to reason, we would expect that the two values would move closer together.

Clearly, the two-value mode of representing uncertainties has an intellectual appeal, and a substantial body of theory called *interval logic* has grown up around it. However, most of us do not usually reason in this complicated a fashion, and FLOPS is content to represent uncertainty as a single number (which we sometimes call a truth value), sometimes a truth value and sometimes (when dealing with fuzzy sets) a grade of membership. All these terms represent pretty much the same thing; our truth value that a datum is valid. FLOPS also prefers to use fuzzy logic for combining uncertainties; we cannot present a totally convincing argument for this, but fuzzy systems theory seems to supply the tools that we need. Especially important is the ability of fuzzy systems theory to deal with ambiguities and contradictions, where fuzzy sets provide the only clean mathematical framework.

In its present incarnation, FLOPS represents truth values as integers between 0 and 1000, rather than as decimal fractions between 0 and 1.

2.8   SUMMARY

Knowledge may be viewed as factual, information that we have stored in memory, or procedural, skills in using the data at hand. In an expert system, factual knowledge is stored as data held in the computer's memory, and procedural knowledge is stored as rules. Production rules are written as "IF (the data satisfy the specified conditions) THEN (perform the specified actions)". The IF part is the rule antecedent; the THEN part is the rule consequent. The antecedent is a fuzzy logical proposition, that is, a statement regarding data whose truth value may be determined. If a rule's antecedent is sufficiently true, and the rule is activated, the rule is said to be fireable.

We are particularly interested in data-driven systems. In such systems, the fireability of a rule is determined by whether the data satisfy the antecedent and by whether the rule has been activated, but does not depend on the position of the rule in the program. Systems in which whether or not a statement will be executed depends on the position of the rule in a program are called procedural; nearly all common computer languages (C++, Fortran, Basic, etc.) are procedural. Data-driven systems are non-procedural.

The interaction between rules and data that occurs when running a fuzzy expert system is considerably more complex than the interaction between statements and data in a procedural language such as C or Fortran. In a rule-based systems, there is a sequence of events: data make rules fireable, and rules are fired creating new or modified data; these data make other rules fireable, and so on. Some of the rules to be fired may serve to control the fireability of individual rules, blocks of rules, or even entire programs; these are called *metarules*. The precise nature of the data-rules-data- sequence depends on whether sequential or parallel rule-firing is in effect.

Parallel rule-firing is simpler in concept than sequential rule-firing. In sequential rule firing, a single rule is picked for firing from all concurrently fireable rules; the rest are stacked for firing if no rules are newly fireable, the backtracking process. In parallel rule firing, all fireable rules are effectively fired concurrently; there are no fireable but unfired rules for backtracking. If information is to be elicited from the user in a context-dependent fashion, so that the next question to be asked depends on the answer to the previous question, sequential rule-firing is appropriate; otherwise, parallel rule-firing is usually to be preferred.

A FLOPS program is made up of a series of commands drawn from a list of about 80. FLOPS programs have two operational modes: *command mode* and *run mode*. In command mode, FLOPS executes commands procedurally, one after another, but rules are not fired. In run mode, FLOPS fires rules, that is, executes the commands in the consequents of fireable rules. If no more rules are fireable, FLOPS reverts to command mode. In command mode, FLOPS operates procedurally, executing commands in the sequence in which they appear in the program; but in run mode, FLOPS is data-driven and non-procedural.

FLOPS begins in command mode, reading a FLOPS program and executing its commands in sequence. When a "rule" command is encountered, the rule antecedent is compiled and the rule entered into FLOPS memory, but the rule is not fired. When a "run" command is encountered, FLOPS switches from command mode to run mode, and begins firing rules. If no more rules are fireable, FLOPS reverts to command mode. (There are also other ways to switch from run to command mode.)

Data-driven production systems can involve much systems overhead in determining which rules are newly fireable. By keeping track of partial matches between rule antecedents and data, the Rete algorithm by Charles Forgy reduces this overhead dramatically. Nevertheless, this systems overhead can still constitute a real problem. Parallel rule firing reduces systems overhead still further.

Expert systems may be forward or backward chaining. In forward chaining systems, we reason from antecedent truth to consequent truth; that is, we reason from facts in the rule antecedent that we know to be true to establish new facts whose truth is implied by the antecedent. Backward chaining reverses this; we attempt to find facts to establish the truth of some goal state. It is quite possible to emulate backward chaining with a forward chaining system.

Modularization of expert system programs is essential for both their construction and their debugging, but is even more important conceptually. At the lowest level, modularization is accomplished by assigning rules to blocks, so that we can view the program organization in terms of the organization of the rule blocks. Metarules are used to activate and deactivate rule blocks. At a higher level, modularization can occur as complete programs, which may be other FLOPS programs or may be procedural language programs. Communication among these programs can be accomplished by a *blackboard*. Blackboard systems may be quite complex, but the essential feature is a common area where the different programs involved can exchange information in a common format.

All fuzzy expert systems and some expert systems not based in fuzzy logic have the problem of representing uncertainties. Most often, a single number between 0 and 1 called truth value, certainty factor, or truth value represents how sure we are that a datum is valid. Sometimes two numbers are used; a lower number representing the extent to which other data support the validity of a datum, and the upper representing the extent to which other data fail to refute the value of a datum. The lower number is called *necessity* in fuzzy systems theory and *belief* in Dempster–Shafer theory; the lower is called *possibility* in fuzzy theory and *plausibility* in Dempster–Shafer theory. The two-valued uncertainty theory is sometimes called *interval logic*.

2.9 QUESTIONS

2.1 We have said that a knowledge base consists of data and rules. Does this give a complete representation of knowledge?

2.2 How should we handle a problem that requires a lot of numerical processing?

2.3 What is the difference between a rule antecedent and a rule consequent?

2.4 What data types should be available in a fuzzy expert system?

2.5 Can the consequent of a rule contain an instruction to create a rule?

2.6 Are there any restrictions on what type of instruction can be included in a rule consequent?

2.7 What is a metarule?

2.8 How do procedural and data-driven programs differ?

2.9 What is the difference between run and command operational modes?

2.10 Under what circumstance is serial rule-firing mode desirable?

2.11 In an expert system, we have goals we wish to reach and data from which to work. How are goals and data related in forward chaining? In backward chaining?

2.12 What purpose does a blackboard system serve?

2.13 How are uncertainties represented in FLOPS?

3 Fuzzy Logic, Fuzzy Sets, and Fuzzy Numbers: I

This chapter is intended to prepare the reader for the basics in fuzzy logic and fuzzy sets that will appear in the rest of the book. We start with classical logic and how fuzzy logic generalizes classical logic. We then discuss fuzzy propositions, fuzzy sets, fuzzy relations, fuzzy comparisons among data, fuzzification, and defuzzification. More advanced fuzzy mathematics are discussed in Chapter 4. In the following sections, we will deal with both single-valued and multivalued data. We will denote a single number from the real line as a scalar number.

3.1 CLASSICAL LOGIC

Fuzzy logic notation and operations are based on classical logic and the propositional calculus, the modern form of notation for classical logic; we first review their foundations.

According to the Random House unabridged dictionary of the English language, logic is "the science that investigates the principles that govern correct or reliable inference". The basic element of logic is a *proposition*, a statement in which something is affirmed or denied, so that it can therefore be characterized as either true or false. A simple proposition might be "the president's first name is William" or "the president's age is 48". A more complex proposition is "the president's first name is William AND his age is 48". Surely, we can determine if these propositions are true or false. In classical logic, propositions are either true or false, with nothing in between. It is often conventional to assign numerical values to the truth of propositions, with 1 representing true and 0 representing false. Important principles of classical logic are the Law of the Excluded Middle, which states that a proposition must be either true or false, and the Law of Non-Contradiction, with states that a proposition cannot be both true and false at the same time. We will denote propositions by capital letters P, Q, R, ... *The truth value of proposition P will be written tv(P), or simply P if the context makes it clear what is meant.* In two-valued logic, truth values must be either 0 (false) or 1 (true).

We will be concerned with two kinds of truth values (Dubois and Prade, 1988). First, we define *possibility* to be the extent to which the available data *fail to refute*

Fuzzy Expert Systems and Fuzzy Reasoning, By William Siler and James J. Buckley
ISBN 0-471-38859-9   Copyright © 2005 John Wiley & Sons, Inc.

a proposition. Possibility measures the extent to which a proposition *might* be true. In the absence of any data to the contrary, the possibility of a proposition is one. (An analogous term is *plausibility.*) Second, we define *necessity* to be the extent to which the available data *support* a proposition. Necessity measures the extent to which a proposition *must* be true. In the absence of any supporting data, the necessity of a proposition is zero. Analogous terms are *credibility* or *belief.*

An example: Suppose that we wish to establish the truth of proposition R. Proposition P supports the truth of proposition R; in the lack of other knowledge, the necessity of R is the truth value of P. On the other hand, proposition Q refutes R; the possibility of R is (NOT Q).

Since this book is concerned with constructing programs to return answers to real-world problems, we will be concerned primarily with necessity; we will want to reach conclusions that are supported by data, not conclusions that might possibly be true.

The truth value of complex propositions is obtained by combining the truth values of the elemental propositions, which enter into the complex proposition. The most common operators (called connectives) are NOT, AND (A AND B is true if both A and B are true) and OR (A OR B is true if either A or B or both are true.)

In this chapter, we will be concerned with *truth-functional* operators. An operator is called truth-functional if the truth value of the resulting proposition is determined solely by the truth values of its operands. That is, the truth value of (say) A AND B is determined only by the truth values of A and B, and no other information is required. Negation, written NOT P, is the simplest example of a truth-functional operator; the truth value of NOT P depends only on the truth value of P, and not on anything else. (For classical logic, this seems obvious; for fuzzy logic, it is not so obvious, as we shall see later in Chapter 4, Section 4.2.2.) We will use throughout this book tv(NOT P) = 1 − tv(P). The two other most common truth-functional operators, also called connectives, are AND and OR. (As we shall see later, these operators are not necessarily truth-functional, although this is seldom admitted!) A set of truth-functional operators that can generate all the others is called a primitive set of operators. It is well known in propositional calculus that all the other truth-functional operators can be constructed from either the NOT and AND or the NOT and OR operators. Computer scientists, electrical engineers, and logicians use different sets of primitive connectives. The NAND operator is defined as A NAND B = NOT (A AND B), and from the NAND operator alone all other logical operators may be constructed; electronic engineers, often take NAND as a primitive, since it is easily implemented in circuitry. Logicians sometimes take the implication operator (A IMPLIES B, defined below), as a member of the primitive set; all other logical operators can be defined from the NOT and IMPLIES operators. Most computer languages furnish AND, OR, and NOT as basic operators. Since our interest is in expert systems implemented in a computer language, we will take AND, OR, and NOT as basic.

3.1.1 Evaluating A AND B and A OR B

The evaluation of tv(P AND Q) and tv(P OR Q), given truth values for P and Q, is shown in Table 3.1, a presentation known as a truth table.

TABLE 3.1   Truth Table for AND and OR Logical Operators

P	Q	P AND Q	P OR Q
0	0	0	0
0	1	0	1
1	0	0	1
1	1	1	1

There are many formulas that can be written to compute algebraically the truth of P AND Q and P OR Q from the truth values for P and Q, all of which will give the same answers as listed in Table 3.1 for classical (crisp) truth values of 0 or 1. (In fuzzy logic, these formulas may give different answers!) Here, we list only three of these formulas for P AND Q, all equivalent for classical (but not for fuzzy) logic. In this and succeeding chapters, we may use the symbol tv(A) to indicate the truth value of A, or may simply use A to denote both a proposition and its truth value. For all fuzzy logic operators,

NOT P = 1−P
P AND Q:

Zadeh operator:

$$P \text{ AND } Q = \min(P, Q) \tag{3.1}$$

Probabilistic operator, assuming independence:

$$P \text{ AND } Q = P * Q \tag{3.2}$$

Bounded difference operator:

$$P \text{ AND } Q = \max(0, P + Q - 1) \tag{3.3}$$

Just as there are many formulas for computing P AND Q, there are also many ways of computing P OR Q, which will all give the same result as in Table 3.1 for classical logic, but that are not equivalent for fuzzy logic. We list three of these in (3.4)–(3.6):

P OR Q:

Zadeh operator:

$$P \text{ OR } Q = \max(P, Q) \tag{3.4}$$

Probabilistic operator, assuming independence:

$$P \text{ OR } Q = P + Q - P * Q \tag{3.5}$$

Bounded sum operator:

$$P \text{ OR } Q = \min(1, P + Q) \tag{3.6}$$

Each formula for P AND Q has a corresponding formula for P OR Q, called a dual operator. In the above, (3.1) and (3.4) are a dual pair, as are (3.2) and (3.5), and also (3.3) and (3.6). If the NOT and AND operators are chosen as primitives, we can derive the OR operator as P OR Q = NOT(NOT P AND NOT Q); if the NOT and OR operators are taken as primitive, we can derive the AND operator from De Morgan's theorems, given in (3.7) and (3.8):

$$P \text{ AND } Q = \text{NOT(NOT } P \text{ OR NOT } Q) \qquad (3.7)$$

or, conversely,

$$P \text{ OR } Q = \text{NOT(NOTP AND NOTQ)} \qquad (3.8)$$

In this way, the formula (3.4) can be derived from (3.1); formula (3.5) can be derived from (3.2); and formula (3.6) can be derived from (3.3). Dual operators satisfy these relationships.

Actually, (3.1) and (3.3), (3.4), and (3.6) represent extremes in the range of fuzzy operators that can be derived from probability theory, and there are similar operator pairs for special purposes that go even beyond these extremes. The problem we now face is—which operator pair do we choose as a default?

Fortunately, there are two approaches to this choice, both of which agree.

First, there are many years of experience by many workers in the field who have chosen the Zadeh operators (3.1) and (3.4) with great success.

Next, there is a theoretical basis. Truth values may be derived from probability theory as the averages of expert binary true–false judgments (Klir and Yuan, 1995, p. 283). If the experts judge two rather than one event, it is likely that their judgments would be strongly positively associated; under this condition, the Zadeh operators are the correct theoretical choice. Of course, under other conditions other operators might be better (Buckley and Siler, 1999).

Exercise AndOrNot—Check on Logic Formulas for AND, OR, and NOT. In this exercise you will calculate NOT A, A AND B, and A OR B from the above formulas. To run the exercise, invoke TFLOPS, load program AndOrNot.fps, and run it as you did the programs in Chapter 2 exercises. AndOrNot.fps will ask you to enter truth values a and b, and will then calculate NOT A, and then calculate A AND B and A OR B by all three sets of formulas above; min-max logic, probabilistic logic and bounded sum/difference logic. To quit the program, enter a negative truth value for b.

We suggest that you first check that for crisp (not fuzzy) logic (truth values 0 or 1), all three logics give the same answers. Then try truth values between zero and one, anticipating fuzzy logic, and see what answers the three logics give. Rule r0 in AndOrNot.fps uses a truth value test. The antecedent (in Data a.cf = 0) checks that the truth value of a in data element Data is zero. This is the case if no value is currently assigned to attribute a. (Note that truth values of attributes are also attributes.)

In rule r2, AndOrNot.fps adds modification of a data element and FLOPS'
calculator to the available tools. Consider the consequent command

```
in 1 Zand = (min(<A>, <B>)) Zor = (max(<A>, <B>))
```

This command will modify attributes in the first data element in the antecedent
(in 1). Attribute Zand will be set to the minimum of variable <A> and variable
<B> by FLOPS' calculator, called by the open parenthesis after "Zand = ", and
closed by the corresponding close parenthesis. min() and max() are among the functions supplied by the calculator.

Rule r3 sets all the truth values in Data to zero by the simple expedient of deleting
the old instance and creating a new instance in which no attri-
butes have been assigned values.

```
:Exercise AndOrNot.fps

message "Compiling AndOrNot.fps";
declare Data
a flt              :truth value a
b flt        :truth value b
Nota flt     :truth value of NOT a
Zand flt     :a AND b using Zadeh logic
Zor flt          :a OR b using Zadeh logic
Pand flt     :a AND b using probabilistic logic and
                 independence
Por flt          :a OR b using probabilistic logic
Band flt     :a AND b using bounded logic
Bor flt;         :a OR b using bounded logic

:rule r0
rule (goal Input a and b truth values)
IF (in Data a.cf = 0)
THEN
  write "Input a",
  read 1 a,
  write "Input b (negative to quit)",
  read 1 b;

:rule r1
rule (goal Quit if b negative)
IF (in Data b < 0)
THEN exit;

:rule r2
rule (goal Calculate Nota, aANDb, aORb by various
multi-valued logics)
```

```
IF (in Data a = <A> AND b = <B> AND Nota.cf = 0 AND b > = 0)
THEN
   in 1 Nota = (1 - <A>),
   in 1 Zand = (min(<A>, <B>)) Zor = (max(<A>, <B>)),
   in 1 Pand = (<A> * <B>) Por = (<A> + <B> - <A> * <B>),
   in 1 Band = (max(0, <A> + <B> - 1)) Bor =
               (min(<A> + <B>, 1));

:rule r3
rule (goal Print results and try again)
IF (in Data Nota = <NOTA> AND Zand = <ZAND> AND Zor = <ZOR>
   AND Pand = <PAND> AND Por = <POR> AND Band = <BAND> AND
Bor = <BOR> AND a = <A> AND b = <B>)
THEN
   write "a <A> b <B>\n",
   write "Min-max Zadehian logic\n",
   write "a AND b <ZAND> a OR b <ZOR> NOT a <NOTA>\n",
   write "Probabilistic logic\n",
   write "a AND b <PAND> a OR b <POR> NOT a <NOTA>\n",
   write "Bounded sum logic\n",
   write "a AND b <BAND> a OR b <BOR> NOT a <NOTA>\n\n",
   delete 1,

make Data;
message "Ready to run";
run;
```

It is easy to see that rule-based systems may not be optimal for efficient numerical computation. By using the advanced feature of recursion, we can solve differential equations, compute factorials, and the like. (Recursion here means computation when one or more rules or rule blocks makes itself refireable until some goal is reached.) But if heavy numerical computation is needed, it is often better to do this in a more numerically oriented language like C or FORTRAN, and to use a blackboard system for inter-program communication and control.

3.1.2 The Implication Operator

Another basic truth-functional operator used in fuzzy logic is logical implication, written P implies Q, $P \rightarrow Q$ or IF P, then Q. Table 3.2 is the truth table for $P \rightarrow Q$. Three different methods for determining $tv(P \rightarrow Q)$, among many other methods listed in Klir and Yuan (1995, p. 309), are

$$tv(P \rightarrow Q) = 1 \quad \text{if } tv(P) \leq tv(Q), \quad \text{else } tv(P \rightarrow Q) = 0 \qquad (3.9)$$

$$tv(P \rightarrow Q) = \min(1, 1 - tv(P) + tv(Q)) \qquad (3.10)$$

$$tv(P \rightarrow Q) = \max(1 - tv(P), \min(tv(P), tv(Q))) \qquad (3.11)$$

TABLE 3.2   Truth Table for Logical Operator P Implies Q

P	Q	P implies Q
0	0	1
0	1	1
1	0	0
1	1	1

Equation (3.11) may also be expressed in terms of OR and NOT as

$$P \to Q = (\text{NOT } P) \text{ OR } Q \tag{3.12}$$

The classical truth table for $P \to Q$ is shown in Table 3.2.

The reader will probably find it difficult to accept that if P is false, $P \to Q$ is true whether Q is true or false. Note that formal logic is not concerned with objective truth in the ordinary sense of the word, but with consistency between premises and conclusions. P being false is consistent with Q being true or false, since if P is false we have no idea what Q might be. $P \to Q$ does not only mean that if P is true, then Q is true; it is a measure of the consistency of the truth value of P with the truth value of Q. (Logicians have had no trouble with this for a very long time!)

Note that the implication operator, of its very nature, returns a possibility, not a necessity. This is clear when we look at truth table 3.2 for the classical implication operator $P \to Q$, where $0 \to 1$ is true. Clearly, if the truth value of P is zero, we cannot conclude that this *requires* the truth value of Q to be one, as would be the case with necessity; on the other hand, if P is false, the truth value of Q *might* be one for all we know, as is the case with possibility. For this reason, the implication operator is of little or no use in a fuzzy reasoning system based on necessity; it is included here because texts of fuzzy theory pay considerable attention to it.

Classical logic now continues using NOT, AND, OR and $\to$ to derive other connectives and prove theorems about disjunctive normal forms, various sets of primitives, and so on. An important tool in classical logic for deriving new propositions from old is the modus ponens, which can be written

$$\text{if P AND } (P \to Q) \text{ then Q} \tag{3.13}$$

which can be read "If P is true and P implies Q then Q is true". Note that the classical modus ponens employs the implication operator.

The formulation of the modus ponens in (3.13) can be (and has been) misleading, because of its strong resemblance to a rule in a rule-based language. However, note that in the modus ponens and its counterpart, the fuzzy modus ponens, discussed in Chapter 4, Section 4.3, both the antecedent (if . . .) and the consequent (then . . .) are logical propositions, and the resulting truth values are possibilities rather than necessities. In a useful rule, we employ necessities rather than possibilities.

This means that the fuzzy modus ponens that employs an implication operator is not applicable to a rule-based system such as we are describing in this book.

Exercise Imply.fps: Evaluating Implications. Program Imply.fps calculates the truth value of using the fuzzy implication operators given in (3.7)–(3.9), and for arbitrary truth values for P and Q. As before, run TFLOPS and load Imply.fps from folder Examples. First, check for crisp values of P and Q to make sure the formulas give the classical values of the implication for crisp inputs. Then check for values of P and Q between zero and one. It will be very quickly obvious that the different formulas are not equivalent, but can produce different values for the truth value of the implication.

When running Imply.fps, try both P and Q = 0. In this case, for all fuzzy implication operators that reduce to the classical values for crisp operands, the truth value of P → Q is 1. This can be interpreted as "If we don't know anything, then anything is possible."

If we use the implication operator to evaluate the truth value of the consequent of the rule "if P then Q", we would conclude that Q is true. In other words, the implication operator returns the possibility that Q might be true, judging from that rule alone. In fuzzy math terms, the implication operator returns the *possibility* that Q might be true, rather than the *necessity* of Q being true. In expert systems that assign a single truth value to data, this could be seriously misleading; in such expert systems, we would ordinarily expect a truth value to reflect the extent to which the data support a conclusion, rather than the extent to which the data fail to refute a conclusion.

The problem is further complicated by the number of fuzzy implication operators available (Klir and Yuan, 1996 list 14), and the lack of any clear guidelines as to which fuzzy implication one should use (Klir and Yuan, 1995, p. 312), "To select an appropriate fuzzy implication for approximate reasoning under each particular situation is a difficult problem". In general, however, if any implication is employed to evaluate a rule, if the antecedent is false the rule will always be fireable; if the antecedent is true the rule may or may not be fireable, depending on the particular implication operator chosen. If the antecedent has truth value 1 and the prior truth value of the consequent is 0, the rule will never be fireable no matter what implication operator is chosen.

All these facts lead us to conclude that the implication operator is of dubious value in a fuzzy expert system.

3.2   ELEMENTARY FUZZY LOGIC AND FUZZY PROPOSITIONS

Like classical logic, fuzzy logic is concerned with the truth of propositions. However, in the real world propositions are often only partly true. In addition, we commonly use terms, which are not sharply defined. It is hard to characterize the truth of "John is old" as unambiguously true or false if John is 60 years old.

In some respects John at 60 is old being eligible for senior citizen benefits at many establishments, but in other respects John is not old since he is not eligible for Social Security. So, we should allow the truth value of (John is old) to take on values in the interval [0, 1], not just 0 or 1.

We shall use the term "truth value" many times in this book; let us define it now. The truth value of a proposition is a measure in the interval [0, 1] of how sure we are that the proposition is true, that is, consistent with its constituent elements. Not only propositions have truth values; data have truth values associated with them, a measure of the extent to which the values of the data are valid; rules have truth values associated with them, a measure of the extent to which the rule itself is valid. In general, then, the truth value of (something) is a measure in [0, 1] of the validity of (something).

As in classical logic, a fuzzy proposition is an assertion whose truth can be tested. Most such assertions are comparisons between observed and specified data values. Unlike classical logic, a fuzzy proposition may be partly true. There are two reasons why a fuzzy proposition may be only partly true. First, the data being tested may be only partly true, that is, may have truth values less than 1; second, the comparison itself may only hold in part, so that the truth value of a comparison may be less than 1.

The structure of fuzzy propositions may be considerably more complex than the structure of crisp (non-fuzzy) propositions. In crisp propositions, data are seldom multivalued, and their truth values (if the data exist) are always 1. Crisp comparisons are all Boolean, returning either 0 or 1. But in fuzzy propositions, single-valued data are accompanied by truth values. Data in a fuzzy system may also be multivalued, as we shall see in Section 3.3.1 on fuzzy sets; and truth values may also be multivalued, as we shall see in Section 3.3.2 on fuzzy numbers. Comparisons among data commonly return truth values other than 0 or 1. Fuzzy propositions will be discussed in more detail in Chapter 4; for the present, let us be content with the simple fact that fuzzy propositions may have truth values anywhere between 0 and 1 inclusive.

Let us see what changes there are, if any, in finding the truth values of NOT P, P AND Q, P OR Q, and P → Q when the truth values can be any number between 0 and 1.

First of all, tv(NOT P) = 1 − tv(P) will always hold in this book.

To compute tv(P AND Q) we cannot use a table like Table 3.1 since the possible values of tv(P) and tv(Q) are now infinite. We must use formulas like equations (3.1)–(3.3). In fuzzy logic, we can use any one of these formulas to determine tv(P AND Q). However, although they all agree when the truth values are 0 or 1, one can now produce different results for truth values in the interval [0, 1]. For example, if tv(P) = 0.8 and tv(Q) = 0.5, then equation (3.1) gives 0.5 for tv(P AND Q) but equation (3.2) produces a value of 0.4. Methods of getting tv(P AND Q) in fuzzy logic are discussed in Section 4.1 when we define what are called t-norms.

For tv(P OR Q) in fuzzy logic, we can use formulas like equations (3.4)–(3.6); such methods are called t-conorms.

In fuzzy logic, any algorithm that gives Table 3.2 when the truth values are 0 or 1 may be used to compute tv(P → Q) if the truth values are now in [0, 1]. So, equations (3.9)–(3.11) can be employed to obtain tv(P OR Q) for tv(P) and tv(Q) since both are in [0, 1].

Up to now we have only looked at simple propositions. Consider the compound proposition

$$P \text{ AND } (Q \text{ OR NOT } R) \tag{3.14}$$

To obtain its truth value let us use the logic originally proposed by Lotfi Zadeh in his seminal 1965 paper on fuzzy sets: min–max fuzzy logic, which means min for AND, equation (3.1), and max for OR, equation (3.4). The truth value of the proposition in equation (3.10) is then

$$\min(p, \max(q, 1 - r)) \tag{3.15}$$

3.3   FUZZY SETS

Let X be a collection of objects called a universal set. The sets we wish to discuss will all be subsets of X.

To explain the transition from regular sets, also called crisp sets, to fuzzy sets we start with crisp subsets of X. Let A be a subset of X. For each x in X we know whether x belongs or does not belong to A. Define a function on X whose values are zero or one as follows: (1) the value of the function at x is one if x is a member of A; and (2) the value is zero if x does not belong to A. We write this function as $A(x) = 1$ if x is in A and $A(x) = 0$ otherwise. This function is called the characteristic function on A and any such function, whose values are either zero or one, defines a crisp subset of X.

Fuzzy sets generalize the characteristic function in allowing all values between 0 and 1. A fuzzy subset F of X is defined by its membership function (a generalization of the characteristic function), also written $F(x)$, whose values can be any number in the interval [0, 1]. The value of $F(x)$ is called the grade of membership of x in fuzzy set F, and is often denoted by $\mu(x)$. If $\mu(x)$ is only 0 or 1, then we get the characteristic function of a crisp, non-fuzzy, set F. Now suppose we have $\mu(x)$ taking on values in [0, 1] besides just 0 and 1. We say x belongs to F if $\mu_F(x) = 1$, x does not belong to F when $\mu_F(x) = 0$, and x is in F with membership $\mu_F(x)$ if $0 < \mu_F(x) < 1$. The universal set always has $\mu_X(x) = 1$ for all x in X, and the empty set is described by its membership function always zero [$\mu_\emptyset(x) = 0$ for all x in X]. Crisp sets are considered special cases of fuzzy sets when membership values are always 0 or 1.

We must be a little careful about the term "membership function". Since fuzzy systems theorists have been almost exclusively concerned with numbers, their fuzzy sets are almost always made up of words describing numbers. In this case, membership functions take a very special form for converting a number into its grades of membership; this form is completely inapplicable to fuzzy sets of non-numeric quantities such as classifications, possible system troubles, or any of the vast varieties of non-numeric fuzzy sets of interest in fuzzy reasoning. In fact, for such fuzzy sets, the term "membership function" itself is only of theoretical interest, and is best avoided in practice. The only universe in which the grades of membership can be calculated by conventional numerical mathematics is the set of real numbers (i.e., the real line), or a subset of the real line such as all non-negative numbers. In this sense, the term "membership function" means specifically a function defined on numbers from the real line. Examples of such membership functions will be given in Sections 3.3.2 and 3.3.3. Grades of membership for universes other than the real numbers are normally calculated by the firing of rules, estimated by an observer or some other method, rather than by membership functions.

At this point, we shall not be concerned with the important topic of how the membership functions are to be determined. We will discuss in later sections and chapters methods of determining memberships and of specifying membership functions. Klir and Yuan (1995) devote a whole chapter to construction of fuzzy sets and operations on fuzzy sets.

There are two very special fuzzy sets needed in fuzzy expert systems: (1) discrete fuzzy sets; and (2) fuzzy numbers. We will now discuss both of these fuzzy sets in detail.

3.3.1 Discrete Fuzzy Sets

If $X =$ is finite, the simplest discrete fuzzy set D is just a fuzzy subset of X. We can write D as

$$D = \left\{ \frac{\mu_1}{x_1}, \frac{\mu_2}{x_2}, \dots, \frac{\mu_n}{x_n} \right\} \tag{3.16}$$

where the membership value of x_1 in D is μ_1. Also, if X is not finite but $D(x) \neq 0$ for only $x = \{x_1, x_2, \dots, x_n\}$ we write D as in equation (3.16). Conventionally, the truth value of a member in a fuzzy set is called its grade of membership.

An example might be a fuzzy set Diagnosis of psychiatric diagnoses, shown in (3.17). This is a non-numeric fuzzy set, since its members describe a non-numeric quantity.

$$\text{Diagnosis} = \left\{ \frac{\mu_1}{\text{depression}}, \frac{\mu_2}{\text{bipolar disorder}}, \frac{\mu_3}{\text{schizophrenia}} \right\} \tag{3.17}$$

Discrete fuzzy sets for fuzzy expert systems may be numeric or non-numeric, depending on whether their members describe numeric or non-numeric quantities. (3.17) shows a non-numeric fuzzy set. As an example of a discrete numeric fuzzy set consider (3.18),

$$\text{Size} = \left\{ \frac{\mu_1}{\text{small}}, \frac{\mu_2}{\text{medium}}, \frac{\mu_3}{\text{large}} \right\} \tag{3.18}$$

whose members describe a numeric quantity, Size. Members of a numeric discrete fuzzy set always describe a numeric quantity. Such discrete fuzzy sets are called *linguistic variables*, with members *linguistic terms*, and are discussed in Section 3.3.3.

3.3.2 Fuzzy Numbers

Fuzzy numbers represent a number of whose value we are somewhat uncertain. They are a special kind of fuzzy set whose members are numbers from the real line, and hence are infinite in extent. The function relating member number to its grade of membership is called a membership function, and is best visualized by a graph such as Figure 3.1. The membership of a number x from the real line is often denoted by $\mu(x)$. Fuzzy numbers may be of almost any shape (though conventionally they are required to be convex and to have finite area), but frequently they will be triangular (piecewise linear), s-shape (piecewise quadratic) or normal (bell-shaped). Fuzzy numbers may also be basically trapezoidal, with an interval within which the membership is 1; such numbers are called fuzzy intervals. Fuzzy intervals may have linear, s-shape or normal "tails", the increasing and decreasing slopes. Figures 3.1–3.4 illustrate fuzzy numbers with these shapes.

Assume that triangular and s-shaped fuzzy numbers start rising from zero at x = a; reach a maximum of 1 at x = b; and decline to zero at x = c. Then the membership function $\mu(x)$ of a triangular fuzzy number is given by

$$\begin{aligned}
\mu(x) &= 0, \quad x \le a \\
&= (x - a)/(b - a), \quad a < x \le b \\
&= (c - x)/(c - b), \quad b < x \le c \\
&= 0, \quad x > c
\end{aligned} \tag{3.19}$$

For trapezoids, similar formulas are used employing b1 and b2 instead of b.

A piecewise quadratic fuzzy number is a graph of quadratics $\mu(x) = c_0 + c_1 x + c_2 x^2$ passing through the pairs of points (a, 0), ((a + b)/2, 0.5); ((a + b)/2, 0.5), (b, 1); (b, 1), ((b + c)/2, 0.5); and ((b + c)/2, 0.5), (b, 0). At the points a, b and c, $d(\mu(x))/dx = 0$. For x < a and x > c, $\mu(x) = 0$.

To derive simple formulas for the quadratic fuzzy numbers, it is best to consider an effective translation of the x axis to the points x = a for the first region, x = b for

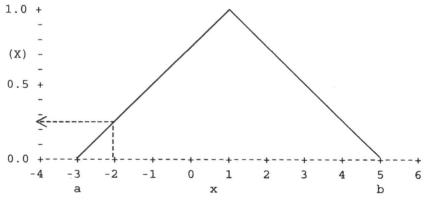

Figure 3.1 Membership function for a triangular fuzzy 1. Membership of −2 is 0.25.

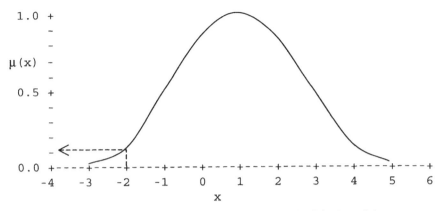

Figure 3.2 An s-shape fuzzy 1. Membership of -2 is about 0.1.

the second and third regions, and $x = c$ for the fourth region. At these three points the first derivatives are 0, and the membership functions are given by

$$\text{For } a \leq x \leq \frac{a+b}{2}; \quad \mu(x) = k_1(x-a)^2$$

$$\text{For } \frac{a+b}{2} \leq x \leq b; \quad \mu(x) = 1 - k_1(b-x)^2$$

(3.20)

$$\text{For } b \leq x \leq \frac{b+c}{2}; \quad \mu(x) = 1 - k_2(x-b)^2$$

$$\text{For } \frac{b+c}{2} \leq x \leq b; \quad \mu(x) = k_2(c-x)^2$$

The constants k_1 and k_2 are easily evaluated by realizing that at $x = (a+b)/2$ and $x = (b+c)/2$, the memberships are 0.5.

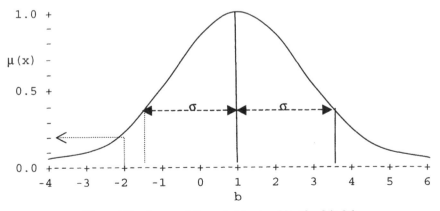

Figure 3.3 A normal fuzzy 1. Membership of -2 is 0.2.

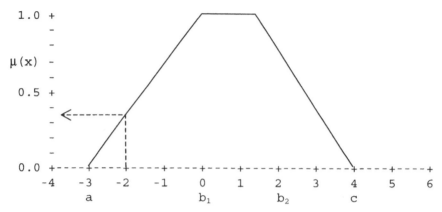

Figure 3.4 Membership function for a trapezoidal fuzzy number. Membership of -2 is 0.34.

We may derive a formula for a normal (bell-shaped) fuzzy number by using the dispersion $\delta/2$ from its central value b to the points where the membership is 0.5. [For the approximating triangular fuzzy number, $(b - \delta)$ corresponds to the point $x = a$ where the membership first begins to rise from zero, b to the central value, and $(b + \delta)$ to the point c where the membership first reaches zero after that.] A normal fuzzy number with dispersion δ and central value b has formula (3.21) for its membership function:

$$\exp\left(\ln(0.5)\left(\frac{x - b}{\delta/2}\right)^2\right) \tag{3.21}$$

The support of a fuzzy number is the interval between the point where the membership first begins to increase from zero and the point at which the membership last returns to zero. Thus in the fuzzy numbers above, the support is the interval from c to a, except for normal fuzzy numbers whose support is infinite.

If $a = b = c$ and $\delta = 0$, the fuzzy number has grade of membership 1 only at $x = b$, and is 0 everywhere else. Such a fuzzy number is called a singleton. A singleton is the precise fuzzy counterpart of an ordinary scalar number, such as (say) 35 or 3.1416. The graph of the membership function of a singleton fuzzy number is not very exciting; it has a single spike from membership zero to membership one (with zero width) at one point, and is zero everywhere else. Note that all the symmetric fuzzy numbers pass through the points where $\mu(x) = 0.5$ at $x = b +/- \delta/2$. Conventionally, membership functions for fuzzy numbers will be normalized, which means that their membership function takes on the value one for some x.

3.3.3 Linguistic Variables and Membership Functions

As mentioned in 3.3.1, some discrete fuzzy sets describe numeric quantities. Numeric discrete fuzzy sets have been formalized as linguistic variables, which

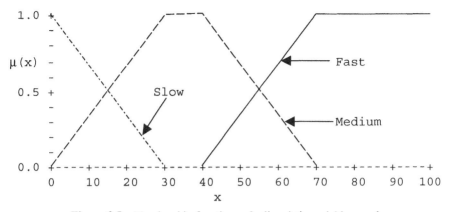

Figure 3.5 Membership functions of a linguistic variable speed.

consist of the name of the discrete fuzzy set; the names of its members, known as linguistic values; and for each linguistic value, a membership function like those for fuzzy numbers. The universe on which the linguistic variable is defined is assumed to be the entire real line, although in specific applications a smaller universe might be needed, such as all non-negative real numbers. (The original definition of a linguistic variable (Zadeh, 1974) was somewhat broader, but our definition will suffice.)

An example of a linguistic variable might be Speed, whose members are Slow, Medium, and Fast, and whose membership functions are shown in Figure 3.5. Linguistic variables have attracted much attention in the fuzzy literature, partly because of their great importance in fuzzy control. The reader is cautioned that in the fuzzy literature, the terminology has not been consistent; linguistic values have also been called linguistic labels and linguistic terms. In addition, while membership functions are of course fuzzy sets with an infinite number of members, we have seen that they are only one kind of fuzzy set. However, because of the great interest in fuzzy control, the term "fuzzy set" in the literature often is assumed to be synonymous with membership function. Usually, the context will make clear what is meant.

3.4 FUZZY RELATIONS

3.4.1 Matrices of Truth Values

We will have several situations in which we deal with arrays of truth values. For example, if we have digitized a membership function by sampling it at discrete values of its numeric argument, we have created a vector of truth values. In the following section on fuzzy relations, we will deal with matrices of truth values. We will call these fuzzy matrices. We now define an important operation we can employ on such arrays. Roughly speaking, the operation of addition in ordinary matrices is analogous to the fuzzy logical OR, and the operation of multiplication on ordinary matrices is analogous to the fuzzy logical AND.

The most important operation on matrices of truth values is called composition, and is analogous to matrix multiplication. Suppose I have two fuzzy matrices A and B. To compose these matrices, they must meet the same size compatibility restrictions as in ordinary matrix multiplication. Let A have l rows and m columns, and let B have m rows and n columns. They are compatible, since the number of columns of A equals the number of rows of B. The composition of A and B is denoted $A \circ B$, and will produce a matrix C having l rows and n columns.

In ordinary matrix multiplication, we would obtain c_{ij} by summing the product $a_{ik} \times b_{kj}$ over k. We could write this as

$$c_{i,j} = a_{i,1} \cdot b_{1,j} + a_{i,2} \cdot b_{2,j} + \cdots + a_{i,n} \cdot b_{n,j}$$

In fuzzy matrix composition, we obtain c_{ij} by repeatedly ORing (a_{ik} AND b_{kj}) over all values of k, using min–max logic by default. This procedure gives:

$$c_{ij} = (a_{i,1} \ AND \ b_{1,j}) \ OR \ (a_{i,2} \ AND \ b_{2,j}) \ OR \ \cdots \ OR \ (a_{i,n} \ AND \ b_{n,j}) \qquad (3.22)$$

The operation of composing matrices A and B is written $C = A \circ B$. For example, suppose we have these two fuzzy matrices to be composed:

$$A = \begin{bmatrix} 0.2 & 0.4 & 0.6 \\ 0.3 & 0.6 & 0.9 \end{bmatrix}$$

$$B = \begin{bmatrix} 0.5 & 1 \\ 0.7 & 0.5 \\ 1 & 0 \end{bmatrix} \qquad (3.23)$$

We first compute $c_{1,1}$, and apply (3.22) to the first row of A and the first column of B. The minimum of 0.2 and 0.5 is 0.2; min(0.4, 0.7) is 0.4; and min(0.6, 1) is 0.6; and the maximum of these minima is 0.6. Continuing this procedure, we obtain C as:

$$C = \begin{bmatrix} 0.6 & 0.4 \\ 0.9 & 0.5 \end{bmatrix} \qquad (3.24)$$

3.4.2   Relations Between Sets

We have two universal sets X and Y. By $X \times Y$ we mean the set of all ordered pairs (x, y) for x in X and y in Y. A fuzzy relation R on $X \times Y$ is a fuzzy subset of $X \times Y$; that is, for each (x, y) pair we have a number ranging from 0 to 1, a measure of the relationship between x and y.

As a simple example of a fuzzy relation let $X = \{John, Jim, Bill\}$ and $Y = \{Fred, Mike, Sam\}$. The fuzzy relation R between X and Y, which we will call "resemblance", might be as shown in Table 3.3.

Fuzzy relations may be given as matrices if the sets involved are discrete, or analytically if the sets are continuous, usually numbers from the real line. The members of X and Y are often the members of fuzzy sets A and B; the fuzzy relation between their members is often a function of their grades of membership in A and in B.

Theoretical fuzzy logical inference involves an important application of fuzzy relations, in which the fuzzy relation is usually an implication, as discussed in Section 3.1. (While this theory is important to fuzzy logicians, it is much less so to builders of fuzzy expert systems, as we shall see below.) First, we must choose an implication operator valid for classical logic. Suppose we picked the one given in equation (3. 8). Next let A and B be two fuzzy numbers with membership functions $A(x)$ and $B(x)$, respectively, shown in Figure 3.6. (Here X = Y = the set of real numbers.) The fuzzy relation, from equation (3.8) is

$$R(x, y) = \min(1, 1 - A(x) + B(y)) \tag{3.25}$$

for x and y any real numbers. Then tv(A → B) = $R(x, y)$ in fuzzy logic. If A and B are the two fuzzy numbers shown in Figure 3.6, the quadrant ($x \leq 0$, $y \geq 0$) of the fuzzy relation $R(x, y)$ is shown in Figure 3.7. (Other quadrants are not shown, since they would obscure the graph.) $R(x, y)$ is symmetric about the (y, R) plane, and is everywhere 1 outside the region ($-4 < x < 4$).

In fuzzy inference, we will need to compose fuzzy relations. If the fuzzy relation exists in matrix form, the procedure in Section 3.4 may be followed. However, the fuzzy relation may be given as a continuous function. Let R be a fuzzy relation on $X \times Y$ and S another fuzzy relation on $Y \times Z$. Then $R(x, y)$ is a number in [0, 1] for all x in X and all y in Y, and $S(y, z)$ has its values in [0, 1] for all y in Y and all z in Z. We compose R and S to get T, a fuzzy relation on $X \times Z$. This is written as $R \circ S = T$. We compute T as follows:

$$T(x, z) = \sup_y \{\min\{R(x, y), S(y, z)\}\} \tag{3.26}$$

In equation (3.26), "sup" stands for supremum, which must be used in place of max for many infinite sets. For example, the sup of x in [0, 1) = 1, but this interval has no max. On the other hand, sup of x in [0, 1] = max of x in [0, 1] = 1. Other AND type operators [eqs. (3.2)–(3.3)] may be used in place of min in equation (3.26).

TABLE 3.3   A Fuzzy Relation

	Fred	Mike	Sam
John	0.2	0.8	0.5
Jim	0.9	0.3	0.0
Bill	0.6	0.4	0.7

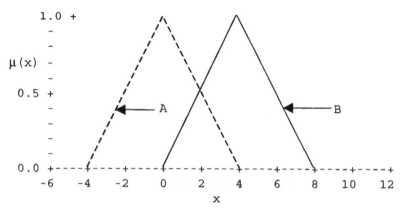

Figure 3.6 Membership functions of two fuzzy numbers A and B.

As an example of composition, suppose the universe X has three members, and the universe Y has two members. Let the relation between X and Y be given in (3.27) as matrix R:

$$R = \begin{bmatrix} 0.4 & 0.8 \\ 0.2 & 0.9 \\ 1 & 0 \end{bmatrix} \tag{3.27}$$

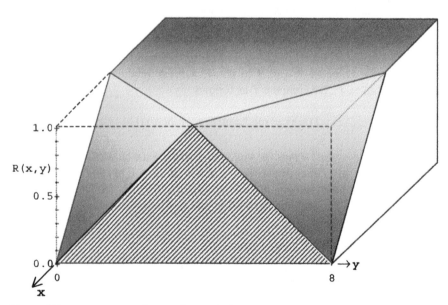

Figure 3.7 Part of one quadrant of fuzzy relation A → B between fuzzy numbers A(x) and B(y) shown in Figure 3.6. Quadrant shown is x < 0, y > 0.

Now suppose that a fuzzy set A, a fuzzy subset of X, has grades of membership

$$A = (0.5 \quad 0.8 \quad 0.2) \tag{3.28}$$

and we wish to compose fuzzy set A with R to get the grades of membership in fuzzy set B, a fuzzy subset of Y. Then

$$B_j = \max(\min(A_1, R_{i,j}), \min(A_2, R_{i,j}) \ldots \tag{3.29}$$

Applying (3.29) to the data in (3.27) and (3.28), we obtain

$$B = (0.4 \quad 0.8) \tag{3.30}$$

3.5 TRUTH VALUE OF FUZZY PROPOSITIONS

A general form of a common simple fuzzy proposition is

$$(A \text{ (comparison operator) } B) \tag{3.31}$$

in which A and B are compatible data items and the comparison operator is compatible with the data types of A and B. Not all data types are compatible; for example, we cannot compare an integer to a character string. The data types also restrict the comparison operators that may be used with them; for example, we may only use Boolean comparisons between scalar numbers, but may use fuzzy (approximate) comparisons if one of the operands is fuzzy. Below we will discuss the most important fuzzy propositions: comparison of single-valued data, including members of discrete fuzzy sets; and comparison of fuzzy numbers.

3.5.1 Comparing Single-Valued Data

Suppose a fuzzy proposition A has the form

$$A: (x = y) \tag{3.32}$$

where x and y are single-valued data, such as integers. Say x has value 3 and truth value 0.8; y has value 3 and truth value 0.7. What is the truth value of proposition A?

It would seem fairly obvious that A cannot have a truth value greater than the truth value of either of its components. The truth value of x is 0.8; the truth value of the comparison is 1.0, since the value of x equals precisely the value of y; and the truth value of y is 0.7. The truth value of A is then

$$tv(A) = \min(0.8, 1.0, 0.7) = 0.7 \tag{3.33}$$

This is easily generalized to

$$tv(x \text{ (comparison operator) } y) = min(tv(x), tv(\text{comparison}), tv(y)) \qquad (3.34)$$

giving us a general way for evaluating the truth value of fuzzy propositions, which involve single-value data. Note that for Boolean comparison operators ($<$, $<=$, $=$, $>=$, $<$, $<>$) the truth value of the comparison will always be
0 or 1.)

Members of discrete fuzzy sets may be tested in the same way. Consider
proposition B:

$$B = (\textit{size is Small}) \qquad (3.35)$$

where *size* is a discrete fuzzy set, of which *Small* is a member. The truth value of the
fuzzy set *size* is one. Since Small is a member of size, the truth value of "is" is also 1.
The truth value of *Small* is its grade of membership in *size*, say 0.75. Then the truth
value of B is given by

$$tv(B) = min(1, 1, (tv(Small))) = 0.75 \qquad (3.36)$$

The truth value of such propositions as (3.35) is always the grade of membership of
the fuzzy set member. (There are cases when a discrete fuzzy set may be a member
of a higher level fuzzy set and its truth value may not be 1, but these are not discussed in this book.)

3.5.2 Comparing Fuzzy Numbers

Comparing fuzzy numbers involves data with multiple values and truth values; the
members of a fuzzy number are numbers from the real line. This comparison may be
carried out using the extension principle:

$$tv(A \sim= B) = max(min(A(x), B(x) \text{ over all } x$$

Let us compare the fuzzy numbers A and B, shown in Figure 3.8, for equality;
that is, we will evaluate the truth value of the proposition (A $\sim=$ B), where $\sim=$
stands for "approximately equals".

A and B intersect at grades of membership 0 and 0.5. The greatest of these
is 0.5; that is, the truth value of the approximate comparison (A $\sim=$ B).
Extension of this method to cover other fuzzy comparisons between fuzzy
numbers, such as (A $\sim<$ B), requires additional mathematics, and will be taken
up in Section 4.6.

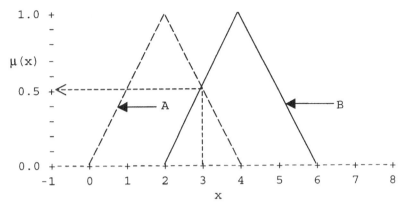

Figure 3.8   Comparing two fuzzy numbers A and B for equality.

3.6   FUZZIFICATION AND DEFUZZIFICATION

3.6.1   Fuzzification

The verb "to fuzzify" has two meanings: (1) to find the fuzzy version of a crisp concept, and (2) to find grades of membership of linguistic values of a linguistic variable corresponding to an input number, scalar or fuzzy. Usually, the term fuzzification is used in the second sense, and it is that sense that we now explore.

Suppose we have a fuzzy number t whose truth values are defined from 0 to 100°C. To fuzzify t means to find grades of membership of linguistic values in a linguistic variable (say Temperature), which are the linguistic equivalent of the number t, over the interval t [0, 100]. The name of the fuzzy set could be Temp with members {low, medium, high}, all defined by membership functions in [0, 100].

The fuzzification operation is quite simple. The grade of membership of each linguistic value is the truth value of the fuzzy propositions

$$\mu(low) = tv(t \sim= low)$$
$$\mu(medium) = tv(t \sim= medium) \tag{3.37}$$
$$\mu(high) = tv(t \sim= high)$$

in which (e.g.) $\mu(low)$ is the grade of membership of low in linguistic variable Temp, and the operator symbol $\sim=$ indicates an approximate comparisons between the operands, defined in Section 3.5.2.

We illustrate fuzzification by showing the membership functions for Temp together with a fuzzy number for t, to be fuzzified into Temp in Figure 3.9.

The input fuzzy number t crosses the membership function of low at a membership value of 0.42; crosses the membership function for medium at two non-zero

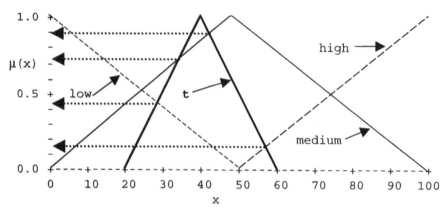

Figure 3.9 Membership functions of a linguistic variable temperature, with an input fuzzy number t to be fuzzified. Grade of membership of low is approximately 0.43; of medium, 0.89; and of high, 0.15.

points, of which the greater is 0.88; and the crosses membership for high at 0.14. The fuzzified membership value of low is 0.42; of medium, 0.88; and of high, 0.14. The fuzzification process is now complete, and Temperature is now this fuzzy set:

$$\text{Temperature} = \left\{ \frac{0.42}{\text{low}}, \frac{0.88}{\text{medium}}, \frac{0.14}{\text{high}} \right\} \tag{3.38}$$

Exercise Fuzzify.par. Program Fuzzify.par illustrates converting a number, the weight of a dog, into a fuzzy set of word descriptors. Membership functions are defined and plotted to represent the validity of the descriptors Small, Medium, or Large as applied to your dog. The input number will be the weight of your dog, real or imagined; the output will be the grades of membership (truth values) of the descriptive terms derived from your input number. Simply invoke TFLOPS, load program Fuzzify.par from the Examples folder and run it. The truth values are given on a zero-1000 scale, rather than 0 to 1.

The critical command, fuzzify, is in rule r2:

```
:rule r2
rule (goal Fuzzifies DogWt into fuzzy set size)
IF (in Data DogWt = <X> AND DogWt > 0)
THEN
message 'Fuzzifying <X>\n',
fuzzify 1 size <X>,
fire block 0 off,
fire block 1 on;
```

Fuzzify.par uses two rule blocks, and activates and deactivates them with the "fire" command.

3.6.2 Defuzzification

At the end of a sequence of rule firings in a fuzzy expert system we may end up with a fuzzy conclusion C that is a linguistic variable, whose values have been assigned grades of membership. Quite often we want to compute a single scalar, which corresponds to these grades of membership. The process of computing a scalar from C is called defuzzification. This is especially needed in fuzzy control because the final conclusion must be communicated to the process, and the defuzzified value is the signal sent to the process.

Defuzzification is a much more complex process than fuzzification; there are several choices to be made, and many different methods have been proposed. We will not attempt to explore the entire array of possibilities; instead, we will lay out the areas where choices must be made, and indicate which choices are most commonly used.

We will assume that at the start of the defuzzification process, the grades of membership of the fuzzy set to be defuzzified are known.

First, we must decide how to modify the membership functions for the linguistic values to reflect the fact that each value probably has a different grade of membership, some of which may be 0, and some of which will in all likelihood not be 1, but somewhere between 0 and 1. Let us call a general linguistic value "value", and the linguistic variable of which value is a member "Lvariable". We will call the membership of real number x in "value" $\mu(x, \text{value})$ and the membership of value in lvar $\mu(\text{value}, \text{Lvariable})$. We now wish to modify the membership function for value to reflect the fact that the membership of value in Lvariable is not necessarily 1. Let us call the modified membership function $\mu'(x, \text{value})$. We usually modify the $\mu(x, \text{value})$ by ANDing the membership function $\mu(x, \text{value})$ with $\mu(\text{value}, \text{lvar})$. This yields

$$\mu'(x, \text{temp}) = \mu(x, \text{temp}) \text{ AND } \mu(\text{temp}, \text{lvar}) \tag{3.39}$$

The most common choices for the AND operator in (3.39) are the Zadehian min(A, B), often known as the Mamdani method because of its early successful use in process control by Mamdani (1976) and the product operator $tv(A) \cdot tv(B)$. In Figure 3.10, we show the membership functions of Figure 3.9 modified to reflect the memberships of their respective linguistic values.

Next, the individual membership functions in Figure 3.10 must be aggregated into a single membership function for the entire linguistic variable. Aggregation operators resemble t-conorms, but with fewer restrictions (Klir and Yuan 1995, p. 88 ff); the Zadehian max OR operator is frequently used. Figure 3.11 shows the aggregated membership functions of Figure 3.10.

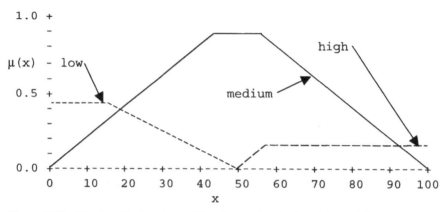

Figure 3.10   Membership functions of linguistic values in linguistic variable temperature, modified by the grades of membership of the linguistic values A AND B = min(A, B).

In the last step, we find a single number compatible with the membership function for Temp in Figure 3.11. This number will be the output from this final step in the defuzzification process.

There are several methods for calculating a single defuzzified number. We will present three: the *average maximum* method, the *weighted average maxima* method, and the method most commonly used, a *centroid* method. In the following, let x represent the numbers from the real line, let $\mu(x)$ be the corresponding grade of membership in the aggregated membership function, let xmin be the minimum x value at the maximum and xmax be the maximum x value at the maximum, and let $\bar{X}$ be the defuzzified value of x.

The simplest is the average maximum method. In Figure 3.11, the maximum grade of membership stretches from x = 43 to x = 55. The average of

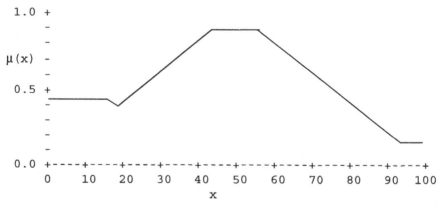

Figure 3.11   Aggregated membership functions of linguistic values in linguistic variable temperature, using Zadehian max(A, B) OR operator.

these is 49; this is the defuzzified value by the average maximum method. The formula is

$$\bar{X}(\text{average maximum}) = (x\ \text{max}_1 + x\ \text{max}_2)/2 \qquad (3.40)$$

Next is the weighted average maxima method. In Figure 3.11, we have two maxima: one stretches from x = zero to x = 15 with grade of membership 0.42, and the second stretches from x = 43 to x = 55 with grade of membership 0.88. We take the average of these two maxima, weight each by its grade of membership, and add the products, and divide this sum by the sum of the grades of membership. The defuzzified value by this method is

$$\bar{X} = \left(\frac{(0+15)}{2} \cdot 0.42 + \left(\frac{43+55}{2}\right) 0.88 \right) \bigg/ (0.42 + 0.88) = 35.6$$

Denote the start and end of each local maximum by $x\text{min}_i$ and $x\text{max}_i$. If we have n local maxima, the general formula is

$$\bar{X}(\text{weighted average maxima}) = \sum_{i=1}^{n} \frac{(x\ \text{max}_i \cdot \mu(x\ \text{max}_i))}{\sum \mu(x\ \text{max}_i)} \qquad (3.41)$$

The final method, preferred by most fuzzy control engineers, is the centroid method. It is

$$\bar{X}(centroid) = \frac{\int_a^b x\mu(x)dx}{\int_a^b \mu(x)dx} \qquad (3.42)$$

In these integrals, we have assumed that the support of the aggregated membership function is the interval [a, b]. In our case, the defuzzified value by the centroid method is 41.8.

The defuzzification process may be made much simpler by assigning singleton membership functions to the output linguistic variable. Remember that a singleton is a fuzzy number with grade of membership one at only one value of its argument, and grade of membership zero everywhere else. In this case, the centroid method reduces to a simple weighted average.

While not usually of interest to control engineers, the idea of reversible defuzzification is sometimes attractive to expert system modelers in other areas. By reversible defuzzification, we mean that if an input number is fuzzified and immediately defuzzified, the defuzzified value equals the input value. Reversible defuzzification is assured if membership functions are triangular, adjacent membership functions intersect at a membership of 0.5, as each membership function begins to decline from 1 the next begins to ascend from 0, and memberships always add to 1 over the admissible range of input numbers. However, fuzzy control engineers routinely shape response surfaces (plots of defuzzified value against the input variables) very carefully to achieve specific quantitative results, and may require the flexibility offered by the numerous variations on the defuzzification theme.

Exercise Defuzz.par. Program Defuzz.par illustrates both fuzzification and defuzzification. A discrete fuzzy set with members Short, Medium, and Tall is declared, and membership functions for these terms are defined. The user enters a height. Defuzz then fuzzifies the height into discrete fuzzy set size and prints out the grades of membership. This newly defined fuzzy set is now defuzzified into a scalar number, which is then printed out. The membership functions are chosen so that fuzzification and defuzzification are reversible.

Of course, non-numeric discrete fuzzy sets cannot be defuzzified since they do not describe numbers.

3.7 QUESTIONS

3.1 Evaluate the following:

    a. Proposition P = A AND B; proposition Q = A OR B. For all crisp truth values for A and B, first construct a truth table for P, for Q, for P AND Q, and for P OR Q.

    b. Proposition R = A IMPLIES B; proposition S = A OR B. For all crisp truth values for A and B, first construct a truth table for P, for Q, for P AND Q, and for P OR Q.

3.2 Let W be a complex logical proposition made up of elementary (atomic) propositions P, Q, R... connected by and, or, implies and using not. For example,

$$W = \text{not } (P \text{ implies (not } Q))$$

W is a tautology if tv(W) = 1 for all values of tv(P), tv(Q),...; the truth table for a tautology W will contain only 1 in its last column. W is a contradiction if tv(W) = 0 for all values of tv(P),...; the truth table for a contradiction W will contain only 0 in its last column. Determine if the following complex propositions are tautologies, contradictions, or neither.

    a. P and (not Q)

    b. (not P) or Q

    c. (P and (P implies Q)) → Q

    d. ((P → Q) and (Q → R)) → (P → R)

3.3 Show that using the tautology (de Morgan's theorem)

$$P \text{ or } Q = \text{not}((\text{not } P) \text{ and } (\text{not } Q))$$

we can obtain

a. (3.4) from (3.1)

b. (3.5) from (3.2)

c. (3.6) from (3.3)

3.4 Derive the formulas for k_1 and k_2 for a piecewise quadratic fuzzy number with membership 0 at x = a, 1 at x = b, and 0 at x = c with a < b < c. Evaluate k_1 and k_2 if a = 0, b = 1 and c = 4, and test that $\mu = 0$ at x = (a + b)/2 and x = (b + c)/2. (See Section 3.3.2.)

3.5 Construct a truth table for the operator NAND: A NAND B = NOT(A AND B) using

a. Equation (3.1) for AND

b. Equation (3.3) for AND

3.6 Assume tv(P) and tv(Q) can be any value in [0, 1]. Show that

a. Equations (3.1) and (3.2) can produce different results.

b. Equations (3.3) and (3.6) can produce different results.

3.7 Evaluate equation (3.11) using (3.3) for AND and (3.6) for OR

3.8 Let A be a 3 × 3 fuzzy matrix and we compute $A^2 = A \cdot A$ using min–max composition as discussed in Section 3.4.1. Let $A^3 = A^2 \cdot A$, $A^4 = A^3 \cdot A$, and so on.

a.

$$\text{If } A = \begin{pmatrix} 0 & 0.2 & 1 \\ 0.4 & 0 & 1 \\ 0 & 1 & 0.3 \end{pmatrix}, \text{ then find } A^2, A^3, A^4, A^5, \ldots$$

b.

$$\text{If } A = \begin{pmatrix} 1 & 0 & 0.2 \\ 0.4 & 1 & 0 \\ 0 & 0.3 & 1 \end{pmatrix}, \text{ then find } A^2, A^3, \ldots$$

c. Make an educated guess on what happens to $A^2, A^3, A^4, \ldots$ for all 3 × 3 fuzzy matrices A.

3.9 Fuzzification in equation (3.31) was done using a fuzzy number for *t*. It can also be done using crisp numbers for t, considering the crisp number as a singleton fuzzy number. Compute the discrete fuzzy set Temperature using Figure 3.9 if

a. t = 50

b. t = 25

c. t = 75

3.10 Defuzzification, as described in Section 3.6.2, is somewhat complicated. To speed up defuzzification assign to each fuzzy number its central value and then find the centroid. In the example in 3.6.2, we obtain the discrete fuzzy set

$$F = \left(\frac{0.42}{0} \quad \frac{0.88}{50} \quad \frac{0.14}{100} \right)$$

from equation (3.31). Find the centroid of F and compare to the value of 41.8 obtained in Section 3.6.2.

4 Fuzzy Logic, Fuzzy Sets, and Fuzzy Numbers: II

4.1 INTRODUCTION

This chapter presents some topics in fuzzy systems theory more advanced than those in Chapter 3. We begin with the algebra of fuzzy sets and fuzzy numbers, followed by a discussion of fuzzy logical inference called approximate reasoning. A discussion of the modifying words called hedges and a treatment of fuzzy propositions is followed by a section on fuzzy arithmetic, which includes a section on the important extension principle. The chapter concludes with a more complete treatment of fuzzy comparisons than that given in Chapter 3. The problems at the end of the chapter are designed to test your knowledge of basic fuzzy logic and fuzzy sets.

4.2 ALGEBRA OF FUZZY SETS

4.2.1 T-Norms and t-Conorms: Fuzzy AND and OR Operators

Given fuzzy sets $A, B, C, \ldots$ all fuzzy subsets of X, we wish to compute $A \cup B, B \cap C$, and so on. What we use in fuzzy logic are the generalized AND and OR operators from classical logic. They are called t-norms (for AND) and t-conorms (for OR). We first define t-norms.

A t-norm T is a function from $[0, 1] \times [0, 1]$ into $[0, 1]$. That is, if $z = T(x, y)$, then x, y, and z all belong to the interval $[0, 1]$. All t-norms have the following four properties:

1. $T(x, 1) = x$ (boundary)
2. $T(x, y) = T(y, x)$ (commutativity)
3. if $y_1 \leq y_2$, *then* $T(x, y_1) \leq T(x, y_2)$ (monotonicity)
4. $T(x, T(y, z)) = T(T(x, y), z)$ (associativity)

T-norms generalize the AND from classical logic. This means that $tv(P \text{ AND } Q) = T(tv(P), tv(Q))$ for any t-norm and equations (4.1)–(4.3) are all examples of

Fuzzy Expert Systems and Fuzzy Reasoning, By William Siler and James J. Buckley
ISBN 0-471-38859-9   Copyright © 2005 John Wiley & Sons, Inc.

t-norms. The basic t-norms are

$$T_m(x, y) = \min(x, y) \tag{4.1}$$

$$T_L(x, y) = \max(0, x + y - 1) \tag{4.2}$$

$$T_p(x, y) = xy \tag{4.3}$$

and $T^*(x, y)$ defined as x if $y = 1$, y if $x = 1$, 0 otherwise.

T_m is called the standard or Zadehian intersection, and is the one most commonly employed; T_L is the bounded difference intersection; T_p is the algebraic product; and T^* is the drastic intersection. It is well known that

$$T^* \le T_L \le T_p \le T_m \tag{4.4}$$

and

$$T^* \le T \le T_m \tag{4.5}$$

for any t-norm T.

If A and B are fuzzy subsets of universal set X, then $C = A \cap B$ is also a fuzzy subset of X and from De Morgan's theorems (3.8) the membership function of C as

$$C(x) = \text{NOT } T(\text{NOT } A(x), \text{NOT } B(x)) = 1 - T(1 - A(x)), 1 - B(x)) \tag{4.6}$$

for all x in X. Equation (4.6) defines the membership function for C for any t-norm T.

t-Conorms generalize the OR operation from classical logic. As for t-norms, a t-conorm $C(x, y) = z$ has x, y, and z always in [0, 1]. The basic properties of any t-conorm C are

1. $C(x, 0) = x$ (boundary)
2. $C(x, y) = C(y, x)$ (commutativity)
3. If $y_1 \le y_2$, then $C(x, y_1) \le C(x, y_2)$ (monotonicity)
4. $C(x, C(y, z)) = C(C(x, y), z)$ (associativity)

The basic t-conorms are

1. $C_m(x, y) = \max(x, y)$ called standard union $\tag{4.7}$

2. $C_L(x, y) = \min(1, x + y)$ called bounded sum $\tag{4.8}$

3. $C_p(x, y) = x + y - xy$ called algebraic sum $\tag{4.9}$

and

   4. $C^*(x, y)$ called drastic union that is defined as:
      x if y $= 0$; y if x $= 0$; and one otherwise   (4.10)

It is well known that

$$C_m \le C_p \le C_L \le C^* \qquad (4.11)$$

and

$$C_m \le C \le C^* \qquad (4.12)$$

for all t-conorms C.
   To compute $A \cup B$ for A and B fuzzy subsets of X, we use a t-conorm. If we let $D = A \cup B$, the we compute the membership function for D as

$$D(x) = C(A(x), B(x)) \qquad (4.13)$$

for a t-conorm C, for all x in X.
   The complement of a fuzzy set A, written A^c, is always determined by

$$A^c(x) = 1 - A(x) \qquad (4.14)$$

for all x in X.
   T-norms and t-conorms are only defined for two variables and in fuzzy expert systems we need to extend them to n variables. Through associativity, the fourth property, we may extend T(x, y) to $T(x_1, \ldots, x_n)$ and C(x, y) to $C(x_1, \ldots, x_n)$ for each x_i in [0, 1], $1 \le i \le n$. T_m and C_m are easily generalized to

$$T_m(x_1, \ldots, x_n) = \min(x_1, \ldots, x_n) \qquad (4.15)$$
$$C_m(x_1, \ldots, x_n) = \max(x_1, \ldots, x_n) \qquad (4.16)$$

Next we have for T_L and C_L

$$T_L(x_1, \ldots, x_n) = \max\left(0, \sum_{i=1}^{n} x_i - n + 1\right) \qquad (4.17)$$

$$C_L(x_1, \ldots, x_n) = \min\left(1, \sum_{i=1}^{n} x_i\right) \qquad (4.18)$$

Also, we easily see that

$$T_P(x_1, \ldots, x_n) = x_1, \ldots, x_n \tag{4.19}$$

but the extension of C_p is more complicated. For n = 3, we see that

$$C_P(x_1, x_2, x_3) = (x_1 + x_2 + x_3) - (x_1x_2 + x_1x_3 + x_2x_3) + (x_1x_2x_3) \tag{4.20}$$

and the reader can see what needs to be done for n = 4.

When one computes $A \cap B$ and $A \cup B$ one usually uses a t-norm T for $A \cap B$ and its dual t-conorm C for $A \cup B$. A t-norm T and t-conorm C are dual when

$$C(x, y) = 1 - T(1 - x, 1 - y)$$

The usual dual t-norms and t-conorms are T_m, C_m and T_L, C_L and T_p, C_p and T^*, C^*.

Using the above operators, fuzzy sets do not enjoy all the algebraic properties of regular (crisp) sets. (In Section 4.2.2, we will see that this problem may be avoided by the use of correlation fuzzy logic.) Once you choose a t-norm T for intersection and its dual t-conorm C for union, some basic algebraic property of crisp sets will fail for fuzzy sets. Let us illustrate this fact using T_m, C_m, and T_L, C_L. For crisp sets, the law of non-contradiction is $A \cap A^c = \varnothing$ (the empty set) and the law of the excluded middle is $A \cup A^c = X$ (the universal set), where A is any crisp subset of X. Using T_m, C_m both of these basic laws can fail. For fuzzy sets, the law of non-contradiction is $A \cap A^c = \varnothing$, where now $\varnothing$ is the fuzzy empty set whose membership function is always zero; the law of the excluded middle would be $A \cup A^c = X$, where X is the fuzzy set whose membership function is always one. In Section 4.2.3, we show that we do not get identically one for C_m. However, in the problems you are asked to verify that the laws of non-contradiction and excluded middle hold if you use T_L and C_L. But, if you choose to use T_L and C_L for fuzzy set algebra, the distributive law fails. This means that for $T = T_L$ for intersection and $C = C_L$ for union, then

$$A \cap (B \cup C) \neq (A \cap B) \cup (A \cap C) \tag{4.21}$$

for some fuzzy sets A, B, and C (see the Questions, Section 4.8).

4.2.2 Correlation Fuzzy Logic

As we have seen, one must be careful when working with equations in fuzzy sets involving intersection, union, and complementation because the equation may be true for crisp sets but false for fuzzy sets. It would be nice to have a method of doing the algebra of fuzzy sets so that all the basic equations for crisp sets also hold for fuzzy sets. This is true of correlation fuzzy logic. In correlation fuzzy logic you can use T_L, C_L in certain cases and T_m, C_m in other cases.

In the papers Buckley and Siler (1998, 1999), we introduced a new t-norm $T^\wedge$ and a new t-conorm $C^\wedge$, which depend on a parameter ρ in $[-1, 1]$, which is the correlation between the truth values of the operands. For example, to compute $D = A \cap B$ we use $D(x) = T^\wedge(A(x), B(x))$ for all x, where the t-norm $T^\wedge$ to be used depends on any prior association between A and B. (In most cases ρ will demand prior knowledge, but if we are combining A and NOT A prior knowledge is not required; we know that A and NOT A are maximally negatively correlated, and their correlation is -1.) Let

$$
\begin{aligned}
a &= tv(A) \\
b &= tv(B) \\
\rho &= \textit{prior correlation coefficient between a and b} \\
\delta &= \sqrt{a(1 - a)b(1 - b)}
\end{aligned}
\tag{4.22}
$$

Then $T^\wedge(a, b)$ and $C^\wedge(a, b)$ are defined by

$$
\begin{aligned}
\delta &= a(1 - a)b(1 - b) \\
\rho_U &= (\min(a, b) - ab)/\delta \\
\rho_L &= (\max(a + b - 1, 0))/\delta \\
&\text{if } \rho < \rho_L \text{ then } \rho' = \rho_L \\
&\text{else if } r > r_U \text{ then } r' = r_U \\
&\text{else } r' = r \\
T^\wedge(a, b) &= a + b - r'\delta \\
C^\wedge(a, b) &= a + b - ab - r'\delta
\end{aligned}
\tag{4.23}
$$

A specification of ρ as 1 is equivalent to specifying the standard min–max fuzzy logic. It is possible to specify values for a, b, and ρ that are incompatible. For example, if a is specified as 0.4 and b as 0.6, a value for ρ of 1 is not possible. In (4.16), ρ_U and ρ_L are the limits of possible values for ρ given a and b. In the event that a value of ρ outside those limits is specified, the possible value of $\rho(\rho\text{Eff})$ nearest the specified value is used. If a value of ρ of 1 is specified, this value of ρEff will always result in the standard Zadehian min–max logic being used, no matter what values a and b have.

The notion of semantic consistency between fuzzy sets was put forward by Thomas (1995). Up to now, we have considered proposition with a single truth value. We may also have to consider combining fuzzy numbers and membership functions defined on the real line. Let one fuzzy number or membership function be defined by $\mu_1(x)$, and the other by $\mu_2(x)$. In this case, we compute the cross-correlation coefficient using the well-known formula

$$
\rho = \mathrm{cov}(\mu_1(x), \mu_2(x))/\sqrt{\mathrm{var}(\mu_1(x)) \cdot \mathrm{var}(\mu_2(x))}
$$

by integrating *over the area of overlap only*. If no overlap, $\rho = -1$.

It was shown that

$$T_L \leq T^\wedge \leq T_M \tag{4.24}$$

$$C_M \leq C^\wedge \leq C_L \tag{4.25}$$

$$T^\wedge = T_p, C^\wedge = C_p, \text{ if } \rho = 0; T^\wedge = T_L, C^\wedge = C_L, \text{ if } \rho = -1 \tag{4.26}$$

and

$$T^\wedge = T_m, C^\wedge = C_m, \text{ if } \rho = 1 \tag{4.27}$$

A computer routine in the C language to calculate a AND b and a OR b using correlation logic is

```c
//Function CorrLogic - given a, b and default r,
//returns aANDb and aORb
//04-17-2004 WS

#include <math.h>

double min(double x, double y);
double max(double x, double y);

bool CorrLogic (double a, double b, double r, double
*aANDb, double *aORb)
{
  double std, ru, rl;

  if (a < 0||a > 1||b < 0||b > 1||r < -1||r > 1)
          return false;

    std = sqrt(a * (1 - a) *b * (1 - b));
  if (std > 0)
  {
    ru = (min(a, b) - a *b)/std;
    rl = (max(a+b) - 1, 0) - a *b)/std;
    if (r < rl)
      r = rl;
    else if (r > ru)
      r = ru;
  }
  *aANDb = a *b+r *std;
  *aORb = a+b - a *b - r *std;
    return true;
}
```

```
double min(double x, double y)
{
    if (x < y)
        return x;
    else
        return y;
}

double max(double x, double y)
{
    if (x > y)
        return x;
    else
        return y;
}
```

There are two basic cases where it is obvious what to choose for ρ. To find $A \cup A, A \cap A$ we *must* use $\rho = 1$ since A and A are maximally positively correlated. Then, $T = T_m$ and $C = C_m$ so that $A \cup A = A, A \cap A = A$. For $A \cup A^c, A \cap A^c$ we *must* use $\rho = -1$ because A and A^c are maximally negatively correlated. Then, we have $T = T_L, C = C_L$ for this value of ρ so that $A \cup A^c = X, A \cap A^c = \varnothing$ and the laws of non-contradiction and excluded middle hold.

We showed that using this new t-norm and t-conorm (correlation logic), and properly choosing the value of the parameter ρ, all the basic laws of crisp set theory also now hold for fuzzy sets, including the laws of excluded middle and non-contradiction.

We may ask: If we have no knowledge of prior associations between A and B, what should the default logic be? We suggest, on the basis of nearly 20 years of experience, that the Zadehian min–max logic is a desirable default. If we are evaluating rules with complex antecedents, with any other logic the truth value of an antecedent with several clauses ANDed together tend to drift off to zero as the number of clauses increases; and when aggregating the truth values of a consequent fuzzy set member by ORing them together, the resulting truth value tends to drift up to one. The Zadeh logic, unless combining B and NOT B, passes a pragmatic test; *it works*, and works well.

4.2.3 Combining Fuzzy Numbers

Since fuzzy numbers are fuzzy sets, we may perform logical operations upon them, such as $A \cap B, A \cup B, A \cap B^c$, and so on, when A and B are fuzzy numbers. Consider the fuzzy number A and its complement NOT A in Figure 4.1.

We now construct the intersection A AND NOT A using the conventional min–max logic, T_m, shown in Figure 4.2. Because segments of membership functions coincide in a number of places, the labeling of the graph is a little complicated.

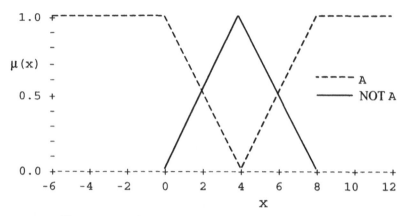

Figure 4.1   A fuzzy number A and its complement NOT A.

The intersection of A and NOT A is not everywhere zero, as we would expect from the laws of classical logic, but has two sharp peaks with $\mu(2)$ and $\mu(6)$ being 0.5. Similarly, the union A OR NOT A is not everywhere one but has two sharp notches, shown in Figure 4.3.

If, however, we use T_L rather than T_M, we obtain $A \cap A^c = \varnothing$ and not Figure 4.2. To evaluate $A \cup A^c$ use C_L, then $A \cup A^c = X$ and we eliminate the notches in Figure 4.3. An occasion when correlation logic is of theoretical importance was caused by a paper by Elkan (1994), which offered a proof that fuzzy logic was only valid for crisp propositions. This paper depended on the fact that standard fuzzy logic, and indeed all multivalued logic, fail to fulfill the laws of excluded middle and non-contradiction. When the appropriate logic is used for combining A and NOT A the excluded middle and non-contradiction laws are obeyed, and Elkan's proof fails.

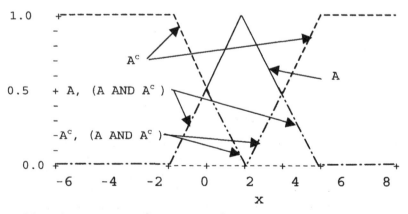

Figure 4.2   A fuzzy number A, A^c and (A AND A^c) using standard min–max fuzzy logic T_m.

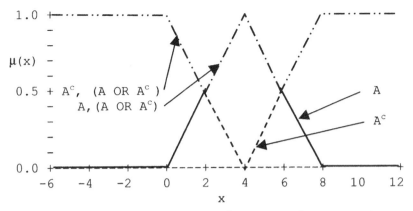

Figure 4.3   A fuzzy number A, its complement A^c, and (A OR A^c) using standard min–max fuzzy logic T_M.

4.3   APPROXIMATE REASONING

Approximate reasoning is the term usually used to refer to fuzzy logical inference employing the generalized fuzzy modus ponens, a fuzzy version of the classical modus ponens discussed in Section 3.1. (Here, we are using "approximate reasoning" in a strict technical sense; the term is also used sometimes in a less technical sense, to mean reasoning under conditions of uncertainty.)

The classical modus ponens is

$$if\ A\ then\ B \tag{4.28}$$

which can be read *if* proposition A is true, *then* infer that proposition B is true. The modus ponens itself is a proposition, sometimes written as "A implies B" or "A → B", where "implies" is a logical operator with A and B as operands whose truth table given in Chapter 3, Table 3.2. The modus ponens is an important tool in classical logic for inferring one proposition from another, and has been used for that purpose for roughly 2000 years.

The fuzzy version of the modus ponens, the *generalized modus ponens*, has been formulated as:

$$If\ X\ is\ A\ then\ Y\ is\ B$$
$$from\ X = A' \tag{4.29}$$
$$infer\ that\ Y = B'$$

in which A and A′ are fuzzy sets defined on the same universe, and B and B′ are also fuzzy sets defined on the same universe, which may be different from the universe on which A and A′ are defined. In fuzzy control, usually the membership functions of fuzzy sets are defined on the real line, and hence are fuzzy numbers.

Calculation of B′ from A, B, and A′ is straightforward. First, a fuzzy implication operator is chosen; implication operators are discussed in Section 3.1. The implication $A(x) \rightarrow B(y)$ defines a fuzzy relation $A \rightarrow B$ between A and B. Next, B′ is calculated by composing A′ with $A \rightarrow B$, following the procedure in Section 3.4.2:

$$B' = A' \circ (A \rightarrow B) \tag{4.30}$$

The fuzzy conclusion B′ is computed using the compositional rule of inference $B' = A'oR$ (Sections 3.4.1–3.4.2). This expression defines the membership function for the fuzzy conclusion B′. The compositional rule of inference is valid for all fuzzy sets; they do not have to be fuzzy numbers. A and A′ must be fuzzy subsets of the same universal set X, and B and B′ must be fuzzy subsets of a universal set Y, which may or may not be the same as X. Let us go through the details of the compositional rule of inference for discrete fuzzy sets. Let

$$A = \left\{ \frac{0.3}{x_1}, \frac{0.7}{x_2}, \frac{1.0}{x_3} \right\}$$

$$B = \left\{ \frac{0.5}{y_1}, \frac{1.0}{y_2}, \frac{0.6}{y_3} \right\} \tag{4.31}$$

and

$$A' = \left\{ \frac{1.0}{x_1}, \frac{0.6}{x_2}, \frac{0.3}{x_3} \right\} \tag{4.32}$$

Choose the implication operator $T(x, y) = \min(1, 1 - x + y)$, called the Lukasiewicz implication operator, in equation (3.8). Then, $R(x, y)$ is shown in (4.33).

$$R = \begin{bmatrix} 1 & 1 & 0.5 \\ 0.8 & 1 & 1 \\ 0.6 & 1 & 0.6 \end{bmatrix} \tag{4.33}$$

We are now ready to obtain B′ from A′oR. Using $T = T_m$, we see

$$B'(y_1) = \max(\min(1, 1), \min(0.6, 0.8), \min(0.3, 0.6)) = 1$$
$$B'(y_2) = \max\{\min(1, 1), \min(0.6, 1), \min(0.3, 1)\} = 1 \tag{4.34}$$
$$B'(y_3) = \max(\min(1, 0.5), \min(0.6, 1), \min(0.3, 0.6)) = 0.6$$

and

$$B' = \left\{ \frac{1.0}{y_1}, \frac{1.0}{y_2}, \frac{0.6}{y_3} \right\} \tag{4.35}$$

The fuzzy sets A and B in approximate reasoning are usually fuzzy numbers (or membership functions defined on the real line).

Approximate reasoning using the generalized modus ponens has been proposed for fuzzy inference from if–then rules. Consider the fuzzy if–then rule

$$\text{If } x \text{ is Big, then } y \text{ is Slow} \qquad (4.36)$$

Where Big is defined by fuzzy number A and Slow is specified by fuzzy number B. Now suppose we are presented with a new piece of information about Big in the form of fuzzy set A′. That is, we are given that $x = A'$ and this new fuzzy number does not have to equal A. Figure 4.4 shows an example of fuzzy numbers A, B and A′. A′ is close to A, but not identical.

Given the fuzzy rule in equation (4.27) and the data $x = A'$, we wish to draw a conclusion about Slow. If the conclusion is $y = B'$, we can apply the generalized modus ponens in (4.24) compute a new fuzzy number B′ for Speed. To do this we must first choose an fuzzy logical implication operator I(x, y) giving the implication relation between A(x) and B(y). I(x, y) could be any function that will reduce to the classical values for implication in Table 3.2 when x and y are 0 or 1, so we could use any of the formulas given in equations (3.7)–(3.9) or any other fuzzy implication operator.

There are many fuzzy implication operators from which to choose; Klir and Yuan (1995, p. 309) list fourteen. Choice, according to Klir and Yuan (1995), will depend on the application. Our application is clear; we wish to employ the implication operator in the generalized fuzzy modus ponens. Let R be the fuzzy relation (A → B). We pick the simplest (Gaines–Rescher), defined by equation (4.28),

$$R(x, y) = tv(A(x) \to B(y)) = 1 \text{ if } tv(A(x)) \le tv(B(y)), \text{ else } R(x, y) = 0 \quad (4.37)$$

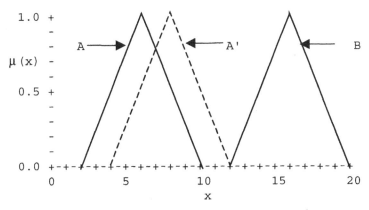

Figure 4.4 Membership functions of fuzzy numbers A, A′, and B.

and obtain B′ by composing A′ with R, using

$$B'(y) = \sup_x\{(A'(x), R(x, y))\} \tag{4.38}$$

where sup denotes supremum, the smallest number that is not exceeded by the arguments. Carrying out the calculation for $0 \le x \le 20$, we obtain the B′ shown in Figure 4.5.

We can see immediately that B′ is nowhere less than 0.5 on the entire real line. Clearly, using the centroid method to defuzzify a membership function that extends from −infinity to +infinity with non-zero membership is not possible. The problem is not caused by the particular implication operator chosen; any implication operator that reduces to the classical for crisp operands has a similar problem.

Another problem is the property of consistency. We say a method of fuzzy reasoning is consistent if whenever $A' = A$, we get the conclusion $B' = B$; that is, if the data matches the antecedent exactly, the conclusion must match the consequent exactly. However, approximate reasoning may, or may not, be consistent. It depends on the implication operator. For some it is consistent and for other implication operators it is not consistent. Klir and Yuan (1995, p. 309) list 14 implication operators, of which 7 do not possess consistency. [The Gaines–Rescher implication in equation (4.28) is consistent.]

A third problem is that if $A' \cap A = \varnothing$ using T_m, we get $B'(y) = 1$ for all y; if the data A′ and the specification A are disjoint, the conclusion is the universal set. We have been assuming that $I(0, y) = 1$ for all y, which is true for most of the usual implication operators (Klir and Yuan, 1995). You are also asked to check this result in the problems. Because of these reasons, and others discussed in Chapter 8, we will not use approximate reasoning in our fuzzy expert system. What is used in practice is not an implication operator, but a fuzzy AND (t-norm). Although of

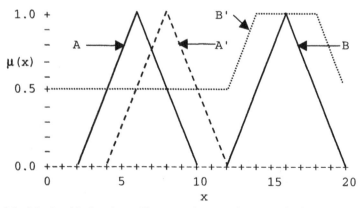

Figure 4.5 Membership functions of fuzzy numbers A, A′, B, and B′. B′ is obtained from A, A′, and B by Approximate Reasoning using Gaines–Rescher implication.

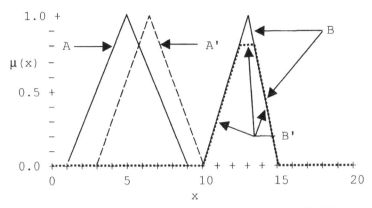

Figure 4.6   Membership functions of fuzzy numbers A, A', B, and B'. B' is obtained by composing A' with (A AND B).

course a t-norm is not an implication at all, the min t-norm used in this context is sometimes called a "Mamdani implication", from its use by Mamdani in fuzzy control.

The above discussion assumed that approximate reasoning was based on fuzzy implications that reduce to the classical for crisp operands. Fuzzy inference may be based on other fuzzy relations R. Going back to equation (4.28), we could define R by

$$R(x, y) = \min(A(x), B(y)) \tag{4.39}$$

We can compose A' with this R to obtain B'. If we do, we get the perfectly reasonable result shown in Figure 4.6. In fact, this general type of fuzzy relation based on t-norms is used almost universally in fuzzy control.

Approximate reasoning may be extended to more complex antecedents and to blocks (multiple) of IF-the rules (Klir and Yuan, 1995). However, we shall not present further results in this book.

4.4   HEDGES

Hedges are modifiers, adjectives, or adverbs, which change truth values. Such hedges as "about", "nearly", "roughly", and so on, are used in fuzzy expert systems to make writing rules easier and to make programs more understandable for users and domain experts. The term was originated by Zadeh (1972), and hedges have been developed and used to great effect by Cox (1999), which is highly recommended. Hedges are indispensible to the builder of fuzzy expert systems in the real world. There are several types of hedges, of which we will consider the two most important.

TABLE 4.1   Hedges that Create Fuzzy Numbers

Hedge	Spread, +/− % of central value at membership 0.5
nearly	5%
about	10%
roughly	25%
crudely	50%

One type of hedge, applied to scalar numbers, changes the scalar to a fuzzy number with dispersion depending on the particular term used. Thus, "nearly 2" is a fuzzy number with small dispersion, and "roughly 2" has a considerably wider spread. The precise meaning of the hedge term will vary from one expert system shell to another.

In FLOPS, each hedge term is associated with a percent of the central value, and specifies the spread of the fuzzy number from the central value to the 0.5 truth value point. [The reason the spread is specified at the 0.5 truth value rather than the support is that normal (bell-shaped, Gaussian) fuzzy numbers in theory have infinite support, and in practice a large support depending on the precision of the floating-point numbers in a particular implementation.]

FLOPS hedges of this type are not untypical of those employed by Cox. The hedge terms and corresponding membership function spread are given in Table 4.1, and are

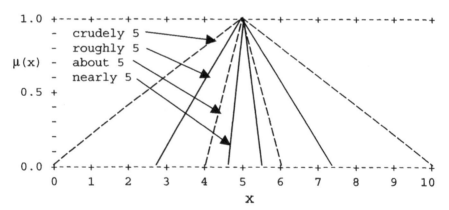

Figure 4.7   A fuzzy 5 created by various hedges.

TABLE 4.2   Hedges to Modify Truth Values

Hedge	Power to which truth value is raised
slightly	cube root
somewhat	square root
very	square
extremely	cube

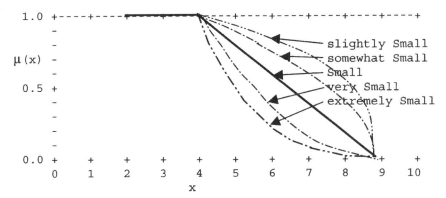

Figure 4.8 A membership function modified by hedges.

shown graphically as a fuzzy 5 in Figure 4.7. We assume that the fuzzy number is symmetrical, with a single value of the argument (the central value) at which the membership is one. The shape of the resulting fuzzy number is assumed separately specified, and may be linear, s-shaped (piecewise quadratic) or normal.

The second type of hedge is applied to truth values. "very Small" reduces the truth value of Small; "somewhat Small" increases the truth value. Usually, the original truth value is raised to a power greater than 1 for terms that reduce truth values, and less than 1 for terms that increase truth values. Table 4.2 defines hedges for modification of truth values, and Figure 4.8 gives a sample membership function modified by hedges. Again, the hedges employed by FLOPS are similar to those used by Cox.

As shown in Figure 4.8, hedges can operate on membership functions producing modified membership functions, and can be used to modify clauses in fuzzy propositions. Consider the fuzzy proposition

```
speed is Fast
```

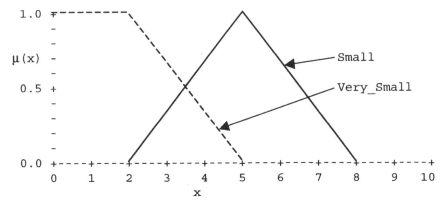

Figure 4.9 Membership function Very_Small created without hedges.

This can be modified by substituting very Fast, somewhat fast, and so on. If the grade of membership of Fast in speed is 0.5, the truth value of (somewhat Fast) would be $0.5^{1/2} = 0.707$, of (slightly Fast) $0.5^{1/3} = 0.794$, of (very Fast) $0.5^2 = 0.25$, and of (extremely fast) $0.5^3 = 0.125$.

However, we have found that in practice such hedges applied to membership functions can be confusing and inflexible. It is possible to use separate linguistic terms such as Slow and Very_slow, each with its own membership function, rather than use hedges applied to membership functions. For example, the membership function for Very_Small in Figure 4.9 cannot be created by using the usual power-based hedges just described.

4.5 FUZZY ARITHMETIC

Fuzzy arithmetic is concerned with the addition, subtraction, multiplication, and division of fuzzy numbers. There are two methods of performing fuzzy arithmetic: (1) from the extension principle; and (2) using alpha-cuts and interval arithmetic.

4.5.1 Extension Principle

The extension principle, due like so much of fuzzy theory to Lotfi Zadeh, is a powerful and very general tool used to fuzzify crisp operations, crisp equations, crisp functions, and so on. To fuzzify arithmetic, let $*$ denote addition, subtraction, multiplication, or division of real numbers. We wish to compute $P = M * N$ for fuzzy number M and N producing fuzzy number P. If $*$ is division we need to assume that zero does not have positive membership in the divisor. So, for $M \div N$ we assume $N(0) = 0$. The membership function for P is determined using the extension principle as follows:

$$P(z) = \sup_{x,y}\{\min(M(x), N(y))|x * y = z\} \qquad (4.40)$$

Suppose we wish to add a fuzzy M and a fuzzy N to yield fuzzy number P. Let us first consider evaluating P(z = 4). We consider all pairs of values of x and y that sum to 4. For each such $x - y$ pair, we calculate M(x) and N(y). We take the minimum of M(x) and N(y). We now take the maximum of all these minima, and that is the value of P(4).

If we can evaluate (4.40) analytically, we have a very general method for generalizing crisp operators to fuzzy operators. However, unless this can be done analytically, the procedure is computationally unfriendly, involving two nested loops. So, let us now present a second procedure that is more easily incorporated into computer programs. After defining this second method, we discuss the relationship between the two procedures.

4.5.2 Alpha-Cut and Interval Arithmetic

First, we will discuss alpha-cuts and then interval arithmetic. If $\alpha \in (0, 1]$, the alpha-cut of A, a fuzzy subset of universal set X, written $A[\alpha]$, is defined to be the crisp set $\{x | A(x) \geq \alpha\}$. This set is the collection of all the x in X whose membership value is at least alpha. We must separately define A[0], because otherwise it will be all of X. A[0] will be simply the base of the fuzzy number. For the triangular fuzzy number A in Figure 3.1, $A[0] = [a, c]$. For the s-shape fuzzy number in Figure 3.2 $A[0] = [a, d]$; and for the trapezoidal fuzzy number in Figure 3.4 $A[0] = [a, c]$. For the normal fuzzy number in Figure 3.3, the support is infinite. Practically, if we assume A(x) is effectively 0 for $x \leq a - 3\sigma$ and for $x \geq a + 3\sigma$, then $A[0] = [a - 3\sigma, a + 3\sigma]$.

The core of a fuzzy number is the set A[1] and the support is the interval A[0]. A fuzzy set is normal if the core is nonempty. All our fuzzy number will be normal. The alpha-cut of a fuzzy number is always a closed, bounded, interval. We will assume that A[0], for normal fuzzy numbers, is the interval given above. So we will write $A[\alpha] = [a_1(\alpha), a_2(\alpha)]$ for fuzzy number A, where the $a_i(\alpha)$ give the end points of the interval that are, in general, functions of alpha. For example, if A is a triangular fuzzy number with base the interval [1, 4], vertex at $x = 2$, and straight line segments for its sides, then we see $A[\alpha] = [1 + \alpha, 4 - 2\alpha]$ for alpha in [0, 1]. If $A[0] = [a_1, a_2]$, then we write: (1) $A > 0$ if $a_1 > 0$; (2) $A \geq 0$ for $a_1 \geq 0$; (3) $A < 0$ means $a_2 < 0$; and (4) $A \leq 0$, whenever $a_2 \leq 0$.

Next we need to review the basic ideas of interval arithmetic. Let [a, b] and [c, d] be two closed, bounded, intervals. If $*$ denotes addition, subtraction, multiplication or division of real numbers, then we extend it to interval as follows:

$$[a, b] * [c, d] = \{x * y | x \text{ in } [a, b], y \text{ in } [c, d]\} \tag{4.41}$$

It follows that

$$[a, b] + [c, d] = [a + c, b + d] \tag{4.42}$$

$$[a, b] - [c, d] = [a - d, b - c] \tag{4.43}$$

$$[a, b] \div [c, d] = [a, b] \cdot \left[\frac{1}{d}, \frac{1}{c}\right] \tag{4.44}$$

if zero does not belong to [c, d], and

$$[a, b] \cdot [c, d] = [\kappa, \nu], \text{ for}$$
$$\kappa = \min\{ac, ad, bc, bd\}$$
$$\nu = \max\{ac, ad, bc, bd\}$$

Multiplication and division may be simplified if we know $a > 0$, $c > 0$ or $b < 0$, $c > 0$, and so on. For example, if $a > 0$ and $c > 0$, then

$$[a, b][c, d] = [ac, bd]$$

but if $b < 0$ and $c > 0$ we see that

$$[a, b][c, d] = [ad, bc]$$

Now we may return to fuzzy arithmetic. For fuzzy numbers A and B let

$$A[\alpha] = [a_1(\alpha), a_2(\alpha)], \quad B[\alpha] = [b_1(\alpha), b_2(\alpha)]$$

Using the alpha-cut and interval arithmetic method we first calculate $P = A + B$ as $P[\alpha] = A[\alpha] + B[\alpha] = [a_1(\alpha) + b_1(\alpha), a_2(\alpha) + b_2(\alpha)]$. This, of course, gives alpha-cuts of the sum P. For $P = A - B$, we get $P[\alpha] = [a_1(\alpha) - b_2(\alpha), a_2(\alpha) - b_1(\alpha)]$. In multiplication $P = AB$ we find P as $P[\alpha] = A[\alpha]B[\alpha]$. If $A > 0$ and $B > 0$, then $P[\alpha] = [a_1(\alpha)b_1(\alpha), a_2(\alpha)b_2(\alpha)]$. When zero does not belong to the support of B, then $P = A \div B$ is defined and alpha-cuts of P are calculated as $P[\alpha] = [a_1(\alpha), a_2(\alpha)] \cdot [1/b_2(\alpha), 1/b_2(\alpha)]$. You are asked to complete some of these calculations in the problems for certain fuzzy numbers.

4.5.3   Comparison of Alpha-Cut and Interval Arithmetic Methods

The alpha-cut and interval arithmetic procedure is easily incorporated into computer programs since we discretize it only computing for say alpha equal to $0.0, 0.1, \ldots,$ 0.9, and 1.0. This is the method we will use for fuzzy arithmetic in this book.

It is well known that the two procedures compute the same value for $A + B$, $A - B$, $A \div B$ *and* $A \cdot B$ for fuzzy number A and B. However, this is not true for the evaluation of all fuzzy expressions. For example, for the fuzzy expression $P = (A + B)/A$ the two methods can calculate different answers for P. Even so, we will be using the alpha-cut and interval arithmetic procedure in this book to do fuzzy arithmetic.

4.6   COMPARISONS BETWEEN FUZZY NUMBERS

4.6.1   Using the Extension Principle

If A and B are two fuzzy numbers, we will need to evaluate the approximate comparisons $A \sim< B$, $A \sim<= B$, $A \sim= B$, $A \sim>= B$, $A \sim> B$ and $A \sim<> B$, the fuzzy equivalents of the conventional Boolean numerical comparisons supplied by most computer languages. The truth value of any one of these comparisons will be a number in [0, 1]. If either A or B is a single-valued scalar number, we simply replace it by a singleton fuzzy number. (In FLOPS, at least one of the numbers to be compared must be initially a fuzzy number.)

The simplest comparison to make is to compare A and B for equality. We use the extension principle in Section 4.5.1, equation (4.40), for this comparison:

$$\text{tv}(A = B) = \sup_{x,y}\{\min(M(x), N(y))|x = y\} \qquad (4.45)$$

Evaluating (4.45) is simpler than it looks for fuzzy numbers that are first monotonic upward, then monotonic downward, as the argument increases; we look for the highest point where the two fuzzy numbers intersect.

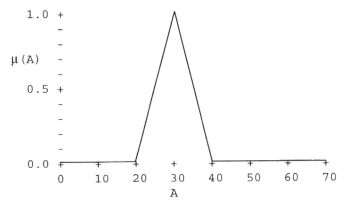

Figure 4.10   A fuzzy number A.

We now consider approximate fuzzy numerical comparisons such as (A $\sim<$ B). This implies that we wish to compare fuzzy number A, shown in Figure 4.10, to another fuzzy number that is less than C. However, the fuzzy literature does not define such a fuzzy number; we now proceed to define a fuzzy number that is approximately less than C. We first create a new fuzzy number C such that C is not equal to A, or C = NOT A, as shown in Figure 4.11.

Next, we create a masking fuzzy number D that is less than A in the Boolean true–false sense. Our truth value for D(x) is 1 so long as A(x) is less than its maximum with x increasing from $-\infty$; from there on, as x increases, D(x) is 0. Denote the value of x at the point where A(x) first achieves its maximum value by x(Amax). This operation results in D $<$ A shown in Figure 4.12.

We now calculate fuzzy number E that is approximately less than A by demanding that E be (NOT A) AND D, shown in Figure 4.13.

To carry out the comparison, we simply test whether the fuzzy number E, $<$A, we have created equals A using equation (4.45).

To carry out the comparison A $\sim>=$ B, we create the fuzzy number F $>=$ B by ORing A and F $<$ A, as in Figure 4.14.

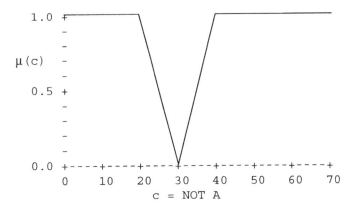

Figure 4.11   A fuzzy number C, unequal to A = NOT A.

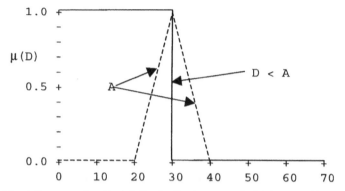

Figure 4.12   A fuzzy number D < A (in the Boolean sense); D(x) = true if x < x(Amax), else false.

4.6.2   Alternate Method

If A and B are two fuzzy numbers we will need to evaluate, in our fuzzy expert system, the approximate comparisons

$$A \sim\leq B, A \sim< B, A \sim= B, A \sim\neq B, A \sim\geq B \text{ and } A \sim> B$$

The truth value of any one of these comparisons will be a number in [0, 1]. We will use the notation v( ) for this value. So, v(A $\sim$< B) is in [0, 1] and the truth value associated with A $\sim$< B is v(A $\sim$< B); that is, tv(A $\sim$< B) = v(A $\sim$< B).

We will first need to specify some auxiliary fuzzy sets and concepts before we can define v( ). This section is based on Klir and Yuan (1995).

For a given fuzzy number A(x), we will construct four other fuzzy sets. Call the core of A the interval over which the membership of x is one. If the core of A is [m, m], a single number m, then set $\delta = m$. If the core of A is an interval [a, b], then $\delta = (a + b)/2$. Define the fuzzy set L to have membership value 1 on the

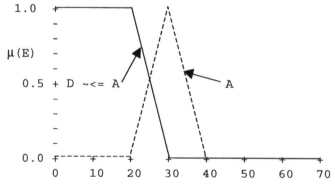

Figure 4.13   A fuzzy number E $\sim$< A = <NOT A AND (E < 30) or E $\sim$<= A.

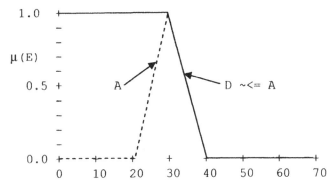

Figure 4.14 A fuzzy number E $\sim<=$ A $=$ $<$NOT A OR b $<$ A, or E $\sim<=$ A.

interval $(-\infty, \delta]$ and zero otherwise. Similarly, fuzzy set R has membership 1 on $[\delta, \infty)$ and 0 otherwise. Then, define fuzzy sets

$$(<A) = A^c \cap L \text{ using } T_m$$
$$(\sim\leq A) = (\sim<A) \cup A \text{ using } C_L$$
$$(\sim>A) = A^c \cap R \text{ for } T_m$$
$$(\sim\geq A) = (\sim>A) \cup A \text{ for } C_L$$

We use C_L for OR since $(\sim<A)$ and A, and $(\sim>A)$ and A, are maximally negatively associated (see Section 4.4.1). Fuzzy sets $(\sim<A)$ and $\sim(\leq A)$ are shown in Figure 4.15 for triangular fuzzy number A.

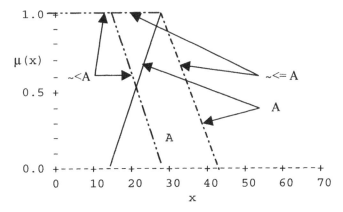

Figure 4.15 Fuzzy numbers A, triangular; $\sim<$ A; and $\sim<=$ A.

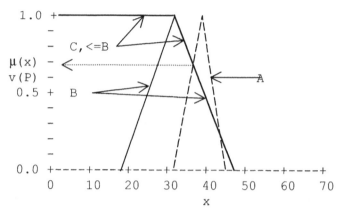

Figure 4.16   Truth value of proposition P = (A $\sim$<= B). Shown are A, B, triangular fuzzy numbers, and C, <= B. Truth value tv(A $\sim$<= B) of proposition (A $\sim$<= B) is 0.7.

If M and N are two fuzzy subsets of the real numbers ht(M, N) stands for the height of their intersection. More formally,

$$ht(M, N) = \sup_x \{ \min (M(x), N(x)) \}$$

Now, we may define v( ), shown in Figure 4.16.

Let us now return to the fuzzy proposition in Example 4 in Section 4.5. Suppose pulse = 56 and "around" 60 produces the triangular fuzzy number A with base on the interval [45, 75], vertex at x = 60, and it has straight-line segment sides. Then the truth value of this fuzzy proposition is v(56, (<A)) = (<A)(56), the membership value of 56 in the fuzzy set (<A). The truth value is evaluated to be 0.27.

4.7   FUZZY PROPOSITIONS

Propositions in a fuzzy expert system are found in the antecedent of rules, where their truth values are combined to yield the antecedent truth value.

Among the simpler propositions are those that test whether a datum exists, ignoring its value. The proposition

$$x \tag{4.46}$$

simply asserts that x exists; that is, it tests whether x has been assigned a value. The truth of that proposition is the truth value of x. If, for example, x had been assigned a value of 36 with truth value 0.75, the truth value of (4.31) would be 0.75. If x does not exist, the proposition's truth value is 0.

Most propositions test the value of a datum against some specified value. Propositions involving single-valued data have been discussed in Chapter 3, Section 3.5. Here, we briefly review that discussion.

A proposition involving only single-valued data (integers, floats, strings) is of the form

$$P = \text{(value of datum)(comparison operator)(comparison value)} \qquad (4.47)$$

and its truth value is

$$\text{tv}(P) = \text{tv(datum) AND tv(comparison) AND tv(comparison value)} \qquad (4.48)$$

Another proposition tests the grade of membership of a member of a discrete fuzzy set. For example,

$$\text{size is Small} \qquad (4.49)$$

where size is a discrete fuzzy set of which Small is a member. size is, of course, multivalued, having several members, of which Small is 1. The truth value of the entire discrete fuzzy set size is 1; the truth value of the comparison is 1, since Small is a member of size; and the truth value of Small is the grade of membership of Small in size, say 0.523. The truth value of the proposition is then $\min(1, 1, 0.523) = 0.523$.

A more complex proposition is frequently used in fuzzy control:

$$x \text{ is fast} \qquad (4.50)$$

where x is a scalar number and fast is a fuzzy number. The truth value of x might be 0.765 (although in the real world it is more likely to be 1); the truth value of the comparison is the grade of membership of x in the fuzzy number fast, say 0.654; and the truth value of the fuzzy number itself is 1. The truth of the proposition is then $\min(0.765, 0.654, 1) = 0.654$.

These comparisons may involve hedges. For example, (4.34) could be modified to read

$$x \text{ is very fast} \qquad (4.51)$$

When evaluating (4.35), we must include the effect of the hedge very. Suppose that *very* has been defined as squaring membership values. *very fast* is another fuzzy number, obtained from fuzzy number fast by squaring its grades of membership. Since the grade of membership of x in fast was 0.654, the grade of membership of x in very fast is $0.654^2 = 0.428$. The truth value of (4.35) is then $\min(0.765, 0.428, 1) = 0.428$.

Similarly, if (4.33) had read

$$\text{size is somewhat Small} \qquad (4.52)$$

and *somewhat* were defined to be a square-root transformation, the truth value of (4.52) would be $\min(1, 1, \sqrt{0.523} = 0.723) = 0.723$.

Fuzzy numbers may be specified as literals using hedges. For example, proposition (4.50) could have been written

$$x \text{ is about } 70 \tag{4.53}$$

in which the hedge *about* changes 70 into a fuzzy number with dispersion say $+/-$ 10% around 70.

Propositions may include approximate comparisons; for example, in

$$\text{speed } \sim < = \text{ roughly } 30 \tag{4.54}$$

the truth value of the comparison is obtained by comparing speed with a fuzzy number $<=$ about 30, as discussed in Section 4.7. Suppose speed is 35, with truth value 1. The membership of 35 in ($<=$ roughly 30) might be 0.7, and the truth value of the fuzzy number itself is 1. The truth value of the proposition is then min(1, 0.7, 1) or 0.7.

Propositions may also involve truth values directly. For example, suppose we have a discrete fuzzy set size that has a member Large. We can test the grade of membership of this discrete fuzzy set member directly, by using the notation size.-Large to represent Large's grade of membership, in proposition

$$\text{size.Large } <= 0.250 \tag{4.55}$$

The truth value of the grade of membership itself is 1, as are the truth values of all truth values. If size.Large is 0, the truth value of the comparison is 1, as is the truth value of the literal 0.250. The truth value of the proposition is then $\min(1, 1, 1) = 1$.

A similar proposition is

$$x.cf = 0 \tag{4.56}$$

which tests whether the truth value of x is 0. Truth values so tested have themselves a truth value of 1. The truth value of the proposition (x.cf = 0) is then the fuzzy AND of the truth value of x.cf, one; the truth value of the Boolean comparison = 1 or 0; and the truth value of 0, set to one by default since it is a literal.

The truth value of complex logical propositions is obtained simply by using the logical connectives AND, OR, and NOT as indicated in Section 4.2.1, evaluating from left to right, using parentheses if necessary. For example, suppose the complex logical proposition P is given by

$$P = A \text{ AND } B \text{ OR NOT } C \tag{4.57}$$

in which the truth values of A, B, and C are, respectively, 0.6, 0.8, and 0.3. Evaluating from left to right, we have

$$
\begin{aligned}
&\text{tv(A)} = 0.6 \\
&\text{tv(A AND B)} = \min(0.6, 0.8) = 0.6 \\
&\text{tv(NOT C)} = 1 - 0.3 = 0.7 \\
&\text{tv(A AND B OR NOT C)} = \min(0.6, 0.7) = 0.6
\end{aligned}
\tag{4.58}
$$

If parentheses are permitted in propositions, we evaluate as in (4.41) within each pair of parentheses, from inmost to outermost as conventional in language compilers.

In the theory of fuzzy logic, Klir and Yuan (1995, p. 220 ff.) define four types of fuzzy propositions. The first type is a proposition of the form given above in (4.34); the second type is a proposition of the form in (4.35).

The third type of proposition is the generalized modus ponens discussed in Section 4.3:

$$
\text{if X is A then Y is B} \tag{4.59}
$$

and the fourth type is the same except that a hedge is introduced:

$$
\text{if X is A then Y is very B} \tag{4.60}
$$

While in logic the modus ponens is indeed a proposition, as we have seen in Section 4.3 such propositions are not usually useful in a fuzzy expert system. In the theory of fuzzy logic, Klir and Yuan (1995, p. 220 ff.) define four types of fuzzy propositions. The first type is of the form

$$
\text{temperature is high} \tag{4.61}
$$

where temperature is a single-valued attribute, and high is a membership function. The truth value of this proposition is the grade of membership of temperature in high.

The second type is of the form

$$
\text{temperature is very high} \tag{4.62}
$$

where "very" is a modifier, a hedge of the type that modifies a truth values such as, for example, by replacing the truth value by its square root.

The third type of proposition is the generalized modus ponens discussed in Section 4.3:

$$
\text{if X is A then Y is B} \tag{4.63}
$$

and the fourth type is the same except that a hedge is introduced:

$$\text{if X is A then Y is very B} \tag{4.64}$$

While in logic the modus ponens is indeed a proposition, as we have seen in Section 4.3 we do not find such propositions useful in a fuzzy expert system.

4.8   QUESTIONS

4.1   Using the property of associativity, derive equations (4.15)–(4.19) for n = 3.

4.2   Show that any t-norm will give the AND table, Table 3.1, if x and y are only 0 or 1.

4.3   Show that tv(P OR Q) = C(tv(P),tv(Q)) for any t-conorm.

4.4   Verify that the laws of non-contradiction and excluded middle hold if you use T_L and C_L.

4.5   Elkan's proof that the Zadehian logic fails except for crisp truth values (0 or 1) is based on the a set of two logical propositions, P and Q, which are equivalent for classical logic:

$$\text{P: NOT (A AND NOT B)}$$
$$\text{Q:B OR (NOT A AND NOT B)}$$

Show that these propositions are not equivalent using Zadehian logic (4.1) and (4.7), but are equivalent using correlation logic. Use the Zadehian min–max logic as a default, but use the bounded logic when appropriate. *Hint*: Alternatively, reformulate Q using the distributive law to isolate B OR NOT B. Then, Try to get an analytic solution. Alternatively, calculate truth tables for P and Q using truth values of A = 0.25 and B = 0.5, first using Zadehian min–max logic, and then using min–max logic as a default and bounded logic where appropriate.

4.6   Consider the fuzzy numbers A, A', and B, using Figure Question 4.6:
Using the theory of approximate reasoning and the fuzzy modus ponens, calculate B' from equation (4.30), B' = A' ∘ (A → B) for selected values of x. *Hint*: Write a computer program for this purpose. Select x values of 1,2,3, ... , 16. Calculate A, Apr, B, the matrix $A \rightarrow B$. Then use min–max composition of A' with the matrix (A → B) to obtain the vector B'.

4.7   Consider two ways of defining the dispersion of a triangular fuzzy number:
a. Dispersion   of   U = <central value>,   <absolute dispersion>, <relative dispersion>, where the net dispersion =

$$\sqrt{<\text{absolute dispersion}>^2 + (<\text{central value}> \cdot <\text{relative dispersion}>)^2}$$

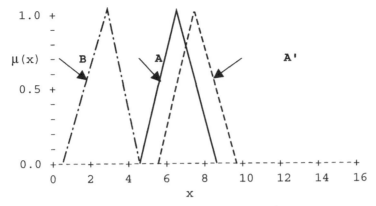

Figure Question 4.6 Fuzzy numbers A, A′, and B.

b. Dispersion of U = <hedge> · <central value>, where the hedge "nearly" represents the decimal number 0.05 or 5%, "about" represents 0.1, "roughly" represents 0.25, and "crudely" represents 0.5.

What are the advantages and disadvantages of these two methods?

4.8 Using the fuzzy numbers A and A′ defined in Problem 4.4, add A and A′ by
a. The extension principle.
b. Alpha cuts.
c. Interval arithmetic.

5 Combining Uncertainties

5.1 GENERALIZING AND AND OR OPERATORS

This chapter will deal with the problem of combining truth values. In Chapter 3, we dealt with definitions of the AND, OR, and NOT operators for multivalued logics, and pointed out that many definitions of these operators can be defined, which reduce to the classical definitions for crisp logic for crisp truth values. In Chapter 4, we presented the mathematics of a family of fuzzy logics that obey the classical laws of Excluded Middle and Non-Contradiction. In this chapter, we will present a general treatment of combining truth values, with the objective of calculating the truth value of rule antecedents. In particular, we discuss use of prior association between operands as a guide to selecting which fuzzy logical operators to use.

The concept of truth-functional operators is based on the idea that the result of applying these operators will yield a value that depends only on the values of the operands. As we have seen in Chapter 3, any of the three definitions of AND and OR are truth functional, and may all give different results; however, we are not given any basis on which to make a choice among the available operators. Certainly, the Zadehian min–max operators are used more often than any other, for a variety of reasons, including some rather nice mathematical properties, and in the real world they can usually be made to work.

Let us back up and ask what properties the classical AND, OR, and NOT operators posses. Among the most basic are the Law of the Excluded Middle and Law of Non-Contradiction. These can be quite simply formulated:

$$\text{Excluded middle: P AND NOT P} = \text{false} = 0 \tag{5.1}$$

$$\text{Non-Contradiction: P OR NOT P} = \text{true} = 1 \tag{5.2}$$

Unfortunately, all the definitions for the AND, OR, and NOT operators except the bounded sum fail to obey these laws. While this can be disturbing to some people, many fuzzy mathematicians seem to regard it as a virtue. In Chapter 4, we developed the mathematical theory for a family of fuzzy logics that does obey these laws; in this chapter, we discuss the origin of this development and its utility.

Fuzzy Expert Systems and Fuzzy Reasoning, By William Siler and James J. Buckley
ISBN 0-471-38859-9 Copyright © 2005 John Wiley & Sons, Inc.

5.1.1 Correlation Logic: A Family of Fuzzy Logical Operators that Obeys Excluded Middle and Non-Contradiction Laws

We felt that the inability to make a rational choice of logical operators and the failure to obey the laws of Excluded Middle and Non-Contradiction creates a rather unsatisfactory situation. Spurred by a paper by Ruspini (1982), we investigated what effect prior associations between the operands of the logical operators might have on the choice of a proper set of operators. We adopted a model for fuzziness presented by Klir and Yuan (1996, pp 283ff). In this model, a number of persons were asked whether a proposition were true, and were restricted to true (1) or false (0) responses. The truth value of the proposition was considered to be the average of all responses. As the number of observers increases without limit, the granularity of our estimate of the truth value vanishes; the estimate of the truth value becomes the probability that an observer would say that the proposition is true. The following treatment is taken from Buckley and Siler (1998b, 1999).

We extend Klir and Yuan's model just above to two propositions simultaneously presented, and find the probability that an observer would report that P is true; that P AND Q is true; that P OR Q is true; and the association between the individual reports of the truth of P and of Q. Table 5.1 gives a sample of such reports.

We found that if the truth values of P and Q were positively correlated as strongly as possible, the Zadehian AND/OR operators were correct in predicting the mean value for P AND Q and P OR Q. If the individual P and Q truth values were maximally negatively correlated, the bounded sum operators gave correct results. If the individual P and Q truth values were uncorrelated, the product-sum operators gave correct results, as would be expected from elementary probability theory. In Table 5.1, the correlation coefficient is 0, and the truth values obtained for P AND Q and OP OR Q are those we would expect from probability, assuming independence.

This approach yielded a family of logical operators with a single parameter; the prior correlation coefficient between the operands. We concluded that a rational

TABLE 5.1 Sample Table of Observer Reports of Truth of Two Propositions, P and Q[a]

Observer	P	Q	P AND Q	P OR Q
1	0	1	0	1
2	1	0	0	1
3	1	1	1	1
4	1	1	1	1
5	0	0	0	0
6	0	0	0	0
7	0	1	0	1
8	1	0	0	1
Average	0.500	0.500	0.250	0.750

[a]Correlation P and Q = 0.

choice among logic operators could be based on information regarding such associations. The family of AND/OR operators returns the truth values of P AND Q and P OR Q given the truth values of P(a) and Q(b) and a single parameter, r, the correlation coefficient between prior values of a and b.

We first place a restriction on the maximum and minimum permissible values of the parameter r, ru, and rl, respectively, and from these restrictions derive a working value for r, r'. The reason for this is that the values of a and b may make some values for r impossible. For example, if a = 0.2 and b = 0.6 it is impossible for these values to be perfectly correlated. If the specified r is less than rl, then the formulas will use the bounded sum operators; if the specified r = 0, the formulas will use the sum-product operators; if the specified r is greater than ru, the formulas will use the Zadehian max–min operators. We first present the formulas for this family of AND/OR operators, then present some numerical examples of their performance. Since we are interested in implementing these operators on a computer, we will present them as statements in BASIC.

$$
\begin{aligned}
&ru = (\min(a, b) - a * b)/ \ SQR(a * (1 - a) * b * (1 - b)) \\
&rl = (\max(a + b - 1, 0) - a * b)/ \ SQR(a * (1 - a) * b * (1 - b)) \\
&\text{if } r > ru \text{ then } r' = ru \text{ else } r' = r \\
&\text{if } r < rl \text{ then } r' = rl \text{ else } r' = r \\
&aANDb = a * b + r * SQR(a * (1 - a) * b * (1 - b)) \\
&aORb = a + b - a * b - p * SQR(a * (1 - a) * b * (1 - b))
\end{aligned}
\tag{5.3}
$$

Table 5.2 gives some typical results of applying these formulas.

Of course, this family of operators is not truth-functional, since other information is required besides the values of the operands. In many cases, that information is lacking and the Zadehian operators are a good default for expert systems, provided that we do not combine A and NOT A. They are the mathematical equivalent of the "a chain is no stronger than its weakest link" common sense reasoning. Further, any other multivalued logic limits the complexity of the rule antecedents that can be used: If several clauses are ANDed together, the resulting truth value tends to drift down to 0; if they are ORd together, the resulting truth value tends to drift up to 1.

TABLE 5.2 Examples of Application of Logic Operator Family Using the Prior Correlation Coefficient

r	a	b	r'	aANDb	aORb	Resulting Logic
−1	0.2	0.6	−0.612	0	0.8	Bounded
0	0.2	0.6	0	0.12	0.68	Product
+1	0.2	0.6	0	0.2	1	Max–min
−1	0.4	0.8	−0.612	0.2	1	Bounded
0	0.4	0.8	0	0.32	0.88	Product
+1	0.4	0.8	0.408	0.4	0.8	Max–min

There are two circumstances under which there is no question as to prior associations. If P and NOT P are the operands, they are maximally negatively associated; if P and P are the operands, they are maximally positively correlated. If we want to use multivalued logic, and wish to retain the laws of Excluded Middle and Non-Contradiction, we can use any multivalued logic we please unless the equivalent of P and NOT P or P AND P appear in the same proposition. We can save Excluded Middle and Non-Contradiction by using the Zadehian max–min logic when combining P and P, and by switching to the bounded-sum operator pair when combining P and NOT P. (We might require rearranging the proposition to bring P and P together, and to bring P and NOT P together.)

In most cases, we will not have prior information available on which to base a choice of which logical operators we should employ. However, we can choose a default set of operators. Let us assume that our observers share a common background. It would seem that in this case, they would tend to agree more than to disagree. They might have more or less strict ideas as to when to say a proposition is true, resulting in individually larger or smaller estimates as to the truth of P and of Q, but if the observer who is more strict says that P is true, it seems likely that the less strict observer would also say that P is true. (Our formulation provides for precisely this contingency.) So it seems likely that the default correlation should be +1, yielding the Zadehian operators; indeed, many years of practice have shown that this choice works.

5.2   COMBINING SINGLE TRUTH VALUES

The most important calculation of truth values takes place when the truth value of a rule's antecedent is evaluated. The basic unit of an antecedent is a clause. Several types of clauses are shown in Table 5.3.

TABLE 5.3   Types of Clauses in a Rule Antecedent

Test Performed	Example	Truth Value
A. Test of truth value of member of discrete fuzzy set	size is Small	Grade of membership of Small in discrete fuzzy set size
B. Test of attribute value against a literal	age < 35	Truth value of age AND truth value of comparison
C. Test of attribute value against a previously defined variable	age < <A1>	Truth value of attribute AND truth value of comparison AND truth value of variable <A1>
D. Test of attribute's truth value against a literal	age.cf > 0	Truth value of comparison
E. Test of attribute's truth value against a previously defined variable	age.cf > <X>	Truth value of comparison AND truth value of variable <X>

A. The truth value of "size is Small" is simply the grade of membership of Small in discrete fuzzy set size. If this is 0.645, then the truth value of the clause is also 0.645.
B. Say the value of age is 32, and its truth value is 0.925. The truth value of the data comparison, 32 ~= fuzzy 35, might be 0.550. The truth value of the fuzzy 35 itself is 1.0 by default, since it is a literal. The truth value of the clause is then min(0.925, 0.550, 1.0) = 0.550.
C. As before, the truth value of age is 0.925. Say the variable <A1> has previously been assigned the value 35 and truth value 0.495. The truth value of the comparison would be 0.550 (as before). The truth value of the comparison value is not 0.495. The truth value of the clause is then min(0.925, 0.550, 0.495) = 0.495.
D. The attribute age.cf (the truth value of age) is 0.925 from B. just above. The truth value of age.cf is 1.0. If age.cf is not 0, the truth value of the comparison is 1. The truth value of the literal comparison value 0 is 1.0 by default. The truth value of the clause is then min(1.0, 1, 1.0) = 0.
E. Age.cf is 0.925 as above, and its truth value is 1.0. Say that <X> has value 0.5 and truth value 0.75. The truth value of the Boolean comparison is 1. The truth value of the clause is then min(1, 1, 0.75) = 0.75.

Antecedent clauses referring to the same declared data element are grouped together into a *pattern*. We list such a pattern, with the truth values of its individual clauses:

```
(in Data x <3 AND (y < 0 OR NOT size is Small))
       (tv 1)    (tv 0.8)     (tv 0.23)
```

or

```
tv = (1 AND (0.8 OR NOT 0.23))
   = (1 AND (0.8 OR 0.77))
   = (1 AND 0.8)
   = 0.8
```

5.3 COMBINING FUZZY NUMBERS AND MEMBERSHIP FUNCTIONS

Fuzzy numbers and membership functions are fuzzy sets, and hence may be combined logically. If Small, Medium, and Large are declared to be fuzzy numbers, we might ask IF (profit is Small OR Medium), or perhaps IF (profit is NOT Large), both requiring logical operations on fuzzy numbers. Another example of combining fuzzy numbers logically is the combining a fuzzy (<2) and a fuzzy 2 in order to make the approximate comparison x~<=2.

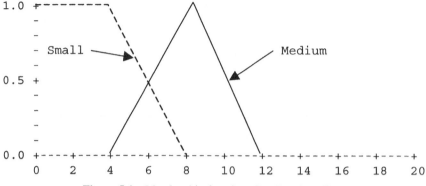

Figure 5.1   Membership functions Small and Medium.

Suppose we wish to combine the membership functions Medium and Large. We define these two functions in Figure 5.1.

Assume that we have adopted the Zadehian AND (min) and OR (max) as defaults. Figure 5.2 shows the fuzzy number that results from ORing Small and Medium using the max OR operator.

The notch in Figure 5.2 is quite counterintuitive. To eliminate the notch, we introduce here the notion of *semantic inconsistency*, first proposed by Thomas (1995). It occurs because we are combining P and NOT P with an inappropriate logic. The Zadehian max–min logic holds if the operands are positively associated as strongly as possible. However, the membership functions for Small and Medium are not so associated; they are *semantically inconsistent*, a notion introduced by Thomas (1995), and the use of min–max logic here is probably invalid.

The proper logic is the correlation logic defined in Section 4.2.2. We simply calculate the cross-correlation between the fuzzy numbers or weighted membership functions being combined, *over the area of overlap*. We then OR the memberships with the formulas in (5.3), using the cross-correlation as the default correlation coefficient.

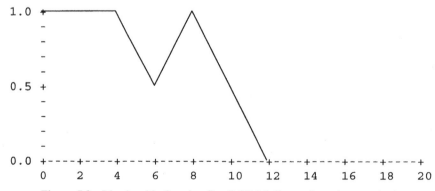

Figure 5.2   Membership function Small OR Medium using min–max logic.

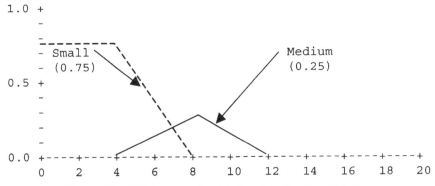

Figure 5.3 Weighted membership functions Small and Medium.

Suppose that our basic membership functions are those shown in Figure 5.1, and that rules have established the truth value of Small as 0.75 and that of Medium as 0.25. Then the functions we must combine are shown in Figure 5.3.

The correlation coefficient calculated over the area of overlap is -1. Using correlation logic, the function Small OR Large is shown in Figure 5.4, which seems intuitively much more acceptable than the functions ORd with max–min logic, shown in Figure 5.5.

Once we begin to apply set-theoretic operations to fuzzy numbers, the failure to obey the laws of Excluded Middle and Non-Contradiction can give quite counter-intuitive results.

There may be restrictions on when the bounded operators can be fruitfully used; this is a topic for future research. Now, control engineers have a great deal of experience in shaping membership functions using presently widely accepted logics, and changing the logics used would invalidate that experience. We do not suggest such a change for fuzzy control problems. There is no such backlog of experience in handling non-numeric data; in this case, we suggest using membership functions that add

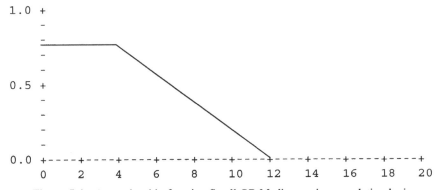

Figure 5.4 A membership function Small OR Medium, using correlation logic.

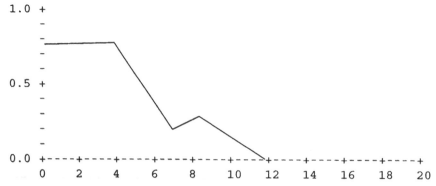

Figure 5.5 Weighted membership functions Small and Medium, ORd by min–max logic.

to one at every point, and using the bounded sum/difference logics when combining membership functions.

FLOPS does not make the bounded sum operator available as such to the user, although it is not difficult to compute the result and the reset command can be used to set the antecedent confidence to the bounded sum confidence. However, in computing the results of fuzzy comparisons involving the OR operator $(x \sim\, <=\, Y$ or $x \sim\, >=\, Y)$, the bounded sum operator is used internally in a fashion transparent to the user.

There is an open question as to which logical OR should be used when combining weighted membership functions prior to defuzzification. The Zadehian OR (max) is commonly used for this purpose, but this tends to produced notched membership functions similar to the notch in Figure 5.2. Control engineers are primarily interested in shaping a response surface, and usually use *ad hoc* methods; these notches have not prevented them from obtaining a desired response. If, however, we are interested in the combined curves to obtain grades of membership in a concept rather than in a defuzzified value, the notches may be worse than annoying. In general, we feel that for a reasonable family of membership functions, the membership function for the entire linguistic value obtained by ORing weighted individual functions should be convex. We define "reasonable" to be that adjacent functions should intersect at no less than the 0.5 membership value, and that the ordered grades of membership of the individual linguistic values should also be convex. This subject is for future research.

5.4 BAYESIAN METHODS

Reverend Thomas Bayes derived his theorem in the eighteenth century, and although mathematically irrefutable it has been attended by controversy ever since. The eminent statistician R. A. Fisher stated that it was his opinion that Bayesian methods are founded upon error, and should be totally rejected. It was the pleasure of one of us to attend a meeting at which two papers on Bayesian methods were presented. The first paper was titled "The applicability of Bayes' theorem to problems of medical diagnosis"; the second, that followed immediately, was titled "The inapplicability of Bayes' theorem to problems of medical diagnosis". Bayes' theorem requires knowledge of prior conditional probabilities, but often that knowledge is lacking. What is in question is Bayes' assumption of the "equal distribution of ignorance" if prior probabilities are not known.

Bayes' theorem has achieved some success in expert systems in the last 20 years, and we will briefly describe it here.

The rule itself is based on conditional probabilities. We write the probability the B is true given that P is true as $p(B|P)$. Bayes' rule reverses this, and is

$$p(A_k|B) = p(B|A_k)\,p(A_k)/\,p(B) \tag{5.4}$$

or eqivalently, since $p(B) = \sum p(B|A_i)\,p(A_i)$,

$$p(A_k|B) = p(B|A_k)\,p(A_k)/\sum p(B|A_i)\,p(A_i) \tag{5.5}$$

In applying Bayes' rule to inference, we say that A_k is a hypothesis we wish to test. With the information we have acquired to date, $p(A_k)$ is the probability that A_k is true. Now, we uncover a new piece of evidence B. We know from past experience that the probability that B is true varies with all the various possible hypotheses A_i, and have a table of prior knowledge of $p(B|A_i)$ and $p(A_i)$ for all possible A_i. This prior knowledge permits us to write Table 5.4.

Table 5.4 shows that our confidence in A_i can either increase or decrease as a result of the new evidence B. It also illustrates the problem with Bayesian methods; where do we get all that prior knowledge? Our table assumes a very simple problem, with only one new piece of evidence and only three possible hypotheses. In the real world, we almost always have many more pieces of evidence and many more hypotheses. It is not often that we can accumulate reliable figures for the prior knowledge Bayes' theorem requires. Instead, subjective estimates are made or some simple rule applied, such as the "equal distribution of ignorance", which assumes that all possibilities are equally likely. It is to the "equal distribution of ignorance" that Fisher objected so violently.

TABLE 5.4 Sample Application of Bayes' Rule to Updating Confidence in P from New Evidence B

$p(B|A_i)$	$p(A_i)$	$p(B|A_i)\,p(A_i)$	$p(A_i|B) = \dfrac{p(B|A_i)p(A_i)}{\sum p(B|A_k p(A_k))}$
0.2	0.3	0.06	0.15
0.4	0.5	0.2	0.5
0.7	0.2	0.14	0.35

5.5   THE DEMPSTER–SHAFER METHOD

Dempster–Shafer methods (Dempster, 1967) use dual truth values: a lower level, called *belief*, representing the extent to which the evidence supports a hypothesis; and an upper level, called *plausibility*, representing the extent to which the evidence fails to refute the hypothesis. These are closely analogous to the dual measures *necessity* and *possibility* in fuzzy systems theory. The method is concerned with combining evidence regarding the truth of a hypothesis from different sources. Our presentation here is paraphrased from that of Jackson (1999), Chapter 21. We seek to establish belief and plausibility of some set of hypotheses from evidence. The representation and manipulation of possibility and necessity in rule-based systems will be taken up in Chapter 8.

A *hypothesis space* in Dempster–Shafer theory is represented by Θ, a space that holds all the individual hypotheses h_i. All hypotheses are assumed to be mutually exclusive, and the set of hypotheses Θ is assumed to be exhaustive. We assume that it is possible to obtain evidence that each single subset of Θ, A_1, A_2, ... , is true. (A subset A_i may be a single hypothesis, or may be the entire hypothesis set Θ.) The hypotheses in each subset may overlap those in other subsets. We also have pieces of evidence y_i, included in a set Ψ. Each piece of evidence will point to a subset A_i of Θ that holds all the hypotheses that are supported by y_j; the subset A_i to which y_j points is called a *focal element*. Since the hypotheses are exhaustive, that is, that there is at least one hypothesis consistent with every evidence, no evidence will point to a null set.

Key to the Dempster–Shafer method is the idea of a *probability assignment*. A *basic probability assignment* (bpa) is defined as a function $m(A_i)$ that maps each subset A_i of the hypotheses to a value included in $[0, 1]$. The sum of all $m(A_i)$ over all subsets of Θ is 1. The belief Bel in any focal element A is the sum of all the basic probability assignments for all subsets of A:

$$\text{Bel}(A) = \sum_{B \supset A} m(B) \tag{5.6}$$

The plausibility Pls of A represents the evidence is consistent with A:

$$\text{Pls}(A) = \sum_{A \cap B} m(B) \tag{5.7}$$

The importance of the Dempster–Shafer method is that it furnishes a method of combining beliefs based on different evidence. Let Bel_1 and Bel_2 denote to belief functions. To these belief functions there will correspond two basic probability assignments, m_1 and m_2. We now wish to compute a new basic probability assignment $m(A) = m1 \oplus m2(A)$ and a new belief $\text{Bel}(A) = \text{Bel}_1(A) \oplus \text{Bel}_2(A)$ based on the combined evidence. Dempster's rule is

$$m(A) = m1 \oplus m2 = \sum_{x \cap y = A} m_1(X)m_2(Y) \Big/ \left(1 - \sum_{X \cap Y = 0} m_1(X)m_2(Y) \right) \tag{5.8}$$

$\text{Bel}(A) = \text{Bel}_1 \oplus \text{Bel}_2$ can now be computed by (5.8).

We might also wish to combine evidence from two different sources. [Our treatment of this topic is taken from Klir and Yuan (1995), pp 183 ff.] We need basic probability assignments m_1 and m_2 for the set of all hypotheses and for all its subsets, the power set of the set of hypotheses Θ. There is no unique way of combining the evidence, but a standard way is given by

$$m_{1,2}(A) = \sum_{B \cap C = A} m_1(B) \cdot m_2(C)/(1 - K) \qquad (5.9)$$

where

$$K = \sum_{B \cap C = 0} m_1(B) \cdot m_2(C) \qquad (5.10)$$

Klir and Yuan (1996) also give a simple example of Bayes' method to a problem of the origin of a painting. They have three hypotheses: the painting is by Raphael (hypothesis R); by a disciple of Raphael (hypothesis D); or a counterfeit (hypothesis C). Two experts examine the painting, and provide basic probability assignments m_1 and m_2, respectively, for the origin of the painting; R, D, C, R $\cup$ D, R $\cup$ C, D $\cup$ C, and R $\cup$ D $\cup$ C. Table 5.5 shows the basic assignments m_1 and m_2, the corresponding measures of belief Bel_1 and Bel_2, and the combined evidence $m_{1,2}$ and belief $Bel_{1,2}$ using the Dempster–Shafer formulas.

An advantage of Dempster–Shafer over Bayesian methods is that Dempster–Shafer does not require prior probabilities; it combines current evidence. However, a great deal of current evidence is required for a sizeable set of hypotheses, and if this is available the method is computationally expensive. For fuzzy expert systems, there is an important failure of Dempster–Shafer; the requirement that the hypotheses be mutually exclusive. Since the members of fuzzy sets are inherently *not* mutually exclusive, this raises doubts as to the applicability of Dempster–Shafer in fuzzy systems. Nevertheless, Baldwin's FRIL system (Baldwin et al., 1995) uses a generalization of Dempster–Shafer to good effect.

TABLE 5.5 Example of Dempster–Shafer Method

Focal Elements	Expert 1		Expert 2		Combined Evidence	
	m_1	Bel_1	m_2	Bel_2	$m_{1,2}$	$Bel_{1,2}$
R	0.05	0.05	0.15	0.15	0.21	0.21
D	0	0	0	0	0.01	0.01
C	0.05	0.05	0.05	0.05	0.09	0.09
R $\cup$ D	0.15	0.2	0.05	0.2	0.12	0.34
R $\cup$ C	0.1	0.2	0.2	0.4	0.2	0.5
D $\cup$ C	0.05	0.1	0.05	0.1	0.06	0.16
R $\cup$ D $\cup$ C	0.6	1	0.5	1	0.31	1

5.6 SUMMARY

A problem faced by users of multivalued logics is to select which of a wide variety of the logical operators AND and OR to use in evaluating a complex fuzzy logical proposition such as those found in the antecedent of fuzzy rules. [Almost everyone uses the same operator for NOT: NOT A = 1 − truth(A).]

Almost all definitions of the AND and OR logical operators fail to obey the classical laws of Excluded Middle (P and NOT P = 0) and Non-Contradiction (P OR NOT P = 1), which some find disconcerting. The Zadehian max−min logic has the advantage that it is idempotent (A AND A = A, A OR A = A) and there is an enormous amount of experience with it. In an attempt to rescue the classical laws for fuzzy logic, we devised a family of operators for AND and OR that preserves the classical laws. The family has one parameter, the correlation coefficient between the truth values of the operands obtained either from past experience or from the structure of the logical expression being evaluated, if the expression contains both A and NOT A, where A is a logical proposition.

If the expression being evaluated does not include both a proposition and its negation, and if there is insufficient historical data to establish a reliable correlation coefficient between elements of the complex proposition, the user has a free choice of any operator pair for AND and OR, without violating either excluded middle or non-contradiction. We suggest that the Zadehian max−min operator pair is a desirable default. The Zadeh operators have the nicest mathematical properties; there is a great deal of experience with them; and they do not restrict the complexity of rule antecedents.

The most important need for fuzzy logic is in evaluating the antecedent of a rule. We list five types of antecedent clauses and discuss the evaluation of their truth values: test of truth value of discrete fuzzy set member; test of attribute value against a literal; test of attribute value against previously defined variable; test of attribute's truth value against a literal; and test of attribute's truth value against a previously defined variable. For an antecedent clause of the type

$$A \text{ (comparison operator) } B$$

the truth value of equal to the truth value of A; the truth value of the comparison; and the truth value of B. In many cases, such as literal values for B, the truth value of B or C will be one by default.

Fuzzy numbers may be combined in a similar fashion, except that the truth values are no longer scalars, but are functions of numbers from the real line. Suppose that fuzzy number A and B are defined as $a(x)$ and $b(x)$, where $a(x)$ and $b(x)$ are the grades of membership of x in A and B, respectively. Then the fuzzy numbers C = A AND B, and D = A OR B are defined by

```
C = A AND B, c(x) = a(x) AND b(x) for all x on real line
D = A OR B, d(x) = a(x) OR b(x) for all x on real line
```

In effect, we calculate the union (or intersection) of two fuzzy numbers point by point.

ANDing or ORing fuzzy numbers using the Zadehian max–min logic can give rather peculiar results. Of particular interest is the combining of fuzzy numbers such as in "less than OR equal to", useful in approximate numerical comparisons. While there is more theoretical work to be done here, the use of the concepts in the parameterized family of logics in Section 5.1.1 can produce more sensible results, as shown in Figures 5.1–5.3, since the laws of Excluded Middle and Non-Contradiction are preserved.

5.7 QUESTIONS

5.1 What properties do the classical logic operators posses that are not shared by fuzzy logic operators?

5.2 When combining the fuzzy numbers A and NOT A, what fuzzy logical operators should be used?

5.3 When combining the fuzzy quantities A and A, what fuzzy logical operators should be used?

5.4 Should the bounded sum and difference operators be used when combining semantically inconsistent membership functions in

    a. Fuzzy control applications?

    b. In general-purpose fuzzy reasoning applications?

5.5 Temperature is a scalar whose value is 78 and whose truth value is 0.6. What are the truth values of the following antecedent clauses?

    a. "Temperature $= 75$"

    b. "Temperature is 78"

    c. "Temperature is $<X>$"

    d. "size is Large". (The grade of membership of Large in fuzzy set size is 0.356.)

    e. "Temperature.cf > 0.5"?

5.6 We have two fuzzy numbers, A and B, shown below in Figure Question 5.6.

    a. What is the truth value of the proposition "A $\sim= $ B"?

    b. Of the proposition "A $\sim< $ B"?

    c. Of the proposition "A $\sim>= $ B"?

5.7 Using the fuzzy numbers A and B in Question 5.6, we wish to construct the fuzzy numbers A AND B and A OR B, with the min–max logic as our default. Should we use min–max or the bounded operators in combining these two fuzzy numbers?

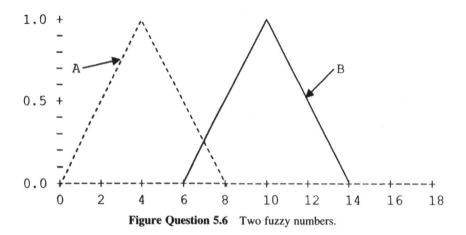

Figure Question 5.6   Two fuzzy numbers.

5.8   Assume that the fuzzy numbers A and B in Question 5.5 are in fact membership functions used to describe the same numeric quantity. Should we use the
default min–max or the bounded operators in combining these two fuzzy
numbers?

5.9   What is the main problem with the use of Bayesian methods?

5.10   What is the relation between Dempster–Shafer methods and fuzzy logic?

5.11   In the lack of any knowledge about a hypothesis, what is its possibility? Its
necessity?

6 Inference in an Expert System I

6.1 OVERVIEW

In this chapter, we are concerned with the theory of the fuzzy reasoning process; drawing conclusions from data and rules that relate data to conclusions, under conditions of uncertainty, ambiguity, and contradictions. This is a very dynamic process; conclusions reached in early stages of the reasoning process may be, and usually are, modified or invalidated as the process continues from one step to the next.

The process of drawing conclusions from existing data is called *inference*; we infer new truths from old. Of course, classical logic propositions have only two truth values, true or false, the process of inference is simplified as compared to fuzzy logic, where we have to be concerned not only with propositions but also with their truth values. Accordingly, both Chapters 6 and 7 are concerned with the ways with which we can determine new truth values.

Much of the literature on fuzzy mathematics is concerned with *possibility*, a measure of the extent to which the data fail to refute a conclusion. In the real world, we are primarily concerned with *necessity*, a measure of the extent to which the data support a conclusion. The reasoning process of establishing *necessary* conclusions is not the same as the process of establishing *possible* conclusions. For example, when we initialize *possible* truth values in the lack of any data, we set them to 1; but when we initialize *necessary* truth values in the lack of any data, we set them to 0. When working with possibility, the fuzzy modus ponens using the implication operator is an important tool; when working with necessity, we employ t-norms rather than the implication operator.

Klir and Yuan (1995, Chapter 8) deal with Fuzzy Logic and various schemes of inference. Unfortunately, their presentation is not geared to the different modes of inference necessary in a rule-based system for fuzzy reasoning. Baldwin et al. (1995) present a discussion of inference in a Prolog system of depth-based search with backtracking, as used in their expert system Fril, which employs backward-chaining Horn clauses. Both of these references deal with approaches sufficiently different from that necessary in FLOPS so that in the next two chapters (Chapters 7 and 8) we essentially develop our own theory from scratch.

Chapters 6 and 7 assume we are working with necessity rather than possibility unless otherwise stated, and are concerned with establishing the process under

Fuzzy Expert Systems and Fuzzy Reasoning, By William Siler and James J. Buckley
ISBN 0-471-38859-9   Copyright © 2005 John Wiley & Sons, Inc.

which modification of data and truth values may take place. Aside from initialization, these modifications will usually take place when a rule is fired, and are performed by consequent instructions. We are specifically concerned with the question of the conditions under which we may permit these consequent instructions to be executed. While the consequent instruction (then) "size is Small" may be viewed as a proposition, viewing it as an instruction is perhaps pragmatically more direct.

In the early days of FLOPS, we used the term "confidence" rather than the term "truth value", and we continue to use these terms interchangeably. Old habits die hard.

In FLOPS, each rule has an associated truth value; by default, each rule is assumed to have full confidence unless otherwise specified. A rule-firing threshold is effective, either specified or set by default. In general, a rule is considered fireable if the antecedent confidence is above the rule-firing threshold; if the rule is actually fired, the consequent instructions are carried out with a confidence equal to the fuzzy AND of the antecedent confidence and the rule confidence.

6.2 TYPES OF FUZZY INFERENCE

We list three types of rule-based inference: *monotonic*, in which consequent truth values may increase but not decrease; *non-monotonic*, in which consequent truth values may increase or decrease; and *downward monotonic*, in which consequent truth values may decrease but not increase. We define four methods of determining consequent truth values from antecedents, including approximate reasoning. We list three desirable properties for each of the three reasoning types. We show that the first three methods possess all desirable properties for the reasoning type for which they were designed, but approximate reasoning fails to possess all desirable properties for any reasoning type.

We will not be concerned with evaluating the truth value of the rule antecedent; we will assume that this has been determined by the methods of Chapters 3 and 4. When the antecedent has been found to be sufficiently true, we are ready to execute the consequent of the rule.

There are many possible consequent instructions, including creation, modification and input or output of data, direction of the flow of the program by metarules, debugging instructions, and so on. Here, we will be concerned only with instructions that change or create values or truth values of data; the other instruction types are ancillary to the main purpose of the program, which is to reason from data to conclusions.

6.3 NATURE OF INFERENCE IN A FUZZY EXPERT SYSTEM

Inference in an expert system involves the modification of data, either its value or its truth value or both, by rules. Whether modification of the value of a datum is permitted or not depends on its existing truth value, the truth value of the new value, and the type of inference being used. Creation of new data is always permitted; the only question here is the confidence that will be assigned to any values specified in the new datum's value. Since truth values are so important here, we first take up the modification and assignment of truth values; following that, modification of the value of data will be discussed.

Since inference is carried out by rules, we first review the structure of fuzzy rules. The most compact form of a rule is

$$\text{IF (P) THEN (Q)} \tag{6.1}$$

in which P (the antecedent) is a fuzzy proposition, and Q (the consequent) is a set of instructions to be carried out if the rule is fired.

The antecedent proposition will make some assertion(s) about data. These assertions may be very simple (that a given datum exists, or even more simply an assertion whose truth value is always true). A somewhat less simple assertion is that the truth value of a datum is true. Very commonly, an antecedent proposition will involve a comparison between value or truth value of a datum and that of either a literal or another datum. Most commonly the antecedent will be a complex proposition made up of two or more elemental propositions connected by AND, OR, and NOT connectives. In all cases, evaluation of the antecedent will yield a single truth value.

There are many types of consequent instructions. In this section, we are interested only in those instructions that modify data.

There are two kinds of data modification. In the first kind, which applies only to single-valued attributes of types integer, float and string, both the datum and its truth value may be changed. In the second kind, which applies to both single- and multi-valued attributes, only truth values are modified. Without loss of generality we may consider rules that modify truth values; if a modification of a truth value is permitted, modification of the value of a single-valued attribute is also permitted. A rule that modifies truth values may be written as

$$\text{IF (P) THEN (B}' = \text{B)} \tag{6.2}$$

P is the antecedent as before; B is an existing datum; and B' is a revised datum, with a different truth value. Our special interest is in deciding whether or not modification of a truth value is permitted

A further development of rule form (6.2) reflects an antecedent that compares data values. In that case, we have

$$\text{IF (A}' = \text{A) THEN (B}' = \text{B)} \tag{6.3}$$

in which A and B are specified prior values, and A' is an observed new value, usually different from the prior value of A. If A is a fuzzy set, then A' must be defined on the same universe as A; similarly, if B is a fuzzy set, then B' must be defined on the same universe as B.

6.4 MODIFICATION AND ASSIGNMENT OF TRUTH VALUES

If the antecedent truth value of rule (6.2) is P, the general principle is that we execute the consequence B with confidence P. Let the modified truth value of B be B'. We have three possible types of inference: *monotonic, non-monotonic, and downward monotonic*. In monotonic inference, the truth value B' may increase or remain unchanged, but not decrease; in non-monotonic inference, the truth value may increase, decrease, or remain unchanged; and in downward monotonic inference, the truth value may decrease or remain unchanged but not decrease.

The rule itself is assigned a truth value, say r. (By default, r is 1.) The antecedent confidence is modified before executing the consequent instructions by replacing P with P AND r to yield the posterior confidence, where usually the Zadehian AND or minimum is used. To avoid cumbersome notation in this chapter, we will assume that whenever the antecedent truth value appears, it will have been ANDed with the rule truth value (by default 1).

6.4.1 Monotonic Inference

In monotonic inference, we assume that the existing truth value of B is firmly based, and cannot be reduced by any new information. (As is customary in AI, we assume that the term unqualified term "monotonic" means that facts believed true will not be invalidated, i.e., truth values of data will not be reduced.) This amounts to the assumption that we have not made any erroneous conclusions up till now. Any new information can only add to our confidence that the value of B is valid.

Suppose we have already established that the grade of membership of B is 0.8. A rule now fires with antecedent confidence 0.5. The argument is that since we already know that B's grade of membership is 0.8, the new information should be discarded, and the rule would fail; B's grade of membership would remain at 0.8.

A formula for B', the new truth value of B', using monotonic inference is

$$B' = P \text{ OR } B \tag{6.4}$$

where P is the antecedent truth value. P may have the form $(A' = A)$, and P will be the confidence that A' and A are approximately equal (discussed in Chapter 3). Suppose A and A' represent single-valued data (integers, floats, strings), with the same value but different truth values A and A', then

$$P = \text{truth value}(A' = A) = \max(A, A') \tag{6.5}$$

If A and A′ are not scalar quantities, that is, discrete fuzzy sets, fuzzy numbers or membership functions, then we can write (6.5) as

$$P = tv(A' = A) = max(A(x), A'(x))\forall x \text{ in } A, A' \qquad (6.6)$$

Similarly, if B and B′ are not scalar quantities, we can write (6.4) as

$$B'(x) = max(P, B(x)) \qquad (6.7)$$

According to (6.7), if P is multivalued and is non-zero, B would be every non-zero also. It appears that monotonic reasoning is then not likely to be useful in modifying a multivalued datum.

6.4.2 Non-monotonic Inference

In non-monotonic inference, we assume that the new information supplied by the firing of a new rule is more reliable than any existing information.

As before, suppose we have already established that the grade of membership of B is 0.8. A rule now fires with antecedent confidence 0.5. Since we believe the new information, we would reduce the truth value of B to 0.5. If, on the other hand, the new rule fires with confidence 0.9, we would increase the truth value of B to 0.9.

For single-valued data, a formula for B′, using non-monotonic inference is

$$B' = P \qquad (6.8)$$

where P is the confidence that A′ and A are approximately equal as given just above.

If B and B′ are not single-valued quantities, non-monotonic reasoning is not useful unless A, A′, B, and B′ are defined on the same universe. In this case, we could write (6.8) as

$$B'j(x) = A'(x) \text{ AND } A(x) \qquad (6.9)$$

but this is of doubtful utility in a fuzzy expert system. Another possibility is two use two levels of fuzziness; that is, we assign P as the truth value of the existing fuzzy number or membership function B. However, this case is usually covered by monotonic downward reasoning, discussed next. The assignment of truth values to other truth values has not been explored to any great extent in working fuzzy expert systems, except in the case of downward monotonic reasoning, discussed next in Section 6.4.3.

6.4.3 Downward Monotonic Inference

Downward monotonic inference may be useful when we believe that the prior truth value of B represents an upper limit on what is possible. This type of inference is useful when modifying multivalued data, necessary when defuzzifying. Suppose our consequent linguistic variable is B, with members the linguistic terms B_j. A sample such data declaration and rule might be

```
declare Data output fzset (Small Medium Large);
rule IF (...) THEN output is Small;
```

where the rule is of the form

$$\text{if } P_i \text{ then } B \text{ is } B_j \tag{6.10}$$

A rule has fired, assigning a grade of membership to B_j. A membership function has been assigned to B_j, since B_j is a linguistic term. We now wish to modify the membership function to reflect its grade of membership. To do this, we employ downward monotonic reasoning.

A formula for B_j', the new truth value of B_j using downward monotonic inference, is

$$B_j' = P \text{ AND } B_j \tag{6.11}$$

The reader will recall that there are many possible definitions for the AND operator. If we adopt the Zadehian min AND operator, we can write (6.11) as

$$B_j' = \min(P, B_j) \tag{6.12}$$

If we adopt the product AND operator, we can write (6.12) as

$$B_j' = P \cdot B_j \tag{6.13}$$

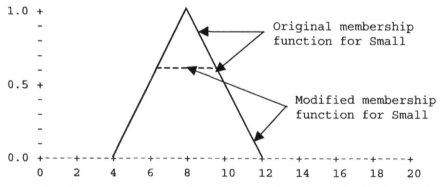

Figure 6.1 Downward monotonic inference; modification of a membership function by firing a rule, prior to defuzzification. Rule is "IF A THEN size is Small"; combined antecedent and rule confidence (pconf) is 0.6.

In Figure 6.1, we illustrate the modification of a membership function using downward monotonic inference and the Zadehian min AND operator.

6.5 APPROXIMATE REASONING

We have discussed the theory of approximate reasoning in Section 4.3. As we have noted, this theory is sometimes suggested for use in fuzzy expert systems. Since the method has already been presented, we will not repeat the procedure here. We will, in Section 6.6, attempt to place approximate reasoning for expert systems in the same general framework as monotonic reasoning (6.4), non-monotonic reasoning (6.8) and downward monotonic reasoning (6.11).

6.6 TESTS OF PROCEDURES TO OBTAIN THE TRUTH VALUE OF A CONSEQUENT FROM THE TRUTH VALUE OF ITS ANTECEDENT

We consider a rule

$$\text{if } X \text{ is } A \text{ then } Y \text{ is } B \tag{6.14}$$

In this rule X and A are fuzzy sets defined on the same universe, as are Y and B. X is observed to be A', a fuzzy set whose truth values may be different from those of A. We denote the fuzzy set Y that corresponds to A' by B'. We now desire to calculate the truth values of the fuzzy set B'. Note that since X and A, Y and B are defined on the same universes, their *values* are the members of those universes; we are concerned here with the calculation of *truth values* only.

$$B' = P \text{ OR } B \text{ (Monotonic reasoning)} \tag{6.15}$$
$$B' = P \text{ (Non-monotonic reasoning)} \tag{6.16}$$
$$B' = P \text{ AND } B \text{ (Downward monotonic reasoning)} \tag{6.17}$$
$$\text{if } X = A \text{ then } Y = B: X = A': \therefore Y = B',$$
$$B' = A' \circ (A \rightarrow B) \text{ (Approximate reasoning)} \tag{6.18}$$

where $\circ$ denotes a fuzzy relation, and $\rightarrow$ denotes a fuzzy implication operator.

6.6.1 Desirable Properties

Given rule (6.14), if P then ($B' = B$), we have now established four methods for inferring truth values of B' given truth values for P and B or, in the case of approximate reasoning, A', A, and B. We now ask what properties these methods should have to be useful in expert systems. We think that the following properties are indispensable for the three different reasoning modes we have defined.

Monotonic reasoning:

$$1. \; B'_j \geq B_j$$
$$2. \; \text{If } A' = \text{NULL, then } B' = B \qquad\qquad (6.19)$$
$$3. \; \text{If } A' \text{ and } A \text{ are disjoint, then } B' = B$$

Non-monotonic reasoning:

$$1. \; B' = P = (A' = A)$$
$$2. \; \text{If } A' = \text{NULL, then } B' = \text{NULL} \qquad\qquad (6.20)$$
$$3. \; \text{If } A' \text{ and } A \text{ are disjoint, then } B' = \text{NULL}$$

Downward monotonic reasoning:

$$1. \; B'_j \leq B_j$$
$$2. \; \text{If } A' = \text{NULL, then } B' = \text{NULL} \qquad\qquad (6.21)$$
$$3. \; \text{If } A' \text{ and } A \text{ are disjoint, then } B' = \text{NULL}$$

6.6.2 Summary of Candidate Methods

In the following, the symbols for propositions represent their truth values.

A. Fuzzy rule "if A then B", monotonic reasoning:

$$B' = (A' = A) \text{ OR } B \qquad\qquad (6.22)$$

B. Fuzzy rule "if A then B", non-monotonic reasoning:

$$B' = (A' = A) \qquad\qquad (6.23)$$

C. Fuzzy rule "if A then B", downward monotonic reasoning (equivalent to Mamdani method);

$$B' = (A' = A) \text{ AND } B \qquad\qquad (6.24)$$

D. Fuzzy rule "if $A' = A$ then $B' = B$", Approximate reasoning:

$$B' = A' \circ (A \to B) \qquad\qquad (6.25)$$

In D, approximate reasoning, $A \to B$ produces the fuzzy relation matrix $[A_i \to B_j]$; the $\circ$ operator denotes composition of A' with $A \to B$ by $B'_j = \max(\min(A'_i, A_i \to B_j)$ for all i in A, A' as defined in Chapter 3.

TABLE 6.1A   Desirable Inference Properties[a]

| | | | | | Desirable Properties | | | | | | | | |
| A | B | A' | A' = A | B' | NonMonotonic | | | Monotonic | | | Downward Monotonic | | |
					1.	2.	3.	1.	2.	3.	1.	2.	3.
0	0	0	0	0	Y	Y	Y	Y	Y	Y	Y	Y	Y
0	0	1	0	0	Y	—	Y	Y	—	Y	Y	—	Y
0	1	0	0	1	N	Y	Y	Y	Y	Y	Y	N	Y
0	1	1	0	1	N	—	Y	Y	—	Y	Y	—	Y
1	0	0	0	0	Y	Y	Y	Y	Y	Y	Y	Y	Y
1	0	1	1	1	Y	—	—	Y	—	—	Y	—	—
1	1	0	0	1	Y	Y	N	Y	Y	Y	Y	N	N
1	1	1	1	1	Y	—	—	Y	—	—	Y	—	—

[a]Method A: monotonic rule: B' = (A' = A) OR B.

6.6.3   Tests of Methods Against Desirable Properties

We now test these four methods on rule (6.14) in the simple case of a fuzzy set with one member, with grades of membership of A, B, and A' 0 or 1, with results in Table 6.1A–D. By using crisp values, we leave open the definitions of AND and OR as any valid t-norm and t-conorm, and of any implication operator that reduces to the classical for crisp values. ("Desirable properties" are defined in Section 6.6.1.)

Methods A, B, and C all satisfy the desirable properties for the type of reasoning they are designed to handle, and fail to satisfy all desirable properties for any other reasoning type. They are not interchangeable.

TABLE 6.1B   Desirable Inference Properties[a]

| | | | | | Desirable Properties | | | | | | | | |
| A | B | A' | A' = A | B' | NonMonotonic | | | Monotonic | | | Downward Monotonic | | |
					1.	2.	3.	1.	2.	3.	1.	2.	3.
0	0	0	0	0	Y	Y	Y	Y	Y	Y	Y	Y	Y
0	0	1	0	0	Y	—	Y	Y	—	Y	Y	—	Y
0	1	0	0	0	Y	Y	Y	N	N	N	N	N	N
0	1	1	0	0	Y	—	Y	Y	—	N	Y	—	N
1	0	0	0	0	Y	Y	Y	Y	Y	Y	Y	Y	Y
1	0	1	1	1	Y	—	—	Y	—	—	Y	—	—
1	1	0	0	0	Y	Y	Y	Y	N	N	Y	N	N
1	1	1	1	1	Y	—	—	Y	—	—	Y	N	N

[a]Method B: non-monotonic rule: B' = (A' = A).

TABLE 6.1C   Desirable Inference Properties[a]

A	B	A′	A′ = A	B′	NonMonotonic			Monotonic			Downward Monotonic		
					1.	2.	3.	1.	2.	3.	1.	2.	3.
0	0	0	0	0	Y	Y	Y	Y	Y	Y	Y	Y	Y
0	0	1	0	0	Y	—	Y	Y	—	Y	Y	—	Y
0	1	0	0	0	Y	Y	Y	N	N	N	Y	Y	Y
0	1	1	0	0	Y	—	Y	N	—	N	Y	—	Y
1	0	0	0	0	Y	Y	Y	Y	Y	Y	Y	Y	Y
1	0	1	1	0	N	—	—	Y	—	—	Y	—	—
1	1	0	0	0	Y	Y	Y	N	N	N	Y	Y	Y
1	1	1	1	1	Y	—	—	Y	—	—	Y	—	—

[a]Method C: downward monotonic rule: B′ = (A′ = A AND B).

The approximate reasoning method fails to satisfy all desirable properties for any type of reasoning: monotonic, non-monotonic, or downward monotonic. Of particular concern is the failure to satisfy property 3. If A′ and A are disjoint so that (A′ = A) is 0, it is quite possible to produce a B′ that is everywhere 1, a very counter-intuitive result.

If the t-norm (Mamdani "implication") A AND B is used instead of the fuzzy implication in the approximate reasoning method, all properties are satisfied for downward monotonic reasoning. This is important, since Castro (1995) has demonstrated that this formulation produces universal approximators for any t-norm used for the AND operator. However, since the Mamdani "implication" does not reduce to the classical implication for crisp values, it is not properly speaking an implication

TABLE 6.1D   Desirable Inference Properties[a]

A	B	A′	A → B	B′	NonMonotonic			Monotonic			Downward Monotonic		
					1.	2.	3.	1.	2.	3.	1.	2.	3.
0	0	0	1	0	Y	Y	Y	Y	Y	Y	Y	Y	Y
0	0	1	1	1	N	—	N	Y	—	N	N	—	N
0	1	0	1	0	Y	Y	Y	N	N	Y	Y	Y	Y
0	1	1	1	1	N	—	N	Y	—	Y	Y	—	N
1	0	0	0	0	Y	Y	Y	Y	Y	Y	Y	Y	Y
1	0	1	0	0	N	—	—	Y	—	—	Y	—	—
1	1	0	1	0	Y	Y	Y	N	N	N	Y	Y	Y
1	1	1	1	1	Y	—	—	Y	—	—	Y	—	—

[a]Method D (approximate reasoning): B′ = A′ AND (A IMPL B).

at all. In the procedure defined for approximate reasoning in (6.25), the fuzzy relation (A → B) is replaced by (A AND B), becoming

$$B' = A' \circ (A \text{ AND } B) \tag{6.26}$$

The method of composing A' with a fuzzy relation between A and B defined by a t-norm is precisely equivalent to our Method C, downward monotonic inference, B' = (A' = A) AND B.

We have demonstrated that for crisp truth values for A, A', and B, the non-monotonic rule method satisfies all properties for non-monotonic logic; the monotonic rule method satisfies all properties for monotonic logic; the downward non-monotonic rule method satisfies all properties for downward non-monotonic logic; and the approximate reasoning method fails to satisfy all desirable properties for any reasoning type. We will be content with the simple assertion that the rule methods also satisfy the corresponding properties for fuzzy truth values, and will forego the proof.

Note that in the definitions of methods A, B, and C for determining B' from A, A', and B summarized in 6.6.2, the antecedent involves only A' and A; the consequent involves only B' and B. Only the antecedent in approximate reasoning method D has a clause that involves both A and B; as we have shown, the approximate reasoning method fails to meet the desirable properties, and hence has little use in an expert system. In an expert system, it is then possible to compute the consequent confidence in two steps, the first of which depends only on the antecedent, and the second of which couples this to the consequent.

6.6.4 Implementation of Choices Among Types of Reasoning

Inference in a fuzzy expert system differs somewhat from conventional logical inference. Logical inference seeks to infer new logical propositions from old. A primary tool for this purpose is the *modus ponens* "if A implies B, and A is true, then B is true", where A and B are logical propositions. Inference in a fuzzy expert system deals not only with establishing the truths of fuzzy propositions, but with the creation or modification of data and their truth values by the firing of rules.

In modifying data by a rule, we must consider the combined antecedent and rule confidences (pconf), and the existing truth value of the data to be modified. We define three types of inference (Table 6.2):

TABLE 6.2 Data Modification Permissible Under Different Types of Inference

Type of inference	Modification permitted if:
Monotonic	Modify if pconf $>=$ old data confidence.
Non-monotonic	Always modify.
Monotonic downward	Modify if pconf $<=$ old data confidence.

Default reasoning is optimistic; we assume that the existing truth value of a consequent datum is well founded, and any additional information can only validate or increase existing consequent truth values. This is monotonic reasoning. However, we occasionally bring in new data in which we have the utmost confidence; in this case, non-monotonic reasoning can be employed. The last circumstance occurs when we are quite pessimistic, and any new data can only reduce existing confidences; we then employ monotonic downward reasoning. The last method is sometimes appropriate when modifying membership functions prior to defuzzification.

Obviously, if different types of reasoning need to be employed under different circumstances, the writer of a fuzzy expert system must provide mechanisms for making this choice. We have seen that the method of approximate reasoning is inapplicable to rule-based fuzzy expert systems. We shall see later that downward monotonic reasoning is employed when modifying membership functions prior to defuzzification; FLOPS employs this type of reasoning by default with the defuzzify command. However, in normal fuzzy reasoning, the knowledge engineer should be given a way of choosing between monotonic upward and non-monotonic reasoning.

FLOPS employs monotonic upward reasoning by default. The default reasoning may be changed to non-monotonic by issuing the TMSoff command, and may restore monotonic upward reasoning by the TMSon command. In addition, when confidence levels are modified inferentially by such consequent commands as area is Small, or x is 33, the default reasoning method is used; when confidence levels are referred to directly, by such consequent commands as area.Small = 0 or x.cf = 0, non-monotonic reasoning is used. It is also possible to use an arbitrary inference method by computing truth values in any desired way; this ability is utilized in a FLOPS program using the Combs' inference method, described in Chapter 7.

6.7 SUMMARY

Inference in an expert system is the process of drawing conclusions from data; that is deriving new data or truth values from input data and truth values. The new data may be the final conclusions, or in multistep reasoning, may be intermediate conclusions that constitute input to the next step.

Inference in a fuzzy expert system differs somewhat from conventional logical inference. Logical inference seeks to infer new logical propositions from old. A primary tool for this purpose is the *modus ponens* "if A implies B, and A is true, then B is true", where A and B are logical propositions. Inference in a fuzzy expert system deals not with establishing the truths of fuzzy propositions, but with the creation or modification of data and their truth values by the firing of rules.

In modifying data by a rule, we must consider the combined antecedent and rule confidences (pconf), and the existing truth value of the data to be modified. We define three types of inference:

Type of inference	Modification permitted if:
Monotonic	Modify if pconf $>=$ old data confidence.
Non-monotonic	Always modify.
Monotonic downward	Modify if pconf $<=$ old data confidence.

Default reasoning is optimistic; we assume that the existing truth value of a consequent datum is well founded, and any additional information can only validate or increase existing consequent truth values. This is monotonic reasoning. However, we occasionally bring in new data in which we have the utmost confidence; in this case, non-monotonic reasoning can be employed. The last circumstance occurs when we are quite pessimistic, and any new data can only reduce existing confidences; we then employ monotonic downward reasoning. The last method is usually appropriate when modifying membership functions prior to defuzzification.

6.7.1   Data Types and Truth Values

Available attribute data types and their truth values may be summarized as:

- Integers, floats and strings. Values are assigned either by user input or as literals within the program. A single truth value is attached to any value these attributes may have. This truth value is itself an attribute, accessed by appending .cf to the attribute name. This truth value itself is assumed to be fully true.
- Fuzzy numbers. Values are any number from the real line. Truth values are defined by a parameterized membership function that maps any real number value onto its truth value (grade of membership). Fuzzy numbers are used primarily in approximate comparisons in a rule antecedent. A full range of approximate comparison operators is available corresponding to the conventional Boolean numerical comparison operators furnished by most computer languages. The truth value of a fuzzy number attribute itself is assumed to be fully true.
- Discrete fuzzy sets. Values are defined as the names of the members of the fuzzy set. To each member a single truth value is attached, the grade of membership of that member in the fuzzy set.
- Membership functions. Values are numbers from the real line. If a discrete fuzzy set is a linguistic variable, whose members are linguistic terms describing a numeric quantity, membership functions are attached, one to each linguistic term. These functions, like fuzzy numbers, map any real or fuzzy number onto the truth value (grade of membership) of the corresponding linguistic term (discrete fuzzy set member). The grade of membership of the linguistic term applies also to its membership function.

6.7.2   Types of Fuzzy Reasoning

Three types of fuzzy inference are defined. These types differ in consequent truth value modifications permissible as a result of firing a rule. In *monotonic reasoning*, consequent truth values may increase or stay the same, but may not decrease; in *non-monotonic reasoning*, consequent truth values may increase, decrease, or stay the same; in *monotonic downward reasoning*, consequent truth values may decrease or stay the same, but may not increase.

We consider a rule that modifies data or truth values as

$$\text{if P then } B' = B \tag{6.27}$$

in which P is the antecedent, B is an existing truth value, and B' is the new truth value modified by the firing of the rule. P may have the form

$$P = (A' = A) \tag{6.28}$$

where A is a specified value, and A' is an observed value. This form is required by the generalized modus ponens used in approximate reasoning.

In data modification by a rule, we consider three types of inference and define these types quantitatively, in terms of the antecedent confidence and the truth value of data to be modified. We also similarly define the Approximate Reasoning method.

- Monotonic reasoning: **$B' = $ P OR B**
  Monotonic reasoning is useful when modifying values of scalar data, or grades of membership of discrete fuzzy sets by such consequent instructions as THEN name = "Jane" or THEN size is Small.
- Non-monotonic reasoning: **$B' = $ P**
  Non-monotonic reasoning is useful when modifying truth values directly, especially when invalidating data previously believed to be true.
- Monotonic downward: **$B' = $ P AND B**
  For membership functions, where x is a scalar argument,

  B'(x) = P AND B(x)

  This type of reasoning is useful when combining the grade of membership of a linguistic term with its membership function prior to defuzzification.
- Approximate reasoning:

  B' = A' o [A IMPLIES B]

  in which o denotes fuzzy composition and IMPLIES denotes any fuzzy implication operator that reduces to the classical for crisp operands.

We define desirable properties for inference in an expert system for these inference types. We then show that the definitions of monotonic, non-monotonic, and monotonic downward reasoning all satisfy the desirable properties for their reasoning types, but the approximate reasoning method fails to satisfy all desirable properties for any type of reasoning. We note that Mamdani inference, which uses a fuzzy AND operator in place of an implication operator, is precisely the same as our monotonic downward method.

6.8   QUESTIONS

6.1   What is the difference between possibility and necessity?

6.2   We have proposition A, but as yet no evidence to support it or refute it. What is Nec(A)? Pos(A)?

6.3   We have created a fuzzy set to hold some preliminary classifications of an object.
   a. To what value should the grades of membership of the fuzzy set members be initialized?
   b. If we are going to employ monotonic reasoning, what advantage does this initialization have?

6.4   What are the differences among monotonic, non-monotonic and downward monotonic reasoning?

6.5   We are employing monotonic reasoning, and have a fireable rule with a consequent instruction that would decrease the truth value of a datum. What happens to that truth value when the rule is fired?

6.6   Under what circumstance should we employ non-monotonic reasoning?

6.7   When should downward monotonic reasoning be employed?

6.8   What type of inference does FLOPS employ by default?

6.9   **a.** Can FLOPS default inference method be changed?
   b. If so, how, and to what method?

7 Inference in a Fuzzy Expert System II: Modification of Data and Truth Values

In Chapter 6, we defined three types of fuzzy inference useful in expert systems. These are *monotonic* (upward), in which consequent truth values can increase or stay the same but cannot decrease; *non-monotonic*, in which truth values may increase, decrease or stay the same; and *monotonic downward*, in which truth values may decrease or stay the same, but cannot increase. Monotonic inference is useful when modifying values of scalar data (integers, floats and string) by such consequent instructions as $x = 13$, where x is an integer, and in inferring grades of membership in discrete fuzzy sets by such instructions as `size is Small`, where `size` is a discrete fuzzy set of which `Small` is a member. Non-monotonic inference is required when invalidating data previously believed to be true, by directly assigning truth values or grades of membership with such instructions as `x.cf = 0`, which sets the truth value of x to 0, and `size.Large = 0`, which sets the truth value of member `Large` of discrete fuzzy set `size` to 0. Monotonic downward inference is useful when modifying membership functions prior to defuzzification.

In this chapter, we will examine how these methods are used in modifying existing data and truth value when firing rules. We will not be concerned with evaluating the truth value of the rule antecedent; we will assume that this has been determined and combined with the truth value of the rule itself using the methods of Chapters 3 and 4. We will refer to this combined truth value as the *antecedent confidence* to simplify our wording. When the antecedent has been found to be sufficiently true, we are ready to execute the consequent of the rule.

There are many possible consequent instructions, including creation, modification and input or output of data, direction of the flow of the program by metarules, debugging instructions, and so on. Here, we will be concerned only with instructions that change or create values or truth values of data; the other instruction types are ancillary to the main purpose of the program, which is to reason from data to conclusions.

Creating new data in the consequent of a rule offers no problems. Scalar data (integer, floats, and strings) and fuzzy numbers are set to the new value with (by default) the truth value set to the antecedence confidence. Fuzzy numbers are

Fuzzy Expert Systems and Fuzzy Reasoning, By William Siler and James J. Buckley
ISBN 0-471-38859-9 Copyright © 2005 John Wiley & Sons, Inc.

set to the specified membership function; since entire fuzzy numbers themselves do not have a truth value, the antecedent confidence is ignored. Grades of membership of discrete fuzzy sets are initialized to 0. Membership functions of linguistic terms are set to the specified values. Default truth values for new scalar data and grades of membership of discrete fuzzy set members may be overridden by direct assignment of these values.

We now consider the major problem: modification of existing data and truth values.

7.1 MODIFICATION OF EXISTING DATA BY RULE CONSEQUENT INSTRUCTIONS

Conventionally, a simple rule of the type

$$\text{IF } (A' = A) \text{ then } (B' = B) \tag{7.1}$$

where A, A', B, and B' are fuzzy numbers, and B' is evaluated setting up a fuzzy relation $[A_i \text{ AND } B_j]$ and evaluating B' by composing A' with this relation, usually using max–min composition:

$$B' = A' \circ [A_i \text{ AND } B_j] \tag{7.2}$$

where the AND operator is a selected t-norm. [In the Mamdani method, the Zadehian t-norm $\min(A_i, B_j)$ is used.]

There are two problems with this approach. First, the method is difficult to apply to complex antecedents. Second, the method involves two nested loops, first over rows, then over columns of the fuzzy relation. Both these problems are easily solved, since (7.2) is precisely equivalent to formulation (7.4), which does not require two nested loops. [See Klir and Yuan (1995), p. 316.]

Let p be the antecedent truth value. Then in rule (7.1),

$$p = \max(\min(A'(x), A(x))) \text{ over } x \tag{7.3}$$

Then,

$$B' = pB = \{\min(p, B'_j)\} \tag{7.4}$$

We can then evaluate our rule (7.1) quite simply, using (7.4):

$$\text{IF } (A' = A) \text{ THEN } (B' = pB) \tag{7.5}$$

in which P is the antecedent truth value, B is the specified prior truth value of B, and B' is the new value of B resulting from firing the rule. If B is a fuzzy set, then B' must be defined on the same universe as B.

7.2 MODIFICATION OF NUMERIC DISCRETE FUZZY SETS: LINGUISTIC VARIABLES AND LINGUISTIC TERMS

Recall that a linguistic variable is a special kind of discrete fuzzy set, such as Speed, that describes a numeric quantity. The members of this discrete fuzzy set are linguistic terms such as Fast, Medium, and Slow. To each linguistic term a membership function is attached that maps numbers from the real line onto grades of membership of the linguistic terms.

In this section, we consider rules with linguistic terms in both antecedent and consequent. This is almost always the case in fuzzy control, and sometimes in more general fuzzy reasoning problems as well.

Consider a special case of rule (7.1) above:

$$\text{if (speed is Slow AND distance is Far) then (power is High)} \qquad (7.6)$$

where speed, distance, and power are numeric attributes.

This type of rule is found in most fuzzy control programs. There are two different ways of defining the syntax of this rule. In typical fuzzy control rule syntax, Slow, Far, and High are membership functions in (unspecified) linguistic variables; speed, distance, and power are floating-point numeric variables. Such rules are almost invariably coupled with many other similar rules.

Firing this rule involves a complex procedure. First, the numeric attributes speed and distance are fuzzified to get the truth value of the antecedent clauses (speed is Slow) and (power is High); these are combined to get the antecedent confidence. The membership function for High is then modified using downward monotonic reasoning. Next, the membership functions relating to power, including High and, for example, Medium, Low, and Zero, are combined, that is, aggregated, using an OR operator. Finally, the combined membership functions are defuzzified using, for example, the centroid method to yield a numeric value for power. This yields an extremely compact rule structure.

There are, however, disadvantages to lumping this entire procedure into one rule, stemming in part from the fact that while linguistic terms are employed, the linguistic variable of which they are members is unspecified. This means that the term Medium, for example, should not be used except in association with speed, since only one membership function can be associated with Medium. Since names of the linguistic variables associated with speed, distance, and power are not specified, they are inaccessible to the programmer if he wishes to use the grades of membership of their members (such as High) in later rules; multistep reasoning becomes more difficult. Fuzzification and defuzzification are automatic and inescapable; it is impossible to use a discrete fuzzy set of classification in the consequent. For these reasons, we prefer to avoid this rule of syntax in general-purpose fuzzy reasoning, and to break out fuzzification and defuzzification (if any) as separate steps in two other rules. For example,

```
declare Data
  fspeed flt
```

```
speed fzset (Slow Medium Fast)
fdistance flt
distance fzset (Short Medium Far)
fpower flt
power fzset (Zero Low Medium High);
```

```
rule block 1
IF (in Data fspeed = <SP> AND fdistance = <D>)
THEN fuzzify 1 <SP> into speed,
   fuzzify 1 <D> into distance;
```

After this rule has fired, the discrete fuzzy sets (linguistic variables) speed and distance will have grades of membership assigned to their respective members. Although the term Medium is used three times, each one belongs to a different linguistic variable, and will have its own membership function.

We are now ready to fire our next set of rules, of the type

```
rule block 2
IF (speed is Slow AND distance is Far) THEN (power is High);
```

```
rule block 2
IF (speed is Fast AND distance is Short) THEN (power is
Zero);
```

When the rules in block 2 have fired (in parallel), the members of linguistic variable power will have been assigned their grades of membership, and we are ready to defuzzify if we wish;

```
rule block 3
IF(Data)
THEN defuzzify 1 power (centroid) into 1 fpower;
```

The grades of membership of the members of linguistic variables speed, distance, and power are accessible to the programmer after the block 2 rules have fired.

We now ask what type of reasoning is appropriate in this problem.

7.3 SELECTION OF REASONING TYPE AND GRADE-OF-MEMBERSHIP INITIALIZATION

A critical element in deciding reasoning type is to decide what we want to do if two or more rules have the same consequent discrete fuzzy set member or linguistic term, firing with different antecedent confidences.

Suppose we have two rules with the same consequent:

```
:rule r1
IF (speed is Slow AND distance is Medium) THEN (power is
Medium);
:rule r2
IF (speed is Medium AND distance is Short) THEN (power is
Medium);
```

and that rule r1 fires with antecedent confidence 0.8, and that rule r2 fires with antecedent confidence 0.6. With monotonic reasoning, rule r1 would succeed in setting the grade of membership of Medium to 0.8, even if rule r2 fires after rule r1. If we allow each rule to set truth values regardless of their existing value, the last rule to fire would succeed.

There are, however, occasions when we wish to modify grades of membership in different ways, employing non-monotonic reasoning; these will be discussed in Section 7.7.

7.4 FUZZIFICATION AND DEFUZZIFICATION

We review briefly fuzzification and defuzzification, discussed more fully in Chapter 3, from the point of view of the choices to be made and their specification in an expert system language.

Overall, we have these steps to carry out; fuzzification and evaluation of antecedent confidence; modification of consequent membership functions; aggregation of membership functions for each consequent linguistic variable; and defuzzification of the aggregated membership functions.

7.4.1 Fuzzification and Evaluation of Antecedent Confidence

Fortunately, almost everyone agrees on how fuzzification should be carried out; in a working expert system. Also, combination of truth values of two or more antecedent clauses is almost always carried out using the Zadehian min–max AND and OR operations. It is probably satisfactory to take the conventional methods as defaults, and not necessary to permit specifying any other choices here.

7.4.2 Modification of Consequent Membership Functions

The modification of membership functions can carried out by

$$B'_j = P \text{ AND } B_j \tag{7.7}$$

but there is not general agreement as to which AND operator should be used. Common choices are the Zadehian min operator (which yields the Mamdani method) and the product operator. The min operator is widely accepted, and is probably a good default, but it lends flexibility to a system if other operators can be specified.

7.4.3   Aggregation of Consequent Membership Functions for Each Consequent Linguistic Variable

Aggregation of all the modified membership functions belonging to a single linguistic variable is usually carried out using the Zadehian max OR operator, and this is probably acceptable as a default at present. However, an argument can be made for employing a different OR operator. Let us take an example and follow it through.

Suppose we have a linguistic variable control in the consequent of a rule, with three members N, Z, and P with these membership functions (Fig. 7.1):

We fire rules that give grades of membership 0 for N, 0.8 for Z and 0.6 for P, and modify the membership functions using the Zadeh AND operator, giving these modified membership functions (Fig. 7.2):

We now aggregate these modified functions using the Zadehian OR operator (Fig. 7.3):

The aggregated membership functions in Figure 7.3 represent a new membership function. We may ask—Membership in what? The answer is that Figure 7.3 represents the truth value that a number between -1 and $+1$ is valid for this particular instance of the linguistic variable control. But the resulting membership function is

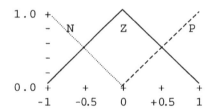

Figure 7.1   Membership functions for linguistic variable control.

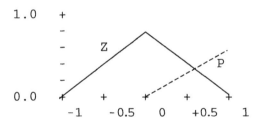

Figure 7.2   Modified membership functions for linguistic variable control.

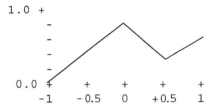

Figure 7.3   Aggregated membership functions using Zadehian OR operator for linguistic variable *control.*

not convex, and the notch in Figure 7.3 at an argument 0.5 seems quite counterintuitive. Why should 0.5 have a lower grade of membership in control than arguments of 0 and 1?

In Chapter 3 we showed that when ORing fuzzy numbers are *logically incompatible,* such as 2 and NOT 2, there is a mathematical (and practical) argument for using the bounded sum OR operator. In aggregating membership functions, we deal with fuzzy numbers that are *semantically incompatible.*

Unfortunately, we do not have a mathematical argument to justify using the bounded sum operator in this, but from a practical viewpoint it seems to work out, at least in this case. In Figure 7.4, we aggregate the membership functions of Figure 7.2 using the bounded sum operator with intuitively pleasing results; the resulting membership function is convex and the annoying notch in Figure 7.3 has been removed.

Figures 7.3 and 7.4 indicate that it might be desirable to furnish a choice of other OR operators than the Zadehian for aggregation of membership functions, provided that the memberships of the unweighted aggregated membership functions satisfy appropriate conditions, such as their sum being one at any point. More research is needed on this point.

7.4.4   Determination of Defuzzified Value for Consequent Attribute

We denote the argument of the membership functions, the number whose defuzzified value is to be obtained by z; its grade of membership by $\mu(z)$; and the defuzzified value by z_{def}.

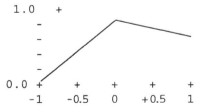

Figure 7.4   Aggregated membership functions for linguistic variable *control.* using the bounded sum OR operator.

Here again different methods are used, described in Klir and Yuan (1996) (books on.fuzzy control). Here, we will describe only the most commonly used defuzzification method, the *centroid* method.

Probably the most commonly used defuzzification method is the *centroid* method, equivalent to calculating the center of area of the aggregated membership function, as shown in Figure 7.3 or 7.4. Analytically, we divide the integral over the range of the membership function of the product of the argument and its grade of membership, and divide this by the integral of the grade of membership; this is very useful when the membership functions are given as parameterized continuous functions, such as piecewise linear, piecewise quadratic or normalized Gaussian:

$$z_{\text{defuzzified}} = \frac{\int_Z z\mu(z)dz}{\int_Z \mu(z)dz} \tag{7.8}$$

The discrete version of this, when the membership functions are given as a discrete set of values, is to sum the products of the arguments and their grade of membership, and divide this by the sum of the grades of membership:

$$z_{\text{defuzzified}} = z_{\text{defuzzified}} = \frac{\sum_i z_i \mu(z_i)}{\sum_i \mu(z_i)} \tag{7.9}$$

In the case where the membership functions are singletons, equation (7.9) becomes a very fast and simple calculation.

7.5   NON-NUMERIC DISCRETE FUZZY SETS

In "What?" problems, the output will usually be non-numeric: A classification such as a disease in problems of diagnosis, a specific trouble as in problems of trouble shooting, identification of an unknown object, or recommendation of a course of action. There are two convenient ways to represent such an output internally: as a discrete fuzzy set of possibilities, or as a character string to be presented to the user. Representation as a discrete fuzzy set has advantages. Fuzzy sets lend themselves well to representation of ambiguities and contradictions, and numeric measures are available for the degrees of fuzziness and ambiguity in a discrete fuzzy set, helping to evaluate how certain we are that a conclusion we have reached is unique and supported by the evidence.

There are rules whose syntax seems at first to be virtually the same as the typical fuzzy control rule (7.6), but used for classification, and which do not involve defuzzification at all. In such rules, the consequent discrete fuzzy set is a fuzzy set of classifications, perhaps preliminary classifications. For example, here is a sample from a simplified program for classification of the famous Iris data of Fisher (1936).

```
declare Data
  N int PL flt PW flt SL flt SW flt;
declare Iris
  N int
  PetalL  fzset (setosa versicolor virginica)
  PetalW  fzset (setosa versicolor virginica)
  SepalL  fzset (setosa versicolor virginica)
  SepalW  fzset (setosa versicolor virginica)
  species fzset (setosa versicolor virginica);
```

In this case PL, PW, SL, and SW are the measured length and width of petal and sepal, and PetalL, PetalW, SepaL, and SepalW, are linguistic variables with three members, one for each of the possible species classifications. Of course, membership functions must be defined; the linguistic term setosa will identify one membership function for petal length, one for petal width, one for sepal length and one for sepal width. Species is a discrete fuzzy set of classification; it is non-numeric, and has no membership functions attached.

Our first classification rule fuzzifies the data, just as in fuzzy control:

```
rule block 0 (goal Fuzzify input data)
IF (in Data N = <N> AND PL = <PL> AND PW = <PW> AND SL =
<SL> AND SW =
    <SW>)
  (in Iris N = <N>)
THEN
    fuzzify 2 PetalL <PL>,
    fuzzify 2 PetalW <PW>,
    fuzzify 2 SepalL <SL>,
    fuzzify 2 SepalW <SW>;
```

Now, we are ready to classify with three rules, one for each candidate species:

```
rule block 1 (goal classify as setosa)
IF (in Iris PetalL is setosa AND PetalW is setosa AND
SepalL is setosa AND SepalW is setosa)
THEN
  in 1 species is setosa;
rule block 1 (goal classify as virginica)
IF (in Iris PetalL is virginica AND PetalW is virginica
AND SepalL is virginica AND SepalW is virginica)
THEN
  in 1 species is virginica;
rule block 1 (goal classify as versicolor)
IF (in Iris PetalL is versicolor AND PetalW is versicolor
AND SepalL is versicolor AND SepalW is versicolor)
```

THEN
```
    in 1 species is versicolor;
```

When these rules have fired, discrete fuzzy set species will hold the grades of membership assigned to each species. Since the classifications are non-numeric, no defuzzification is required, or even possible.

7.6   DISCRETE FUZZY SETS: FUZZINESS, AMBIGUITY, AND CONTRADICTION

When we desire to output results as a discrete fuzzy set of possibilities, it is most often the case that more than one fuzzy set member will have an appreciably non-zero grade of membership. For example, in the iris classification problem described above, our output fuzzy set might be

Fuzzy Set Species	Grade of Membership
Setosa	0.024
Versicolor	0.895
Virginica	0.910

(7.10)

Or, if we want to describe the speed of a car:

Fuzzy Set Speed	Grade of Membership
Slow	0.024
Medium	0.895
Fast	0.910

(7.11)

In (7.10), the classifications are mutually exclusive; the specimen must be one species only. A plant cannot belong to two species at the same time. We have, therefore, a contradiction between Versicolor and Virginica, which we will have to resolve one way or another.

In (7.11), however, it is quite possible for a car to share the characteristics of speed Medium and speed Fast. On an expressway a car traveling just below the speed limit of 65 mph might be considered to be going Fast, but a state trooper would probably consider that speed to be Medium. We have here not a contradiction, but an ambiguity.

7.6.1   Fuzziness and Ambiguity

We might want to know quantitatively to what extent the members of the fuzzy set fail to have crisp memberships, either 0 or 1. We now measure *fuzziness*, the extent to which a fuzzy set is not crisp. First, we present a very simple measure of fuzziness:

$$\text{fuzziness1} = \sum_i (1 - abs(2\mu_i - 1)) \tag{7.12}$$

The fuzziness measure returns the effective number of fuzzy set members that have complete fuzziness, that is, grade of membership 0.5. For example, the fuzziness of $\{0.5, 0.5, 0.5\}$ is 3; the fuzziness of $\{0, 0.5, 1\}$ is 1 and the fuzziness of $\{0.75, 0.75, 0.25\}$ is 1.5. For the two fuzzy sets just above, the fuzziness is 0.436. A sounder fuzziness measure that is based on information theory requires normalization of grades of membership to a sum of 1:

$$\mu'_i = \frac{\mu_i}{\sum_i \mu_i}$$

$$\text{fuzziness} = \exp\left(-\sum_i (\mu_i \log \mu_i - (1 - \mu_i) - \log(1 - \mu_i))\right)$$

(7.13)

Note that *fuzziness* does not measure how decisively the grades of membership in a fuzzy set point to one and only one member; instead, it measures how sure we are of the various degrees of membership. For measures of our ability to distinguish one valid member from others, we have to consider *ambiguity*.

7.6.2 Ambiguities and Contradictions

We now consider the extent to which more than one member of the output fuzzy set has a non-zero grade of membership; in other words, the effective number of members to which the memberships point. Of course, an ambiguity of one is great; only one member can be considered to be valid.

Ambiguity can be measured in a similar fashion to fuzziness. We present a simple measure of ambiguity corresponding to the measure of fuzziness in (7.12). For this simple measure of ambiguity, the first step is to determine the maximum grade of membership $\max(\mu)$. We then normalize the original grades of membership to a maximum of one:

$$\mu'_i = \frac{\mu_i}{\max(\mu_i)}$$

(7.14)

The total ambiguity is then simply the sum of the normalized grades of membership:

$$\text{ambiguity} = \sum_i \frac{\mu_i}{\max(\mu_i)}$$

$$\text{ambiguity} = \sum (\mu'_i)$$

(7.15)

Examples of measured fuzziness and ambiguity are given in Figure 7.1. The ambiguity measure returns the effective number of fuzzy set members that cannot be distinguished from each other as the best choice. For example, the ambiguity of $\{1, 1, 0\}$ is 2; the ambiguity of $\{0.5, 0.5, 0\}$ is 2; and the ambiguity of $\{0.9, 0.1, 0.1\}$ is 1.22. For the two fuzzy sets (7.1, 7.2) the ambiguity is 0.436.

TABLE 7.1   Examples of Fuzziness and Ambiguity

Fuzzy set grades of membership: {0, 1}: fuzziness 0; ambiguity 1
Fuzzy set grades of membership: {0.5, 0.5}: fuzziness 2; ambiguity 2
Fuzzy set grades of membership: {0.25, 0.75}: fuzziness 1; ambiguity 1.333

Let us look again at the two fuzzy sets in Section 7.6:

Fuzzy Set Species	Grade of Membership
Setosa	0.024
Versicolor	0.895
Virginica	0.910

Fuzzy Set Speed	Grade of Membership
Slow	0.024
Medium	0.895
Fast	0.910

While there is no difference in the mathematics of these two identical sets, their interpretation and how we handle them is quite different. Note that for a single sample, valid memberships in the members of fuzzy set species are mutually exclusive; only one correct membership can be assigned to a single sample. If (say) we have similar high grades of membership in Versicolor and Virginica, we have a *contradiction*: They cannot both be true. However, for a single sample, the memberships in fuzzy set speed are *not* mutually exclusive. It is quite likely that a single speed measurement would not correspond exactly to our concepts of speed as Slow, Medium, or Fast, and might be (e.g.) half-way between what we think of as Slow and what we think of as Medium. In that case, since more or less equally high grades of membership in Slow and Medium would be quite acceptable, we now have an *ambiguity* rather than a contradiction.

7.6.3   Handling Ambiguities and Contradictions

Retaining Ambiguities.   The action we take with regard to ambiguities and contradictions is quite different. In general, there are several reasons to retain ambiguities and not try to reduce them to a single valid member. Suppose that in fuzzy set speed, we had membership of Slow 0.56, Medium 0.52, and Fast 0, and that we had decided to resolve the multiple grades of memberships by retaining only the largest. We would now have Slow 0.56, Medium 0, and Fast 0. Now we transmit an inaccurate picture to later reasoning stages or to the user; if we were then to defuzzify speed, we would get again quite an inaccurate value. Later rules that should fire if (say) Medium were at least 0.10 would now fail to fire, perhaps leading us to a catastrophically wrong final result, such as failing to brake sufficiently hard and smashing into the car ahead of us. Similarly, with classification problems. It is not at all unusual to have more than one preliminary classification with respectable truth values for the same object; and it infrequently happens that the preliminary classification with the highest truth value turns out to be incorrect. So, we need have no fear of ambiguities; they often lend robustness to a line of reasoning.

Resolving Contradictions. Contradictions, however, should be resolved if possible when they arise. Of course, the simplest method is to take the highest grade of membership as the only valid one, and if two grades of membership are identical, possibly to spin a random number to decide. This can clearly lead us to results that are at least suspicious if not downright wrong. It is better first to detect whether the grades of membership are appreciably contradictory; the measure of ambiguity given in (7.14) and (7.15) above is one suitable way to do this. If we find that contradictions can occur (which is usually the case), we have a choice of several ways in which to proceed. In any case, we must recognize that the rules we have written so far have not produced final results, but have produced *preliminary results.*

We should always review the rules and membership functions we have used so far to see if we can produce better preliminary results. It is conceivable, but unlikely, that this step will solve our problem.

The next step is to see if we can use or acquire additional data to distinguish among the contradictions. For example, an image analysis program for ultrasound images of the heart to detect the various heart regions such as left atrium and right ventricle initially classifies the regions based on region area and position in the image. While this detects a lot of regions correctly, it is virtually guaranteed to produce contradictions, since the rules to detect a ventricle and merged atrium and ventricle (mitral valve open) are identical!

The succeeding steps resolve contradictions. For example, suppose a rule has classified a region as both left ventricle (LV) and merged left ventricle and left atrium (LA + LV). We now look to see if in the same frame a region has been classified as left atrium (LA). If this is true, clearly the classification as LA + LV is wrong, and the classification as LV is correct. If, however, no region has been classified as LA, the classification as LV is wrong and LA + LV is correct.

It is true that the rules for determining preliminary results might possibly be written so as to simultaneously rule out contradictions, but this would make the rules more difficult to write, to debug, and to maintain, and is not advisable.

If our efforts to resolve a contradiction fail, we should report this to the user (or later stages of the program) so that the data are available for determining a course of action.

7.7 INVALIDATION OF DATA: NON-MONOTONIC REASONING

Let us suppose that after obtaining preliminary classifications, we find that an unacceptable degree of ambiguity exists among classifications that are mutually exclusive. (It is not always the case that classifications are mutually exclusive. For example, two or more diseases may be concurrently present in a patient.) Since the classifications are mutually exclusive, ambiguity in the fuzzy set of classifications represents a contradiction that we must now resolve.

It is fairly common, in this case, to accept the classification that has the highest grade of membership. This is easily done, but somewhat dangerous. We have on a number of occasions found that the classification with the highest degree of membership was, in fact, not the correct one. Resolving contradictions requires non-monotonic reasoning; we wish to invalidate something previously believed to be true, and write rules for this purpose. The antecedent of such a rule represents our criteria for rejecting the preliminary classification. But our default reasoning is monotonic, and we must now implement non-monotonic reasoning. This is accomplished by setting values for truth values directly. Truth values of data, including grades of membership in fuzzy sets, are attributes themselves, and can have values set to whatever we desire by the consequent of a rule. Suppose we have declared a discrete fuzzy set of classifications:

```
declare Data
  class fzset (class1 class2 class3);
```

and have written classification rules

```
rule r1 IF (antecedent A) THEN class is class1;
rule r2 IF (antecedent B) THEN class is class2;
rule r3 IF (antecedent C) THEN class is class3;
rule r4 IF (antecedent D) THEN class is class1;
```

The confidence in antecedent A is 0.6, in antecedent B is 0.8, in antecedent C is 0, and in antecedent D is 0.9. Rule r1 fires, setting the grade of membership of class1 to 0.7. Rule r2 fires, setting the grade of membership of class2 to 0.8. Rule r3 fails to fire, leaving the grade of membership of class3 at its initialized value of 0. Finally, rule r4 fires, resetting the grade of membership of class1 to 0.8 since our default reasoning is monotonic.

In the next block of rules, we have written a rule specifically to detect and correct contradictions. This rule is

```
IF (in Data class is class1 AND class is class2 AND
correction clauses here)THEN in 1 class.class1 = 0;
```

The last rule sets the membership of class1 to 0. When modifying truth values and grades of membership directly as attributes, reasoning is non-monotonic. This is a very important point. When modifying data values or grades of membership in fuzzy sets by such consequent clauses as

```
in 1 x is 4;in 2 class is class1;
```

reasoning and management of truth values is monotonic. But if truth values are modified directly, as in

```
in 1 x.cf is 0;in 2 class.cf is .5;
```

reasoning is non-monotonic and the specified value for truth value or grade of membership will be stored regardless of its prior value.

7.8 MODIFICATION OF VALUES OF DATA

Modification of data values is a fairly simple matter. The default reasoning is monotonic; replacement of a data value by a new value is not permitted if the truth value of the new value is less than that in the existing value.

Replacement of data if the truth value of the new value is greater than that of the existing value is easily justified. [wec1]Replacement of an old value by a new value if truth values are equal [wec2]is justified on two scores. First, the new value is more recent than the old. Second, if replacement of equal truth value is not allowed, it becomes very difficult to write a working program at all; replacement on equal values because of recency is extremely common, and accomplishing it[wec3] when necessary would require considerable extra code. We would have to reset the old truth value directly by the non-monotonic reasoning permitted when truth values are directly manipulated, then carry out the replacement in a second rule, fired after the truth value had been reset.

There is a command available to reset the antecedent confidence to any desired value; in the consequent of a rule, the command

```
reset;
```

sets the antecedent confidence to full. If it is desired to set the antecedent confidence to another value, say $\langle N \rangle$, this can also be accomplished by the reset command;

```
reset <N>;
```

By using the reset command, data values may be replaced even if the antecedent confidence is less than the existing truth value of the old value.

7.9 MODELING THE ENTIRE RULE SPACE

Up to this point, we have been concerned with modeling a single rule of the general type

$$\text{if p then q} \tag{7.16}$$

where p is an antecedent, usually complex, and q is a consequent that modifies an attribute of type integer, float, string, fuzzy number, or member of a discrete fuzzy set. The consequent has not been a complete discrete fuzzy set; we have implicitly assumed that when we are trying to establish a new complete discrete fuzzy set, that we have a number of rules of the general type

$$\text{if } p_i \text{ then } q'_j = q_j \qquad (7.17)$$

where p_i is a member of the set of antecedents P, q_j is a member of the consequent discrete fuzzy set Q with grades of membership defined prior to firing the rule set, and q_j' is a member of the consequent discrete fuzzy set Q' with grades of membership defined after firing the rule set. A rule confidence r_i is associated with each such rule; if omitted from the rule, r_i is assumed to be 1.

It may be more efficient to look at a whole collection of rules of type (7.17) rather than to look at single rules when solving a problem. We now deal with modeling the entire space of such rules. We assume that we have N input variables represented by N discrete fuzzy sets, each with M members, and one output variable, represented by a discrete fuzzy set with Q members. We will also assume that there is a confidence associated with each rule. Each rule may be uniquely identified by the antecedent and consequent subscripts. The rule confidences are the elements $r_{i,j}$ of the rule confidence matrix R. *The R matrix is of great importance; it relates inputs to output for a particular problem.*

There are several steps involved in evaluation of a rule set. (Note that fuzzification and defuzzification are broken out as separate steps.) Step 1: Any fuzzification necessary takes place so that numeric attributes are mapped onto the grades of membership of discrete fuzzy sets. Step 2: The truth values of the antecedents are determined. Step 3: The *antecedent truth values* are combined with *rule confidences* to yield *antecedent confidences*, now representing the consequent confidence with which consequent may be executed, the *consequent confidences*. Step 4: The consequent confidences are combined with existing truth values of consequent discrete fuzzy set members to yield their new grades of membership. If defuzzification is to take place, in Step 5 the grades of membership of consequent fuzzy set members are combined with their membership functions to yield modified membership functions. Step 6: The modified membership functions of the consequent discrete fuzzy set, a linguistic variable, are combined to yield a membership function for the entire consequent linguistic variable. Step 7: A single numeric floating-point variable is derived from the combined membership functions.

In this section, we assume that Step 1, fuzzification, has already taken place. Methods of Step 2, determining truth values of the antecedents, has been covered in Chapters 3–5. Steps 5–7 have already been covered in Sections 7.2, 7.3, and 7.8. In this section we will be concerned with Steps 3 and 4; determination of new grades of membership q'_j of consequent fuzzy set members from antecedent truth values, rule confidences and prior grades of membership of consequent fuzzy sets in an entire rule set. We will use a notation that is suitable for an entire rule set. As noted in Section 7.3, monotonic reasoning is indicated as a default reasoning type for modification of grades of membership of discrete fuzzy sets.

For monotonic reasoning, that is often used when determining grades of membership for discrete fuzzy sets,

$$Q' = (P \circ R) \text{ OR } Q \qquad (7.18)$$

We define non-monotonic reasoning as

$$Q' = P \circ R \tag{7.19}$$

and monotonic downward reasoning as

$$Q' = (P \circ R) \text{ AND } Q \tag{7.20}$$

Non-monotonic reasoning is most often used only when invalidating data; rules of this type are extremely unlikely to fit into this framework. Monotonic downward reasoning is usually incorporated in the defuzzification process; since defuzzification is deferred to the next rule-firing step, monotonic downward reasoning is also unlikely to be used in this framework.

7.9.1 Conventional Method: The Intersection Rule Configuration (IRC)

Conventionally, each input discrete fuzzy set is represented by members that describe the input variable. For example, a numeric input variable `velocity` might be represented by discrete fuzzy set speed with members `Slow`, `Medium`, and `Fast`. A typical rule might be

$$\text{IF } (A_1 \text{ is } a_{1,i1} \text{ AND } A_2 \text{ is } a_{2,i2} \text{ AND } A_3 \text{ is } a_{3,i3} \dots) \text{ THEN } Q \text{ is } q_j \tag{7.21}$$

in which A_1, A_2, ... are input discrete fuzzy sets and Q is an output discrete fuzzy set.

With N input discrete fuzzy sets, each with M members, and Q members of the output fuzzy set, we would have N^M antecedents and Q consequent fuzzy set members. If a single consequent fuzzy set member is associated with each antecedent, we have N^M rules. In general, we could have up to $N^{M}*Q$ rules. If the R matrix is sparse, the actual number of rules could be considerably less. In either case, the rule set could be evaluated by (7.14), (7.15), or (7.16), depending on the type of reasoning employed.

The well-known problem with systems using rules of this type is the exponential growth in the number of rules as the number of input variables increases. Assume an economical formulation in which there is only one consequent fuzzy set member associated with each antecedent. Say each of the input discrete fuzzy sets has five members. For two input discrete fuzzy sets, we have 25 rules; for three input sets, we have 125 rules; for 4 input sets, we have 3125 rules, an exponential increase. This makes it exceedingly difficult or impracticable to use this type of rule with a large number of input variables.

We now consider an alternate model of the entire rule set, quite different from (7.21).

7.9.2   The Combs Union Rule Configuration

William Combs of the Boeing Company has devised a method to avoid the exponential growth in the number of rules as the number of input variables increases (Combs and Andrews, 1998). Combs proposes a Union Rule Configuration or URC. The structure of the rules in the Combs method exploits the following equivalence in the propositional calculus:

$$[(\text{p1 and p2}) \text{ implies } q] \text{ is logically equivalent to } [(\text{p1 implies } q) \text{ or } (\text{p2 implies } q)] \tag{7.22}$$

Rules written in the conventional style, which Combs calls the IRC, are similar to this:

$$\text{IF (U is } A_i \text{ AND V is } B_j \text{ AND W is } C_k) \text{ THEN Z is } D_{Rn} \tag{7.23}$$

where D_{Rn} denotes the output fuzzy set member assigned to the nth rule. This rule becomes three in the simplest implementation of the Combs method URC:

$$\text{IF (U is } A_i) \text{ THEN Z is } D_{R1}$$
$$\text{IF (V is } B_j) \text{ THEN Z is } D_{R2} \tag{7.24}$$
$$\text{IF (W is } C_k) \text{ THEN Z is } D_{R3}$$

The truth value of D is obtained by averaging D_{Rn} over N;

$$D = \frac{1}{N} \sum_n D_{Rn} \tag{7.25}$$

where N is the number of rules in which D_{Rn} appears in the consequent.

If we have N input variables X, Y, . . . , i, j, and k in range from 1 to M, and we wish to include rules with all combinations of i, j, and k, the IRC will require M^N rules. The URC will require M*N rules. The number of rules in the IRC goes up exponentially with the number of input variables N; the number of rules in the URC goes up linearly with N. For control systems with a large number of input variables, the Combs URC system offers considerable economy in the number of rules, as illustrated in Table 7.2.

In practice, the "OR" operator in (7.22) is defined to yield the mean of the operands. More advanced formulations of the URC (Weischenk et al., 2003) deal successfully with the questions of precise equivalence between the IRC and URC methods by employing more than one block of rules and rule-firing step. Nevertheless, the simple formulation of the URC in (7.24) and (7.25) works quite well in many if not most applications.

The utility of the Combs method for classification programs is less clear than for control programs, and depends on the type of fuzzy set chosen for the input variables. If numeric input variables are fuzzified into fuzzy sets with members such as Small, Medium, and Large [as done in Kasbov (1998, p. 219)], and these in

TABLE 7.2   Number of Rules Required by IRC and URC methods[a]

Number of Input Variables									
1		2		3		4		5	
IRC	URC	IRC	URC	IRC	URC	IRC	URC	IRC	URC
3	3	9	6	27	9	81	12	243	15

[a]We assume that there are three members to each input variable (fuzzy set); that rules are required for each combination of the input fuzzy set members; and that each rule has one consequent clause.

turn are used in rules similar to (7.23), the reduction in number of rules provided by the Combs method may be realized. If, however, the membership functions are tailored to the classifications, with input fuzzy set members such as Class_1, Class_2, and Class_3, the URC method may actually produce a greater number of rules than the IRC. For example, in the famous Iris classification problem, the IRC program iris.par requires three rules of the type

```
IF (in Data PL is setosa AND PW is setosa AND SL is
setosa AND SW is setosa) THEN Class is setosa;
```

and the URC program iriscombs.par requires 12 rules of the type
    IF (in Data PL is setosa) THEN Class is setosa;

7.9.3   Performance of the Combs Method

We were originally somewhat doubtful of the validity of the Combs method, since its justification is based on rules formulated using the implication operator, as does the Theory of Approximate Reasoning. (We have previously demonstrated that the Theory of Approximate Reasoning is not useful in a fuzzy expert system.) Additional concern was caused by the unusual OR operator Combs uses to combine grades of membership. We subjected the Combs method to two kinds of tests; a fuzzy control problem and two classification problems, comparing the Combs Union Rule Configuration (URC) method, with one antecedent clause per rule, against the conventional Intersection Rule Configuration method (IRC). (In the Exercises for this chapter, programs are provided for the reader to perform his/her own tests.) We found that although the precise performance of the URC differed slightly from the IRC, the performance of the two systems was nearly identical.

7.9.4   Sample IRC and URC Programs

Exercises IRC and URC. IRC.EXE and URC.EXE are very simple compiled BASIC programs for control of a simulated nonlinear process. The original BASIC programs, IRC.BAS and URC.BAS, may be viewed from TFLOPS. Both programs may be run from TFLOPS by two one-line FLOPS programs, IRC.FPS and URC.FPS. Simple text plots show the membership functions used. Simple text output is used, one data sample at a time. To run the programs, invoke TFLOPS, then (in the Examples folder) open and run programs IRC.FPS for the conventional intersection rule configuration and URC.FPS for the Combs union rule configuration. To see the original BASIC programs, open IRC.BAS and URC.BAS in the Examples folder. At first, take the default values for the program parameters, and observe the programs' performances; then you may try different program parameters to see their effect. With default parameter values, both the IRC and URC methods reduce the error to zero (to two significant decimal places) in 12 steps.

For problems of classification, we classified a test set of data from a real-world application, the echocardiogram program echo.par. Members of the output fuzzy set of classifications were ranked in order of their grades of membership for both IRC and URC methods, from highest to lowest. The highest ranking classification, that with the highest degree of membership in the classification fuzzy set, was the same with both methods. However, the grades of membership of lower ranking classifications were better separated from the highest and from each other by the intersection rule method.

An additional classification test was furnished by the classical Iris classification data of Fisher. These data are well known as being difficult to classify correctly. Program IrisCombs.par uses the Combs URC method; program iris.par uses the conventional IRC method, and is discussed more fully in Chapter 11. Using identical unsophisticated membership functions derived from a training set of even-numbered data, the IRC method showed a slight advantage, misclassifying 5 out of 150 specimens as opposed to 6 out of 150 by the URC program.

7.9.5 Exercises Iris.par and IrisCombs.par

Both programs in this exercise are written in FLOPS, and are in the Examples folder. The membership functions used are triangular, and quite unsophisticated. Invoke TFLOPS, load Iris.par and IrisCombs.par, and compare their performances.

The membership functions are defined by the memfunct FLOPS command, and may be viewed when running the programs by the drawmemf command. The syntax of these commands is given in the Manual help file. The membership functions so defined may be modified in two ways: by changing their shape using the linear, s-shape and normal options, or by changing the specified values. Try changing the shape and values of the membership functions to see if the number of incorrect classifications can be reduced. The original triangular membership functions were derived from the minimum, mode, and maximum of even-numbered specimens by setting the grade of membership of the mean to 0.5; the grade of membership of the mode to 1; and the grade of membership of the maximum to 0.5. This places the left-hand corner, peak, and right-hand corner of the triangle at:

Left-hand corner (membership zero): 2*minimum − mode
Peak (membership one): mode
Right-hand corner (membership zero): 2*maximum − mode

In this case, the greater number of rules required by the Combs union rule configuration, as compared with the conventional IRC method, would seem to be a disadvantage. Where expert knowledge is sufficient, problems with a discrete set of possible non-numeric outputs (such as classification, decision support, and trouble-shooting) may require a much smaller number of rules, as described in Section 7.10. In such cases, it is often not necessary to write rules that cover all combinations of the input discrete fuzzy sets and their members. The seldom-realized ideal in classification is to have one rule for each classification, giving Q rules rather than $M^{N*}Q$.

7.9.6 Data Mining and the Combs Method

In problems of data mining, when we deduce the rules from a test data set rather than employing expert knowledge, the Combs method offers much promise. In many or most data-mining problems, we must deal with databases that have many variables, and the rules we seek to deduce are likely to have many input variables. In such cases, the number of possible conventional (IRC) rules could be extremely difficult or even virtually impossible to handle, due to the combinatorial explosion of antecedent clauses. The Combs method (URC) does not suffer from this disadvantage, since the number of rules goes up linearly with the number of input variables. In addition, the Combs method offers a remarkably simple way of handling missing data, making it unnecessary either to delete entire observations or to attempt to predict them. Only those rules with non-zero input variable values contribute to the calculation of the output truth value. Combs has successfully classified a number of such real-world problems in addition to several commonly used test data sets.

7.9.7 Combs Method Summary

In short, we believe the linear increase in the number of rules with the number of input variable values furnished by the Combs method means that it has an important role to play, especially in situations where all combinations of input variable values must be used, as in fuzzy control and in data mining. For classification problems, when there is already a good base of expert conceptual knowledge and a limited number of input variables, and if the rule-reduction techniques described in Section 7.10 are applicable, then the intersection rule matrix will probably continue to be employed. We think that the importance of the Combs method warrants intensive research.

7.10 REDUCING THE NUMBER OF CLASSIFICATION RULES REQUIRED IN THE CONVENTIONAL INTERSECTION RULE CONFIGURATION

We now illustrate a method of reducing the number of rules required by the conventional rule format in classification problems. In this method, we do not simply create rules with all combinations of input variables, such as {Slow, Medium, Fast}.

Instead, we try to tailor our rules to a fuzzy set of output variables, such as {Class_1, Class_2, Class_3, ...}.

Consider the well-known Iris classification problem, using the data of Fisher (1936). We have data on values of four attributes: petal length, petal width, sepal length, and sepal width, together with the correct classification of 150 samples as one of three species of the genus Iris: setosa, versicolor, and virginica.

The conventional approach is to define four discrete fuzzy sets (linguistic variables), say PL, PW, SL, and SW, with several members each, say {Small, Medium, and Large} as in done in Kasabov (1998), pp. 152 ff. We also define a discrete fuzzy set of classifications, say species, with three members: {setosa, versicolor, virginica}. We then have a possible $3^4 = 81$ rules of the type

```
IF (PL is Small AND PW is Medium AND SL is Large AND SW
is Medium)
THEN species is setosa;
```

and seek to establish membership functions for our input linguistic terms, perhaps from a training set, that will maximize the number of correct classifications predicted.

It is likely that the data would permit omitting a number of rules of this type, perhaps half, so that the actual number of rules might be around 15 or 20.

There is, however, another approach that will reduce the number of rules to three. We achieve this by revising the linguistic terms for our input variables. We now define these linguistic terms (members) for input discrete fuzzy sets PL, PW, SL, and SW as setosa, versicolor, and virginica. (Ofcourse, the membership function for setosa in linguistic variable PL would be different from the membership function for setosa in linguistic variable PW, e.g.) Our three rules now become:

```
IF (PL is setosa AND PW is setosa AND SL is setosa AND SW
is setosa)
THEN species is setosa;
```

Determination of membership functions from test data becomes easier. We can simply determine the distribution of the input variables for each of the three species, and use these data to derive our membership functions.

In general, our method for reducing the number of rules to a manageable minimum amounts to the top-down method of defining the problem by first defining our outputs, then defining our inputs, and their discretization in a way relevant to the desired outputs. Combinations of the discretized inputs that do not relate to a desired output are simply omitted from our rule set as irrelevant to our goal.

7.11   SUMMARY

Inference in an expert system is the process of drawing conclusions from data that is deriving new data or truth values from input data and truth values. The new data may be the final conclusions, or in multistep reasoning, may be intermediate conclusions that constitute input to the next step.

7.11.1   Data Types and Their Truth Values

Available attribute data types and their truth values may be summarized as:

- Integers, floats, and strings. A single truth value is attached to any value these attributes may have. This truth value is itself an attribute, accessed by appending .cf to the attribute name.
- Fuzzy numbers. Values are any number from the real line. Truth values are defined by a parameterized membership function that maps any real number value onto its truth value (grade of membership). Fuzzy numbers are used primarily in approximate comparisons in a rule antecedent. A full range of approximate comparison operators is available corresponding to the conventional Boolean numerical comparison operators furnished by most computer languages.
- Discrete fuzzy sets. Values are defined as the names of the members of the fuzzy set. Each member has a single truth value, its grade of membership of that member in the fuzzy set.
- [wec4]Membership functions. If a discrete fuzzy set is a linguistic variable, whose members are linguistic terms describing a numeric quantity, member-ship functions are attached, one to each linguistic term. These functions map any real or fuzzy number onto the grade of membership of the corresponding linguistic term. The grade of membership of the linguistic term is the truth value of its membership function.

7.11.2   Types of Fuzzy Reasoning

We assume that the truth value of an antecedent has been determined and combined with the truth value of the rule itself to furnish the antecedent confidence P. We will denote the truth values of data to be modified as B', the modified truth value, and B, the existing truth value.

In data modification by a rule, we consider three types of inference and define these types quantitatively, in terms of the antecedent confidence and the truth value of data to be modified.

- Monotonic reasoning. Here truth values in the consequent are nondecreasing.

  B' = P OR B

  Monotonic reasoning is useful when modifying values of scalar data, or grades of membership of discrete fuzzy sets.
- Non-monotonic reasoning. Here truth values in the consequent may increase, decrease or stay the same.

B′ = P

Non-monotonic reasoning is useful when modifying truth values directly, especially when invalidating data previously believed to be true.

- Monotonic downward. Here truth values in the consequent are nonincreasing.

B′ = P AND B

This type of reasoning is useful when combining the grade of membership of a linguistic term with its membership function prior to defuzzification.

- Approximate reasoning, defined as

B′ = A′ o [A IMPLIES B]

in which o denotes fuzzy composition and IMPLIES denotes any fuzzy implication operator that reduces to the classical implication for crisp operands.

We define desirable properties for inference in an expert system for these inference types. We then show that the definitions of monotonic, non-monotonic, and monotonic downward reasoning all satisfy these desirable properties for their reasoning types, but the approximate reasoning method fails to satisfy all desirable properties for any type of reasoning. We note that Mamdani inference, which uses a fuzzy AND operator in place of an implication operator, is precisely the same as our monotonic downward method.

The question of inference in a fuzzy expert systems boils down to the defining of the way in which values and truth values of consequent data are inferred when a rule is fired, knowing the prior truth values of the antecedent and of consequent data.

7.12   QUESTIONS

7.1   We have the rule "If A′ = A then B′ = B", where A′, A, B′, and B are the discrete fuzzy sets

$$A = \left\{ \frac{0}{a1}, \frac{0.5}{a2}, \frac{1}{a3} \right\}, \quad A' = \left\{ \frac{0.25}{a1}, \frac{0.75}{a2}, \frac{0.75}{a3} \right\},$$

$$B = \left\{ \frac{0}{b1}, \frac{0.5}{b2}, \frac{1}{b3} \right\}, \quad B' = \left\{ \frac{?}{b1}, \frac{?}{b2}, \frac{?}{b3} \right\}$$

Calculate B′ by

a. Composing A′ with [A$_i$ AND B$_j$] (7.2).

b. B′ = pB, where p is the antecedent truth value of A′ = A (7.4).

7.2   What are the advantages and disadvantages of using separate rules for fuzzification and defuzzification of discrete fuzzy sets?

7.3 We wish to classify regions of an image from several numeric measurements. We set up linguistic variables for the input data, and a non-numeric discrete fuzzy set if possible region classifications. The input variables have been fuzzified. We have several rules whose consequent would set the grade of membership of classification Artifact. Two of these rules are concurrently fireable; of these, one would set the truth value of Artifact to 0.7, and one would set it to 0.4,

   a. What is the default inference method?

   b. What will the truth value of Artifact be after the rules have fired?

   c. What rationale can you give for using the default inference method?

7.4 We wish to use the information from a physiological monitor to evaluate the condition of a patient in an intensive care unit. The data include heart rate, systolic and diastolic blood pressures, percent of oxygen saturation in both arterial and venous blood, and temperature. We set up linguistic variables for each of these measurements, with five linguistic terms in each linguistic variable, and fuzzify the input data. The data are collected nearly continuously (1 sample every 2 s), so we can calculate rates of change for each input variable, and set up corresponding linguistic variables for the rates of change.

   Our output consists of two discrete fuzzy sets, one for present condition (good, fair, poor, bad) and one for changes (improving. stable, deteriorating). We write rules whose consequents are present condition (condition is good), and other rules whose consequents are rate of change (state is deteriorating). We have several rules that have the same consequent. Rule A would set the grade of membership of "deteriorating" to 0.1; rule B would set its grade of membership to 0.2; and rule C would set its grade of membership to 0.5. Since our rules are fired in parallel, all three rules are fired concurrently. To what value should we set the grade of membership of "deteriorating"?

7.5 We have five input variables with four possible values for each, and six output variable values.

   a. How many rules will be required using the conventional IRC method?

   b. How many rules will be required by the Combs Union Rule Configuration method?

8 Resolving Contradictions: Possibility and Necessity

Chapters 6 and 7 dealt with the modification of data and truth values under the assumption that the truth values represent *necessity*, the extent to which the data support a proposition. In this chapter, we also will treat truth values that represent *possibility*, the extent to which a truth value represents the extent to which the data fail to refute a proposition. We denote the necessity of proposition A by Nec(A), and its possibility by Pos(A). Here, we will consider the dynamics of a multistep reasoning process. In such a process, we often proceed first to establish plausible preliminary conclusions that are supported by the relevant data. If the conclusions so reached are mutually exclusive, we then proceed to rule out preliminary conclusions that are refuted by additional data or by existing data looked at more deeply. In the first of these steps we consider the extent to which the data support a conclusion, that is, necessity; in the second step, we consider whether any data refute a proposition, that is, possibility, and any effect a change in possibility of a proposition might have on its necessity.

While we accept the definition of possibility and necessity given by Dubois and Prade (1988), we do not accept that all the axioms used to develop conventional possibility theory [Klir and Yuan (1995), Chapter 7] are valid for fuzzy reasoning with rule-based systems. In particular, we do not accept the axiom that the propositions involved are nested $(A \Rightarrow B \Rightarrow C \cdots)$, nor the use of min−max logic when combining A and NOT A. This last objection is especially valid since a family of fuzzy logics has been constructed that does obey these fundamental laws (Buckley and Siler, 1998b and 1999). Since it is well known that min−max logic does not obey the law of the excluded middle (A and NOT A = 0), its use in combining A and NOT A to yield min(a, 1-A) is invalid. For these reasons, the treatment of possibility and necessity developed here differs substantially from conventional theory; hence, it is somewhat controversial. Aside from theoretical considerations, the theory here has one big advantage: it works.

Fuzzy Expert Systems and Fuzzy Reasoning, By William Siler and James J. Buckley
ISBN 0-471-38859-9 Copyright © 2005 John Wiley & Sons, Inc.

8.1   DEFINITION OF POSSIBILITY AND NECESSITY

Dubois and Prade define possibility and necessity as:

> *Necessity* of a proposition (Nec) is the extent to which the data support its truth.
>
> *Possibility* of a proposition (Pos) is the extent to which the data fail to refute its truth.

The term "necessity" is closely analogous to the term *credibility* in Dempster–Shafer theory, and the term "possibility" is closely analogous to their term *plausibility*.

Both possibility and necessity are truth values in [0, 1]. Clearly we are dealing with two different kinds of truth values. For example, suppose that we have only this information about proposition A: its current necessity is 0.3, and its current possibility is 1.0; the truth value (necessity) of proposition P that supports A is 0.4, and the truth value (necessity) of proposition Q that refutes A is 0.2. Nec(A), the necessity that A is true, is then max(0.3, 0.4) = 0.4. Since Q refutes A, the extent to which Q fails to refute A is NOT Nec(Q), or 0.8. Then, considering these new data, Nec(A) = 0.4, and Pos(A) = 0.8.

If our fuzzy reasoning language permits it, we could specify the truth value of a proposition by the two values, possibility and necessity. However, few if any current rule-based fuzzy languages permit storing more than one truth value, usually necessity. But since we can calculate the possibility of a proposition from the necessities of refuting data, we can deal with the most important aspect of possibilities within a necessity-based system.

8.2   POSSIBILITY AND NECESSITY SUITABLE FOR MULTI-STEP RULE-BASED FUZZY REASONING

We now develop formulas for possibility and necessity that are suitable for complex multistep forward-chaining rule-based fuzzy reasoning systems. (We concur with Anderson (1993) that rule-based systems offer a very powerful way of emulating human reasoning.) At the ith reasoning step, we denote Nec(A) as $Nec(A)_i$, and Pos(A) by $Pos(A)_i$. (If a relationship is always true the i subscript is omitted.)

8.2.1   Data Types and Their Truth Values

First, we consider the way in which our system uses truth values. Most truth systems maintain only one truth value, necessity; if we are to maintain both possibility and necessity, each truth value consists of these two values.

Now consider the different types of data that we might have. There are scalar or single-valued data; typically these include integers, floats, and strings; to each of these a truth value is attached. We also have discrete fuzzy sets, whose members are words; to each member a truth value is attached. If these words describe numbers, they are linguistic terms, and their parent fuzzy set is a linguistic variable;

to each linguistic term there is attached a membership function that maps all or part of the real line onto truth values for the corresponding linguistic term.

At this point, we can see that systems that maintain both possibility and necessity could have a problem; the membership function should return two values, both possibility and necessity. In fact, we know of no such dual-valued membership functions; necessity is returned, and the possibility is assumed to be one.

We will also have fuzzy numbers with attached membership functions similar to the membership functions for linguistic terms.

Now consider initialization of data values and truth values. As in such computer languages as C, there are two steps in creating a datum in most computer languages.

First, a template is declared, that tells the compiler what data it can expect. In C, for example, such a data declaration might be

$$\text{flt x[20];} \tag{8.1}$$

This declaration tells the compiler to expect an array x of 20 floating-point numbers, and the compiler will assign sufficient memory to accommodate that array.

A more complex declaration provides for a data structure. Such a structure might be, in the C language,

$$
\begin{aligned}
&\text{struct Date} \\
&\{ \\
&\quad \text{day int;} \\
&\quad \text{month int;} \\
&\quad \text{year int;} \\
&\};
\end{aligned} \tag{8.2}
$$

This declaration tells the compiler what to expect in structure Date, but does not assign memory as yet.

FLOPS uses data declarations similar to (8.2), but not identical. A typical FLOPS declaration of a data element Region might be

```
declare Region
rnum int
Area flt
Size fzset (Small Medium Large)
Xbar flt
Xpos fzset (Left Center Right)
Ybar flt
Ypos fzset (Low Center High);
```
(8.3)

Like (8.2), (8.3) does not actually assign any memory for an instance of Region. (There may be several instances of Region, probably with different values of rnum.) Memory is allocated for an instance of Region by the FLOPS *make* command:

$$\text{make Region;} \tag{8.4}$$

8.2.2   Initialization of Data and Truth Values

When command (8.4) is executed, memory locations are assigned for the values and truth values of all attributes. Since no data values are specified, by default numbers are initialized to 0 and strings to blanks. If the truth value of an integer, float, or string is initially unknown, then its necessity is 0 (nothing supports it) and its possibility is 1 (nothing refutes it). Similarly, the necessity (grade of membership) of a fuzzy set member is initialized to zero. Possibilities are explicity (for dual-truth-value systems) or implicitly (for necessity-based systems) initialized to 1.

However, the *make* command may specify values and truth values, if desired. For example,

$$\text{make Region rnum = 1;} \tag{8.5}$$

will assign a value of 1 to that instance of Region. If a value is specified in a make command but no truth value is specified, by default its necessity will be set to 1. If we wish, we may specify a different truth value, as in

$$\text{make Region Area = 25 Area.cf = 800;} \tag{8.6}$$

{Of course, since in FLOPS truth values range from 0 to 1000, in (8.6) the necessity of Area is actually 0.8 on a [0, 1] scale.}

Parameterized membership functions for fuzzy numbers are specified when the fuzzy number is created. Parameterized membership functions for linguistic terms are created by the memf command.

8.3   MODIFICATION OF TRUTH VALUES DURING A FUZZY REASONING PROCESS

In the following, A is a proposition; $\text{Nec}(A)_0$ and $\text{Pos}(A)_0$ are its initial truth values. We assume that, as reasoning progresses,

$$\text{Nec}(A) >= \text{Nec}(A)_0 = 0 \tag{8.7}$$

$$\text{Pos}(A) <= \text{Pos}(A)_0 = 1 \tag{8.8}$$

$$\text{Nec}(A) <= \text{Pos}(A) \tag{8.9}$$

Note that adding supporting evidence may affect necessity, but not possibility; adding refuting evidence can affect possibility, and by (8.9) can also affect necessity.

Almost any nontrivial reasoning problem will require multiple reasoning steps. Denote the reasoning step by subscript i, where i is initially 0. For multistep reasoning, when we go from the ith reasoning step to the $(i + 1)$th step, we assume

$$\text{Pos}(A)_{i+1} <= \text{Pos}(A)_i \tag{8.10}$$

Equation (8.10) follows from the fact that added supporting evidence can affect necessity but not possibility, and adding refuting evidence can never increase possibilities.

Instead of assuming (8.10), we could have assumed

$$\text{Nec}(A)_{i+1} >= \text{Nec}(A)_i \tag{8.11}$$

The choice between (8.10) and (8.11) becomes important when considering refuting evidence. If we choose (8.11), so that necessities can never decrease, it becomes impossible to admit that we made a mistake! This is especially important when resolving contradictions by ruling out incorrect preliminary conclusions.

At the end of the ith step we have determined $\text{Nec}(A)_i$. Consider the effect on $\text{Nec}(A)_i$ of proposition P, that supports the truth of A, and of proposition Q, that tends to refute it. We denote the effect of P alone on $\text{Nec}(A)_i$ by $\text{Nec}_P(A)_{i+1}$, and assume

$$\text{Nec}_P(A)_{i+1} = \text{Nec}(A)_i \cup \text{Nec}(P) \tag{8.12}$$

With several supporting propositions P_j (8.12) becomes

$$\text{Nec}_P(A)_{i+1} = \text{Nec}(A)_i \bigcup_j \text{Nec}(P_j) \tag{8.13}$$

The effect of Q, which refutes A, is more complex. Denote the effect of Q alone on the necessity of A by $\text{Nec}_Q(A)_{i+1}$, and on the possibility of A by $\text{Pos}_Q(A)_{i+1}$. Q tends to reduce the possibility of A. We assume

$$\text{Pos}_Q(A)_{i+1} = \text{Pos}(A)_i \cap \text{Nec}(\neg Q) = \text{Pos}(A)_i \cap (\neg \text{Nec}(Q)) \tag{8.14}$$

If we have several refuting propositions Q_k, then (8.14) becomes:

$$\text{Pos}_Q(A)_{i+1} = \text{Pos}(A)_i \bigcap_k (\neg \text{Nec}(Q_k)) \tag{8.15}$$

By (8.9), (8.15) places an upper limit on $\text{Nec}_Q(A)_{i+1}$. Then, combining

$$\text{Nec}_Q(A)_{i+1} = \text{Nec}(A)_i \cap \text{Pos}_Q(A)_i = \text{Nec}(A)_i \cap \text{Pos}(A)_i \bigcap_k (\neg \text{Nec}(Q_k)) \tag{8.16}$$

Since $Nec(A)_i <= Pos(A)_i$, (8.16) reduces to

$$Nec_Q(A)_{i+1} = Nec(A)_i \bigcap_k (\neg Nec(Q_k)) \qquad (8.17)$$

Combining (8.13) and (8.17),

$$Nec(A)_{i+1} = (Nec(A)_i \bigcup_j Nec(P_j)) \bigcap_k (\neg Nec(Q_k)) \qquad (8.18)$$

8.4 FORMULATION OF RULES FOR POSSIBILITY AND NECESSITY

If $Nec(Q) = 1$, $Nec(\neg Q_k) = 0$, and rules with NOT Q in the antecedent will not fire. On the other hand, rules with Q in the antecedent will not fire if $Nec(Q) = 0$. Rules based on (8.18) can be written, with header "rule ⟨rule name⟩ block ⟨block number⟩",

```
rule support block k
IF (A AND P₁ AND P₂)                              (8.19)
THEN Nec(A)=(Nec(A) OR Nec(P₁) OR Nec(P₂))
```

```
rule refute block k+1
IF (A AND (Q₁ OR Q₂))
THEN Nec(A)=Nec(A) AND NOT (Q₁ OR Q₂),           (8.20)
  Pos(A)=(Pos(A) AND NOT (Q₁ OR Q₂));
```

Equations (8.19) and (8.20) cannot be fired concurrently in parallel; rules in block k must be fired before those in block $k + 1$. If $Nec(Q_1)$ and $Nec(Q_2)$ both $= 0$, (8.20) will not fire; this is okay, since if there are no refuting data $Nec(A)$ and $Pos(A)$ remain unchanged. In a single-truth-value system based on necessity, we cannot store $Pos(A)$, and the second consequent clause in (8.20) need not be written.

8.5 RESOLVING CONTRADICTIONS USING POSSIBILITY IN A NECESSITY-BASED SYSTEM

An example of the use of possibility in a necessity-based system to resolve contradictions is given by example program echo.par. In this program, we wish to determine the anatomical significance of regions in an echocardiogram, noisy cross-sectional ultrasound images of a beating heart. To do this, the major steps are first, fuzzify the input data; next, determine preliminary classification using supporting data and necessities; last, rule out contradictory preliminary classifications using refuting data and calculated possibilities.

8.5.1 Input Data: Useful Ambiguities

Our critical input data are numerical values of the area, x- and y-centroid of each image region. Since the image is noisy, these values are somewhat uncertain, and are represented by fuzzy numbers. These values are fuzzified into three fuzzy sets; size (TINY SMALL MEDIUM LARGE HUGE), xpos (FAR-LEFT LEFT CENTER RIGHT FAR-RIGHT), and ypos (VERY-HIGH HIGH MIDDLE LOW VERY-LOW). Usually, more than one member of each of these fuzzy sets will have non-zero truth values; since the members are not mutually exclusive, ambiguities are almost certain to be present. Such ambiguities are a very good thing; they lend robustness to the reasoning process.

In addition, we have a simple string attribute "border", which has value "YES" if a region touches the border of the image, and "NO" if the region does not touch the border.

8.5.2 Output Data: Contradictions

Our output data, the region classifications, are represented by fuzzy set class {ARTIFACT LUNG LA (left atrium) LV (left ventricle) LA + LV (merged left atrium and ventricle) RA (right atrium) RV (right ventricle) RA + RV (merged right atrium and ventricle) LA + LV + RA + RV (all four chambers artifactually merged)}. These members are mutually exclusive; if more that one member has a non-zero truth value, we have a contradiction that will have to be resolved.

8.5.3 Reaching Preliminary Classifications Using Supporting Evidence and Necessities

Rules for determining preliminary classifications all employ supporting data, and hence employ necessities, the default truth value for the FLOPS language. An example is

```
IF (in Region area is LARGE AND xpos is RIGHT AND ypos
is MIDDLE AND border = "NO")
THEN in 1 class is LV;
```

(In echo.par the preliminary classification rules are created automatically from a classification definition database; this permits modification of the classification definitions without rewriting the program. However, this makes the rules more difficult to access; the "prule" command must be used to inspect them.)

Since the rules for classification as LV and LA + LV (and RV and RA + RV) have identical antecedents, we can be sure that there will be contradictory preliminary classifications.

Suppose there are more than one rule whose consequent is "class is LV". Since the default reasoning is (upward) monotonic, the aggregation procedure will store the largest of the existing and new truth values as the grade of membership of LV in fuzzy set class.

8.5.4   Resolving Contradictions Using Refuting
Evidence and Possibilities

Here, we will consider the rules for resolving the contradiction when a region has been classified both as LV and as LA + LV. In this case, if another region in the same image frame has been classified as LA, we can be sure that the LA + LV classification is wrong, and the LV classification is right; if in that frame no other region has been classified as LA, then we are sure that the LV classification is wrong and the LA + LV classification is right. The refuting data for LA + LV is then the presence of an LA region; the refuting data for LV is the absence of an LA region. Our rule antecedents will then read

```
    rule (goal Refute LA+LV)
    IF (in Region frame = <FR> AND class is LA)            (8.21)
        (in Region frame = <FR> AND class is LA+LV)
    THEN ...
    rule (goal Refute LV)
    IF (in Region frame = <FR> AND NOT class is LA)        (8.22)
        (in Region frame = <FR> AND class is LV)
    THEN ...
```

We must now think about how to formulate the consequent. Then antecedent is a complex proposition, say Q, that refutes a proposition; the antecedent will then assign a (possibly) new truth value(s) to that proposition. In a necessity-based system, the new truth value will be the proposition's necessity.

The new truth value itself can be obtained from (8.17). This requires using the complement of the truth value of the antecedent. We must now employ non-monotonic reasoning; this can be done by storing truth values directly. In FLOPS, the combined truth value of antecedent and rule is available as the system-furnished variable <pconf>. Since the truth value of the rule is 1.0 (1000 in FLOPS), the truth value of ¬Q for a particular rule instance is given by

$$\texttt{tv(¬Q) = (1 − <pconf>)}$$

Rules (8.21) and (8.22) then become:

```
rule (goal Refute LA+LV)
IF (in Region frame = <FR> AND class is LA)               (8.23)
    (in Region frame = <FR> AND class is LA+LV)
THEN class.LA+LV = (min(class.LA+LV, (1 - <pconf>)));...
rule (goal Refute LV)
IF (in Region frame = <FR> AND NOT class is LA)           (8.24)
    (in Region frame = <FR> AND class is LV)
THEN class.LV = (min(class.LV, (1 - <pconf>))));...
```

The truth value of the antecedent represents how sure we are that the LV or LAV + LV classification should be refuted; its complement represents the possibility of the LV or LAV + LV classification.

8.6 SUMMARY

Necessity represents the degree to which the evidence considered to date supports the truth of a proposition or datum; possibility represents the extent to which the evidence considered to date fails to refute a proposition or datum. Initially, in the lack of any data supporting or refuting a datum, its necessity is 0 and its possibility is 1. As more and more supporting data are considered the necessity of a datum tends to increase monotonically, always subject to the restriction that the necessity of a datum must be equal to or less than its possibility; as more and more refuting data are considered, the possibility of a datum tends to decrease monotonically.

In systems that maintain two truth values, possibility and necessity, a datum of which we have no knowledge at all has necessity 0 and possibility 1. A datum that is known to be completely false has both necessity and possibility 0. A datum that is known to be completely true has both necessity and possibility 1.

In systems that maintain a single truth value, necessity, we cannot distinguish between a datum about which nothing is known from a datum known to be false, since both have necessity 0. In such systems, we consider a datum to be false until supporting evidence is found.

Even though necessity-based systems do not maintain the possibility of data, it is possible to calculate the possibility of a datum from refuting evidence; if the calculated possibility is less than its existing necessity, the necessity must be reduced to obey the restriction that necessity is less than or equal to possibility. However, supporting evidence considered in subsequent firing of block of rules could increase the reduced necessity. It is then advisable first to fire blocks of rules to arrive at preliminary conclusions, which may be ambiguous or contradictory. We then resolve any contradictions by considering refuting evidence in rule blocks fired later in the reasoning process.

8.7 QUESTIONS

8.1 We have said that if there is no supporting or refuting evidence for a datum, its necessity is 0 and its possibility is 1. Why is this?

8.2 We have postulated the relationship

$Nec(A) <= Pos(A)$

Suppose that at the end of a rule-firing step, we have calculated $Nec(A) = 0.6$, and $Pos(A) = 0.4$. To maintain that relationship, we can either decrease $Nec(A)$ to 0.4 or can increase $Pos(A)$ to 0.6. Which should we do? Why?

8.3 Why should we consider supporting evidence before considering refuting evidence?

8.4 What is the basis for rejecting the conventional possibility axiom that in theory, when considering several propositions A, B, C, ..., that A, B, and C are nested so that $(A \Rightarrow B \Rightarrow C \cdots)$?

8.5 What is the basis for rejecting the conventional possibility axiom that A AND NOT A = $\min(A, 1 - A)$?

9 Expert System Shells and the Integrated Development Environment (IDE)

9.1 OVERVIEW

In the days when languages such as FORTRAN were first coming into use, one first wrote a high-level program using a text editor; compiled the program to an assembler language by running a compiler program; assembled the resulting assembler code to machine language by running an assembler program; then ran the machine language program. Usually, the program would not work, so additional statements were added to locate the error, and back to square one. The painfulness of this procedure is obvious. Now virtually all high-level languages are implemented with an *Integrated Development Environment* (IDE) that permits the programmer to refer to help files giving details of the language, write his program with a built-in program editor, compile it with compilation errors reported, run the program with debugging tools such as breakpoints and inspection variable values during the run of program, correct any errors in the source code, and immediately rerun the program to see if the bug has been corrected. Important features of a language development environment are listed in Table 9.1.

We must differentiate two types of rule-based fuzzy systems: those used for general-purpose fuzzy reasoning, and those used for fuzzy control. General-purpose rule-based fuzzy systems usually are implemented as a language; application programs are written in that language; input and output may be either numeric or linguistic, and are more often linguistic. Fuzzy control systems are much more stereotyped than general-purpose fuzzy reasoning systems; their rules employ a very restricted syntax; input and output are almost always numeric.

The restricted range of fuzzy control systems means that their development environments may be quite different from those for general-purpose systems. Entire systems may be specified as block diagrams rather than as explicit rules; rule syntax is especially designed for numeric input and output. Membership function manipulation and display receives much attention, and three-dimensional display of system inputs and outputs is common. The relative simplicity of control systems means that help files need not be extensive, and program debugging receives very little attention.

Fuzzy Expert Systems and Fuzzy Reasoning, By William Siler and James J. Buckley
ISBN 0-471-38859-9 Copyright © 2005 John Wiley & Sons, Inc.

TABLE 9.1   Important Features of a Well-Designed Integrated Program Development Environment

Text editor for writing programs, with color-coding of reserved words and syntax features
Help files with language manual and syntax details, general language features, and sample
   programs
Messages for syntax errors
Ability to run and debug the program being edited

In this chapter, we will focus out entire attention on development environments for general-purpose fuzzy reasoning systems. Table 9.2 lists the IDE operations provided as tool-bar buttons:

Run-time options include setting an output file name, to which all FLOPS text output is routed; setting a debug trace level; setting a default rule-firing confidence level; option to display the output file in the text editor on return from the FLOPS run, an option to control the output-file font, and an option, not run-related, to set two hot-keys to paste text into the file being edited.

The "General" options are selected by icons on the task bar, just below the menu bar at the top of the TFLOPS screen. Placing the cursor on an icon will display the word identification of that option.

TABLE 9.2   TFLOPS Menubar Button Operations

File options:
   Open new file
   Open existing file
   Save file
   Print file
Edit options:
   Cut
   Copy
   Paste
   Undo
   Redo
   Find
   Repeat
   Find previous
   Replace
Run options:
   Run FLOPS with no program file (disabled)
   Run FLOPS with program file being edited
   Set run-time options
General:
   Relabel rules
   Check syntax of program being edited
   Run FLEDIT to edit blackboard data files

While the option to check the syntax of rules in the program being edited is fairly complete, there are a few syntax errors TFLOPS will not pick up; these will be picked up by FLOPS when the program is run.

The option to relabel rules is very useful when the program is being written and debugged, when (as is usual) all or most rules are automatically labeled by FLOPS itself. **Caution**: When FLOPS discovers and error in a rule and returns an error message, the number of the offending rule returned is not necessarily the number assigned in a comment statement before the rule in the program. It is instead the rule number that TFLOPS would have assigned by the "relabel rules" option. Frequent rule relabeling is therefore important.

The FLEDIT option is very useful when blackboard files are used to communicate information to a program or between programs. FLEDIT presents a friendly way to construct, review or modify blackboard files.

9.2 HELP FILES

Both the FLOPS IDE and FLOPS itself provide a variety of help files. These include a FLOPS overview, language manual, a fuzzy math review, a review of the syntax of FLOPS rules, a description of the sample FLOPS programs provided, a short manual on building fuzzy expert systems, a glossary, some help on getting started, a section on on-line real-time work, and how to obtain technical support. A list of the help files in FLOPS and TFLOPS is given in Table 9.3.

Programmers used to procedural languages face some real problems in adjusting to a data-driven, parallel fuzzy language, and extensive help files are essential to help overcome these problems.

9.3 PROGRAM EDITING

All text editors provide the ability to save or abandon text entered. A program editor is different from a general-purpose text editor in that programs are written in a specific formal language with a specific syntax. It is very desirable to color-code

TABLE 9.3   FLOPS Help Files

FLOPS overview
Manual of FLOPS language
Fuzzy math review
Rule syntax review
Description of sample FLOPS programs
Manual on Building Fuzzy Expert Systems
Glossary
Help on getting started
On-line real-time work
Technical support

the text according to the specific language syntax; this helps the programmer master the syntax and correct errors. Every language will have certain reserved words. These should be separately color-coded for easy identification and error-avoidance, to help avoid using a reserved word when a nonreserved word should be used, or incorrectly typing in a desired reserved word. Other desirable features include separate color-coding for character strings and numbers, and perhaps more advanced color-coding depending on the specific language syntax. If rules may be assigned names by default, an automatic rule-relabeling feature is quite desirable. For production systems, it is quite desirable to be able to check program syntax prior to a program run.

In TFLOPS, the FLOPS IDE, reserved words are colored blue; strings are colored red; symbols enclosed in angle brackets (variables and FLOPS reserved data symbols) are colored green. Comments are shown in gray rather than black. Rule names may be specified by the programmer or automatically provided by the IDE. Toolbar buttons are provided to check program syntax and to relabel rules that have been automatically labeled. Of course, the usual array of edit function such as search and replace is provided.

In addition to the source code editor, TFLOPS provides an editor FLEDIT for FLOPS blackboard data files.

The FLOPS IDE differs substantially from those designed to create fuzzy control programs. Being oriented toward extremely general-purpose use, the FLOPS IDE resembles those for such languages as C++, also designed for general-purpose use.

9.4 RUNNING THE PROGRAM

It should be possible to run the program being edited directly from the IDE without saving the program to disk. The IDE should provide for setting run-time options prior to the run, such as setting level of detail for program tracing, output to a debug file in addition to screen output, and setting a rule-firing threshold to be used other than the default value. Errors found during a run should be reported back to the programmer, with pointers to offending source code.

9.5 FEATURES OF GENERAL-PURPOSE FUZZY EXPERT SYSTEMS

Fuzzy rule-based systems designed for general-purpose fuzzy reasoning are considerably more complex in concept than most programs in procedural languages such as C++.

First, most general-purpose fuzzy expert systems are *data-driven*; that is, which rules are fireable depends only on the available data, and not in the position of the rules in the program. This is true even of sequential rule-firing programs; the fact that they fire their rules sequentially, one by one, does not mean that the program is written in a procedural program language. Second, most fuzzy expert systems fire their rules in parallel rather than sequentially, the way in which procedural languages execute their statements. This means that we are dealing with a data-driven non-procedural language with parallel capabilities, rather than the conventional sequential languages. If the program is quite simple, as are many fuzzy control programs, this difference may be easily implemented. However, if the program is to be manually operated, it is quite possible we may need to extract information from a user in a context-dependent fashion, so that the next question to be asked may depend on the answer to the previous question. In this case, sequential rule-firing may be better adapted to the task at hand. If, however, the data needed by the program are automatically available, such as in database analysis or in real-time on-line problems, parallel programming is probably superior.

Clearly, if we wish to maintain a high degree of flexibility, both sequential (procedural) and parallel (non-procedural) rule-firing methods should be provided. Another difference is that rule-based system programs require not only rules, but also instructions that are directly executed, such as definitions of data elements, membership functions, unconditional output to and input from the user and the like; that gives us to running modes, one in which unconditional instructions are executed (*command mode*), and run in which rules are fired (*run mode*). This nomenclature (command and run modes) is our own, and not standard. For example, Earl Cox calls rules in our sense *conditional rules* (fired conditionally on the validity of the antecedent); in his terms, *unconditional rules* (always fired) correspond to our unconditional instructions.

The most important bug-susceptible items in a FLOPS program are (1) the data automatically created, and (2) the rules themselves. The most important symptoms that bugs can cause are errors in the data, or errors in the rule firing order. Clearly, the most important tools are those that permit detecting that a bug exists by inspecting the existing data and the newly fireable rule stack.

9.6 PROGRAM DEBUGGING

The first step in debugging a program is to correct syntax errors in the source code. In most computer languages, detection of syntax errors is done during program compilation. While this is also true of FLOPS, TFLOPS provides its own syntax checker that may be run at any time during program edit. An additional debug feature furnished by TFLOPS is the setting of FLOPS program run-time options. These options are shown in Table 9.4.

TABLE 9.4   Run-Time Options Set in TFLOPS

Enable and name output file to log screen output
Set debug trace level, 0–3
Set rule-firing threshold
Display output file on return to TFLOPS

TABLE 9.5   Some Debugging Commands Built Into the FLOPS Run-Time Module

prdata/ldata—displays or lists current data
prstack—lists newly fireable rules and any rules on the backtracking stack
run N—runs for a selected number of rule-firing steps
breakpoint—sets breakpoints at selected rules or lists current breakpoints
debug—sets level of program trace
explain—shows why rules are or are not fireable, and gives the source of current data
history—list of previously fired rules
keyboard/resume—temporarily exits run mode and accepts keyboard commands
prule—displays rule source code

FLOPS differs from most computer language development environments in that most debugging features are built into the FLOPS language itself, and are interactively available during a program run. FLOPS provides three types of debugging commands: data inspection (six commands); rule inspection (six commands); and rule firing (six commands). If an output log file is enabled, debugging results are returned to TFLOPS when the program run is concluded for use in modifying source code. The process of debugging non-procedural programs such as FLOPS is discussed in Chapter 10, Program Debugging. Major debugging commands built into the FLOPS run-time module are shown in Table 9.5.

9.7   SUMMARY

A most important step forward in computer programming was the development of the IDE in the 1980s, which made it possible for the programmer to work interactively and conveniently in program development. In an IDE, the programmer can switch back and forth between program editing, compiling, and debugging, substantially reducing the time, effort, and aggravation that program development entails. Help files made it possible to access language manuals during program development while never leaving the IDE. IDEs for procedural languages are highly developed and their availability is taken for granted among most programmers.

Since general-purpose expert systems involve languages, it is natural to expect an IDE for program development. For a program editor, no special problems are involved. The lack of experience of most programmers in data-driven parallel fuzzy systems means that more extensive help files are needed than for procedural languages. Program debugging constitutes a very different problem for a parallel fuzzy production system than for a procedural language. Except for syntax checking, FLOPS incorporates most debugging tools into the language itself for use at run time, including display of membership functions.

An IDE for a fuzzy control system offers great opportunities for making program development easy. Most importantly, the stylized nature of fuzzy control rules makes it possible to use tables and block diagrams for program development and test. For general-purpose fuzzy reasoning, however, the greatly expanded rule syntax means that the IDE must be more like that of (say) the C language than a fuzzy control IDE, and the IDE should furnish appropriate features for that kind of program development.

9.8 QUESTIONS

9.1 What is the primary advantage to using an IDE when writing and debugging programs as compared to using a text editor?

9.2 What features of language and IDE are absolutely necessary?

9.3 How does TFLOPS, the FLOPS IDE, differ from IDEs for procedural languages?

9.4 What debugging aids are built into the FLOPS run-time module?

9.5 Why are some debugging aids built into the FLOPS run-time module?

9.6 How can we check the syntax of a FLOPS program being edited?

9.7 How can we trace program execution?

9.8 Screen output during a FLOPS run disappears when the FLOPS run terminates. How can we review the FLOPS output after a FLOPS run is over?

10 Simple Example Programs

10.1 SIMPLE FLOPS PROGRAMS

In this chapter, we will introduce three very simple FLOPS programs. The first, numbers.fps, tests whether one number is less than, equal to, or greater than another. The .fps suffix to the program name, number.fps, tells us that this is a sequential FLOPS program. Next we compare two programs for adding a column of numbers, one written as a sequential and the other as a parallel program.

Remember the general sequence of major program sections. First, we have the data declarations. Next, there are the rules. Then there are the commands to create initial data for the program run; last, we have a run command to start the actual program run. In complex FLOPS programs, this sequence may be more complicated; for example, a rule can be written that will automatically create other rules. We will not deal with this ability in this chapter.

10.2 NUMBERS.FPS

We begin with program NUMBERS.FPS.

10.2.1 Program Listing

```
:********************************************************
:program NUMBERS.FPS for Boolean tests on two scalar numbers
:********************************************************
write 'compiling program numbers.fps...\n';
:-------------------------------------------------------------------------------
:DECLARATIONS
declare Numbers
  num1 flt
  num2 flt;
:-------------------------------------------------------------------------------
:RULES
:rule r0
rule rconf 0 (goal Inputs numbers to be compared.)
```

Fuzzy Expert Systems and Fuzzy Reasoning, By William Siler and James J. Buckley
ISBN 0-471-38859-9 Copyright © 2005 John Wiley & Sons, Inc.

```
IF (in Numbers num1.cf = 0)
THEN
  message nocancel 'Enter two numbers to be compared\,
0 0 to quit.',
  reset,
  input "First number?" 1 num1,
  input "Second number?" 1 num2,
  make Numbers;
:rule r1
rule (goal Tests for zeroes, quits.)
IF (in Numbers num1 = 0 AND num2 = 0)
THEN
  message nocancel 'Terminating NUMBERS.FPS.',
  stop;
:rule r2
rule (goal Tests for equality.)
IF (in Numbers num1 = <N1> AND num2 = <N2> AND num2 =
<N1> AND num1 > 0)
THEN
  message '<N1> equals <N2>',
  delete 1;
:rule r3
rule (goal Tests for N1 < N2.)
IF (in Numbers num1 = <N1> AND num2 = <N2> AND num1 <
<N2>)
THEN
  message '<N1> less than <N2>',
  delete 1;
:rule r4
rule (goal Tests for N1 > N2.)
IF (in Numbers num1 = <N1> AND num2 = <N2> AND num1 >
<N2>)
THEN
  message '<N1> greater than <N2>',
  delete 1;
:---------------------------------------------------------------------------------------------
:MAKES
make Numbers;
string = "NUMBERS.FPS does Boolean comparison of two numbers,
num1 and num2";
string + " for num1 = num2, num1 > num2 or num1 < num2.\n\n";
string + "Here is an extremely simple program, illus-
trating ";
string + "basic principles of a rule-based data-driven
system. ";
```

```
string + "After you have run the program, look it over in
the ";
string + "TFLOPSW editor.\n\n";
string + "If you like, comment out the run command by
placing a colon ";
string + "in front, thus - '\:run'. You can then enter
'prstack\;' to see ";
string + "which rules are fireable\; 'prdata\;' to
inspect the data\; and ";
string + "run 1\;' to execute one rule-firing
step.\n\n";
string + "ready to run...";
message "<string>";
run;
:****************************************************************
```

10.2.2   Program Structure

First, we note that there are three main sections to the program, as is typical of
FLOPS programs. The first section is "Declarations", in which the data structures
(data elements in FLOPS) are defined. Next comes the "Rules" section, where we
define our rules. After that comes the "Makes" section, in which the initial data are
created by make commands or read from the blackboard by the transfer
command. Finally, after everything is set up for the run, we issue a fairly long
message to the user, followed by a run command.

  This sequence is not completely arbitrary. To write a rule, we must be able to
refer to data, which in turn must be previously defined by declare commands.
Finally, we cannot run the program and execute the rules unless at least some
data have been created. The important fact that dictates that creation of rules
must precede creation of data is that *a rule*, *when first created*, *does not know*
about any data previously created. While this may seem capricious, in complex
programs it permits isolating newer rules created during the program run from
earlier and perhaps outmoded data.

10.2.3   Running the Program

Let us run NUMBERS.FPS to see what it does. We first invoke TFLOPS any way
that is convenient. With TFLOPS running, we edit NUMBERS.FPS by clicking on
FILE, OPEN, EXAMPLES, and finally NUMBERS.FPS. The numbers program
now appears on the screen. We run the program by clicking on RUN and then on
"Run numbers.fps". FLOPS now begins to run the program.

  After a brief "Compiling numbers.fps" written to the top of the screen, the long
message set up at the end of the program appears in a dialog box. We click on OK;
the dialog box disappears, its message is transferred to the screen, and a new dialog
box appears, inviting us to enter two numbers to be compared. We click on OK, and
again the dialog box disappears, its message is transferred to the screen, and a new

dialog box appears in which we can enter the first of the two numbers. We enter the first number, then the second in a new dialog box. FLOPS then reports the result of checking the two numbers, and we are ready to enter two more.

In every case, the contents of a dialog box are transferred to the screen as the dialog box is closed. This permits us to scroll up and review the program run from earlier stages, even from the beginning if we so desire.

After trying out several different number pairs during the program run, we are ready to quit. By repeated tries, we find out that if we press the Cancel button in an input dialog box, FLOPS immediately terminates, but if we press the Cancel button in a message box, FLOPS stops running rules and issues a FLOPS prompt >>. There is some reason behind the apparently completely arbitrary behavior. If an input command is executed, in general FLOPS cannot proceed without the input value, so it terminates. If a message dialog box is canceled, FLOPS can interrupt its run, issue a `keyboard` command to itself, and revert to command mode in which we can do almost anything we want. If we press Cancel in a message dialog box, and we wish to quit the run, we can exit by entering an `exit;` command, by clicking on the menu button FILE and then EXIT, by clicking on the X button just below the menu bar, or by clicking on the X button in the upper right-hand corner.

10.2.4   Using Basic Debugging Commands

Now that we see how the Numbers program runs, let us look at the run in more detail. To do this, when in TFLOPS and editing NUMBERS.FPS, we comment out the `run;` command by placing a colon inform of it, thus: `:run;`. When we now run the program, it behaves very differently. Our first dialog box with the long message appears, and its contents transferred to the screen when it is closed. But now the second dialog box does not appear; instead, after a "ready to run" message, we see the FLOPS prompt >>. FLOPS is now in command mode, waiting for us to tell it what to do. Fortunately, this message has been issued also:

If you like, comment out the run command by placing a colon in front, thus ":run". You can then enter "prstack;" to see which rules are fireable; "prdata;" to inspect the data; and "run 1;" to execute one rule-firing step.

We have already commented out the run command. The suggestion now is to enter prstack; prdata; and `run 1;` in succession. We proceed to do this, and get first:

```
>>prstack;
LOCAL STACK (partially ordered)
******* STACK TOP     *********
rule r0 Time Tags 1 pconf 0
******* STACK BOTTOM *********

PERMANENT STACK
******* STACK TOP     *********
******* STACK BOTTOM *********
>>
```

We see that only one rule is newly fireable (LOCAL STACK), rule r0, and that no rule instances have been placed on the backtracking stack (PERMANENT STACK).

We go ahead by entering prdata;, and see

```
>>prdata;
(Numbers (
  ('tt',1)))
>>
```

Our only data are an instance of data element Numbers, which has been assigned time tag 1, and no other values.

We can now proceed with run 1; and see that our dialog boxes input the two numbers to be compared, and return to command mode and the FLOPS prompt >>.

We enter prstack; again.The next time we enter prstack; we get

```
>>prstack;
LOCAL STACK (partially ordered)
******** STACK TOP    *********
rule r3 Time Tags 3 pconf 1000
rule r0 Time Tags 4 pconf 0
******** STACK BOTTOM *********
PERMANENT STACK
******** STACK TOP    *********
LOCAL STACK (partially ordered)
******** STACK BOTTOM *********
```

Two rules are now newly fireable, one with pconf = 1000 and one, r0, with confidence pconf = 0. This situation requires a brief digression.

10.2.5   Confidence Terminology: Antecedent Confidence, Rule Confidence, and Posterior Confidence (pconf)

Here, we are concerned with three confidences (truth values). One is the *rule confidence*, assigned when the rule is created. The second is the *antecedent confidence*, determined when the truth value of the antecedent is evaluated with actual data. The third is the posterior confidence (pconf), evaluated by taking the fuzzy AND (minimum) of the rule and antecedent confidences.

Rule instances are selected for firing if the antecedent confidence is sufficiently high, that is, equal to or greater than the rule-firing threshold. Newly fireable rules are ordered according to their pconf values, with the highest pconf being on top of the stack. When a rule is fired, the consequent instructions are executed with confidence pconf, which may be zero. (The pconf value can be reset to any desired value between zero and full confidence by the reset command.)

To return to our two fireable rules. If we were in parallel mode, both rules would be fired; but we are in sequential mode, so one rule will be picked for firing, and any others stacked for backtracking. The rule with pconf 1000 will be selected for firing, and rule r0 with pconf zero will be placed on the backtracking stack for possible firing when no rules are newly fireable.

We finish our sequence with `run 1`; which writes our conclusion about the numbers to the screen, and follow with prdata; and prstack;

```
>>prstack;
LOCAL STACK (partially ordered)
******** STACK TOP     *********
******** STACK BOTTOM *********

PERMANENT STACK
******** STACK TOP     *********
rule r0 Time Tags 4 pconf 0
******** STACK BOTTOM *********
```

No rules are newly fireable, so we pop the rule on top of the backtracking stack off the track and execute it. In our case, there is only one rule on the backtracking stack, r0, so we pop r0 off the stack, and fire it, thus beginning a new loop through our rules.

We can continue the prdata; prstack; `run 1`; sequence until we get bored. To avoid boredom, however, note that there are a bunch of other debugging commands we might use. For example, entering debug 1; will print out the names and goals of the rule instances as they are fired, and prule <rule name>; will list rule <rulename> to the screen. If we click on the HELP menu item, then on Manual, then on Debugging Commands, we will see a list of the debugging commands available; clicking on a command will bring up a description of the command's syntax and purpose.

10.3 SUM.FPS

In program Sum.fps we load a sequence of numbers into memory before the run begins, then total this sequence. This is a reasonable task when the sequence of numbers has been generated automatically, as from a cash register, and stored in the computer; at the end of the day we run our totals.

10.3.1 Program Listing

```
:*********************************************************
:program SUM.FPS to illustrate recursive arithmetic in
serial FLOPS
:10-15-86 WS
:instances of NUMBER are added sequentially to SUM TOTAL
:*********************************************************
```

```
string = "Program SUM.FPS computes the sum of s recur-
sively";
string + " in several sequential steps, one for each
number to be added.\n";
string + "Compiling program SUM.FPS";
message "<string>";
:-------------------------------------------------------------------------------------
:DECLARATIONS
declare Number
  num flt;
declare Sum
  total flt;
:-------------------------------------------------------------------------------------
:RULES
:block 0 - accumulates sum recursively in many sequen-
tial steps
:rule r0
rule (goal Accumulates sum recursively in many sequen-
tial steps)
IF ( in Number num <N> )
  ( in Sum total <T> )
THEN
  delete 1,
  message "adding <N> to <T> getting \(<N> + <T>\)",
  in 2 total (<T> + <N>);
:rule r1
rule rconf 0 (goal Prints out total when no more
instances of r0 are fireable)
IF ( in Sum total <T> )
THEN
  message "total of all is <T>\n",
  clear backtrack,
  halt;
:-------------------------------------------------------------------------------------
:MAKES
make Number num 12.34 ;
make Number num 23.45 ;
make Number num 34.56 ;
make Number num 45.67 ;
make Number num 56.78 ;
make Number num 67.89 ;
make Number num 78.90 ;
make Number num 89.01 ;
make Number num 90.12 ;
make Number num 01.23 ;
```

```
make Number num 32.10 ;
make Number num 21.09 ;
make Number num 32.10 ;
make Number num 43.21 ;
make Number num 54.32 ;
make Number num 65.43 ;
make Sum total 0 ;
message "Ready to run sum.fps";
run;
message "Sum.fps finished";
;*****************************************************
```

There are only two memory elements: Number, instances of which will hold the numbers to be totaled; and Sum, to hold the sum as it is developed. There are also only two rules, r0 to accumulate the sum, and r1 to print out the total when no more instances of r1 are fireable.

Note that rule r0 is recursive; whatever the value of total was (<T>), we add the value of num (<N>) to it to get a new total. Symbols in the antecedent enclosed in angle brackets are called *variables*, and are assigned a value when they first appear in the antecedent. Thus in rule r0 the value of num is assigned to <N>, and the value of total is assigned to <T>. Variables retain these assigned values throughout the firing of the rule; thus both <N> and <T> are available in the consequent for arithmetic operations or printing.

10.3.2   Running sum.fps

When we run sum.fps, we see nothing out of the ordinary. Program SUM.FPS computes a sum of numbers recursively in several sequential steps, one for each number to be added. Here is the program output:

```
Compiling program SUM.FPS
Ready to run sum.fps
adding 12.34 to 0 getting 12.34
adding 23.45 to 12.34 getting 35.79
adding 34.56 to 35.79 getting 70.35
adding 45.67 to 70.35 getting 116.02
adding 56.78 to 116.02 getting 172.8
adding 67.89 to 172.8 getting 240.69
adding 78.9 to 240.69 getting 319.59
adding 89.01 to 319.59 getting 408.6
adding 90.12 to 408.6 getting 498.72
adding  1.23 to 498.72 getting 499.95
adding 32.1 to 499.95 getting 532.05
adding 21.09 to 532.05 getting 553.14
adding 32.1 to 553.14 getting 585.24
adding 43.21 to 585.24 getting 628.45
```

```
adding 54.32 to 628.45 getting 682.77
adding 65.43 to 682.77 getting 748.2
total of all is 748.2
Sum.fps finished
```

If at the end of the run we enter the debug command history; we see that the number of rule instances fired equals the number of data points plus one rule for outputting the sum, which seems very reasonable.

```
>>history;
Fired Rule History, first to most recent
******** STACK TOP     **********
rule r0 Time Tags 17 1 pconf 1000
rule r0 Time Tags 18 2 pconf 1000
rule r0 Time Tags 19 3 pconf 1000
rule r0 Time Tags 20 4 pconf 1000
rule r0 Time Tags 21 5 pconf 1000
rule r0 Time Tags 22 6 pconf 1000
rule r0 Time Tags 23 7 pconf 1000
rule r0 Time Tags 24 8 pconf 1000
rule r0 Time Tags 25 9 pconf 1000
rule r0 Time Tags 26 10 pconf 1000
rule r0 Time Tags 27 11 pconf 1000
rule r0 Time Tags 28 12 pconf 1000
rule r0 Time Tags 29 13 pconf 1000
rule r0 Time Tags 30 14 pconf 1000
rule r0 Time Tags 31 15 pconf 1000
rule r0 Time Tags 32 16 pconf 1000
rule r1 Time Tags 33    pconf    0
******** STACK BOTTOM **********
```

10.3.3   Running sum.fps with Debugging Commands prstack; and Run 1;

To get a picture of the systems overhead going on, comment out the run command at the end of sum.fps by placing a colon in front of the command and then run the program with a sequence of prstack; and run 1; commands.

The first prstack command produces a screen output like this:

```
LOCAL STACK (partially ordered)
******** STACK TOP     **********
rule r0 Time Tags 17 16 pconf 1000
rule r0 Time Tags 17 15 pconf 1000
...
rule r0 Time Tags 17 1 pconf 1000
rule r1 Time Tags 17 pconf 0
******** STACK BOTTOM **********
```

```
PERMANENT STACK
******** STACK TOP     **********
******** STACK BOTTOM **********
```

The "LOCAL STACK" lists the newly fireable rule instances at this point in the run; the "PERMANENT STACK" lists those rule instances that had been found fireable but were not fired, the backtrack stack. If no rules were newly fireable, when a run command is executed a rule would be popped off the backtrack stack and fired. (Since in parallel FLOPS all newly fireable rule instances are fired concurrently, backtracking only occurs in serial *.fps FLOPS programs.)

In this list, we first give the name of the rule eligible for firing (e.g., rule r0). Next, we list the identifying time tags of the data that made the rule fireable. Finally, we list the value of pconf, the combined rule and antecedent confidence. Note that rule r1 has a pconf value of zero, but is nevertheless fireable. A rule is made fireable if its antecedent confidence is greater than the rule-firing threshold; in this case rule r1 has full antecedent confidence, but the rule confidence is zero. Rule instances are fired in the order of their pconf values; a pconf of zero places the rule at the bottom of the stack, so it will not fire until all rules with greater pconf values have fired. Since we have not yet executed any rule-firing steps, no rules have had an opportunity to be placed on the backtrack stack.

After the first 'run 1;' we execute prstack and find 16 rule instances on the backtracking stack; after the second 'run 1;' we have 31; after the third 'run 1;' we have 45 rule instances stacked; and so on, increasing every time until we have a couple of hundred rule instances stacked. Since this is a very simple program and computers are now very fast, we do not notice the increased systems overhead; but if our program were considerably more complex and we had a lot more data, the time used up by the system in processing all the extra rules could be very appreciable, even though almost none of the rules are ever fired.

Note that there are a number of other debugging commands available. For example, if prstack shows that rule r1 is fireable and we want to know what r1 does, we can enter (at the command prompt) >>explain goal r1; and the goal of r1 will be written to the screen. If we wish even more information, >>prule r1; will cause the entire rule to be written out. If prstack tells us that rule r1 is made fireable by the data with time tag 33, we can print out this data by entering >>prmem 33;. It is helpful to click on HELP, Manual and then Debugging Commands to see what commands are available to you.

10.4 SUM.PAR

When we open sum.par in TFLOPS, it is hard to detect any differences from sum.fps. Rule r1 is placed in its own block 1, while r0 remains in block 0. The program itself is listed in Section 10.4.1.

10.4.1 Program Listing

```
:*************************************************************
:program SUM.PAR to illustrate recursive arithmetic in
parallel FLOPS
:instances of are added in one parallel step to SUM TOTAL
:*************************************************************

string = "Program SUM.PAR computes the sum of s recur-
sively";
string + " in one parallel step.\n";
string + "Compiling program SUM.PAR";
message "<string>";


:-------------------------------------------------------------------------------
:DECLARATIONS

declare Number
  num flt;

declare Sum
  total flt;


:-------------------------------------------------------------------------------
:RULES
:block 0 - accumulates sum recursively in one parallel
step

:rule r0
rule (goal Adds num to sum recursively)
IF (in Number num = <N>)
  (in Sum total = <T>)
THEN
  write "adding <N> to $<T> getting \(<N> + $<T>\)\n",
  modify 2 total = ($<T> + <N>),
  fire block 0 off,
  fire block 1 on;

:-------------------------------------------------------------------------------
:block 1 - final answer

:rule r1
rule block 1 (goal Prints final sum)
IF (in Sum total = <T>)
```

```
THEN
  message "total of all is <T>\n";
  halt;

make Number num 12.34;
make Number num 23.45;
make Number num 34.56;
make Number num 45.67;
make Number num 56.78;
make Number num 67.89;
make Number num 78.90;
make Number num 89.01;
make Number num 90.12;
make Number num 01.23;
make Number num 32.10;
make Number num 21.09;
make Number num 32.10;
make Number num 43.21;
make Number num 54.32;
make Number num 65.43;
make Sum total 0;
fire block 1 off;

message "ready to run SUM.PAR\n";
run;
message "SUM.PAR finished.";
:*********************************************************
```

10.4.2   Running sum.par

When sum.par is run, the output seems virtually identical to that from sum.fps.

```
Program SUM.PAR computes the sum of s recursively in one
parallel step.
Compiling program SUM.PAR
ready to run SUM.PAR
adding 65.43 to 0 getting   65.43
adding 54.32 to 65.43 getting 119.75
adding 43.21 to 119.75 getting 162.96
adding 32.1 to 162.96 getting 195.06
adding 21.09 to 195.06 getting 216.15
adding 32.1 to 216.15 getting 248.25
adding 1.23 to 248.25 getting 249.48
adding 90.12 to 249.48 getting 339.6
```

```
adding 89.01 to 339.6 getting 428.61
adding 78.9 to 428.61 getting 507.51
adding 67.89 to 507.51 getting 575.4
adding 56.78 to 575.4 getting 632.18
adding 45.67 to 632.18 getting 677.85
adding 34.56 to 677.85 getting 712.41
adding 23.45 to 712.41 getting 735.86
adding 12.34 to 735.86 getting 748.2
total of all is 748.2
SUM.PAR finished.
```

As before, at the end of the run we enter history;, and get this list of fired rule instances.

```
>>history;
Fired Rule History, first (stack top) to most recent
(stack bottom)
******** STACK TOP    **********
rule r0 Time Tags 17 16 pconf 1000
rule r0 Time Tags 17 15 pconf 1000
rule r0 Time Tags 17 14 pconf 1000
rule r0 Time Tags 17 13 pconf 1000
rule r0 Time Tags 17 12 pconf 1000
rule r0 Time Tags 17 11 pconf 1000
rule r0 Time Tags 17 10 pconf 1000
rule r0 Time Tags 17 9 pconf 1000
rule r0 Time Tags 17 8 pconf 1000
rule r0 Time Tags 17 7 pconf 1000
rule r0 Time Tags 17 6 pconf 1000
rule r0 Time Tags 17 5 pconf 1000
rule r0 Time Tags 17 4 pconf 1000
rule r0 Time Tags 17 3 pconf 1000
rule r0 Time Tags 17 2 pconf 1000
rule r0 Time Tags 17 1 pconf 1000
rule r1 Time Tags 33 pconf 1000
******** STACK BOTTOM **********
```

So far, there appears to be no advantage to parallel mode.

10.4.3 Running sum.par with prstack; and run 1; Commands

We now run sum.par by repeating the prstack; and run 1; command sequence, with this output;

Program SUM.PAR computes the sum of s recursively in one
parallel step.
Compiling program SUM.PAR
ready to run SUM.PAR
>>prstack;
LOCAL STACK (unordered)
******** STACK TOP   **********
rule r0 Time Tags 17 16 pconf 1000
rule r0 Time Tags 17 15 pconf 1000
rule r0 Time Tags 17 14 pconf 1000
rule r0 Time Tags 17 13 pconf 1000
rule r0 Time Tags 17 12 pconf 1000
rule r0 Time Tags 17 11 pconf 1000
rule r0 Time Tags 17 10 pconf 1000
rule r0 Time Tags 17 9 pconf 1000
rule r0 Time Tags 17 8 pconf 1000
rule r0 Time Tags 17 7 pconf 1000
rule r0 Time Tags 17 6 pconf 1000
rule r0 Time Tags 17 5 pconf 1000
rule r0 Time Tags 17 4 pconf 1000
rule r0 Time Tags 17 3 pconf 1000
rule r0 Time Tags 17 2 pconf 1000
rule r0 Time Tags 17 1 pconf 1000
******** STACK BOTTOM **********
>>run 1;
adding 65.43 to 0 getting 65.43
adding 54.32 to 65.43 getting 119.75
adding 43.21 to 119.75 getting 162.96
adding 32.1 to 162.96 getting 195.06
adding 21.09 to 195.06 getting 216.15
adding 32.1 to 216.15 getting 248.25
adding 1.23 to 248.25 getting 249.48
adding 90.12 to 249.48 getting 339.6
adding 89.01 to 339.6 getting 428.61
adding 78.9 to 428.61 getting 507.51
adding 67.89 to 507.51 getting 575.4
adding 56.78 to 575.4 getting 632.18
adding 45.67 to 632.18 getting 677.85
adding 34.56 to 677.85 getting 712.41
adding 23.45 to 712.41 getting 735.86
adding 12.34 to 735.86 getting 748.2
>>prstack;
LOCAL STACK (unordered)
******** STACK TOP   **********
rule r1 Time Tags 33 pconf 1000

```
******* STACK BOTTOM *********
>>run 1;
total of all is 748.2
>>prstack;
LOCAL STACK (unordered)
******* STACK TOP    *********
******* STACK BOTTOM *********
```

In the entire program sum.par, only 17 rule instances have been found fireable, as compared to hundreds of rules in sum.fps. It is very well known that in production systems such as FLOPS, the bulk of the program run time (outside of I/O) is used up by the system in determining which rules are fireable. The improvement in running time achieved by parallel FLOPS over serial FLOPS can be dramatic.

10.5 COMPARISON OF SERIAL AND PARALLEL FLOPS

Conceptually, serial FLOPS amounts to a depth-first search of a decision tree, and parallel; FLOPS amounts to a breadth-first search. In practice, if information must be elicited from a user, when the next question to be asked depends on the answer to the previous question, serial FLOPS is appropriated; if the information comes in automatically, or is present at the beginning of the program run, parallel FLOPS is appropriate. In the sum problem, all the information is available at the beginning of the run, so the parallel program sum.par is to be preferred. If a problem can be solved with either serial or parallel FLOPS, the lower overhead of parallel FLOPS is usually the way to go.

10.6 MEMBERSHIP FUNCTIONS, FUZZIFICATION AND DEFUZZIFICATION

10.6.1 Membership Functions in FLOPS/

Membership functions in FLOPS are specified by the memf command. This permits the programmer to specify the point at which the membership function first begins to rise from zero; the point at which it first reaches 1; the point at which it first starts down from 1; and the point at which the function reaches zero again. If the function stays at 1 from -infinity until it starts to drop, the first parameter is set to $-1e6$; if the function remains at 1 after rising from 0, the last parameter is set to $-1e6$. An additional parameter is the shape of the membership function; piecewise linear, piecewise quadratic, or normally distributed (Gaussian). (In the case of normal functions, the first and last parameters are the point at which the membership function reaches 0.5.)

Membership functions are displayed by the drawmemf command. Figure 10.1 shows a typical membership function plot.

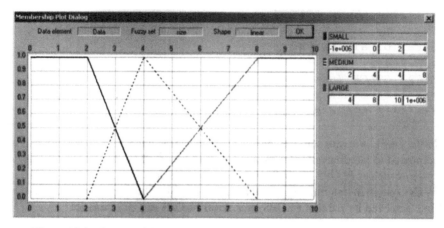

Figure 10.1 Output of drawmemf command to display membership functions.

The example program drawmemf.fps illustrates the use of the drawmemf command.

```
:**************************************************************
:DRAWMEMF.FPS - illustrates drawmemf command
:**************************************************************
message "Program DRAWMEMF.FPS to illustrate the drawmemf
command.";
:Specifications for the individual functions are given in the
:memfunct command. The first number is the point where the
:function first begins to rise from zero; the second number is
:the point where the function reaches 1000. The third number is
:the point where the function begins to decline from 1000; the
:fourth number is the point where it reaches zero again.

:If the first number is -1e6, the function starts at 1000 for
all
:values less than the third number, where it begins to decline
:toward zero; the only effect of the second number is to tell
:drawmemf where to start its plot.

:Similarly, if the fourth number is 1e6, the function never
:declines toward zero after its initial rise to 1000 at the value
:given by the second number; the only effect of the third number
:is to tell drawmemf where to stop its plot.

message "First membership functions are linear." ;
```

```
declare Data size fzset (SMALL MEDIUM LARGE);

memfunct Data size linear
  SMALL -1e6 0 2 4
  MEDIUM 2 4 4 8
  LARGE 4 8 10 1e6 ;

drawmemf Data size;

message "Next membership functions are s-shape." ;

memfunct Data size s-shape
  SMALL -1e6 0 2 4
  MEDIUM 2 4 4 8
  LARGE 4 8 10 1e6 ;

drawmemf Data size;

message "Last membership functions are normal.";

memfunct Data size normal
  SMALL -1e6 0 2 4
  MEDIUM 2 4 4 8
  LARGE 4 8 10 1e6 ;

drawmemf Data size;
message "DRAWMEMF.FPS finished." ;
:exit ;
*************************************************************
```

10.6.2 Fuzzifying Numbers in FLOPS

Fortunately, there is only one generally accepted way of fuzzifying a number. As we have shown, fuzzifying takes place as shown in Figure 10.2.

The FLOPS command `fuzzify` is used to fuzzify a number into grades of membership of a discrete fuzzy set. (A fuzzy set whose members describe a number is called a *linguistic variable*.)

Program fuzzify.par illustrates the use of the `fuzzify` command.

```
:*************************************************************
:program FUZZIFY.PAR - fuzzifies
:*************************************************************

thresh 1;

declare Data x flt size fzset (small medium large);
```

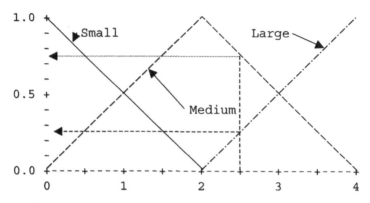

Figure 10.2 Fuzzifying 2.5; Small 0.25, Medium 0.75, Large 0.

```
memfunct Data size normal
  small -1e6 1 2
  medium 1 2 2 3
  large 2 3 1e6;

:rule r0
rule (goal Fuzzifies x into fuzzy set size)
IF (in Data x = <X> AND x <= 3.5)
THEN
  message 'Fuzzifying <X>\n',
fuzzify 1 size <X>,
fire block 0 off,
fire block 1 on;

:Permit firing rules with zero confidence in fuzzy set
member
TestFsetOff;

rule block 1 (goal Prints out results of fuzzification)
IF (in Data x = <X> AND size.small = <S> AND size.medium = <M>
  AND size.large = <L>)
THEN
  message '<X> fuzzified: small <S> medium <M> large
  <L>\n',
  reset,
  in 1 x = (<X> + 0.5),
  fire block 1 off,
  fire block 0 on;
```

```
make Data ^x 0.5 ;

string = "Program fuzzify.PAR\n";
string + "We have only two rules, one to fuzzify, one to
print results.\n" ;

string + "Rule r0 will fuzzify several values of an
input, x, ";
string + "Into a fuzzy set size with three members\:
small,
medium, large.\n";
message "<string>";
prule r0;
fire block 1 off;
message 'Here are the membership functions for fuzzy set
size:\n';
drawmemf Data size;
message 'Ready to run\n' ;
:run ;
:message 'Fuzzification demonstration finished.\n' ;
:exit ;
:************************************************************
```

10.6.3 Defuzzification in FLOPS

Unlike fuzzification, there are many methods of defuzzification. FLOPS provides
the popular *centroid* method; and also the *average maximum* method. The FLOPS
`defuzzify` command in FLOPS makes defuzzification simple. Program
defuzz.fps illustrates the defuzzification method. Because FLOPS only stores confidences with a resolution of one part in a thousand, the defuzzified value may differ
slightly from the original fuzzified value.

```
:++++++++++++++++++++++++++++++++++++++++++++++++++++++++++
:program DEFUZZ.PAR
:++++++++++++++++++++++++++++++++++++++++++++++++++++++++++

message 'Compiling program DEFUZZ to fuzzify and defuz-
zify height of a person\n' ;

thresh 1 ;

declare Data
  height flt
  defuzz flt
```

```
    size fzset
      ( Short Medium Tall) ;

memfunct Data size linear
    Short -1e6 4 4.5 5.5
    Medium 4.5 5.5 5.5 6.5
    Tall 5.5 6.5 7 1e6 ;

message 'Membership functions for fuzzy set size\:\n' ;
drawmemf Data size ;

:rule r0
rule (goal Enter height data)
IF ( in Data height.cf = 0 )
THEN
    input "Enter person\'s height in feet\, 0 to quit\n" 1
height ;

:rule r1
rule (goal Quit on entry of zero height)
IF ( in Data height 0 )
THEN
    message nocancel 'Terminating program DEFUZZ\n' ,
    exit ;

:rule r2
rule (goal Fuzzify height into fuzzy set size)
IF ( in Data height <H> AND height > 0 )
THEN
    message 'Height before fuzzification: <H>\n',
    fuzzify 1 size <H> ,
    fire block 0 off ,
    fire block 1 on ;

:enable firing rule with zero confidence in fuzzy set
members
TestFsetOff ;

rule block 1 (goal Print fuzzy set size\, defuzzify into
defuzz)
IF (in Data defuzz.cf = 0 size.Short <S> size.Medium <M>
size.Tall <T>)
THEN
    message 'Fuzzified height:\nShort <S> Medium <M> Tall
<T>\n',
```

```
defuzzify 1 size maxav 1 defuzz;

rule block 1 (goal Print defuzzified value\,
re-initialize program)
IF (in Data defuzz <X>)
THEN
   message 'Defuzzified value <X>\n' ,
   in 1 defuzz.cf = 0 height.cf = 0 ,
   fire block 1 off ,
   fire block 0 on ;

make Data ;
fire all off ;
fire block 0 on ;
message 'Program DEFUZZ ready to run\n' ;
:run ;
```

:++

10.7 SUMMARY

Even extremely simple programs such as those in this chapter can illustrate fundamental features of writing, running, and debugging FLOPS programs. The basic
structure of these programs is typical of more complex programs: declaration of
data structures; rules, commonly partitioned into numbered blocks; and creation
of data by make (or data acquisition) commands.

There is a very substantial difference between the ways in which sequential and
parallel programs are executed. Suppose that we have eight rules concurrently fireable. In sequential mode, one of these is picked for firing according to some criteria
(usually called a *rule conflict algorithm*); the rest are placed on a stack for firing if
no rules are newly fireable, called *backtracking*. In parallel mode, however, all fireable rules are fired effectively in parallel; since there are no unfired rules, there are
no rules to place on a backtrack stack.

If parallel FLOPS can be used, it is much more efficient than sequential FLOPS,
since systems overhead is greatly reduced. Parallel FLOPS is especially appropriate
for discrete fuzzy sets, since all fuzzy set members are processed effectively simultaneously, making the programming relatively simple and unconvoluted compared
to sequential programs. In either case, FLOPS has two operational modes; *run
mode*, in which rules are fired and their consequent instructions executed; and
command mode, in which FLOPS command are executed one at a time, from the
FLOPS program or from the keyboard. Executing commands from the keyboard
is especially convenient for interactive debugging.

In seems to be axiomatic that newly written programs will not run, and FLOPS is
not an exception. Debugging in a data-driven language is not the same as debugging
a procedural program, and special techniques are required. FLOPS has the ability to

single-step through a program using the `run 1;` command, or to halt the program when desired by setting rule breakpoints or using the `run N;` command, where N is the number of rule-firing steps to execute before reverting from run-to-command mode. Probably the two most important debug commands to use together with `run 1;` are `prdata;` for inspecting data, and `prstack;` for seeing which rules are newly fireable. There are a number of other very useful debug commands available that should not be neglected.

10.8   QUESTIONS

10.1   In a simple FLOPS program we have three major program sections and a run command. What are the three program sections?

10.2   In what order must these section and the run command appear in the program?

10.3   Why must the data declarations come first?

10.4   Why must rule commands precede data creation?

10.5   Three important debugging commands are (a) `prstack`, (b) `prdata`, and (c) `run N`. What purpose do these commands serve?

10.6   **a.** What is the :LOCAL stack in FLOPS?

       b. In what order are the rules on the LOCAL stack listed?

       c. What is the meaning of the `pconf` symbol?

10.7   What are the LOCAL and PERMANENT rule stacks?

10.8   In what order are the rules on the LOCAL and PERMANENT stacks listed?

10.9   What information about the rules is presented by the `prstack` command?

10.10   What is the primary difference between serial and parallel FLOPS?

10.11   In terms of availability of information, how do we choose between serial and parallel FLOPS?

11 Running and Debugging Fuzzy Expert Systems I: Parallel Programs

11.1 OVERVIEW

Conventional procedural languages such as C have one operating mode, sequential; compiled machine language instructions are executed in source code order, except for specific transfers of command. FLOPS, on the other hand, has two quite different operational modes: command mode, which is sequential, and run mode, which is data-driven and non-procedural. Run mode, in turn, can operate either serially, in which one rule is fired at a time before modifying data and checking to see if any rules are newly fireable, or in parallel, in which all fireable rules are effectively fired at once before resolving any conflicts for data modification and actually modifying the data, and only then checking to see which rules are newly fireable. These different operational modes give FLOPS a great deal of power and flexibility, but also make writing and debugging programs more difficult.

There are several general steps in debugging a program. First, language syntax errors must be found and corrected; these can be found either using a syntax-checking option in the IDE, or when the program is compiled. Second, any run-time bugs should be isolated to a relatively small part of the program. Last, the program defect itself is found and corrected.

The most challenging task is frequently the isolation of the bug. The same features of FLOPS that make it powerful—the data-driven rules, the fuzzy logic, fuzzy sets and fuzzy numbers, and the parallel rule firing, make it more difficult to debug. In this chapter, we will deal with general debugging techniques.

Unlike most languages, the major debugging tools are built into FLOPS itself rather than into the IDE; this makes interactive debugging during run time very convenient.

11.2 DEBUGGING TOOLS

The debugging process is begun in the IDE by invoking the syntax-check toolbar feature. (At present, the syntax checking provided by the TFLOPS IDE detects

Fuzzy Expert Systems and Fuzzy Reasoning, By William Siler and James J. Buckley
ISBN 0-471-38859-9 Copyright © 2005 John Wiley & Sons, Inc.

most but not all syntax bugs; a few may be detected during the FLOPS run.) After syntax has been checked OK, the serious debugging begins when the program is actually run.

Certain debugging tools may be specified within the IDE TFLOPS for a program run by using the Options menu bar item or by clicking on the Options toolbar button. These include specification of an output log disk file, setting a debug trace level, and setting a rule-firing threshold.

FLOPS provides four general types of debugging commands: data inspection (six commands); rule inspection (six commands); rule firing (seven commands, including a program trace at selectable levels of detail); and output logging (two commands). The Integrated Development Environment TFLOPS provides syntax checking and selection of run-time options; these options include copying FLOPS output to an output file, choice of four different levels of program trace, and specification of FLOPS rule-firing threshold. The debugging commands available are listed in Table 11.1.

All these debugging commands are legal FLOPS commands to be executed by FLOPS. Usually, these commands are most conveniently executed from the keyboard in command mode, although debugging commands may be placed in the FLOPS program as well. If FLOPS is not already in command mode with keyboard entry, it may be placed in command mode with keyboard input in several different ways:

- At the end of executing a specified number of rule-firing commands (for example, "run 3").
- Execution of a "keyboard" or "halt" command.
- By encountering a rule breakpoint, set by, for example, "breakpoint r23".
- By clicking the <Cancel> button in a message box.
- By placing a debug command in the consequent of a rule.

If keyboard or halt debug commands are placed in the consequent of a rule, they must be the last command in the consequent, or else the results are unpredictable. The same effect may often be more flexibly achieved by a rule breakpoint.

11.3   DEBUGGING SHORT SIMPLE PROGRAMS

We will illustrate the debugging process by a simple program that has a number of bugs, Guess.fps. The user tries to guess a number; Guess tells the user if the guess is too high, too low, or correct.

Syntax errors, often called compile-time errors, should be checked in TFLOPS before attempting to run a program. Syntax is easily checked by clicking on the "syntax check" icon on the TFLOPS tool bar, $\sqrt{}$. Errors and warnings are then listed at the bottom of the TFLOPS screen. Information on syntax of FLOPS commands can be accessed through the Manual help file. Run-time errors are often more difficult to correct, and require using the FLOPS debug commands in Table 11.1. Most hard-to-find bugs in a fuzzy expert system (other than simple language

TABLE 11.1   FLOPS Debugging Commands

Data inspection:
    prdata [optional data element names] – prints all or selected data with all attribute values and time tags.
    ldata [optional data element names] – lists all or selected data with data element names and time tags only.
    prmem <time tag> (in command mode); <element number in antecedent> (on RHS of rule).
    source tt <time tag> – gives source of specified datum.
    prdes – prints complete data declarations.
    ldes – lists data declarations, data element names only.

Rule inspection:
    prstack – lists newly fireable rules and backtrack stack with time tags of data which make each rule fireable.
    why <rulename> – explains why <rulename> is fireable.
    why not <rulename> – explains why <rulename> is not fireable.
    prule [optional rule names and rule block numbers] – prints all or selected complete rules.
    lrule [optional rule names and rule block numbers] – lists all or selected rules, rule name and goal only.
    fire status – lists rule blocks with On/Off firing status.

Rule firing commands:
    debug N – selectable level of trace. 0, no trace. debug 1 lists rule about to be fired; debug 2 also lists each FLOPS command as it is about to be executed; debug 3 also lists memory before and after modification.
    breakpoint <rulename> turns breakpoint on, -<rulename> turns breakpoint off, no rule names lists active rule breakpoints – returns temporarily to command mode when breakpointed rule is about to be fired. "resume" commands returns to run mode.
    run N – runs for N rule-firing steps, then reverts to command mode. If N not specified, runs until finished, or when keyboard or halt command is executed.
    resume – returns to run mode after breakpoint is hit or keyboard command is executed.
    keyboard – stops program, takes command input from keyboard until "resume" command is executed.
    halt – reverts to command mode from run mode.
    thresh <N> – sets rule-firing threshold to <N>.

Output logging:
    outfile <filename> – copies screen output to output disk log file <filename>.
    close <outfile> – closes <outfile>.

errors, usually reported by the program compiler) are concerned with rule fireability; rules fire that should not, do not fire when they should, or fail to enable the proper rules for firing next.

Exercise: Guess.fps: basic debugging. We illustrate program debugging by a simple program guess.fps. Guess asks the user to guess a number that is randomly assigned at the start of the program. After the user inputs his guess, Guess reports if the guess is too high, too low, or OK. If the user's guess is wrong, another chance is offered until the number is guessed. The original program, complete with bugs, is listed below.

guessing game: try to guess a number.

```
declare Guess
x int
ok int;

:rule r0
rule (goal Input guess)
IF (x = 0)
THEN
  write "What is your guess for the number ?\n",
  read 1 x,
  srand,
  in 1 ok = (rand * 10);

:rule r1
rule (goal Guess too low)
IF (ok = <OK> AND x ~< <OK>)
THEN
  write "Your guess is too low - guess again\n",
  delete 1;

:rule r2
rule (goal Guess too high)
IF (ok = <OK> AND x ~> <OK>)
THEN
  write "Your guess is too high guess again\n",
  delete 1;

:rule r3
rule (goal Guess correct - stop)
IF (ok = <OK> AND x ~= <OK>)
THEN
  write "Your guess is correct! Thanks for the game\n",
  halt;

run;
```

We invoke TFLOPS and load Guess.fps. The initial debugging step is to run the syntax check, with this result:

```
ERROR lines 1-4: 'guessing' is not a FLOPS' command.
ERROR lines 7-11: 'x' has not been declared.
ERROR lines 14-18: 'x' has not been declared.
ERROR lines 21-25: 'x' has not been declared.
ERROR lines 28-32: 'x' has not been declared.
0 warning, 5 errors
```

We see that Line 1 is supposed to be a comment describing the program, but that it has not been commented out by a colon. We insert a colon at the beginning of Line 1, and check syntax again:

```
ERROR lines 7-11: 'x' has not been declared.
ERROR lines 14-18: 'x' has not been declared.
ERROR lines 21-25: 'x' has not been declared.
ERROR lines 28-32: 'x' has not been declared.
0 warning, 4 errors
```

We see that lines 7–11 are rule r0:

```
rule (goal Input guess)
IF (x = 0)
THEN...
```

We have forgotten to include the name of the data element in all four rules. We revise r0 and the other rules to read:

```
IF (in Guess...)
```

and check syntax once more., getting:

```
0 warning, 0 error
```

We comment out the run command at the end of the program, and run FLOPS with program Guess.fps:

ERROR lines 14–18 Rule r1 element # 1 attribute x – fuzzy parameters mis-specified

FLOPS has uncovered a syntax error which TFLOPS missed. We Exit FLOPS, returning to TFLOPS, and inspect rule r1:

```
:rule r1
rule (goal Guess too low)
IF (in Guess ok = <OK> AND x ~< <OK>)
```

```
THEN
  write "Your guess is too low - guess again\n",
  delete 1;
```

Rule r1 has specified an approximate comparison when neither of the comparison operands is fuzzy. We remove the tilde "~" from all rules. A TFLOPS syntax check shows no errors, so we run Flops again.

```
>>prstack;
LOCAL STACK (partially ordered)
******** STACK TOP     *********
******** STACK BOTTOM *********

PERMANENT STACK
******** STACK TOP     *********
******** STACK BOTTOM *********
>>
```

No rules fireable are newly fireable. We therefore check data:

```
>>prdata;
>>
```

There are no data; we have forgotten to create any. We return to TFLOPS, add make Guess x = 0 to make rule r0 fireable, and run again:

```
>>prstack;
LOCAL STACK (partially ordered)
******** STACK TOP     *********
rule r0 Time Tags 1 pconf 1000
rule r1 Time Tags 1 pconf 1000
******** STACK BOTTOM *********

PERMANENT STACK
******** STACK TOP     *********
******** STACK BOTTOM *********
>>
```

We have two rules fireable instead of only r0. We look at the rules:

```
>>prule r0 r1;

rule r0 rconf 1000 ON block 0 ON
  (goal: Input guess)
IF
  (in Guess x = 0)
```

```
THEN
  write "What is your guess for the number ?\n",
  read 1 x;

rule r1 rconf 1000 ON block 0 ON
  (goal: Guess too low)
IF
  (in Guess x < 6)
THEN
  write "Your guess is too low - guess again\n",
  delete 1;
>>prdata;
(Guess (
  ('tt',1)
  ('x',0,1000)))
>>
```

We have not planned well. We could restrict the range of guesses to exclude 0 by revising the r1 antecedent to read (in Guess x < 6 AND NOT x = 0). Alternatively, we could create an empty instance of Guess, and test x.cf for zero in rule r0; that is better, since it does not place any restrictions on tests on the value of x carried out by other rules. We return to TFLOPS and change x to x.cf in the antecedent of rule r0, and eliminate x = 0 from the make command:

```
rule r0 rconf 1000 ON block 0 ON
  (goal: Input guess)
IF
  (in Guess x.cf = 0)
THEN
  write "What is your guess for the number ?\n",
  read 1 x;

make Guess;
```

We run our program again, but this time we simply run with debug 1 in effect to trace the rules as they fire:

```
>>debug 1;
>>run;

*** firing rule r0 pconf 1000
goal Input guess

What is your guess for the number ?
  5
```

```
Updating Memory and Partial Matches

*** firing rule r1 pconf 1000
goal Guess too low

Your guess is too low - guess again
Updating Memory and Partial Matches
>>
```

Our run has stopped for no apparent reason. We check the fireable rule stack:

```
>>prstack;
LOCAL STACK (partially ordered)
******* STACK TOP     *********
******* STACK BOTTOM *********

PERMANENT STACK
******* STACK TOP     *********
******* STACK BOTTOM *********
>>
```

Since rules are made fireable by data, we check data:

```
>>prdata;
>>
```

We have no data. The last rule that fired was r1, so we check it:

```
>>prule r1;

rule r1 rconf 1000 ON block 0 ON
  (goal: Guess too low)
IF
  (in Guess x < 6)
THEN
  write "Your guess is too low - guess again\n",
  delete 1;
>>
```

We deleted the old data, but did not supply any new data to take its place. We have two ways of correcting this situation: we can add "make Guess" after "delete 1", or can change the delete command to "in 1 x.cf = 0". Since the second method is neater, we return to TFLOPS and revise Guess.fps accordingly. We run again:

```
>>run;
What is your guess for the number ?
  5
Your guess is too low - guess again
What is your guess for the number ?
  7
Your guess is too high guess again
What is your guess for the number ?
  6
Your guess is correct! Thanks for the game
>>
```

11.4   ISOLATING THE BUG: SYSTEM MODULARIZATION

The absolutely essential factor in bug isolation is program modularization—debugging begins when the program is written in such a way that bugs can be isolated.

In a blackboard system, the top level of modularization is the division of the task into separate programs, component expert systems, and (if advisable) programs written in procedural languages, so that each of the blackboard programs performs a well-defined task. At the top level, then, isolating any bugs is a matter of determining whether each program is performing its task satisfactorily. Test sets of input data, with expected results for each program, are required.

Each individual program is in turn modularized; procedural programs into separate functions, and expert system programs into blocks. When an offending program is detected, we can then proceed to see if each individual function or block is working properly. Again, test sets of input data can be used.

The simplest bug is a program syntax defect detected by FLOPS but missed by TFLOPS that causes FLOPS to issue a syntax error message. In this case, we can return immediately to TFLOPS, where the error message will be displayed and the defect corrected.

One of the simplest debugging techniques is to execute a program trace. FLOPS supplies four trace levels, as shown in Table 11.1.

In production systems, common errors are when a rule or rule block makes itself improperly refireable, or when a rule or rule block is not fireable when it should be so. The **run N**, **prstack**, and **fire status** commands are critical here. Errors can be caused by defects in rules, improper data, or improper metarules to control rule and block firing.

11.5   THE DEBUG RUN

As noted above, the first thing we need is a test set of input data, a knowledge of the expected sequence of fireable rules and rule blocks, and a knowledge of the data modifications expected to occur as rule and rule blocks are successively fired.

We run TFLOPS, the FLOPS IDE, and read our program either from the keyboard or from a previously created disk program file. We make sure that any run commands in the program are either preceded by ":keyboard" commands or, if there is only one run command at the end of the program, it has been commented out by inserting a colon (:) in front of the run command. It is a good idea to route output to a debug file, as provided by the "Options" menu item dialog box. In this dialog box, we can enter the name of our debug file and select an option to display the debug file in TFLOPS at the end of the run. Now, we click the "Run" menu item, and the "Run <filename>" sub-menu item; the FLOPS run commences.

FLOPS begins by compiling the program; that is, it compiles the rule antecedents to an efficient pseudo-code. (Note that in similar expert systems, the bottleneck is evaluating the rule antecedents to see which rules are new fireable, so the compilation is directed at the most time-consuming part of the program.) If the program encounters any compilation errors, these are returned to TFLOPS for correction of the source code. If the program compiles satisfactorily, and no gross errors are encountered, the program will pause in command mode, indicated by the FLOPS prompt ">>". We can now proceed to perform our checks, one by one.

We have two possible problems; incorrect rules fireable, or incorrect data. Both problems are often simultaneously present. Incorrect data are often the cause of incorrect rule fireability.

First, we can make sure that we have the proper data by entering "prdata;" at the FLOPS prompt, and by comparing the actual data with the desired data on our debugging list. If everything seems OK, we can check whether the proper rules are fireable by entering "prstack". This will not only list the newly fireable rules, but will also give the confidence with which they are fireable.

If all the proper rules are fireable and none other, all is well; we can enter "run 1;" and begin again with the first step in the preceding paragraph, executing the debug procedure repetitively until an error is encountered.

If all is not well, we may have rules that are not fireable when they should be; rules that are fireable when they should not be; or both. We can review the rules with questionable fireability by entering "prule <rulename>;" at the command prompt ">>", and can review the data by entering "prdata <data element name>;". (Data elements in FLOPS correspond to data structure names in C; all data in FLOPS are held in data elements.) For rules that should be fireable but are not, we enter (at the command prompt) "explain why not <rulename>;" or simply "why not <rulename>;". An explanation of why the rule is not fireable will be written to the screen (and to our debug output file). Similarly, for rules that are fireable when they should not be, we enter "explain why <rulename.;" or "why not <rulename>;". We then exit FLOPS and return to the IDE, TFLOPS, to correct the problem. We can compare thoughtfully and at leisure the actual situation as given by our debug file with what it should be.

This debugging procedure, repetitively entering "prdata", "prstack", and "run 1" to isolate the bug, and using the other debugging commands to pin it down, is simple to execute if we know what the program status (data and rule fireability) should be at each rule-firing step, and not too many rule-firing steps are involved.

11.6 INTERRUPTING THE PROGRAM FOR DEBUG CHECKS

If a run is of even modest complexity, a sequence of `prstack`, `prdata`, and `run 1` commands may be too painfully slow to carry out if the difficulty is manifest after a number of rule-firing steps. If so, it may be desirable to interrupt the program and return control to the keyboard at some point to inspect data and rule stacks. FLOPS furnishes a number of ways to do this.

The simplest way is to execute a `run N` command, where `N` is the number of rule-firing steps to take before returning from run mode to command mode. After inspecting the data and fireable rule stack, and entering any other desired debugging command, we can enter a new `run N` followed by a `resume` command to start firing rules again.

If it is known that firing a certain rule causes things to go awry, the `break point <rule name>` command will return to command mode whenever that rule becomes fireable, just before it would fire. After executing debug or any other FLOPS commands, the `resume` command will return us to run mode. (Almost all FLOPS commands may be executed during a breakpoint, but a few are not allowed.)

A quick way to enter command mode is to click the <Cancel> button on a message box. This will immediately place us in command mode; as before, the `resume` command will return FLOPS to run mode.

Finally, the `keyboard` command will place us in command mode, with FLOPS expecting the next command to be entered from the keyboard. The keyboard command is useful if we want to interrupt FLOPS when executing commands from a program file in command mode rather than when FLOPS is firing rules in run mode.

11.7 LOCATING PROGRAM DEFECTS WITH DEBUG COMMANDS

11.7.1 Program Structure

The first step is a clear understanding of program structure and function. If the entire project consists of two or more different programs, whether FLOPS programs or executable files written in other languages, we must know what each program is supposed to do, and understand the sequence in which they are to run. Checking the input and output of each subprogram will help isolate the offending program.

Suppose that the offending program is a FLOPS program. We have already seen the general structure of a FLOPS program: data declarations, rules organized into blocks, and data creation. Inside a rule block we have individual rules. Our first step is to see that the rule blocks are fulfilling their tasks by firing one or more blocks at a time, and seeing that the data transformations and changes in rule and block firing status are being properly carried out. From this, we attempt to isolate in which block of rules the trouble occurs; from there, to the individual rules and rule-specific data and control modifications.

We will illustrate these steps by running a program that has no bugs, echo.par. We strongly suggest that at this point you run TFLOPS, open examples\echo.par and start running it.

11.7.2 Sample Debugging Session

Exercise: echo.par. Erroneous data may be encountered from several sources. They may be entered through keyboard, created by a command mode make command, read in from a file or other external data source, or modified by a rule. Erroneous data may have any of several effects. They may cause rules to be fireable when they should not, or cause rules not to be fireable when they should be, or may simply result in incorrect conclusions.

Data errors that cause errors in rule firing require first detecting when a rule or rules are incorrectly fireable, or when incorrectly not fireable. This condition is most readily detected by the prstack command. To illustrate this, run echo.par until a message box appears starting with "Ready to create new rules and process input data —".

At this point, we can enter command mode with keyboard input by simply clicking the <Cancel> button. A message box appears starting with "Execute keyboard commands or scroll—enter 'resume; to return to program control'." We click "OK", and are now in command mode with keyboard input. We now enter prstack; and see that a lot if instances of both r0 and r1 and one instance of r23 are fireable.

Suppose that r0 should not be fireable, and we want to know why. We enter explain why r0;, or more simply just why r0;. FLOPS replies

```
>>why r0;
Newly fireable instance 1 of rule r0:
r0 in block 0 newly fireable:
Rule confidence 1000 antecedent confidence 1000
Goal Moves input data to "Region", converts to fuzzy
numbers
Made fireable by these data:
(Data (
   ('tt',1)
   ('frame',1,1000)
   ('rnum',1,1000)
   ('area',98,1000)
   ('xbar',185,1000)
   ('ybar',298,1000)  ('border','NO',1000)))
time tag 1 made in command mode
Rule and block turned ON for firing.
>>
```

We can tell from this that both r0 individually and block 0 in which r0 appears are fireable, and that the data with time tag 1 has been created in command mode. The time tag 1 data are an instance of data element Data, with contents as listed. We now have several possibilities for r0 being "incorrectly" fireable, as we have supposed. If r0 should not be fireable, the block or rule may have been incorrectly made fireable by default or by improper use of the fire command; the instance of Data may have been prematurely created, fail to have been deleted, or may have incorrect values; or there may be something wrong with the rule itself.

To check the firing status of the rule and block, if we wish, we can enter fire status;. We do so, and FLOPS replies

```
block 0 status ON
block 1 status OFF
block 2 status OFF
block 3 status OFF
block 4 status OFF
block 5 status OFF
block 6 status OFF
block 7 status OFF
block 8 status OFF
block 20 status ON
>>
```

Suppose that so far, all seems OK. Since the instances of Data were created in command mode, we would like to check where they came from, preferably without leaving the FLOPS run. We can do this by clicking on "TFLOPS – echo.par" on the tack bar at the bottom of the desktop. We do so, look for Data in data creation section at the bottom of the echo.par program, and find that the instances of Data were transferred from the file "echodata.dat". We have already seen the contents of Data instance with time tag one; suppose that the contents are OK.

We are now reduced to finding something wrong with rule r0. We go back to the FLOPS run by clicking on FLOPSW on the task bar at the bottom of the desktop, and inspect rule r0 by entering "prule r0;", We do so, and see:

```
rule r0 rconf 1000 ON block 0 ON
   (goal: Moves input data to "Region", converts to fuzzy
numbers)
IF
   ( in Data frame = <F> AND rnum = <N> AND area = <A> AND
xbar = <X>
   AND ybar = <Y> AND border = <B> )
```

```
THEN
  make Region frame = <F> rnum = <N> area = <A> 10 0.1
xbar = <X> 20 0
  ybar = <Y> 20 0 border = "<B>";
>>
```

This rule requires that there be an instance of Data; that the data have values for attributes frame, rnum, area, xbar, ybar, and border. (These values, whatever they are, will be transferred to variables <F>, <N>, <A>, <X>, <Y>, and <B> respectively.) Although the values in time tag 1 have been printed out previously, we would like to verify them. To do this, we enter

```
>>prmem 1;
```

and the contents of time tag one are printed out:

```
(Data (
  ('tt',1)
  ('frame',1,1000)
  ('rnum',1,1000)
  ('area',98,1000)
  ('xbar',185,1000)
  ('ybar',298,1000)
  ('border','NO',1000)))
>>
```

We observe that all attributes are numeric, except for "border" which is a character string. As a final check, we print out the data descriptor (declaration) for Data by entering

```
>>prdes Data;
```

and get

```
declare Data
  tt type int
  frame type int
  frame.cf type conf
  rnum type int
  rnum.cf type conf
  area type flt
  area.cf type conf
  xbar type flt
  xbar.cf type conf
```

```
ybar type flt
ybar.cf type conf
border type str
border.cf type conf
>>
```

This shows us that all values of the attributes of Data stored in time tag one are consistent with the data declaration. We have not been able to find anything wrong. (Of course, there wasn't anything wrong in the first place!)

Now suppose that rule r3 should have been fireable, but is not. To check the reason for this, we enter

```
>>why not r3;
```

FLOPS then tells us:

```
No newly fireable instances of rule r3
Rule r3 status ON
Block 1 status OFF
block turned off for firing
Pattern 1 not fireable
>>
```

We see that there are two reasons why r3 is not fireable. It is in Block 1, that has been turned off; and Pattern 1, the first data element in the antecedent of r3, is not consistent with the data.

To check the firing status of r3, we return temporarily to TFLOPS and check the fire command that turned off block 1. We see that our program has these `fire` commands to be executed in command mode, and none others at the bottom of echo.par:

```
fire all off;
fire block 0 on;
fire block 20 on;
```

The only way block one can be turned on for firing with our existing program is by firing r23, which will increment the active block by one when fired. However, rule 23 was on the list of newly fireable rules printed out by the prstack command that we previously entered, but has not yet fired.

The other reason why r3 is not fireable is that pattern 1, the first data element in r3, is not consistent with the r3 antecedent. To check this, we print out r3 by

```
>>prule r3;
```

and get

```
rule r3 rconf 1000 ON block 1 OFF
  (goal: Writes out data converted to fuzzy numbers)
IF
  (in Region rnum = <N>)
THEN
  write "Raw data for region <N> (fuzzy numbers) -\n",
  prmem 1 rnum area xbar ybar;
>>
```

R3 requires an instance of data element Region with some value for attribute rnum. To check this, we list any instances of Region by entering

```
>>ldata Region;
```

which evokes a message box telling us

```
WARNING Can't find instances of data element 'Region'
>>
```

Remember that a bunch of instances of r0 and r1 are newly fireable, but have not been fired. We print out r0:

```
>> prule r0;
rule r0 rconf 1000 ON block 0 ON
  (goal: Moves input data to "Region", converts to fuzzy
numbers)
IF
  ( in Data frame = <F> AND rnum = <N> AND area = <A> AND
xbar = <X>
  AND ybar = <Y> AND border = <B> )
THEN
  make Region frame = <F> rnum = <N> area = <A> 10 0.1
xbar = <X> 20 0 ybar = <Y> 20 0 border = "<B>";
```

Of course, there are no instances of Region—they are created by r0, that has not fired as yet!

At this point, we might stop thinking that r3 should be fireable, check our program logic, and find that in fact it should *not* be fireable yet. If there had been something wrong, we would have found it by now.

11.8 SUMMARY

In FLOPS, debugging is conveniently accomplished interactively during the FLOPS run by using special debugging commands. When first debugging a FLOPS program, it is well to prepare a list of modules containing desired data and rules to be newly fireable for at least a few initial rule-firing steps. We must now make sure that it is possible to execute the program one rule-firing step at a time, returning to command mode after each rule-firing step. The "keyboard;" command is most useful here. The execution in repeated succession of **prdata, prstack, fire status**, and **run 1**, combined with the options set in TFLOPS of routing the screen output to a debug file and viewing this file in TFLOPS after the FLOPS run will not only find many bugs, but will help the newcomer to FLOPS appreciate the steps that are gone through in a FLOPS run.

For more sophisticated debugging, it may be desirable to interrupt program execution at selected points. The use of `run N` or the unrestricted `run` command combined with rule breakpoints, followed by execution of the appropriate debug commands from the complete list, will help find any remaining or more subtle bugs. Besides the `run N` command, ways of interrupting program execution and returning temporarily to command mode with keyboard input include clicking the <Cancel> button on a FLOPS message box, and the `keyboard` command to interrupt FLOPS when executing a program in command mode.

11.9 QUESTIONS

11.1 Why is debugging FLOPS programs more difficult than debugging programs written in conventional procedural computer languages such as C?

11.2 Can debugging be initiated from TFLOPS, the FLOPS IDE?

11.3 How is debugging carried out during a FLOPS run?

11.4 How can a FLOPS run be interrupted by entry of debug commands from the keyboard?

11.5 How can a FLOPS run be resumed after having been interrupted for entry of debug commands from the keyboard?

11.6 What are the three general types of debugging commands?

11.7 What are the three indispensable and most generally useful debugging commands?

11.8 When it is observed that a program has a defect, what is the first step in debugging?

11.9 What general technique is used to isolate a program defect?

11.10 After a program defect is isolated, what techniques can be used to find the bug itself?

12 Running and Debugging Expert Systems II: Sequential Rule-Firing

The topic of knowledge acquisition is a major one in AI circles. The most difficult part of knowledge acquisition in the AI sense is acquiring expert knowledge from a domain expert in order to construct the expert system itself. Jackson (1999) deals with this topic in Chapter 10; Scott et al. (1991) deal with it in detail. Since much has been written about knowledge acquisition in this sense, we will not attempt to cover it. Instead, we will deal here with the more mundane topic of acquiring data from a human user during a program run, and of the properties of sequential rule-firing programs in general.

In programs that interact with humans by a repeated question–answer sequence, parallel programs, as dealt with in Chapter 11, do not work well. Instead, programs that fire their rules sequentially, as in serial FLOPS, do quite well. There are certain other problems for which sequential rule-firing works better than parallel; we will briefly consider some of these.

12.1 DATA ACQUISITION: FROM A USER VERSUS AUTOMATICALLY ACQUIRED

Many expert systems acquire their data from a human user in a context-dependent fashion; that is, the next question to be asked depends on the answer to the previous question. Other expert systems acquire their data automatically, notably real-time on-line programs in which the computer is wired to the source of data. Between these two extremes there are other possibilities, such as reading data from disk files, or asking questions of a user in which the sequence of questions is fixed. In this chapter, we will consider the first data acquisition task, asking questions of a user when we do not know what question to ask next until the previous question has been answered. In this context, we decide to write our program in serial FLOPS and to fire our rules sequentially, one at a time.

In serial FLOPS, after each rule is fired we will reassess rule fireability. If one or more rules is newly fireable, we will select the rule to be fired by our rule-conflict

Fuzzy Expert Systems and Fuzzy Reasoning, By William Siler and James J. Buckley
ISBN 0-471-38859-9 Copyright © 2005 John Wiley & Sons, Inc.

algorithm and stack the rest on top of the backtrack stack; if no rule is newly fireable, we will pop a rule off the top of the backtrack stack and fire it. If there are no rules on the backtrack stack, we will revert to command mode. Clearly, the rule-conflict algorithm must be well understood. The FLOPS rule conflict algorithm is, at top level, quite simple; rules are first ranked by their pconf (combined rule and antecedent confidence) values, with the highest pconf at the top. In case of a tie, rules with the largest number of antecedent clauses rank highest; if there is still a tie, one of the highest ranking rules is randomly selected for firing. Jackson (1999) discusses rule-conflict algorithms under means-end analysis.

Note that each yes/no question we ask can be viewed as an attempt to verify an hypothesis. Questions that permit multiple discrete replies can be viewed as an attempt to verify one of a number of hypotheses. Questions such as "How old are you?" receive an answer, but do not by themselves test a hypothesis, and the reply does not directly affect the flow of program control, although subsequent rules may branch to different rules depending on analysis of the reply. In this chapter, we are establishing the basics of the repeated question–answer process, and will consider primarily the yes/no type of question. Once the basics are well understood, the reader can extend the treatment to more complex problems.

We can formulate the Q/A process more formally as a depth-first search of a decision tree, where each node in the tree corresponds to a hypothesis to be tested about our problem and a rule or rules to test whether this hypothesis is valid. (If we were using parallel FLOPS, we would have a breadth-first search.) The problem we will try to solve is finding out why an auto will not start.

The dynamics of the solution lend themselves to a graphical description shown in Figure 12.1, where R_i is the rule that tests H_i, the ith hypothesis.

Table 12.1 lists the preceding hypothesis (the last hypothesis verified), the next hypothesis to be tested, the verifying question, and the reply that verifies the hypothesis.

In Table 12.1 we begin at **Top**, where the initial data have made R1, R2, and R3 all newly fireable. R1 is picked and R2 and R3 are placed on the backtrack stack for

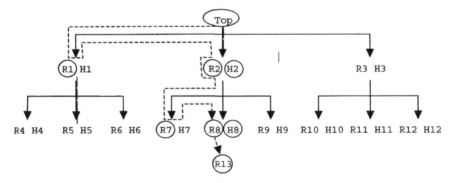

Figure 12.1   Decision Tree structure; hypotheses and rules, with typical rule-firing path in a sequential rule-firing program. A circle around a rule indicates rule firing; a circle around a hypothesis indicates hypothesis validation.

TABLE 12.1   Hypotheses in Decision Tree for auto2.fps

Preceding Hypothesis	Next Hypothesis	Question, Verifying Reply
TOP	engine won't turn over	Does your engine turn over, 'n'
engine won't turn over	dead battery	Do your lights come on, 'n'
engine won't turn over	blown fuse	Are any of your fuses blown, 'y'
engine won't turn over	battery connectors	Are your battery connectors loose, 'y'
TOP	no fuel to engine	Do you smell gas around carburetor, 'n'
no fuel to engine	out of gas	Does your gas gauge read empty, 'y'
no fuel to engine	bad fuel filte	Is your fuel filter clogged, 'y'
TOP	no spark	Can you see spark between plug and lead, 'n'
no spark	points misadjusted	Do your distributor points open slightly, 'n'
no spark	raining	Is it raining, 'y'
raining	ignition wet	Is your distributor or ignition wiring wet, 'y'

firing if our current path turns out to be the wrong one. R1 is fired, asking the user a question; the reply does not validate H1, and no rules are newly fireable. We reject that path and backtrack, firing R2. H2 is validated; so far, so good. Now R7, R8, and R9 are newly fireable. We pick R7 and fire it; the user's response does not validate H7 and no rules are newly fireable. We backtrack and fire R8; H8 is validated, and R13, the terminating rule, is made fireable. Hypothesis H8 is our answer. (If R8 had not verified H8, we would have continued to backtrack.) We have conducted a depth-first search of our decision tree.

In such a decision tree, it is very likely that several rules will be newly fireable concurrently. Very often we will have an idea of which of these rules initiates the path most likely to lead to our answer. Blind tree searches can be very time-consuming; it is much better to direct the search along the most likely paths. There is a very easy way to direct our search; given that (say) H1, H2, and H3 may be ranked in descending order of likelihood as H1, H3, and H2. We simply assign rule confidences to R1, R3, and R2, the highest going to R1, next highest to R3, and the lowest to R2. Alternatively, if our hypotheses are implemented as data items, we assign descending truth values to H1, H2, and H3. If we wish to compute truth values on the fly as the program run progresses, we can reassign computed truth values to the hypothesis data items. The ability to conduct a directed search is extremely important in expert systems.

12.2   WAYS OF SOLVING A TREE-SEARCH PROBLEM

The frequent backtracking makes it clear that this problem should be solved with sequential FLOPS. (If we used parallel FLOPS, we would ask three questions at once, very confusing for the user.) We will take up two ways of handling this problem.

The first way is based on the conventional notion that expert knowledge is embodied in rules. We will write separate rules for each hypothesis to be tested. This method obviously requires at least one rule for each hypothesis, plus one or two more for housekeeping and communication with the user. Auto1.fps is such a program; although it is very simple, it requires 14 rules. If the decision tree were more realistic, many more rules would be required; we would need one rule for each node in the decision tree, plus a rule to check that we have verified a terminal hypothesis, a rule to check if a non-terminal hypothesis is verified, and a rule to check if a non-terminal hypothesis is invalidated.

The second way of writing the program is based on a different concept of knowledge representation. We hypothesize that there are two kinds of expert knowledge; knowing what action to take given the available data, properly stored in rules, and expert factual knowledge, properly stored in databases. We will store the data for each node in a simple database, where each node will include the last hypothesis verified, the current hypothesis which the node is testing, the question to be asked, and the answer that will verify the hypothesis. If we have a database of expert knowledge, we will need rules to interpret the database. The rules in Auto2.fps are written to interpret the database. It requires only five rules to search a decision tree of any width or depth: one rule to ask the user an hypothesis-verifying question; one rule to fire if an hypothesis is verified; one rule to fire if an hypothesis in invalidated; a rule to fire if a terminal hypothesis is verified; and a rule to fire if we are unable to verify any hypothesis.

In either case, we direct the search path by assigning truth values to the various hypotheses, the most likely being given the highest truth values.

12.3   EXPERT KNOWLEDGE IN RULES; AUTO1.FPS

12.3.1   Auto1.fps Program: Partial Listing

```
:*******************************************************
:program AUTO1.FPS - why doesn't the auto start ?
:all knowledge stored in rules
:total rules = 14 = number of nodes in decision tree + 3
:number of rules goes up as complexity of tree increases
:*******************************************************

string = "Trouble diagnosis\: auto will not start.\n" ;
string + "Auto1.fps has 14 rules - expert knowledge in
rules.\n";
string + "compiling program auto1.fps...\n" ;
message "<string>";

declare Answer
  reply str
  verify str ;
```

```
declare Hypothesis
   working str ;

:++++++++++++++++++++++++++++++++++++++++++++++++++++++++++++++
:tests whether engine turns over
:rule r0
rule rconf 999 (goal Check whether engine turns over)
   IF (Answer)
      (in Hypothesis working.cf = 0)
   THEN
      reset ,
      input "Does the starter turn your engine over (y/n)
?\n" 1 reply lcase y n,
      in 1 verify = "n",
      in 2 working = "engine will not turn over";
:tests battery
:rule r1
rule rconf 999 (goal Check if dead battery)
   IF (in Answer reply = <R> AND verify = <R>)
      (in Hypothesis working = "engine will not turn over")
   THEN
      reset ,
      input "Do your lights come on (y/n) ?\n" 1 reply
      lcase y n,
      in 1 verify = "n" ,
      in 2 working = "dead battery" ;

:(Other similar rules, up through rule r10)


:-----------------------------------------

:report trouble found if at end of path
:rule r11 rule rconf  0  (goal Terminal hypothesis
verified - print trouble) IF (in Answer reply = <R> AND
verify = <R>)
      (in Hypothesis working = <H>)
   THEN
      message 'Your trouble is <H>\n' ,
      stop ;

:report failure to find trouble
:can't find the trouble
:rule r12
rule rconf  0  (goal Hypotheses all rejected - can not
find trouble)
   IF (in Answer reply.cf = 0)
```

```
      (in Hypothesis working.cf = 0)
    THEN
      message 'Cannot find the trouble. Call a tow
      truck.\n',
        exit ;

: - - - - - - - - - - - - - - - - - - - - - - - - - - - - - - - - - - - - - - - - - - - - -

:backtracks if answer not verified
:rule r13
rule rconf 999 (goal Backtracks if hypothesis rejected)
  IF (in Answer reply = <R> AND verify <> <R>)
    (in Hypothesis working = <X>)
  THEN
    reset ,
    write 'Checked <X> NG and backtracking\n' ,
    delete 1 ,
    delete 2 ;

:++++++++++++++++++++++++++++++++++++++++++++++++++++++++++++++

make Answer ;
make Hypothesis ;
message 'AUTO1.FPS ready to run -\n' ;
:run ;
:*******************************************************************
```

We can already see a major difference between this sequential program and the parallel program echo.par in Chapter 11. In the parallel program echo.par, we control the rule-firing by placing the rules in different blocks, and turning individual blocks on and off for firing. In the sequential programs auto1.fps and auto2.fps, all rules are by default in block zero, and we control the rule-firing sequence by controlling the confidences of the data and hence the antecedent confidence of the rules.

12.3.2   Running auto1.fps

Dynamics of running auto1.fps are illustrated by a program log, started after the program has been loaded and before any run; commands have been issued.

```
>>prstack;
LOCAL STACK (partially ordered)
******** STACK TOP      *********
rule r0 Time Tags 2 1 pconf 999
rule r4 Time Tags 2 1 pconf 998
rule r7 Time Tags 2 1 pconf 997
```

```
rule r12 Time Tags 2 1 pconf 0
******** STACK BOTTOM *********


PERMANENT STACK
******** STACK TOP     *********
******** STACK BOTTOM *********
>>
```

To begin with, four rules are fireable. Three of these test hypotheses at the top of the tree, and one (with pconf 0 so it will be the last to fire) reports that we have been unable to find an answer. We pick r0 for firing.

```
>>run 1;
```

Does the starter turn your engine over (y/n) ?

```
Y
```

Since the hypothesis being tested by r0 is given by its goal (goal Check whether engine fails to turn over), we have failed to validate the hypothesis and fire rule r13 (goal Backtracks if hypothesis rejected).

```
>>prstack;
LOCAL STACK (partially ordered)
******** STACK TOP     *********
rule r13 Time Tags 5 4 pconf 999
******** STACK BOTTOM *********

PERMANENT STACK
******** STACK TOP     *********
rule r4  Time Tags 2 1 pconf 998
rule r7  Time Tags 2 1 pconf 997
rule r12 Time Tags 2 1 pconf 0
******** STACK BOTTOM *********
>>run 1;
Checked engine will not turn over NG and backtracking
>>prstack;
LOCAL STACK (partially ordered)
******** STACK TOP     *********
******** STACK BOTTOM *********

PERMANENT STACK
******** STACK TOP     *********
rule r4  Time Tags 2 1 pconf 998
rule r7  Time Tags 2 1 pconf 997
```

```
rule r12 Time Tags 2 1 pconf 0
******** STACK BOTTOM *********
>>
```

After firing rule r13, we are forced to backtrack and fire rule r4 (goal Check if no fuel to engine).

```
>>run 1;
Do you smell gas at your carburetor (y/n) ?
N
>>prstack;
LOCAL STACK (partially ordered)
******** STACK TOP     *********
rule r5 Time Tags 8 7 pconf 999
rule r6 Time Tags 8 7 pconf 998
rule r11 Time Tags 8 7 pconf 0
******** STACK BOTTOM *********

PERMANENT STACK
******** STACK TOP     *********
rule r7 Time Tags 2 1 pconf 997
rule r12 Time Tags 2 1 pconf 0
******** STACK BOTTOM *********
>>
```

The hypothesis has been validated, and three rules are newly fireable; r5 (goal Check if no gas in tank), r6 (goal Check if clogged fuel filter) and r11 (goal Terminal hypothesis verified – print trouble).

```
>>run 1;
Does your gas gauge read empty (y/n) ?
y
>>
```

The hypothesis of an empty gas tank has been validated.

```
>>prstack;
LOCAL STACK (partially ordered)
******** STACK TOP     *********
rule r11 Time Tags 11 11 pconf 0
******** STACK BOTTOM *********

PERMANENT STACK
******** STACK TOP     *********
rule r6 Time Tags 8 7 pconf 998
rule r11 Time Tags 8 7 pconf 0
```

```
rule r7 Time Tags 2 1 pconf 997
rule r12 Time Tags 2 1 pconf 0
******** STACK BOTTOM **********
>>
```

Only one rule is newly fireable, r11 (goal: Terminal hypothesis verified – print trouble). We fire it.

```
>>run 1;
Your trouble is out of gas
Terminating FLOPS: 0 warnings, 0 errors
```

And our run is completed.

Incorrect rule-firing order is a major source of bugs in serial FLOPS programs, and the `prstack` debugging command is of paramount importance. If the rule-firing order observed is incorrect, we can rely on the debugging techniques developed in Chapter 11 for parallel programs to isolate the problem. Usually incorrect rule-firing order is due to incorrect data assignments, since we are using the data and their truth values to control the order in which rules are fired.

12.4   EXPERT KNOWLEDGE IN A DATABASE: AUTO2.FPS

While the approach taken by auto1.fps of placing expert knowledge in rules works, the resulting program is not easy to maintain; any change or addition requires modifying the program. The number of rules can be fairly large; one for each node in the decision tree plus three additional housekeeping rules, adding up to 14 rules in this very simple program. We now consider an alternate approach; placing expert knowledge in a database, and writing rules to interpret that database. This approach, used in auto2.fps, gives a five-rule program that is independent of the size of the decision tree. If we had a thousand nodes in our decision tree, we would still have only five rules. Our decision tree structure remains that of the hypotheses in Table 1; however, the multiple rules are different. In auto2.fps, we have only one hypothesis-verifying rule; r0. The other rules are housekeeping rules, to ensure that the rules are fired in the proper order and to tell the user what is going on.

12.4.1   Expert Knowledge Database Structure

First, let us consider the database itself. Each record represents a single node, defined by

```
declare Node        :library data
   hypo1 str        :preceding hypothesis
   hypo2 str        :current hypothesis
   question str     :hypothesis-verifying question
   verify str ;     :hypothesis-verifying response
```

If the preceding hypothesis hypo1 has been verified, then our database says that we should check whether hypo2 is true. To do this we ask question; if the reply is verify, then hypo2 has been verified. Any other reply invalidates hypo2.

Clearly, this is expert knowledge; knowing what tests should be made, and in what order, and how to verify if the test was passed or not is a matter for the skilled person. We have one other small database of messages to tell the user if a terminal hypothesis is verified:

```
declare Messages
   hypo str               :verified hypothesis
   message str;           :message to send
```

12.4.2   auto2.fps Program Listing

In the following listing, we have deleted some more-or-less cosmetic features.

```
:**********************************************************
:program AUTO2.FPS - general tree search program
:**********************************************************
:DECLARATIONS
declare Answer      :element to store user's reply
   reply str ;
declare Node        :library data
hypo1 str           :preceding hypothesis
hypo2 str           :current hypothesis
question str        :hypothesis-verifying question
verify str ;        :hypothesis-verifying response

declare Messages
   hypo str          :verified hypothesis
   message str ;     :message to send

declare Working     :working hypothesis at the moment
   hypo1 str         :preceding hypothesis
   hypo2 str         :hypothesis under test
   verify str ;      :hypothesis-verifying yresponse
:+++++++++++++++++++++++++++++++++++++++++++++++++++++++++++
RULES
:rule r0
rule (goal Sets up hypotheses, gets user response to
question)
IF (in Answer reply.cf = 0)
   (in Working hypo1 = <H1>)
   (in Node hypo1 = <H1> AND hypo2 = <H2> AND question = <Q>
AND
verify
    = <V>)
```

```
THEN
  reset,
  input "<Q> (y/n) ?\n" 1 reply lcase y n,
  in 2 hypo1 "<H1>" hypo2 "<H2>" verify "<V>",
  delete 3;
:rule r1
rule (goal fires if hypothesis accepted)
IF (in Answer reply = <R>)
  (in Working hypo1 = <H1> AND hypo2 = <H> AND verify =
  <R>)
  (in Node hypo1 = <H> AND hypo2 = <H2>)
THEN
  reset ,
  write 'Verified <H>, next hypothesis <H2>\n' ,
  in 1 reply.cf 0 ,
  in 2 hypo1 "<H>" hypo2 "<H2>";
:rule r2
rule (goal fires if hypothesis rejected)
IF (in Answer reply = <R>)
  (in Working hypo2 = <H> AND verify <> <R>)
THEN
  write 'rejected <H> and backtracking\n',
  delete 1 ,
  delete 2 ;
:writes out verified hypothesis and quits
:rule r3
rule rconf 0 (goal writes out verified terminal
hypothesis and quits)
IF (in Answer reply <R>)
  (in Answer reply = <R>)
  (in Working hypo2 = <H2> AND verify = <R>)
  (in Messages hypo = <H2> AND message = <M>)
THEN
  write 'Verified hypothesis <H2>\n' ,
  message nocancel '<M>\n' ,
  write 'Auto2 finished\n' ,
  exit;
:rule r4
rule 0 (goal fires if can\'t find the trouble)
IF (in Working hypo2.cf = 0)
THEN
  message 'Can\'t verify any hypothesis. Better call a
  mechanic!\n' ,
  exit ;
:++++++++++++++++++++++++++++++++++++++++++++++++++++++++
```

```
:MAKES
:expert knowledge database
transfer Node from node2.dat ;
transfer Messages from messages.dat ;

:internal memory elements
make Answer;
make Working hypo1 "TOP" ;
message 'AUTO2.FPS ready to run -\n' ;
:run ;
:exit ;
:**********************************************************
```

Our program maintains the same basic structure—declarations, rules, and makes, although this time we transfer data from two FLOPS data files using the `transfer` command. Since the ability to transfer knowledge to and from expert knowledge databases or to transfer structured data from one program to another is important, FLOPS furnishes a standard database format for such transfers, and a special program (FLEDIT) for creating and editing such files. Files node2.dat and messages.dat are such files, created and edited by FLEDIT. Since we are now relying on data external to the raw program itself, the expert-knowledge data files are an important source of possible bugs.

Here, we have departed from the traditional AI view that expert knowledge is embodied in rules. We divide expert knowledge into two categories; *skills* and *factual knowledge*. Skills are realized in rules; factual knowledge is stored in data bases. Anderson (1993) has independently come to the same conclusion. We have a basis for this distinction; one dictionary definition of learning is "the act or process of acquiring knowledge or skill". One important skill is the ability to interpret factual knowledge; the rules in auto2.fps embody precisely this skill.

To view the most important file, node2.dat, we must first invoke TFLOPS, then open auto2.fps. Next click on the TOOL menu item, then on FLEDIT. The main FLEDIT screen appears, with auto2.fps in the Flops File box. That is fine—we must now open our data file. Click on File, Open, and (in the Examples folder) node2.dat. The first record now pops up on our screen. We can now navigate in the database by clicking on First, Previous, Next, and Last, insert new records, create a new database, and other options that are more-or-less obvious. If we wish, we can also view messages.dat. We cannot view a data file until FLEDIT knows the corresponding FLOPS program, since the data declarations are stored there rather than in the data file.

12.4.3   Running and Debugging auto2.fps

As usual, we begin by commenting out the run; command at the bottom of the program. After one or two preliminary messages, the FLOPS prompt appears, and we begin with `prstack;`

```
>>prstack;
LOCAL STACK (partially ordered)
******** STACK TOP    **********
rule r0 Time Tags 24 1 23 pconf 1000
rule r0 Time Tags 24 5 23 pconf 996
rule r0 Time Tags 24 8 23 pconf 993
rule r4 Time Tags 24 pconf 0
******** STACK BOTTOM **********


PERMANENT STACK
******** STACK TOP    **********
******** STACK BOTTOM **********
```

We have three instances r0 newly fireable. We check what r0 is supposed to do:

```
>>explain goal r0;
Goal of rule r0 is:
Sets up hypotheses, gets user response to question
```

There is a slight disadvantage to this method; before, we could check the goal of a rule to find out exactly what it was trying to do, but now rule r0 tests all our hypotheses. We can, however, check the data that made the rule fireable to see what the hypothesis is that is being checked. We note that in the three instances of r0 up for firing, that the only data time tag not in common is the middle one, tt 1. We then enter

```
>>prmem 1;
(Node (
  ('tt',1)
  ('hypo1','TOP',1000)
  ('hypo2','engine won't turn over',1000)
  ('question','Does your engine turn over',1000)
  ('verify','n',1000)))
>>
```

Very good. We continue;

```
>>run 1;
Does your engine turn over (y/n) ?
Y
>>prstack;
LOCAL STACK (partially ordered)
******** STACK TOP    **********
rule r2 Time Tags 26 25 pconf 1000
******** STACK BOTTOM **********
```

```
PERMANENT STACK
******** STACK TOP     **********
rule r0 Time Tags 24 5 23 pconf 996
rule r0 Time Tags 24 8 23 pconf 993
rule r4 Time Tags 24 pconf 0
******** STACK BOTTOM **********
>>
```

What does r2 do?

```
>>explain goal r2;
Goal of rule r2 is:
fires if hypothesis rejected
>>run 1;
rejected engine won't turn over and backtracking
>>prstack;
LOCAL STACK (partially ordered)
******** STACK TOP     **********
******** STACK BOTTOM **********

PERMANENT STACK
******** STACK TOP     **********
rule r0 Time Tags 24 5 23 pconf 996
rule r0 Time Tags 24 8 23 pconf 993
rule r4 Time Tags 24 pconf 0
******** STACK BOTTOM **********
```

No rules are newly fireable, so we will pop another instance of r0 off the stack
and test another hypothesis.

```
>>run 1;
Do you smell gas around carburetor (y/n) ?
n
>>prstack;

LOCAL STACK (partially ordered)
******** STACK TOP     **********
rule r1 Time Tags 28 27 6 pconf 995
rule r1 Time Tags 28 27 7 pconf 994
rule r3 Time Tags 28 27 16 27 pconf 0
******** STACK BOTTOM **********
PERMANENT STACK
******** STACK TOP     **********
rule r0 Time Tags 24 8 23 pconf 993
rule r4 Time Tags 24 pconf 0
******** STACK BOTTOM **********
```

```
>>explain goal r1;

Goal of rule r1 is:
fires if hypothesis accepted
>>run 1;
Verified no fuel to engine, next hypothesis out of gas
>>prstack;
LOCAL STACK (partially ordered)
******** STACK TOP    **********
rule r0 Time Tags 30 6 29 pconf 995
rule r0 Time Tags 30 7 29 pconf 994
******** STACK BOTTOM **********
PERMANENT STACK
******** STACK TOP    **********
rule r1 Time Tags 28 27 7 pconf 994
rule r3 Time Tags 28 27 16 27 pconf 0
rule r0 Time Tags 24 8 23 pconf 993
rule r4 Time Tags 24 pconf 0
******** STACK BOTTOM **********
>>run 1;
Does your gas gauge read empty (y/n) ?
y
>>prstack;

LOCAL STACK (partially ordered)
******** STACK TOP **********
rule r3 Time Tags 32 31 17 31 pconf 0
******** STACK BOTTOM **********
PERMANENT STACK
******** STACK TOP    **********
rule r0 Time Tags 30 7 29 pconf 994
rule r1 Time Tags 28 27 7 pconf 994
rule r3 Time Tags 28 27 16 27 pconf 0
rule r0 Time Tags 24 8 23 pconf 993
rule r4 Time Tags 24 pconf 0
******** STACK BOTTOM **********
>>explain goal r3;
Goal of rule r3 is:
writes out verified terminal hypothesis and quits
>>run 1;
Verified hypothesis out of gas
Fill 'er up!
Auto2 finished
Terminating FLOPS: 0 warnings, 0 errors
```

And our run is over.

12.4.4   Advantages of Database-Defined Tree Search Method

The primary advantages of the "expert knowledge in the database" method for decision tree searching are *maintainability, flexibility* and *ease of debugging*. A decision-tree searching programming is likely to require maintenance by adding, deleting, or modifying the node structure. The one-rule-per-hypothesis method of auto1.fps requires program modification by changing or adding rules, with all the error possibilities that this entails. The expert-database method of auto2 leaves the program intact, and requires only modification of the database. Further, the availability of FLEDIT as a database editing tool means that we have available a database editor automatically customized for our particular application.

Flexibility comes about with the ability of the program to learn, if we wish, although the programming involved is not simple. We can modify the search direction by assigning hypothesis truth-values under program control. We even have the ability to add, delete, or modify hypotheses from the database under program control.

Ease of debugging is achieved by the availability of FLEDIT to debug our database, since FLEDIT is automatically customized for each data item in each data element involved.

12.5   OTHER APPLICATIONS OF SEQUENTIAL RULE FIRING

So far, we have dealt with the search of a decision tree, with particular application to the simple problem of determining why an auto will not start. The same general scheme can be applied to more complex problems.

12.5.1   Missionaries and Cannibals

We have on one bank of a river a certain number of missionaries, an equal number of cannibals, and a boat with limited carrying capacity. The problem is to get everyone to the other side of the river using the boat. The restriction is that neither in the boat nor on either bank can the cannibals outnumber the missionaries.

The problem is solved by simulation. After initialization, inputting the number of missionaries (and cannibals) and getting the boat capacity we check to see if the boat is big enough to solve the problem, and we begin the simulation.

The general scheme is to load missionaries and cannibals into the boat, starting on the left bank. The first passenger will always be a missionary; after that we use one rule to load a missionary and another rule to load a cannibal. These rules have equal priority, so one will be chosen at random, and the other placed on the backtrack stack. When the boat is ready to sail, we check to see if the cannibals outnumber the missionaries on shore or on the boat. If so, we fire a rule that prints a warning, but does not make any rules newly fireable; in consequence, we will pop the rule that loads the other kind of passenger, and check again. This time we should pass the check, and the cycle repeats until the boat is fully loaded. When this occurs, a rule becomes fireable that will cause the boat to sail to the right bank and unload.

If everyone has been carried to the right bank, we are done; if not, we repeat the loading/sailing cycle on the right bank (now loading only two passengers), then on the left bank, and so on, until we have finished our task.

While MC.FPS employs backtracking and rule confidences to help direct the search like the AUTO programs, its backtracking scheme is more complex.

Here is the output of an MC.FPS run.

```
Enter number miss (= # cann)
3
Enter max in boat
4
rule r1 - initializing
rule r2 - loading first missionary on left
rule r4 - loading cannibal on left
rule r4 - loading cannibal on left
rule r4 - loading cannibal on left
rule r8 - miss will get eaten on left in boat, backtracking
```

[rule r3 will now be popped off the backtrack stack.]

```
rule r3 - loading missionary on left
Boat holds miss 2 cann 2 total 4
leaving miss 1 cann 1 total 2
rule r5 - ready to sail from left
rule r19 - checking new bank totals on right
rule r20 - unloading on right
Trip complete - now miss 2 cann 2 on R bank
rule r10 - loading missionary on right
rule r11 - loading cannibal on right
Boat holds miss 1 cann 1 total 2
leaving miss 1 cann 1 total 2
rule r14 - ready to sail from right
rule r16 - checking new bank totals on left
rule r17 - unloading on left
Trip complete - now miss 2 cann 2 on L bank
rule r2 - loading first missionary on left
rule r4 - loading cannibal on left
rule r4 - loading cannibal on left
rule r3 - loading missionary on left
Boat holds miss 2 cann 2 total 4
leaving miss 0 cann 0 total 0
rule r5 - ready to sail from left
rule r19 - checking new bank totals on right
rule r20 - unloading on right
Trip complete - now miss 3 cann 3 on R bank
```

```
Missionaries and Cannibals finished
Terminating FLOPS 1: 0 warnings, 0 errors
```

This was a fairly lucky run—we only had to backtrack once.

Exercise MC.FPS. Open TFLOPS, then open examples/MC.FPS. Explore the flow of the program in detail, something like this:

```
>>prstack;
LOCAL STACK (partially ordered)
******** STACK TOP      **********
rule r4 Time Tags 9 8 4 pconf 1000
rule r3 Time Tags 9 8 4 pconf 0
******** STACK BOTTOM **********

PERMANENT STACK
******** STACK TOP      **********
******** STACK BOTTOM **********
>>goal r4;

Goal of rule r4 is:
Load a cannibal on left
>>goal r3;

Goal of rule r3 is:
Load another missionary on left
>>run 1;

rule r4 - loading cannibal on left
>>prdata Boat;

(Boat (
  ('tt',11)
  ('miss',1,1000)
  ('cann',1,1000)
  ('total',2,1000)
  ('state','L',1000)))
>>prstack;
...
LOCAL STACK (partially ordered)
******** STACK TOP      **********
rule r4 Time Tags 11 4 10 pconf 1000
rule r5 Time Tags 11 4 10 pconf 999
rule r3 Time Tags 11 4 10 pconf 0
******** STACK BOTTOM **********
PERMANENT STACK
```

```
******** STACK TOP    **********
rule r3 Time Tags 9 8 4 pconf 0
******** STACK BOTTOM **********
>>
```

Use any other debugging commands that might help illuminate the flow of the program.

12.6 RULES THAT MAKE THEMSELVES REFIREABLE: RUNAWAY PROGRAMS AND RECURSION

Rules can make themselves refireable very simply; by modifying an antecedent datum so that the modified data still satisfy the antecedent. This can be the source of an annoying bug causing a runaway program, or can be the basis of a powerful technique, *recursion*. In recursion, the same rule or rules fire over and over again with something different each time they fire until some criterion is met that terminates the process.

We have two example programs to illustrate recursion, but will not go into them in any detail; the student may run and explore them at will.

Program LOGIST.FPS solves a simple ordinary differential equation, that for logistic growth or a population. The differential equation is

$$\frac{dP}{dt} = rs\left(1 - \frac{s}{K}\right)dt$$

where P is the size of the population, r is the growth rate for an individual, K is the population size at equilibrium (carrying capacity), and t is time.

The program has three rules, one of which is to terminate the run. Rule r0 calculates the time derivative of the population; rule r1 updates the population size from the first derivative. These two rules fire recursively until either of two termination criteria is met. At that point, rule r2 fires and notifies the user that the run is over.

Program HANOI.FPS is also recursive, but a bit hairier than LOGIST. Hanoi solves the Tower of Hanoi problem. In this problem, we have three vertical spindles, and a number of disks with holes in their center placed on one spindle in decreasing order of size. The problem is to move the disks one at a time from one spindle to another until all disks are on spindle 3. The restriction is that a larger disk can never be placed on a smaller one.

HANOI has five rules. Rule r0 simply inputs the number of disks to be moved; r1 quits when finished; r2, r3, and r4 do the work recursively. The processing rules are made fireable recursively when r3 creates a new instance of the data that made the rules first fireable, or r4 modifies that instance; rule r2 deletes the new instance when we are finished with it. Running HANOI with three or four disks will give a good picture of its recursion scheme in operation; it is not all that simple!

Note that recursion is not limited to systems that fire their rules sequentially by default, as do FLOPS programs with a .fps suffix. A simple recursive program like LOGISTIC.FPS can simply be renamed LOGISTIC.PAR, and will operate identically when run as a parallel program. But this is unusual; for example, HANOI.FPS will not run properly at all as a parallel program.

However, since FLOPS can switch back and forth between serial and parallel modes, we can utilize this capability to embed serial recursion in a parallel program. HANOI.PAR starts out in parallel mode, and fires its first rule (r0) in that mode. But r0 has the command `parallel;` in its consequent, and the recursive rules are fired in serial mode.

12.7 SUMMARY

When our expert system wants to work interactively with a user to acquire information, so that the next question to be asked depends on the answer to the previous question, sequential rule-firing is clearly indicated. However, sequential rule-firing is only required during the data acquisition phase; if it seems desirable, we can switch to parallel rule-firing after the information has required us to analyze it.

We now consider the choice of methods between having one rule for each hypothesis (auto1.fps) and having one data element instance for each hypothesis (auto2.fps). It may well be better to write and debug our first prototype program like auto1.fps, with only a few hypotheses to be tested, with one rule for each hypothesis. After this small prototype is debugged, we can switch to the more concise and easily maintainable method of placing our hypotheses and related information in a database, with rules to interpret the database (auto2.fps). The availability of FLEDIT as an automatically customized database edit helps make the database method more user-friendly.

12.8 QUESTIONS

12.1 How is acquiring data from a human user different from automatically acquiring data from some instrument?

12.2 What are the nodes in a decision tree?

12.3 In a depth-first search of a decision tree, what happens if a hypothesis is accepted?

12.4 What is a rule conflict algorithm? What is its relevance to a depth-first search of a decision tree?

12.5 Under what circumstance does backtracking take place?

12.6 What happens during backtracking?

12.7 What two different concepts of knowledge representation can be used when writing rules to conduct a depth-first search or a decision tree?

12.8 What are the advantages and disadvantages of placing knowledge in rules or in databases?

12.9 How can we determine whether a problem is best solved by a depth-first (sequential rule-firing) or breadth-first (parallel rule-firing) search of possibilities?

13 Solving "What?" Problems when the Answer is Expressed in Words

13.1 GENERAL METHODS

As noted previously, fuzzy control problems expect a numerical answer. Because of the tremendous success of fuzzy control, fuzzy systems people, with a few exceptions, notably Earl Cox (1999), James Baldwin et al. (1995), and Combs and Andrews (1998), have concentrated on that field. When problems demand a non-numeric answer, they have often been "solved" by getting a numeric answer, then relating this number to a word response. However, this is quite a dangerous method. Suppose, for example, that we have a problem in medical diagnosis, where the three remaining possibilities are disease A, disease B, and disease C. We assign 1 to disease A, 2 to disease B, and 3 to disease C. We run our program, defuzzify fuzzy set disease, and find that the answer is 2; we confidently report that the patient has disease B. In fact, our data rule out disease B, but are unable to distinguish between disease A and disease C. Our answer, the average of 1 and 3, is completely wrong.

How should we handle this problem correctly? There are two general ways. In the first way, we set up a discrete fuzzy set, say Disease, with members {A, B, C}. We use our program to assign grades of membership (truth values, truth values) to A, B, and C. After the program is run, we report the memberships in fuzzy set Disease: A (500), B (0), C (500). The conclusion, that either the patient has both diseases or more tests should be run for differential diagnosis between A and C, is very obvious. If our results are not so clear cut and we wish a general idea as to how confident we are that we have ruled out all but a single disease, we can check the ambiguity and fuzziness of fuzzy set Disease.

It can happen that we do not know in advance what the possible outcomes are. We note that it is possible to declare a fuzzy set at run time, by including the data declaration in the consequent of a rule.

In the second way, we set up a string variable named Disease, and let our analysis create instances of Disease with the appropriate truth values as the data indicate.

Fuzzy Expert Systems and Fuzzy Reasoning, By William Siler and James J. Buckley
ISBN 0-471-38859-9   Copyright © 2005 John Wiley & Sons, Inc.

This method is less convenient than the discrete fuzzy set method just above, but may be more flexible in some cases. This is especially true for our program if the possible outcomes are initially unknown and the program discovers what the possible outcomes might be one by one as the program run progresses.

In general, fuzzy sets are useful for storing preliminary conclusions, and for output when more than one outcome is concurrently possible (as in medical diagnosis); strings are useful for storing final conclusions when only one outcome is possible, and sometimes for storing preliminary conclusions when for some reason it is inconvenient to define the fuzzy set of possible outcomes in advance.

The domain of problems whose answers are expressed in words is enormous. The limitation imposed by restricting answers to numeric can be imagined if you could understand everything that was said to you, but could only respond in numbers. So far, we have no generally agreed-upon name for this class of problems; we sometimes call them non-numeric problems, sometimes classification problems. Lately, Lotfi Zadeh has used the term "Approximate X", where X can be almost anything.

We will present three FLOPS programs to handle "What?" questions: iris.par, to classify Iris plants; echo.par, to classify regions of ultrasound images of a beating human heart; and schizo.par, to derive preliminary psychological diagnoses from a set of behavioral traits. Iris.par uses four numeric input data; echo.par uses three numeric and one non-numeric data; and schizo.par uses only the truth values of non-numeric data.

13.2   IRIS.PAR: WHAT SPECIES IS IT?

Since classification is a very common problem, a number of test data bases are commonly available. One is the famous Iris data base (Fisher 1936), difficult to classify correctly. The database has six items for each of 150 Iris plant specimens: an identifying specimen number; four numeric features: petal length, petal width, sepal length and sepal width; and correct species name (setosa, versicolor, or virginica). Our program will try to classify each of the 150 specimens properly, with as few rules as possible.

We will use parallel rule firing, since it is not necessary to elicit information from a user; all the information, the values of the features of the 150 specimens, will be available at the beginning of the run from a disk file.

Overall, our plan will be to set up a discrete fuzzy set species with members setosa, versicolor, and virginica; fuzzify the input features; determine the species from the fuzzified features; and output the results to the user.

Remember that our default rule-firing threshold is 500. That will not work for us—we need to fire just about everything fireable, so we set our rule-firing threshold to 1 by

```
Thresh 1:
```

13.2.1 Planning Our Data Elements and Membership Functions

First, we will need a data element to hold the input data. This choice seems easy:

```
declare Data N int PL flt PW flt SL flt SW flt orig str;
```

where N is the specimen ID number, PL is the petal length, PW petal width, SL sepal length, SW sepal width, and orig the correct species of this specimen as biologically determined.

We also need another data element (say Iris) to hold processed data about our specimen, including the discrete fuzzy set representation of input numbers PL, PW, SL, and SW. Most people familiar with fuzzy control might choose fuzzy sets something like this:

```
declare Iris
  PetalL fzset (Small Medium Large)
  PetalW fzset (Small Medium Large)
...
```

While this seems quite reasonable at first glance, in fact it is far from the best choice. We do not really care whether a petal length is Small, Medium, or Large; we want to know whether it is characteristic of setosa, versicolor or virginica. The following is much better:

```
declare Iris
  PetalL fzset (setosa, versicolor, virginica)
  PetalW fzset (setosa, versicolor, virginica)
...
```

These fuzzy sets will serve us well when we have to define membership functions for fuzzifying the input data; we can draw our membership functions from the characteristics of plants belonging to the three species.

In addition to the fuzzified features PetalL ..., we need a fuzzy set of classifications:

```
Species fzset (setosa versicolor virginica)
```

and a place to store the original correct classification for checking our results, and (since we can expect contradictory classifications to be reported) a place to put a final crisp classification.

We can now lay out our next data element in detail.

```
declare Iris
  N int  :specimen ID number
  PetalL fzset (setosa versicolor virginica)
  PetalW fzset (setosa versicolor virginica)
  SepalL fzset (setosa versicolor virginica)
  SepalW fzset (setosa versicolor virginica)
```

```
species fzset (setosa versicolor virginica)
orig str    :correct classification
final str;  :final classification
```

Note that we do NOT use the common linguistic terms such as Small, Medium, Large. Instead, we use the names of the species that we are seeking to determine.

Here is the DECLARATIONS section of our program, less cosmetics:

```
declare Data N int PL flt PW flt SL flt SW flt orig str;
declare Iris
  N int  :specimen ID number
  PetalL fzset  (setosa versicolor virginica)
  PetalW fzset  (setosa versicolor virginica)
  SepalL fzset  (setosa versicolor virginica)
  SepalW fzset  (setosa versicolor virginica)
  species fzset (setosa versicolor virginica)
  orig str    :correct classification
  final str;  :final classification
```

Now we must provide membership functions for our fuzzy sets of features. We could spend a lot of time on this, but for our purposes, we will simply take the lowest, highest, and median values for each feature and species from a training subset of the data, even-numbered specimens. We will use normal (bell-shaped) membership functions, with the peak being at the median point, the lower 0.5 membership point being at the midpoint minus twice the distance to the lowerpoint, range, and the higher zero point being at the midpoint plus twice the distance to the lowerpoint. This way, the range of the membership function is twice the range of the training set, giving a reasonable certainty that we will not miss anything. We show in Figure 13.1 the stylized membership functions for PetalL, shown as triangular rather than normal for clarity.

The membership function definitions for PetalL are

```
memfunct Iris PetalL normal
: Training set, even numbers
  setosa 3.60 5.00 5.00 6.40
  versicolor 3.90 5.90 5.90 7.50
  virginica 5.00 6.50 6.50 9.30;
```

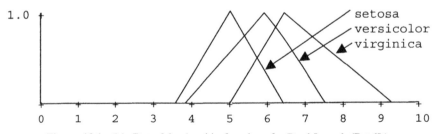

Figure 13.1 Iris Data. Membership functions for Petal Length (PetalL).

13.2.2 Writing Our Rules: Getting Started

We have accomplished our first task, defining our data. Now we can lay out a general outline not of individual rules, but of the rule block structure. The structure below in Table 13.1 may seem very simple, but it does what we need to do.

In Block 0, we need one rule to create instances of Iris corresponding to the input raw data, and one rule to fuzzify the input data, for a total of two. In block 1, we need one rule for each classification, or three rules. In block 2, we need one rule to detect incorrect classifications, and one rule to detect specimens that we failed to classify at all, or two rules. This gives us a total of seven rules we must write.

We have supplied a FLOPS data file, iris.dat that we can use to read in the data after we have compiled our rules, but before we have actually run any. Note that a rule does not know anything about data read in *before* the rule is compiled. So we assume that memory element Data will have its 150 sets of values read in from a disk file before we start to fire any rules.

Reading in the data has created 150 instances of memory element Data, but we have no instances of our most important data element, Iris. We need to create one instance of Iris for every instance of Data, and need to copy the original classification and the specimen ID number from Data to Iris. Our first rule does this:

```
:rule r0
rule block 0 (goal Make instances of Iris from instances
of Data)
IF (in Data N = <N> AND orig = <ORIG>)
THEN
  write "Making instance of specimen <N>\n",
  make Iris N = <N> orig = "<ORIG>";
```

When we start to fire this rule, there will be 150 instances of Data in working memory, and 150 fireable instances of rule r0. Since we are running parallel FLOPS, all instances will fire effectively at once with minimal systems overhead.

Now that the data are in and our instances of Iris created, we can fuzzify our input data. After that we will be ready to classify our specimens. We will place our classification rules in a separate rule block 1. Instead of writing separate metarules to control rule firing, we will place the rule firing controls directly in the rule consequents,

```
:rule r1
rule block 0 (goal Fuzzify input data)
IF (in Data N = <N> AND PL = <PL> AND PW = <PW> AND SL = <SL>
```

TABLE 13.1 Rule Block Structure for iris.par

Block	Function	Number of Rules
0	Makes instances of Iris, fuzzifies input data	2
1	Classifies specimens	3
2	Detects incorrect or missing classifications	2

```
  AND SW = <SW>)
  (in Iris N = <N>)
THEN
  write "Fuzzifying specimen <N>\n",
  fuzzify 2 PetalL <PL>,
  fuzzify 2 PetalW <PW>,
  fuzzify 2 SepalL <SL>,
  fuzzify 2 SepalW <SW>,
  fire block 0 off,
  fire block 1 on;
```

13.2.3   Writing Our Rules: Classifying the Specimens

Now we are ready for our classification rules. Our forethought in fuzzifying the input data into linguistic terms such as "setosa" instead of terms like "Medium" makes this task very easy. We do have to remember to activate the next rule block for analysis of our results.

Since the Iris database is well known for its difficulty, we expect to have many contradictions. The simplest method of resolving contradictions is also the least reliable, but for the sake of simplicity we will adopt it and take the most likely of the classifications as being the correct one. To do this, each classification rule tries to set the value of final in Iris to a string representing the classification at which the rule has arrived, by the consequent command in 1 final is "Iris-setosa" (versicolor, virginica). We now depend on FLOPS' monotonic reasoning to store the most likely value. If the old value of final has a truth value less than the new value, the old value will be replaced; but if the old value of final has a truth value greater than the new value, the old value will not be replaced. (If the two truth values happen to be precisely equal, the old value will be replaced anyhow. Handling equal truth values differently can also be done, but it takes more programming than we want to get into right now.)

```
:rule r2
rule block 1 (goal classify as setosa)
IF (in Iris PetalL is setosa AND PetalW is setosa AND
   SepalL is setosa AND SepalW is setosa)
THEN
  write "Classifying as setosa conf <pconf>\n",
  in 1 species is setosa,
  in 1 final is "Iris-setosa",
  fire block 1 off,
  fire block 2 on;
```

```
:rule r3                                                        (13.1)
rule block 1 (goal classify as versicolor)
IF (in Iris PetalL is versicolor AND PetalW is versicolor
    AND SepalL is versicolor AND SepalW is versicolor)
```

```
THEN
  write "Classifying as versicolor conf <pconf>\n",
  in 1 species is versicolor,
  in 1 final is "Iris-versicolor",
  fire block 1 off,
  fire block 2 on;

:rule r4
rule block 1 (goal classify as virginica)
IF (in Iris PetalL is virginica AND PetalW is virginica
  AND SepalL is virginica AND SepalW is virginica)
THEN
  write "Classifying as virginica conf <pconf>\n",
  in 1 species is virginica,
  in 1 final is "Iris-virginica",
  fire block 1 off,
  fire block 2 on;
```

13.2.4   Writing Our Rules: Reporting Results

We do not really need to report correct answers, since our program is supposed to detect these and anyway, there would be too many of them unless we have a really gross bug. So, let us be content with reporting classification incorrect classifications and failures to reach any classification at all. We need two rules for these reports.

```
:rule r5
rule block 2 (goal detect incorrect classifications)
IF (in Iris N = <N> AND final = <FL> AND orig = <ORIG> AND final
  <> <ORIG>)
THEN
  prmem 1,
  message "Specimen <N> incorrect\: <FL> should be <ORIG>\n";
:rule r6
rule block 2 (goal detect unclassified specimens)
IF (in Iris N = <N> AND species.setosa = 0 AND species.
  versicolor = 0 AND species.virginica = 0)
THEN
  message "Specimen <N> unclassified\n";
```

13.2.5   Setting Our Initial Data

This is a fairly easy task, since all out data are held in one FLOPS data file; iris.dat. Iris.dat is a FLOPS blackboard data file, readable by FLEDIT, and created from the original data file downloaded from the Internet by adding one additional field to the beginning of each record. That field is "Data", the name of the data element. (FLOPS needs this name to know what to do with the data in the rest of the record.)

```
transfer -conf Data from myiris.dat;
fire all off;
fire block 0 on;
```

We have used a new command, `transfer`, that reads FLOPS blackboard data files from disk or writes them to the disk. The −conf in the transfer command means that truth values are omitted, and assumed to be maximum. In blackboard files, the first field in each record is the name of the data structure that holds the description of the contents of the record. In our case, the data descriptor is Data, with the declaration

```
declare Data N int PL flt PW flt SL flt SW flt orig str;
```

The data record itself has "Data" in the first field to identify the data format, and then has the rest of the data in the same sequence as the data declaration. Here is the first record of myiris.dat:

```
"Data", 1, 5.10, 3.50, 1.40, 0.20, "Iris-setosa"
```

The input data are crisp, so we use the −conf flag to tell FLOPS that the data in this file are crisp and do not require truth values; all truth values are 1000.

Our program is now ready to run.

13.2.6 Running iris.par

Since this is a parallel program, all rules concurrently fireable will be concurrently fired. Since we have 150 instances of data, we will usually have at least 150 rules fireable at the same time, and "run 1;" will usually run 150 or more rules at once. To help the user understand the program run better, we have added a sequence of alternating message and run 1; commands at the end of the program, thus:

```
message "IRIS.PAR ready to run and classify 150 specimens";
message "Block 0 - creating instances of Iris\n";
run 1;
message "Block 0 - fuzzifying data\n";
run 1;
message "Block 1 - classifying data\n";
run 1;
message "Block 2 - detecting errors\n";
run 1;
message "Iris.par finished";
exit;
```

We go ahead and run the program. We see right away that a lot of rules are being fired. We can cut down the amount of output by commenting out the write commands, so we do this. While we are at it, we also comment out the prmem command in the rule that detects incorrect classifications. Our stripped-down output is now:

```
IRIS.PAR ready to run and classify 150 specimens
Block 0 - creating instances of data
Block 0 - fuzzifying data
Block 1 - classifying data
Block 2 - detecting errors
Specimen 78 incorrect: Iris-virginica should be
Iris-versicolor
Specimen 84 incorrect: Iris-virginica should be
Iris-versicolor
Specimen 53 incorrect: Iris-virginica should be
Iris-versicolor
Specimen 107 incorrect: Iris-versicolor should be
Iris-virginica
Specimen 71 incorrect: Iris-virginica should be
Iris-versicolor
Iris.par finished
Terminating FLOPS: 0 warnings, 0 errors
```

Our output now makes it clear what steps the program takes to solve the problem. We also see that for a very simple program with very simple membership functions, we have not done badly on a problem well known for its difficulty; our first attempt classified 97% of all specimens correctly.

13.2.7 Improving iris.par

There are several ways of improving the performance of a classification program. First, we can tune our membership functions. Next, we can improve our resolution of contradictions, possibly by adding more attributes; in the Iris program, we could try adding the petal and sepal aspect ratios. We can look for a modified approach to our classification rules; Abe defined an ellipsoidal membership space, rather than the rectangular box most workers have used. All three methods have been employed by other workers attempting to classify the Iris data, but we will be satisfied with having achieved a respectable preliminary classification rate and will proceed to a real-world problem. In fact, FLOPS was originally written to solve the next problem!

13.3 ECHOCARDIOGRAM PATTERN RECOGNITION

When attempting to diagnose heart problems, cardiologists frequently examine ultrasound images of the heart; very fuzzy cross-sectional images, recorded about

20 times a second. Our cardiologists (busy as most doctors are) wanted to have a computer look at digitized echocardiograms to determine the volume changes throughout the heart cycle. We will look here at a somewhat simplified version of the expert system for classifying regions of the image according to their anatomical significance (Siler et al., 1987).

In classical image processing of this nature, there are usually three steps: *segmentation, feature extraction*, and *classification*. We decided to perform the first two by conventional procedural language programs. First, we mapped out regions of interest in the heart image. Next, we extracted numerical features of these regions: area, x- and y-centroid coordinates, and measures of shape (not needed in the final classification program). Finally, we planned a fuzzy expert system to classify the regions. FLOPS was originally written as a fuzzy superset of an AI-based non-fuzzy expert system shell written by Charles Forgy of Carnegie-Mellon University, OPS5 (Brownston et al., 1985).

The segmentation program was based on using a cell-automation algorithm that worked quite successfully. Region feature extraction, into area; centroid position; and whether the region touched the border of each region, was a straightforward task. Now came the FLOPS region classification program.

13.3.1 Echocardiogram Pattern Recognition: Data Declarations

Since we could not be sure what classifications would be needed, we could not use the technique of iris.par of fuzzifying numeric features into a fuzzy set whose members were classifications; instead, we used the conventional {Small, Medium, Large} type of discrete fuzzy set representation of our features.

The first data declaration is straightforward, simply the raw data for each region.

```
:raw data
declare Data
   frame int    :image frame number
   rnum int     :region number within frame
   area flt     :region area, pixels
   xbar flt     :region x-centroid, pixels from left border
   ybar flt     :region y-centroid, pixels from top border
   border str;  :"Y" if region touches border, else "N"
```

Now we declare the region data used in classification.

```
:region characteristics
declare Region   :global region characteristics
   frame int     :frame number
   rnum int      :region number within frame
   area fznum    :global region features
   size fzset    :word equivalent of area
      (TINY SMALL MEDIUM LARGE HUGE)
```

```
xbar fznum          :x-centroid
xpos fzset          :word equivalent of xbar
  (FAR-LEFT LEFT CENTER RIGHT FAR-RIGHT)
ybar fznum          :y-centroid
ypos fzset          :word equivalent of ybar
  (VERY-HIGH HIGH MIDDLE LOW VERY-LOW)
border str          :YES or NO
class fzset         :classifications
  (
  ARTIFACT          :artifact
  LUNG              :lungs
  LA                :left atrium
  LV                :left ventricle
  LA + LV           :merged left atrium and ventricle
  RA                :right atrium
  RV                :right ventricle
  RA + RV           :merged right atrium and ventricle
  LA + LV + RA + RV :all four chanbers artifactually
                     merged
  )
final str;          :final classification
```

A few more classifications were actually used, but most are included above.

We also add a declaration, used by a metarule to control rule block firing that holds the currently enabled rule block:

```
:rule firing control
declare Enable
  block int;
```

and a data element to sequence output by region numbers:

```
:printout control
declare Print
  rnum int;
```

To simplify the program, we used the technique first met in auto2.fps of putting expert knowledge in a database. But this time we will use the database knowledge to generate the actual rules for classification automatically. Remember that a rule can have any FLOPS command in its consequent; this includes the rule command itself, so a rule can generate other rules.

```
:definitions for creating classification rules
declare Classdef
```

```
goal str size str xp str yp str class str borderop str
border
    str;
```

The data in Classdef are all strings that will be assembled into the actual rules.

13.3.2 Echocardiogram Pattern Recognition: Creating Classification Rules from a Database

A typical hand-coded classification rule might be

```
rule r0 (goal Classify region as LV)
IF (in Region size is LARGE AND xpos is RIGHT
    AND ypos is MIDDLE AND border = "NO")
THEN class is LV;
```

We can use this rule to construct a template for classification rules, using variables for actual attribute values:

```
rule r1 (goal <G>)
IF (in Region size is <SZ> AND xpos is <X> AND ypos is
<Y> AND border <OP> <B>)
THEN class is <CL>;
```

The actual values of variables <CL>, <SZ>, <X>, <Y>, <OP>, and <B> are taken from the entries in our classification rule database. Typical database entries are shown in Table 13.2.

The data in the first row of Table 13.2 define a rule for classifying a region as RV (Right Ventricle). When the values are substituted for the variables in the rule template given in rule r1, we get this rule:

```
rule (goal Classify region as LV)
IF (in Region size is LARGE AND xpos is RIGHT
```

TABLE 13.2 Typical Entries in Database for Creating Classification Rules

goal <G>	Class <CL>	Size <SZ>	Xpos <XP>	Ypos <YP>	borderop <OP>	border <B>
"Classify region as LV"	LV	LARGE	RIGHT	MIDDLE	" = "	"NO"
"Classify region as RA"	RA	SMALL	LEFT	LOW	" = "	"NO"
"Classify region as ARTIFACT"	ARTIFACT	TINY	""	""	"<>"	""

```
    AND ypos is MIDDLE AND border = "NO")
THEN class is LV;
```

"borderop" is included in Table 13.2 to take care of classes in which we do not care whether the region touches the border or not; all we demand is that there be some entry for border, even a blank.

The main reason for automatically creating rules from a database is to improve program simplicity and especially maintainability. If we wish to modify the classification rules, there is no need to rework the program; just modify the database. And the convenience of editing the database with FLEDIT makes interfacing with non-programmer personnel much easier. We have not taken this all the way; a small text file would permit automatically generating the data declarations, making it easy to add (or subtract) classifications.

There are also data declarations used for run control, discussed in the next sections.

```
:rule firing control
declare Enable
  block int;

:printout control
declare Print
  rnum int;
```

13.3.3 The Organization of echo.par

Data element Enable just above is often useful for sequencing sequential firing of blocks of rules. Program echo.par has 10 rule blocks: 0–8 for the actual image processing rules, and block 20 for a metarule to control which rules are enabled for firing and another rule to switch from parallel to serial rule-firing mode when it is time to print out our answers.

The list of rule blocks and their functions is given in Table 13.3.

13.3.4 Metarules to Control Activation of Rule Blocks

Block firing control here is a very simple matter—we turn off the block number currently active, increment the block number, and activate the new block. When we have finished block 7, we will switch to serial mode for firing block 8. After block 8 is fired, we are all done.

In AI parlance, *metarules* are rules to control the rule-firing sequence. A metarule is sometimes quite complex, but in iris.par it is extremely simple—it sequences firing of rule blocks sequentially. Here is the very simple metarule of block 20:

```
:rule r23
rule block 20 (goal Enables blocks sequentially)
```

TABLE 13.3   Rule Block Functions in echo.par

```
:Block 0 - creates preliminary classification rules,:converts
  data to fznums
:Block 1 - fuzzifies data, writes out data converted to fuzzy
  numbers
:Block 2 - write out fuzzy sets, get preliminary
  classifications
:from block 2 classification rules created by r1
:Block 3 - writes preliminary classifications to screen
:Block 4 - commences resolution of contradictions
:Block 5 - more conflict resolution
:Block 6 - more conflict resolution
:Block 7 - checks that all chambers are present,
:stores final classifications
:Block 8 - writes classifications to screen in serial mode
:Block 20 - block firing control
```

```
IF (in Enable block = <B> AND block < 8)
THEN
  write 'Turning off rule block <B>, activating next
    block\n',
  fire block <B> off,
  in 1 block = (<B> + 1),
  fire block (<B> + 1) on;
```

Rule r23 is perfectly straightforward; we turn the current block (<B>) off, increment the block number in Enable, and turn the next block on.

```
:rule r24
rule block 20 (goal Switches to serial mode after block 7
fires)
IF (in Enable block = 7)
THEN
  make Print rnum = 1,
  message "Switching from parallel to serial mode for
  printout\n",
  serial;
```

This rule works in concert with the previous rule when Block 7 has been fired. We make an instance of the print control data element Print and initialize it, then switch from parallel rule-firing to serial rule-firing, so we can control the firing of individual rules conveniently.

Metarules can be very much more complex than this, so program flow can be directed as the progress of the program and the data dictate.

13.3.5 New Features of Rules in echo.par

Changing Crisp But Uncertain Input Numbers to Fuzzy Numbers. We have already covered the most important new rule feature, the creation of new rules from a database of expert knowledge. Another new feature is the creation of fuzzy numbers from crisp numbers. Consider this rule:

```
rule block 0 (goal Moves input data to "Region", converts to
fuzzy numbers)
IF (in Data frame = <F> AND rnum = <N> AND area = <A>        (13.2)
  AND xbar = <X> AND ybar = <Y> border = <B>)
THEN
  make Region frame = <F> rnum = <N> area = <A> 10 0.1
    xbar = <X> 20 0 ybar = <Y> 20 0 border = "<B>";
```

The antecedent of this rule assigns variable names to some crisp input numbers. Of these, the frame and region number are inherently crisp, being known to complete precision. However, this is not true of the area and centroid coordinates xbar and ybar; these are quite subject to errors of measurement, and should more properly be represented by fuzzy numbers. The rule consequent takes care of this. The instruction make Region ... area $= <A> 10\ 0.1$ ... creates an area in an instance of Region that is a fuzzy number. The new area will be an s-shaped fuzzy number with absolute uncertainty 10 ($+/-$ 10 pixels) and a relative uncertainty of 10% [$0.1 * <A>$ (area) pixels]. Similarly for the centroid measurements; the crisp xbar and ybar in Data are transformed into fuzzy numbers in Region with absolute uncertainty 20 pixels and zero relative uncertainty. These fuzzy numbers have uncertainties that are consistent with the process of feature extraction from noisy echocardiogram images.

Resolving Contradictions. Of more importance are the rules to resolve contradictory preliminary classifications. We are virtually guaranteed to have contradictions; the rules for classifying as RV (right ventricle) and as RA + RV (merged right atrium and right ventricle have identical antecedents. Here, we cannot use the cavalier approach of taking the most likely classification that we used in iris.par. Instead, we use logic and an additional piece of information; the frame in which the Region appears.

Suppose that in the same frame we have a region classified both as RA + RV and RV. If in the same frame we also have a region classified as RA, then the classification as RV is correct and that as RA + RV is wrong; the RA cannot appear twice in a single frame. Our rule for this purpose is

```
rule block 4 (goal Rule out RA+RV if RV and RA+RV and RA)
```

$$(13.3)$$

```
   IF (in Region frame = <FR> AND rnum = <N1> AND class is
      RV AND class is RA + RV)
      (in Region frame = <FR> AND rnum = <N2> AND rnum <>
      <N1> AND class is RA)
THEN
   reset ,
   write 'Frame <FR> Region <N1> - Ruling out RA + RV in
      favor of RV and RA\n',
   in 1 class.RA + RV = 0 ;
```

In the consequent, we use the reset command to make sure that our actions will override any previously assigned truth values. We then override the default monotonic reasoning of FLOPS by directly assigning a truth value of zero to member $RA + RV$ in fuzzy set class. We do this by the symbolism class.$RA + RV$ to represent the grade of membership of member $RA + RV$, and set it to zero. Suppose we had written

```
THEN
   reset 0,
   in 1 class is RA + RV;
```

The reset command will set pconf to zero, but the command `class is` $RA + RV$; is subject to monotonic reasoning restrictions, and if the existing truth value in $RA + RV$ is greater than 0 (as will certainly be the case), setting its truth value to a lesser value will be rejected by the system. However, the consequent command

```
in 1 class.RA + RV = 0 ;
```

will be unconditionally obeyed.

As a final check on classifications so far, we make sure that we have accounted for all heart regions in each frame before reporting our final classifications. One of these rules is

```
rule block 7 (goal Checks for LA, LV, RA, RV in same frame)   (13.4)
IF (in Region frame = <FR> AND class is LA)
   (in Region frame = <FR> AND class is LV)
   (in Region frame = <FR> AND class is RA)
   (in Region frame = <FR> AND class is RV)
THEN
   reset ,
   write 'LA, LV, RA, RV present in frame <FR>\n' ,
```

```
in 1 final = "LA" ,
in 2 final = "LV" ,
in 3 final = "RA" ,
in 4 final = "RV" ;
```

13.3.6 Running echo.par

Echo.par is already set up to do a sequence of run 1; commands, pausing for a message between blocks. To be able to execute debug commands after each run 1; it is only necessary to click the "Cancel" button on a dialog box; this will return us temporarily to command mode, and we can execute such debugging commands as ldata and prstack, returning to run mode by the resume command. By now the reader should have enough experience with debug commands to get along without detailed guidance.

13.4 SCHIZO.PAR

This program was originally written by graduate student Jeff Jones at the University of Texas at Arlington, with guidance from a University psychologist. It was tested and used by a psychologist at the University of Alabama at Birmingham for several years, and worked out very well in practice. Its purpose is to do a preliminary psychological screen for subjects who might be in need of a professional psychologist, and was designed to be run by a technician. The technician is asked to what extent 30 behavioral manifestations are characteristic of a subject, with grades from 0 to 1000. The program rules then analyze these 30 scores to determine grades of membership in a fuzzy set of diagnoses: major depression, bi-polar disorder, paranoia, and several types of schizophrenia. These preliminary diagnoses are used by the psychologist to help determine if treatment is needed, and to help formulate treatment if needed.

13.4.1 Data Declarations in schizo.par

We have three data structures used in the schizo.par diagnosis process, and one for block firing control.

The first is Fact, a very simple structure to hold the behavioral traits being graded. The score for each behavior becomes the truth value of the corresponding fact. The strings for instances of fact are held in a tiny FLOPS file.

```
declare Fact
  fact str ;
```

The next structure, Symptoms, uses the scored facts to assign truth values to a fuzzy set of generalized symptoms; depressive, manic, and schizophrenic.

```
declare Symptoms
  symptom fzset
```

```
(
has_depressive_symptoms
has_manic_symptoms
has_schizophrenic_symptoms
) ;
```

Finally, the facts and generalized symptoms are used to secure preliminary diagnoses. Since these are preliminary diagnoses in a complex field, we make no attempt to arrive at a single diagnosis; final diagnosis (or diagnoses) is left up to the physician or clinical psychologist.

```
declare Diagnosis
  dx fzset
  (
major_depression
manic_depressive_psychosis
schizophrenia
schizophrenia_disorganized_type
schizophrenia_catatonic_type
schizophrenia_paranoid_type
paranoid_disorder
  ) ;
```

The final declaration is similar to that in echo.par, and serves the same purpose; controlling firing of rule blocks.

```
declare enable
  block int;
```

13.4.2   Structure of schizo.par

We have already indicated the general structure of shizo.par. Now we will look at this structure in more detail. We have six rule blocks, whose functions are given in Table 13.4.

TABLE 13.4   Rule Blocks in schizo.par and Their Functions

Block	Function	Number of Rules
0	Gets truth values in the facts (the behavioral traits)	1
1	Gets generalized symptoms from facts	12
2	Gets first diagnoses from symptoms and facts	7
3	Updates diagnoses	3
4	Outputs final diagnoses	1
5	Enables and disables rule blocks	1

13.4.3   Rules for schizo.par; Block 0, Inputting Data

The decision to handle the data input as a set of facts (the behavioral traits) whose truth values represent the degree to which each behavioral trait is characteristic of a subject is quite workable. The facts themselves will already be in memory, since we will insert, at the end of the rules, the command

```
transfer -conf Fact from facts.dat;
```

Since the facts all have initially full truth value, we can use the −conf option in the transfer command to dispense with putting truth values in the data file. Typical facts are

```
"Fact", "has sad face"
"Fact", "has depressed mood"
"Fact", "loses interest in usual activities"
"Fact", "has euphoria"
"Fact", "is overactive"
```

Our rule to permit the technician to input the truth values that he will assign to each trait is simple and straightforward:

```
:rule r0
rule (goal Gets truth value levels in facts)
IF (in Fact fact <FA> )
THEN
   input "<FA> (0 - 1000) ? " 1 fact.cf ;
```

where, of course, <FA> is replaced by the current fact, such as

```
loses interest in usual activities ? (0 - 1000)
```

13.4.4   Rules for schizo.par; Block 1, Getting Truth Values of Generalized Symptoms

The diagnosis rules for schizo are not obvious; they depend on having a cooperative and dedicated expert available, as Jeff Jones had.

The next block has the rules for translating some of the facts into general symptom classes; depressive, manic, and schizophrenic. Even a non-psychologist can understand some of these rules, for example,

```
:rule r1
rule rconf 400 block 1 (goal Finds symptom is
has_depressive_symptoms)
IF (in Fact fact is "has sad face")
   (in Fact fact is "has depressed mood")
   (Symptoms)
```

```
THEN
  write 'has depressive symptoms ', pconf ,
  in 3 symptom is has_depressive_symptoms ;
```

We are not altogether sure that this rule is valid; the rconf value of 400 means that this rule can assign a truth value of has_depressive_symptoms of no more than 400. (A number of rules have less than full truth value.)

The write command uses a system-furnished symbol pconf whose value is the truth value with which the consequent command is executed, so that the output tells how sure this rule is that the symptom is valid. There is likely to be more than one rule attempting to assign truth values to the symptoms, so FLOPS monotonic logic will let the highest truth value succeed.

13.4.5   Rules for schizo.par; Block 2, Getting Basic Diagnoses

Here we are making the first pass at diagnoses for our subject. These rules attempt to derive only the basic diagnoses: major depression, manic-depressive psychosis, schizophrenia, and paranoid disorder. The rules use a combination of facts and symptoms, as in this rule for diagnosing major depression:

```
:rule r14
rule rconf 800 block 2
  (goal Finds diagnosis is major_depression)
IF (in Symptoms symptom is has_depressive_symptoms)
  (in Fact fact "symptoms have lasted for at least one month")
  (Diagnosis)
THEN
  write 'diagnosis major depression ', pconf,
  in 3 dx is major_depression ;
```

13.4.6   Rules for schizo.par; Block 3, Getting Final Diagnoses

The basic diagnoses have been established; now we can look into differential diagnosis among different types of schizophrenia. Our rules for getting truth values of symptoms used the truth values of the facts; the rules for basic diagnoses used truth values of facts and symptoms; and now we can use the truth values of the basic diagnoses in addition to facts and symptoms final diagnoses. Here is one such rule:

```
:rule r20
rule rconf 800 block 3
  (goal Updates diagnosis to schizophrenia_disorganized_
type)
IF (in Diagnosis dx is schizophrenia)
  (in Fact fact is "has incoherent thought and speech" )
  (in Fact fact is "has markedly illogical thoughts" )
```

```
(in Fact fact is "has inappropriate affect" )
THEN
  write 'diagnosis disorganized schizophrenia ', pconf ,
  in 1 dx is schizophrenia_disorganized_type ;
```

13.4.7 Rules for schizo.par; Block 4, Output of Diagnoses

The authors have frequently heard that fuzzy systems should possess crisp outputs. Often people in engineering and the hard sciences have trouble dealing with fuzzy outputs. But this is much less likely to be true of workers in the medical and biological fields; they live with uncertainty all the time, and are more likely to try to reduce the uncertainty rather than to get rid of it altogether. Certainly in the psychological field, it is not uncommon to find patients who suffer from more than one ailment at the same time. In any event, a physician appreciates having possibilities presented with relative likelihoods rather than a single definite computer-generated answer. Consequently, we present as output the entire range of possible illnesses together with their likelihoods. Any attempt to view the presence of more than one concurrent diagnosis as a contradiction rather than as an ambiguity would be a bad error. This makes our output rule very simple:

```
:rule r23
rule block 4
   (goal Writes fuzzy set of final diagnoses with truth
values)
IF ( Diagnosis )
THEN
  message "final diagnoses -\n" ,
  prmem 1 ;
```

A quite reasonable output might be

```
final diagnosis -
(Diagnosis (
  ('tt',71)
  ('dx',((('major_depression',400) ('paranoid_disorder',
  200)))))
```

Of course, this output could be prettied up, but that is another matter.

13.4.8 Rules for schizo.par; Block 5, Block Firing Control

Block firing control in this program is really trivial—we simply have to execute blocks 0–4 in sucession. Our last rule does this:

```
:rule r24
rule block 5 (goal Controls block firing sequence)
```

```
IF (in enable block <N> block < 6)
THEN
  in 1 block ( <N> + 1 ) ,
  fire block <N> del ,
  fire block ( <N> + 1 ) on ;
```

The consequent command `fire block <N> del` does not only turn block <N> off; the `del` keyword tells FLOPS that we are completely finished with this rule block, and not to test its rules for fireability throughout the rest of the run.

13.4.9 Running schizo.par with Debugging Commands

Certainly, the easiest way to run schizo.par with debugging commands is to comment out the `run;` command at the end of the program and to proceed completely manually by entering the desired FLOPS commands at the FLOPS command prompt $>>$ as we have done before. Check out all the debugging commands in the online manual help file, and try out as many of them as seem appropriate.

13.5 DISCUSSION

We have programmed three problems of the "What?" type, none trivial, and all arising from real-world problems. Iris.par for speciating iris plants used 7 rules; echo.par and schizo.par used 25 programmer-written rules each, although echo.par automatically generated another dozen or so rules from its expert knowledge database. We think this demonstrates that a well-written fuzzy expert system can solve well-defined nontrivial tasks with a relatively few number of rules.

Of course, in these programs we are not trying to solve difficult intellectual tasks like theorem proving. (As a matter of fact, few humans can prove theorems!) But when we add the ability to learn, we are really well on our way to emulating human thought.

All these programs input data, and if the data are numeric we put it in word form as soon as possible. All our data words will have truth values attached, whether computed or assigned subjectively by humans. We are very quickly led to ambiguities, which we treasure; good ambiguities lead to robustness of our program. If it is necessary to give a crisp output, we use resolution of contradictions with as much smartness as we can muster, either looking at existing data more critically or acquiring new data. But it is not always advisable to give crisp answers, particularly if we have not embodied sufficient knowledge and skills into our program, and very seldom with medical diagnoses. If a program can significantly narrow down the range of uncertainty, it has done a good job.

13.6 QUESTIONS

13.1 What fuzzy operation is almost always carried out in problems where the answer is a number, but seldom carried out if the answer is a word?

13.2 Is fuzzification frequently carried out when the answer is a number, or when the answer is a word, or both?

13.3 The members of a discrete fuzzy set are usually words. When is such a set a linguistic variable, and when is it not?

13.4 What is a good data type for output when the answer is in words?

13.5 What is the difference between an ambiguity and a contradiction?

13.6 What are the major steps in arriving at a conclusion expressed in words?

13.7 As a program proceeds from earlier-to-later reasoning steps, what should be done about resolving ambiguities? About resolving contradictions?

14 Programs that Can Learn from Experience

14.1 GENERAL METHODS

As we mentioned in Chapter 1, The Random House unabridged dictionary gives a definition of learning as "the act or process of acquiring knowledge or skill". In this chapter, we will see how expert systems can learn in two very simple ways. The first way will add new facts to the programs knowledge base; the second way will add new rules. The field of machine learning has received much attention for many years; see for example, Mitchell (1997) and Kecman (2001). We will restrict ourselves in this chapter to two basic and fundamentally different ways in which a rule-based system can learn. In one technique, we write our rules to interpret a database, and add facts to the database as the program learns from experience; in the other technique the program creates new rules from its experience.

The programs to illustrate these two techniques are different ways of solving the same problem: pavlov1.par and pavlov2.par, which emulate learning by Pavlovian classical conditioning. Pavlov1 learns by adding rules to deal with important external stimuli; Pavlov2 learns by adding stimulus data to a database. Each technique has its own programming advantages and disadvantages. The learning techniques are so simple that they might seem trivial, but the importance of Pavlovian learning is exceedingly well known. The combination of simplicity and power is sometimes called elegance, and these simple and elegant techniques have a lot of power.

The idea of Pavlovian learning, often called classical conditioning and more recently behavior modification, came originally from Pavlov's experiment on ringing a bell, then offering food to a dog. The dog soon learned to associate the sound of the bell with food, so that as soon as the bell was rung he began to salivate. The great American psychologist Skinner generalized this to nearly all animal species from worms to humans, and learning theorists have intensively examined the connection between conditioning and learning. Most would agree that conditioning is a simple and basic form of learning.

The two FLOPS programs for learning from experience resemble each other quite a bit. The reason is because the conditions under which one learns are identical in both cases. We have a body of stimuli to which we have already associated a response, at birth wired-in and mostly learned after birth, called unconditioned

Fuzzy Expert Systems and Fuzzy Reasoning, By William Siler and James J. Buckley
ISBN 0-471-38859-9   Copyright © 2005 John Wiley & Sons, Inc.

stimuli. We normally encounter a wide variety of apparently neutral stimuli. If a stimulus with established response occurs very quickly after a neutral stimulus, and this response sequence is repeated soon and often enough, we will learn to associate the neutral stimulus with the stimulus whose response is known, and will exhibit the response after the neutral stimulus without waiting for the other stimulus to occur. Thus Pavlov's dog learned to salivate after hearing the bell and before food was offered.

It requires some programming to establish these sequences. Our program then has two sorts of tasks: keeping track of stimuli and their relation to each other; and keeping track of time and memory. We provide for immediate experience; transfer of stimuli to short-term memory, and transfer of stimulus associations to long-term memory. We must establish time limits on how quickly the unconditioned stimulus must occur after the neutral stimulus, and how long we remember stimuli, and define the circumstances under which learning will occur. This programming tends to be about the same for both programs. They differ mainly on whether the learning is implemented as a new skill (adding rules) or as new facts to be remembered (adding data). It is interesting that two programs whose behavior is virtually identical emulate entirely different neurological implementations.

14.2   PAVLOV1.PAR: LEARNING BY ADDING RULES

14.2.1   Data for Pavlov1.par

We have a very limited response repertoire in the Pavlov programs: "Run!" for bad stimuli, such as "burn", and "Whee!" for good stimuli, such as "food". We will need two main types of data elements: some to deal stimulil, and some to do with time; some will deal with both.

Our initial biologically determined stimulus–response data can be stored in Wired-in:

```
declare Wired-in      :library of unconditioned stimuli
                       and response types
  id str              :stimulus id
  response str;       :stimulus response
```

A place to store a new stimulus, with its response (if known) and the time when it was received:

```
declare NewStimulus   :record of new stimuli
  id str              :stimulus ID
  time int            :time when stimulus received
  response str ;      :NULL (neutral), WHEE (positive),
                       RUN (aversive)
```

We store recent stimuli in short-term memory as Stimulus:

```
declare Stimulus        :record of stimuli
   id str               :stimulus ID
   time int             :time received
   response str;        :NULL (neutral), WHEE (positive),
                         or RUN (aversive)
```

Now we need a data element to store stimulus pairs, that is, received in fairly rapid succession:

```
declare Pair            :observed stimulus pair
   id1 str              :earlier stimulus (response " ")
   id2 str              :later stimulus (response + or -)
   T1 int               :time of stimulus id1
   T2 int               :time of stimulus id2
   TF int;              :forget pair after this time
```

For time management, we need a clock (biological or otherwise) to know when a stimulus was received. We also tuck into this data element parameters regarding remembrance of stimuli;

```
declare Time            :Internal clock
   time int             :current time
   pairTime int         :pair with stimulus no earlier than
                         this time
   forget int;          :forget anything earlier than this
                         time
```

and a data element to keep track of how when two stimuli have been paired:

```
declare Count    :
   id1 str
   id2 str
   N int
   time int;
```

In Forget, we store some memory management parameters:

```
declare Forget
   delPT int            :time interval allowed to pair
                         incoming stimuli
   delFT int;           :time interval before stimulus &
                         pairs forgotten
```

We have a feeling that although this program works, time could be handled more compactly than it is.

Final housekeeping data elements:

```
declare Rulemade
  id1 str
  id2 str;
```

and our familiar place to store which rule block is currently fireable:

```
declare Fire              :block firing control
  block int;
```

14.2.2 Rules for Pavlov1.par

We organize the program itself by block numbers, something like this:

0. Let the user input the next stimulus into a NewStimulus data element.
1. Quit on null input, or put the time into into the NewStimulus data element.
2. Associate the new stimulus with a wired-in response if appropriate.
3. Report the response if known. If not, fire any rules that associate the stimulus with a response. Here is where our created rules to associate stimulus with response will go. Forget any stimuli too old to be remembered.
4. If we can, pair new stimulus with wired-in response to recent neutral stimulus. Move new stimulus to short term memory (will be soon forgotten).
5. If the latest stimulus has a wired-in response and is paired with more than one recent neutral stimulus, keep most recent pairing and forget the older.
6. Count recent stimulus pairs
7. If the stimulus pair data indicate that a new rule should be made to associate them, don't make a new rule if one already exists.
8. Generate new stimulus-association rule if ready to do so.
9. Rule firing control: activate next block (block <8) or return to block 0.

As we can see, the most important block is Block 8, which actually creates the new rule from the data at hand. While we have seen automatic rule creation before in echo.par, there was no learning there; the rules were constructed from a preexisting database of expert knowledge. In Pavlov1.par, no one can predict in advance what rules (if any) will be created during a program run; that depends entirely on the user's experiences during a program run.

The critical rule is

```
:rule r14
rule block 8 (goal Generates rule for response to
conditioned stimuli)
```

```
IF (in Count id1 = <ID1> AND id2 = <ID2> AND N > 2 )
   (in Wired-in id = <ID1> AND response = <R> )
THEN
   message 'New rule - conditioning <ID1> to <ID2>
   response <R>\n',
   delete 1,
   make Rulemade id1 = "<ID1>" id2 = "<ID2>",
```

The new rule itself, created by r14, might be

```
rule r20 rconf 1000 ON block 3 ON
IF
   ( in NewStimulus id = "bell" )
THEN
   message 'bell - LOOK OUT - food coming\, DROOL!\n';
```

The conditions under which the rule is fired is that stimulus id1 has been associated with stimulus id2 on at least two previous occasions, sufficiently recently, and that stimulus id1 is associated with a wired-in response. If this is true, then element Count (which kept track of id1-id2 pairings up to now) is deleted as no longer needed, we make an instance of Rulemade so that we will not make any more instances of this rule, and create the rule itself, stored in Block 2.

The sequence of operations is

0. Let the user input the next stimulus into a NewStimulus data element and increment time.
1. Quit on null input, or put the time into into the NewStimulus data element.
2. Associate the new stimulus with a wired-in response if appropriate. Store new rules here.
3. Report the response if known. If not, fire any rules which associate the stimulus with a response. Here is where our created rules to associate stimulus with response will go. Forget any stimuli too old to be remembered.
4. If we can, pair new stimulus with wired-in response to recent neutral stimulus. Move new stimulus to short term memory (will be soon forgotten).
5. If the latest stimulus has a wired-in response and is paired with more than one recent neutral stimulus, keep most recent pairing and forget the older.
6. Count recent stimulus pairs
7. If the stimulus pair data indicate that a new rule should be made to associate them, do not make a new rule if one already exists.
8. Generate new stimulus-association rule if ready to do so.
9. Rule firing control: activate next block (block <8) or return to block 0.

We implement this sequence in this way:

```
:rule r0 block 0 Inputs stimulus and updates time
:Block 1 - Puts input into new stimulus record or quits
on null stimulus
    :rule r1 - Quits on null stimulus
    :rule r2 - Puts time and null response into new stimulus
record
:Block 2 - associates new stimulus with wired-in
response if appropriate
    :rule r3 - Associates new stimulus with wired-in
response if possible
    :conditioned response rules go here
:Block 3 - reports response, forgets old data,
    :rule r4 - Reports response to unconditioned stimulus
    :rule r5 - Forgets old stimuli
    :rule r6 - Forgets old stimulus pairs
    :rule r7 - Forgets Count of how many old Pairs we have had
:Block 4 - stimulus with known response paired with previous
neutral
    :stimulus, moves NewStimulus into short-term memory
    :rule r8 - If response known, pairs with previous
neutral stimuli
    :rule r9 - Moves NewStimulus into short-term memory
:Block 5 - if latest stimulus paired with more than one
neutral stimulus,
    :select latest one
    :rule r10 - Picks latest neutral stimulus paired with
current one
    :rule r11 - Picks latest instance of count)
:Block 6 - counts recent stimulus pairs
    :rule r12 - Counts number of recent stimulus pairs
:Block 7 - stops making new rule if one already exists
    :rule r13 - Stops making new rule if one already made
:Block 8 - generates new rule if ready
    :rule r14 - Generates rule for response to conditioned
stimuli
    :rule r15 - Deletes instance of count - no longer needed)
:Block 10 - sequences rule blocks
    :rule r16 - Sequences rule blocks for firing
    :rule r17 - Restarts rule firing sequence after stimulus
processed
    :rule r18 - Turns off block 3 if new rule created)
    :rule r19 - Fires once to report stimuli with wired-in
responses
```

Run control is very simple; run through the blocks from beginning to end, then restart at the beginning again. The only complication is the necessity of turning off the new block 3 rule when it is created. (FLOPS turns on a rule and its block when the rule is created.)

14.2.3   Exercise: Pavlov1.par

A straight-through run of Pavlov1 can produce this output. (User input is bold face.)

```
Compiling program PAVLOV.FPS...
Simulation of pavlovian conditioning.
```

A stimulus, with no response associated, coming just before a second stimulus with known response, tends to associate the known response to the first stimulus.

```
Known stimuli with wired-in responses -
Stimulus burn response RUN
Stimulus food response WHEE
Stimulus girls response WHEE
```

There are two basically different approaches to this problem. One way is to generate a new rule if a new stimulus becomes associated with a previous stimulus with known response: that is what this program does. We could instead modify the database on which the rules operate.

Try seeing if the burnt child dreads the fire. For example, enter fire followed by burn three or four times in a row, and see what happens. You can of course enter stimuli not in the library.

```
PAVLOV.PAR Ready to run
>>run;
Enter any stimulus, <CR> to quit
fire
Enter any stimulus, <CR> to quit
burn
burn - RUN!
Enter any stimulus, <CR> to quit
fire
Enter any stimulus, <CR> to quit
burn
burn - RUN!
Enter any stimulus, <CR> to quit
fire
Enter any stimulus, <CR> to quit
burn
```

```
burn - RUN!
New rule: conditioning burn to fire response RUN
Enter any stimulus, <CR> to quit
```
fire
```
fire - LOOK OUT - burn coming, RUN!
Enter any stimulus, <CR> to quit
```
(<CR>)
```
Exiting PAVLOV --
Terminating FLOPS: 0 warnings, 0 errors
```

Suppose we would like to run the program without stopping until we are ready to create a new rule. We comment out the run command at the end of the program, and use TFLOPS to open schizo.par. We run schizo.par. FLOPS compiles the program, reads its data from the blackboard, and at the end of the program prints out the FLOPS prompt >>. Now we enter

```
>>breakpoint r14;
>>run;
```

and FLOPS runs happily until it is ready to make a new rule, then reverts temporarily to command mode. At that point we can inspect data, fireable rule stack, and execute whatever other debugging commands we wish. When finished, we enter **return;**, and the program continues from where it stopped.

With judicious use of breakpoints; prstack; prmem, ldata and prdata; lrule and prule, you can get deeper insights into how pavlov1.par functions.

14.3 PAVLOV2.PAR: LEARNING BY ADDING FACTS TO LONG-TERM MEMORY

The overall structure of Pavlov2 is almost the same as Pavlov1. Following our discussion of Pavlov1.par, we begin with differences in the data declarations; next we will look at differences in rule structure.

14.3.1 Data for Pavlov1.par

First, we list the data elements declared in both programs.

- Stimulus—short-term memory for recent stimuli.
- NewStimulus—stores latest stimulus received.
- Pair—short-term memory of stimulus pairs received in fairly rapid succession. The earliest stimulus is neutral (not wired-in or conditioned response), and the latest is a wired-in stimulus–response pair.
- Wired-in—long-term memory of wired-in stimulus response pairs, like "food—whee".

- Time—record of current time, earliest time to pair stimuli, and latest time to forget stimuli.
- Count—record of recent stimulus pairs.
- Forget—time before forgetting received stimuli and max time before stimulus–stimulus pairs are forgotten.
- Fire—record of currently activated rule block. While both programs have a data element Fire to keep a record of currently activated rule block, but Fire in Pavlov1 has an extra attribute NewRule to inform the fire control rule that a new rule has been made and the new rule should be turned off.

Pavlov1 has a data element RuleMade to avoid making duplicate new rules. The corresponding task in Pavlov2, avoiding making duplicate entries in Conditioned, is easily accomplished by a single rule that scans instances of Conditioned to see if a candidate entry has already been made. Element RuleMade is not required in Pavlov2.

14.3.2 Rules for Pavlov2.par

Comparison of the rule block functions in Pavlov1.par and Pavlov2.par shown in Table 14.1 shows immediately that there is very little difference between the two programs; of the 10 program blocks, only three (blocks 3, 7, and 8) show any differences.

TABLE 14.1   Rule Block Functions in Pavlov1.par and Pavlov2.par

Rule Block	Pavlov1.par	Pavlov2.par
Block 0	stimulus input	stimulus input
Block 1	Quit or put time into new stimulus record	Quit or put time into new stimulus record
Block 2	associate new stimulus with wired-in response if appropriate	associate new stimulus with wired-in response if appropriate
Block 3	reports response, forgets old data, holds generated stimulus-response rules	reports response, forgets old data
Block 4	stimulus with known response paired with previous neutral stimulus, moves NewStimulus into short-term memory	stimulus with known response paired with previous neutral stimulus, moves NewStimulus into short-term memory
Block 5	if latest stimulus paired with more than one neutral stimulus, select latest one	if latest stimulus paired with more than one neutral stimulus, select latest one
Block 6	counts recent stimulus pairs	counts recent stimulus pairs
Block 7	prevents making new rule if one already exists	prevents making new library data if one already exists
Block 8	generates new rule if ready	generates new library entry if ready
Block 10	sequences rule blocks	sequences rule blocks

Block 3 differs between the two programs in that the Pavlov1 block holds the learned rules to associate conditioned stimuli with wired-in stimulus and response. However, the same block in Pavlov2 holds a single rule to associate a conditioned stimulus with its learned response, using the learned data. Block 3 in both the Pavlov1 and Pavlov2 perform the same function of associating a conditioned response with the wired-in stimulus to which it was conditioned.

Similarly, Block 7 in both Pavlov1 and Pavlov2 perform the function of avoiding crowding memory with duplicate information. In Pavlov1, Block 7 avoids making duplicate rules; in Pavlov2, Block 7 avoids making duplicate entries long-term memory.

14.3.3 Running: Pavlov2.par

Running Pavlov1.par and Pavlov2.par produces almost identical results, except for a message telling the user that a new rule or new datum is being created. We list outputs in Table 14.2 for both programs. The introductory messages are skipped, since they are identical for both programs. (Data entered by the user are listed in bold type.)

Pavlov2 has a big advantage over Pavlov1: the learned responses can be stored without modification of the program itself. The skills embodied in Palov1 are

TABLE 14.2 Comparing Runs of Pavlov1.par and Pavlov2.par

Pavlov1.par	Pavlov2.par
Enter any stimulus, <CR> to quit **fire**	Enter any stimulus, <CR> to quit **fire**
Enter any stimulus, <CR> to quit **burn**	Enter any stimulus, <CR> to quit **burn**
burn – OUCH!	burn – OUCH!
Enter any stimulus, <CR> to quit **fire**	Enter any stimulus, <CR> to quit **fire**
Enter any stimulus, <CR> to quit **burn**	Enter any stimulus, <CR> to quit **burn**
burn – OUCH!	burn – OUCH!
Enter any stimulus, <CR> to quit **fire**	Enter any stimulus, <CR> to quit **fire**
Enter any stimulus, <CR> to quit **burn**	Enter any stimulus, <CR> to quit **burn**
burn – OUCH!	burn – OUCH!

New rule: conditioning fire to burn
    response OUCH
	New data – conditioning fire to burn
	    response OUCH

Enter any stimulus, <CR> to quit **fire**	Enter any stimulus, <CR> to quit **fire**
fire – LOOK OUT – burn coming, OUCH!	fire – LOOK OUT – burn coming, OUCH!
Enter any stimulus, <CR> to quit **<CR>**	Enter any stimulus, <CR> to quit **<CR>**
Exiting PAVLOV – –	Exiting PAVLOV – –

very specific, relating each new stimulus to the appropriate response individually. Pavlov2 has a different and more powerful skill; it knows how to interpret the knowledge it has stored, and how to add to that stored knowledge. Is it possible to conduct a learning experiment to see which of these techniques we animals use? Possibly. Certainly, if the question "What stimuli produce a flight response?" is asked, there is less processing if the Pavlov2 method is used than if the Pavlov1 method is used. We leave experimental tests to the cognitive psychologists.

14.4 DEFINING NEW DATA ELEMENTS AND NEW: RULEGEN.FPS

Sometimes the definition of new rules as given above is not sufficiently flexible, since it requires that data elements involved be predefined. Actually, FLOPS provides more flexibility than the PAVLOV programs would seem to provide. Program RULEGEN.FPS illustrates not only deriving new rules, but also adding a new data element descriptor.

RULEGEN first defines a prototype data element:

```
declare Proto
  element str
  attr str
  type str ;
```

To simplify the program, the attributes in `Proto` are entered from the keyboard rather than having their values set by a running program. This is done by rule r0. Initially, only rule r0 is fireable. After r0 has fired, we know the name of the new data element, the attribute and attribute type; now rules r1 and r2 are fireable. These data are now stored in `Proto`:

Next, rule r1 fires. R1s consequent declares the data element whose characteristics we have inut in r0. r1 does not create our new rule directly; instead, it creates a rule-generating rule that can create our new rule by establishing its format.

Rule r2 fires next, and makes an instance of the data element declared by r1. R2 must fie after r1, since a rule does not know about data that existed prior to the rule's creation.

R3 is now ready to fire, input the data for the new data element and generating our new rule for which r1 created the template.

At this point, we have generated a new data element, created a new rule with that new element in its consequent, created an instance of the new data element, and are ready to go: Our new rule is now fireable.

Finally, we fire out new rule r4 that simply prints out the rules and data to date.

14.4.1   Running: RULEGEN.FPS

This exercise is straightforward, but the output is not easily digested.

Open TFLOPS, then open RULEGEN.FPS in the examples folder. Comment out everything after "`make Proto;`" by inserting preceding colons "`:`". Now run the program by repeating this command sequence, entered from the keyboard:

```
>>prdata;
<output>
>>lrule;
<output>
>>prstack;
<output>
>>run 1;
<output>
```
(repeat until program finished.)

The problem here is to grasp the sequence of rule-firing steps, what has taken place in each step, and why the rule-firing sequence is necessary.

14.5   MOST GENERAL WAY OF CREATING NEW RULES AND DATA DESCRIPTORS

While the rule- and data descriptor generating method in RULEGEN.FPS is superior to that used in the PAVLOV programs, it is still restricted to maximum number of attributes specified in the Proto data descriptor. A completely general way of generating new data elements and rules depends on the use of the FLOPS system-furnished variable <string>. A string can be initialized by the command

```
string = "..."
```

and assembled by concatenating substrings using the command

```
string + "..."
```

where `"..." is whatever` text you desire. In this way, one can assemble any desired FLOPS command with complete freedom and maximum flexibility. An extremely simple example is given by program StringRule.fps in the TFLOPS examples folder.

14.6   DISCUSSION

The two programs, Pavlov1.par and Pavlov2.par, represent two very different basic models of how we learn. The fact that their performance is identical illustrates the difficulty of trying to learn how the brain works by constructing computer models divorced from neurophysiological data. Nevertheless, while we have learned little about how the brain actually works in simple learning, we do have two different techniques for *emulating* learning that could be quite useful in practice.

It is easy to criticize such simple programs on the grounds of their simplicity. This is quite an error; the important thing about these simple programs is the power of the methods employed. To get an idea of this power, let us examine how these programs could be made more realistic. Note that both programs are based on Aristotelian True/False logic; we have not taken any advantage of the fuzzy capabilities of FLOPS.

An obvious extension is to include a measurement of intensity with each new stimulus; for example, this intensity could be used to affect how long a stimulus is remembered, and how long before a new rule or datum is created to implement a new stimulus association. We could also include a measurement of intensity with the response associated with wired-in responses, to be used in selecting the course of action that follows a particular response.

While Pavlov2.par performs equally well as Pavlov1.par, the method of writing one rule to interpret a library of stored data is somewhat more limited than the method of creating new rules. New data element declarations can also be created, and new rules can be more powerful than new data. When new data are added as a result of experience, as in Pavlov1, we can only couple new stimuli to old responses. This is learning of the simplest possible sort, that can be done by many lower animals, even worms. The construction of new rules, coupled with addition of new data and the ability to construct both rules and data declarations from information received during the course of a program run, offers advanced learning possibilities.

14.7   QUESTIONS

14.1   What are the two basic things that humans can learn?

14.2   What are the two basic ways in which programs can learn?

14.3   What is the simplest way to form new rules?

14.4   Give an example of a new rule formed as in Question 14.3.

14.5   What FLOPS commands relevant to learning can be executed in the consequent of a rule?

14.6   What kinds of rules are needed if expert knowledge is stored in a database rather than in rules? Which of the example programs use such rules?

14.7   We have said that programs can learn from experience either by adding new rules or by adding to a database of expert factual knowledge. If either of these methods could be employed in a particular problem, which method is to be preferred? Why?

14.8   Suppose that the rule or datum we have learned does not fit into a predefined format. What technique can we use to create completely arbitrary rules or data?

15 Running On-Line in Real-Time

15.1 OVERVIEW OF ON-LINE REAL-TIME WORK

There are several different scenarios in which a real-time on-line expert system may be desirable. Of course, there are the many fuzzy control systems; their huge success first put fuzzy systems theory on the map. Other real-time systems may involve watching the data as they come in and waiting for a significant event to happen or significant condition to occur. This may involve asking for human intervention, as in alarm systems, or activation of another computer program to deal with the situation.

In any event, there are certain tasks that must almost always be performed. The input data must be acquired from one or more of a variety of input devices; the data must be processed in a timely fashion; and output must be delivered to the real world. The programmer must know how the processing program can be tested and debugged. Program planning then begins with the input data to be acquired. Processing algorithms must be defined. Processing speed must be estimated to see if speed requirements can be met. Finally, the way in which output data will be presented to the outside world must be decided.

Fuzzy control systems nearly always run on-line in real-time. If they are relatively simple, compared to more general-purpose data-driven fuzzy reasoning systems, they may be able to do this with few difficulties. Data-driven expert production systems are much more flexible and powerful than fuzzy control systems, but tend to run more slowly. Examples of noncontrol on-line real-time applications include alarm detection systems and fault detection and diagnosis programs. But now that personal computers are very much faster than in the past, this speed disadvantage is of less importance. Another disadvantage of production systems for real-time on-line work has been that most non-fuzzy production systems run in serial mode, and keep all data in the computer's memory for backtracking and reference in debugging and explanation. Most fuzzy expert systems run in parallel mode, much faster than sequential programs. Since parallel programs do not backtrack, it is not necessary to keep all data in memory; this means that parallel systems can run indefinitely without overflowing memory. FLOPS furnishes an "erase ON/OFF" command; when erase is ON, data that a program no longer needs are removed from memory, and the space is returned to the operating system.

Fuzzy Expert Systems and Fuzzy Reasoning, By William Siler and James J. Buckley
ISBN 0-471-38859-9   Copyright © 2005 John Wiley & Sons, Inc.

Running parallel expert systems on-line in real-time then becomes an option available to the knowledge engineer.

Many, if not most, real-time on-line programs are *closed loop*; that is, the program not only takes input from an external source, but also returns data to the process that generates the data. The problem here is that errors in the program can seriously affect the process, perhaps disastrously so.

Sometimes programs that interact with a user via mouse or keyboard are called real-time or on-line. In this chapter, we consider primarily programs that are hard-wired to processes that generate program input and (when closed-loop) accept program output. Programs that depend on interaction with a human user have much more tolerance for delays than most hard-wired programs. A human will normally tolerate a delay of 6 or 7 s between human input and computer response; hard-wired programs often require responses in milliseconds or even faster. Also, if a human is constantly interacting with the program, it is difficult for a runaway program to remain undetected; hard-wired programs with defects can have catastrophic results.

15.2 INPUT/OUTPUT ON-LINE IN REAL-TIME

There is a great variety of ways in which data can be transferred automatically to a running program, including RS232 and its descendants, parallel ports, Ethernet, hard disk, USB, the Web, and so on with an ever-increasing number of options. Further, each application will have its own data formats. It is asking a lot of a programming language to furnish configurable drivers for all the possible I/O channels, and it is virtually impossible for an expert system shell to furnish built-in drivers to accommodate all the various I/O possibilities and data formats. There are a number of hardware and software packages available for using a wide variety of input/output channels. It is very likely that driver code must be written in a language like C or C++ to get our data in and out. The expert system shell should furnish links to user-written functions to do the I/O, with sample functions to provide guidelines for the users to write their own I/O routines.

For on-line data input, FLOPS provides the "acquire" command, which links to a "getdata( )" or "putdata( )" function that does the hardware-specific data input/output. The acquire command syntax is

```
acquire <command> (parameters)
```

<command> is used to control the getdata() function, by specifying the operation to be performed. Permissible values are INIT, READ, REREAD, WRITE, REWRITE, and END. Only four commands cause data transfers other than device status; READ, REREAD, WRITE, and REWRITE. In all cases, device status will be returned as a status attribute value if possible.

If <command> is INIT or END, the parameters are user-determined to initialize or close the input device. For example, if data are to be read from disk the only parameter might be the name of the disk file. (Disk-recorded data are very useful when debugging or calibrating a program.)

When all the data records have the same format, the READ command syntax is

```
READ <data element number> <attribute 1> <attribute 2>···
```

<data element number> is the pattern number if the acquire command appears on the RHS of a rule, as in "in 2 attrib = ...". If the acquire command is used from the command line, then <data element number> is the time tag of the data element. The data element must contain an attribute `status` of type `str`, to hold the device status on completion of the I/O operation. If not, an error message will be issued and program execution will halt.

The WRITE command will simply have as parameters the values to be written

```
WRITE <value1> <value2>···
```

REREAD and REWRITE are used when the records have different formats; in that case, a READ command inputs a record and returns information to determine the format; the REREAD command then rescans the input record according to its format, and returns actual data values to the FLOPS program. Similarly, for output the WRITE command holds the output format, and the REWRITE command actually outputs the data. The syntax of these commands is usually

```
READ <data element number> <format string>
WRITE <format string>
REREAD <data element number> <attribute 1> <attribute 2>···
REWRITE <value 1> <value 2>···
```

The acquire command is almost always held in the consequent of a rule.

Sample getdata( ) functions for disk data input are SIMPLE.CPP (when all input records have the same format) and RECTYPES.CPP (when input records may have different formats) are provided with FLOPS. Either routine may be linked in using the Microsoft Visual C++ linker, and alternative getdata( ) functions may be programmed and linked also using Microsoft Visual C++. In the educational version of FLOPS furnished with this book, the getdata( ) function in SIMPLE.PAR is linked in to FLOPS; the corresponding output function putdata( ) is not included.

15.3 ON-LINE REAL-TIME PROCESSING

Fuzzy control programs are often embedded in other systems, and many are written for special-purpose microprocessors in assembly language. Such programs are virtually always procedural, and their development requires special control-oriented program development environments. FLOPS is not really suitable for this work. However, FLOPS can be used for more complex control programs, when a PC can be used to run the program. (One of the first FLOPS programs was written to control drug injection to stabilize blood pressure of patients in an intensive care unit.)

Real-time on-line programs usually begin with more-or-less extensive initialization, of input/output routines and program variables. We then enter the processing loop itself.

15.3.1   Detection of Obvious Artifacts in the Input Data Stream

The input data should be scanned to check for unreasonable values. The simplest check, which should always be performed, is a range check on input values. A range check can also be performed on rates of change of input values; this usually requires data smoothing, discussed in Section 15.3.2.

15.3.2   Data Smoothing and Time Delays and Baselines: Exponential Smoothing

It is very common for the input data to require smoothing. This is especially true if rates of change of input data are to be determined; while integration of an input variable is little affected by noise, differentiation tends to multiply noise in the input data, usually requiring that the input data be smoothed.

There are several different smoothing techniques, including a class called *moving averages.* One of the simplest and most effective has an unwieldy name— *exponentially mapped past average*, equivalent to passing analog input data through a low-pass filter. (We will call it simply *exponential smoothing*.) Assume that we have a stream of data points y_i coming in at equally spaced times t_i. We have a single parameter, TC (for time constant) that controls the degree of smoothing. The smoothed value of y, say ys_i, is given by

$$ys_i = (y_i + TC \cdot ys_{i-1})/(TC + 1) \tag{15.1}$$

ys is initialized to the first value of y. If TC is 0, ys simply equals y. As TC increases, the smoothing becomes more and more heavy.

Simple FLOPS code for exponential smoothing might be

```
declare Data
  x flt
  xSmooth flt
  TC flt;

rule (goal Smooth x)
IF (in Data x = <X> AND xSmooth = <XS> AND TC = <TC>)
THEN in 1 xSmooth = ((<X> + <XS> * <TC>)/(1 + <TC>);
```

It is well to initialize xSmooth to the initial value of *x*.

TABLE 15.1   Exponential Smoothing with Various Time Constants.[a]

y_i	ys, TC 1	ys, TC 2	ys, TC 4
1	1.00	1.00	1.00
1.5	1.25	1.17	1.10
0.5	0.88	0.94	0.98
1	0.94	0.96	0.98
1.5	1.22	1.14	1.09
0.5	0.86	0.93	0.97
1	0.93	0.95	0.98
1.5	1.21	1.14	1.08
0.5	0.86	0.92	0.96
1	0.93	0.95	0.97

[a]y is the noisy input signal; ys is the smoothed value; TC is the smoothing time constant.

Consider some examples of this smoothing. Suppose that y is a constant one with intermittent noise of ± 0.5. Then for values of TC $= 1, 2$ and 4, we have Table 15.1.

It is obvious that the greater the time constant TC, the greater the smoothing for a steady-state signal with superimposed noise.

We now consider the case where the input signal is not steady state, but is steadily increasing, as shown in Table 15.2.

It is easy to see from Table 15.2 that after 20 samples, the smoothed value with time constant 1 closely represents the unsmoothed value 1 time sample ago; the smoothed value with TC $= 2$ represents the value 2 samples ago; and the smoothed value with TC $= 4$ represents the unsmoothed value 4 time samples ago. If the rate of change itself is reasonably constant, the moving average method furnishes a delay approximately equal to the time constant expressed in numbers of samples.

Another example of a time delay resulting from exponential smoothing is shown graphically in Figure 15.1.

Table 15.2 and Figure 15.1 indicate that after a few time constants have passed, the smoothed value approaches the input value with a delay of about one time constant. Thus at time 5 and thereafter, the smoothed value with time constant 1 closely approaches the input value 1 time unit previously. At time 10 and thereafter, the smoothed value with time constant 2 closely approaches the input value 2 time units previously; and at time 20 (and thereafter), the smoothed value with time constant 4 closely approaches the input value 4 time units previously. Exponential smoothing not only smooths the input but also introduces a time lag approximately equal to the smoothing time constant. This permits the programmer economically to compare a current input value to a smoothed past value without storing a table of previous values, quite useful in looking for events signaled by sudden changes in the input value.

TABLE 15.2   Exponential Smoothing of a Steadily Increasing Input[a]

T	y(t)	ys, TC 1	ys, TC 2	ys, TC 4
1	1	1.00	1.00	1.00
2	2	1.50	1.33	1.20
3	3	2.25	1.89	1.56
4	4	3.14	2.59	2.05
5	5	4.06	3.40	2.64
6	6	5.03	4.26	3.31
7	7	6.02	5.18	4.05
8	8	7.01	6.12	4.84
9	9	8.00	7.08	5.67
10	10	9.00	8.05	6.54
11	11	10.00	9.03	7.43
12	12	11.00	10.02	8.34
14	14	12.00	11.02	9.27
14	14	14.00	12.01	10.22
15	15	14.00	14.01	11.18
16	16	15.00	14.00	12.14
17	17	16.00	15.00	14.11
18	18	17.00	16.00	14.09
19	19	18.00	17.00	15.07
20	20	19.00	18.00	16.06

[a]y is input; ys is the smoothed value; and TC is the smoothing time constant.

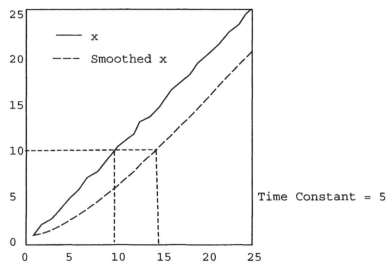

Figure 15.1   Exponential smoothing of a ramp function, showing time delay of smoothed function approximately equal to the time constant 5.

An important use for the smoothed and delayed input values produced by exponential smoothing is to furnish values for a "wandering baseline". In some processes, baseline values for measurements may be subject to changes due to changes in the process. For example, consider the heart rate of a patient in an intensive care unit measured on a beat-by-beat basis. Over the course of a day, this rate will change slowly due to patient activity level, and considerably more rapidly due to any heart-rate arrhythmias. Exponential smoothing with a suitable time constant (perhaps 20–40 s or so) will produce a baseline heart rate that varies slowly with activity level, but is insensitive to momentary changes due to onset and cessation of arrhythmias. Comparison of the momentary heart rate to the smoothed baseline value offers a way to detect the onset and cessation of hear-rate arrhythmias.

If an exponentially smoothed baseline is used for detection of an event that causes the input signal to depart significantly from the baseline, it is desirable to avoid updating the baseline until the event is over.

15.3.3 Rates of Change: Differentiating Noisy Data

Reliable numerical differentiation of a noisy input is not easy to accomplish, but may be needed for a variety of reasons, including artifact detection, process control, and event detection. A quick but crude determination of instantaneous rate of change may suffice to exclude obvious artifacts.

Let us compare some very simple ways of getting a first derivative of a noisy input signal.

First, we could use the original unsmoothed input values:

$$rate1 = (y_i - y_{i-1})/\Delta t \tag{15.2}$$

We could also use adjacent smoothed values:

$$rate2 = (ys_i - ys_{i-1})/\Delta t \tag{15.3}$$

We could also smooth the raw rates:

$$rate3_i = (rate1_i + rate1_{i-1})/2 \tag{15.4}$$

Table 15.3 gives examples of steadily increasing data subject to random fluctuations. In this table, y is the original data, and y smoothed is the original data smoothed with a time constant of one. Rates of change rate 1, rate 2, and rate 3 are obtained using formulas (15.2), (15.3), and (15.4) above. While the mean rates of change for the various methods do not differ very much, the fluctuations in the rates of change are considerably greater when using the unsmoothed data than when either using smoothed y values to determine the rate or when smoothing the rates obtained with unsmoothed input.

TABLE 15.3   Rates of Change of Noisy Data Obtained With and Without Smoothing[a]

y	y Smoothed	rate 1 (15.2)	rate 2 (15.3)	rate 3 (15.4)
3.080	2.324	1.046	0.756	0.937
3.790	3.057	0.710	0.733	0.878
4.802	3.929	1.012	0.873	0.861
6.275	5.102	1.473	1.173	1.243
6.514	5.808	0.239	0.706	0.856
8.261	7.034	1.747	1.226	0.993
9.314	8.174	1.054	1.140	1.400
10.209	9.192	0.895	1.017	0.974
10.545	9.869	0.336	0.677	0.615
11.914	10.891	1.369	1.023	0.852
14.363	12.127	1.449	1.236	1.409
14.290	14.209	0.928	1.082	1.188
14.874	14.041	0.583	0.832	0.755
16.462	15.252	1.588	1.210	1.086
17.371	16.311	0.909	1.060	1.249
17.556	16.934	0.185	0.622	0.547
19.450	18.192	1.893	1.258	1.039
19.864	19.028	0.414	0.836	1.154
	Mean	0.991	0.970	1.002
	StdDev	0.519	0.217	0.244
	Range	1.708	0.636	0.862

[a]See formulas 15.2, 15.3, and 15.4.

15.3.4   Rates of Change: Differentiating Wandering Data

It frequently happens that while the input data have very little random fluctuations, they may follow a curvilinear path with varying curvature. Formulas for differentiating data of this type are then required to give reasonably accurate rates of change without time lags. To get an estimate of rate of change of wandering curvilinear data, assume that the input is a function of time, realized as a time series of measurements taken at equal time intervals Δt. Expand this function into a McClauren series;

$$f(t - \Delta t) = f(t) - f'(t)\Delta t + f''(t)(\Delta t^2) - \cdots \qquad (15.5)$$

We can also write

$$f(t - 2\Delta t) = f(t) - f'(t)(2\Delta t) + f'(t)(2\Delta t)^2 - \cdots \qquad (15.6)$$

Dropping the terms after the second derivative, we manipulate these two equations to eliminate the second derivative term, and obtain

$$f'(t) = (3f(t) - 4f(t - 1) + f(t - 2))/(2\Delta t) \qquad (15.7)$$

The third derivative can also be eliminated by

$$f'(t) = \frac{-11F(x) + 18F(x + \Delta x) - 9F(x + 2\Delta x) + 2F(x + 3\Delta x)}{6\Delta X} \tag{15.8}$$

Equation (15.7) corrects the input stream for presence of a (constant) second derivative, and assumes that the third and all higher derivatives are zero; (15.8) corrects also for a third derivative. There is no time lag in the result. Deriving similar formulas that eliminate the effect of higher order derivatives is a straightforward but somewhat tedious task.

While formulas like (15.7) and its higher order counterparts correct for the presence of 2nd and higher order derivatives in the input data stream, they are virtually useless for eliminating the effects of random noise in input data.

15.4 TYPES OF RULES USEFUL IN REAL-TIME ON-LINE WORK

15.4.1 Fuzzy Control Rules

The field of fuzzy control has been discussed in depth in many excellent books; see, for example, Pedrycz (1995), deSilva (1995) .... Since our main interest is the use of fuzzy expert systems in other than control applications, we will only outline the main features of fuzzy control rules.

A typical fuzzy control rule has this format:

$$\text{IF (x1 is Small and x2 is Slow) THEN y is Positive;} \tag{15.9}$$

Ordinarily $x1$, $x2$, and y are scalar numbers, although it is not uncommon for $x1$ and $x2$ to be fuzzy numbers. Small, Slow, and Positive are members of discrete fuzzy sets properly called linguistic variables, in which each member such as Small has an associated membership function. Usually, there are several such rules, fired in parallel.

Rule (15.9) is much more complex than it appears; many steps and several choices are involved before its evaluation is complete.

The first step is fuzzification; that is, the input values x_i are used with the membership functions to determine the grades of membership of Small, Slow, and so on in their respective linguistic variables. Next, the truth values of the input clauses (x1 is Small, x2 is Slow ...) are combined, usually using a t-norm operator, to get truth values for the antecedents of the various rules to be fired together. The combined antecedent truth values now become the truth value of the consequent, and in (15.9) the truth value of Positive. We are now ready to start the defuzzification process, and determine a numeric value for y. The membership function for Positive is modified by taking the fuzzy AND of the membership function truth values with the antecedent truth value. Now the consequents of the various rules must be aggregated, which means combining the membership functions together to form a single complex fuzzy number (not necessarily convex) defined on the real line. We then use one of the methods available (most often the centroid method) to derive a value for y.

While the notation of rule (15.9) is quite compact, it is quite inflexible, and not really useful for general-purpose fuzzy reasoning. In FLOPS, for flexibility and clarity we break out fuzzification and defuzzification as separate consequent operations. We also refer specifically to the names of input and output linguistic variables (discrete fuzzy sets). The complete FLOPS code for such a control rule might be

```
:----------------------------------------------------------
:Data declarations
declare Data
  x1 flt
  x2 flt
  y flt
  size fzset (Small Medium Large)
  speed fzset (Slow Medium Fast)
  output fzset (Negative Zero Positive;
:----------------------------------------------------------
:Define membership functions
memfunct Data size linear
  Small.....;
:----------------------------------------------------------
:Fuzzify inputs
rule block 1 (goal Fuzzify inputs)
IF (in Data x1 = <X1> AND x2 =  < X2)
THEN
  fuzzify 1 size <X1>,
  fuzzify 1 speed <X2>,
  fire block 1 off,
  fire block 2 on;
:----------------------------------------------------------
:Fuzzy inference
rule block 2 (goal Rules to get output fuzzy sets from
input fuzzy sets)
IF (in Data size is Small AND speed is Slow)
THEN
  in 1 output is Positive,
  fire block 2 off,
  fire block 3 on;
:----------------------------------------------------------
:Defuzzification to get output
```

```
rule block 3
IF (Data)
THEN
  defuzzify 1 output centroid 1 y ;
```

Note that FLOPS syntax permits using the linguistic term Medium in two different contexts; fuzzy control rules do not often permit this, since their linguistic terms such as Medium are not usually associated with a specific linguistic variable, in this case `size` and `speed`.

The point to having fuzzification and (especially) defuzzification as separate operations is that the discrete fuzzy sets and the grades of membership of their members are available for use elsewhere in the program, either as input to succeeding stages of reasoning or as output to the user. It is not always necessary to have a defuzzification rule; programs that have their output in words rather than in numbers may not have any defuzzification taking place at all.

This rule scheme requires definition of the input (and output) linguistic variables, the discrete fuzzy sets, their members, and membership functions, at some time before the rules are fired. Although it is possible to define these fuzzy sets as the program runs, using information acquired during the run, in practice the input and output fuzzy sets are almost always defined when the program is written, rather than during the course of a run.

A potential problem with this type of rule is the "combinatorial explosion" in number of rules as the number of input variables and input fuzzy set members increases. Suppose we have N input numeric variables and (correspondingly) N input linguistic variables, each of which has M members We then have M^N possible combinations of input linguistic variable members, and M^N possible rules; there is an exponential increase in the number of rules with the number of input variables. The Combs method, although requiring more rules for a small number of input variables, has a linear rather than exponential growth in the number of rules as the number of input variables increases.

15.4.2 Focused Control-Type Rules and Focused Membership Functions

It is well known that in control programs utilizing the standard type of fuzzy control rules, that the number of rules goes up exponentially with the number of input variables, the "combinatorial explosion" problem.

This is because if we have N input variables fuzzified into N linguistic variables (discrete fuzzy sets describing numbers) with M linguistic terms (fuzzy set members) each, we construct rules with all combinations of the linguistic terms for each variable. This gives us M rules for one variable, M^2 rules for two variables, and M^N rules for N rules.

If the objective of our program is to detect particular events in which we are interested, we may be able to use rules to detect the events in which we are interested and to ignore others, with a substantial reduction in the number of rules required.

For example: in program ECHO.PAR to classify regions of an echocardiogram, we have these input fuzzy sets:

```
declare Region
   size fzset (TINY SMALL MEDIUM LARGE HUGE)
   xpos fzset (FAR-LEFT LEFT CENTER RIGHT FAR-RIGHT)
   ypos fzset (VERY-HIGH HIGH MIDDLE LOW VERY-LOW)
   class fzset (ARTIFACT LUNG LA LV LA+LV RA RV RA+RV
   LA+LV+RA+RV) ;
```

The rules are focused on detecting the output fuzzy set members. A rule for detecting one kind of artifact is

```
IF (size is TINY) THEN class is ARTIFACT;
```

All TINY regions, regardless of placement, are artifacts. This single rule replaces 25 generic rules of the control type. Similarly, a different type of artifact is detected by the rule

```
IF (size is SMALL AND ypos is VERY-HIGH) THEN class is
artifact;
```

This rule replaces 25 generic rules.

It is possible to reduce the number of rules and to increase their effectiveness by not only focusing the rules on the desired outputs, but also by focusing the membership functions. Program IRIS.PAR, presented in Chapters 7 and 12, illustrates this technique. In this program we have four input numeric variables (petal length, petal width, sepal length, and sepal width) and three possible outputs (setosa, versicolor, and virginica). Instead of fuzzifying the inputs into discrete fuzzy sets with members such as (Small, Medium, Large), our input fuzzy sets have members (setosa, versicolor, virginica). The membership functions for these linguistic terms are derived from the characteristics of the corresponding plant species. There are only three classification rules:

```
IF (petal-L is setosa AND petal_W is setosa AND sepal-L
is setosa AND sepal-W is setosa)
THEN class is setosa;

IF (petal-L is versicolor AND petal_W is versicolor AND
sepal-L is versicolor AND sepal-W is versicolor)
THEN class is versicolor;

IF (petal-L is virginica AND petal_W is virginica AND
sepal-L is virginica AND sepal-W is virginica)
THEN class is virginica;
```

The technique here is not to use such generic input fuzzy set members and membership functions as in Section 15.4.1, but to use input fuzzy set members and membership functions that are directly related to the desired outputs.

15.4.3 Fuzzy Reasoning with Approximate Numerical Comparisons

In 15.3.1 we have discussed the determination of a varying baseline using exponential smoothing. It is quite possible that we would like to compare an input to some number (like a varying baseline) that is determined during the course of a run in order to detect an event.

It is possible to revise membership functions during the course of a run and fuzzify an input number using the revised membership functions, but this is somewhat awkward. It is often simpler and more direct to use approximate numerical comparisons for this purpose.

We will take advantage of a real-world program to detect malfunctions of an instrument used in a hospital intensive care unit to measure indirectly blood pressure in the left atrium of a patient's heart after open-heart surgery. Blood pressure is measured from an intravenous catheter that runs through the right heart into the pulmonary artery.

These data are sometimes very noisy, with artifacts caused by patient movement, coughing, and the like, so detection of all artifacts is an almost hopeless task. We do get rid of the worst artifacts, but our main reliance is on rules focused on the events we wish to detect.

We have kept track of a pressure baseline by using exponential smoothing of the input pressures with a fairly large time constant. In our program notation, the pressures are

PAPs = systolic pulmonary artery pressure

PAPd = diastolic pulmonary artery pressure

PP = pulse pressure

MPAPs = systolic pulmonary artery pressure moving average

MPAPd = diastolic pulmonary artery pressure moving average

MPP = pulse pressure moving average

Here is a summary of the rules for event detection:

```
:Block 11 detect abnormal data
:r56 (goal Event PAPinRV if PP ~= PAPs and PAPs unchanged)
:r57 (goal Event PAPinRV if PAPs same AND PAPd ~< MPAPd)
:r58 (goal Event PAPinRV if 1st good sample & PP ~= PAPs)
:r59 (goal Event Wedged if PP ~< MPP & PAPs ~< MPAPs & PAPd
     ~<= MPAPd)
:r60 (goal Event Overwedged if PP ~< MPP & PAPs ~> MPAPs)
:r61 (goal Event Damped if PAPd ~= PAPs)
:r62 (goal Event Damped if PP ~< MPP)
```

You will note that every rule is focused on the event to be detected and makes use of approximate numerical comparisons between the current pressures and the wandering baseline moving averages. (The actual rules are more complicated, and take care of such features as not too much noise in the data and some bookkeeping chores.)

15.5   MEMORY MANAGEMENT

Data-driven production systems firing their rules sequentially usually retain all data created or modified in the computer's memory. This is critical in sequential rule-firing programs. When backtracking, the data that made a rule on the backtrack stack originally fireable may have been subsequently modified or deleted by the time the backtracked rule is popped off the stack for firing. If these data are referred to in the rule's consequent, they must be recovered and made available when the rule is finally fired. In addition, in both sequential and parallel programs it may be desirable for old data to be recovered for inspection for debugging or explanation purposes.

However, keeping old data indefinitely is not practical for programs that may run indefinitely, such as real-time on-line programs. Fortunately, such programs are virtually always run in parallel mode; since there is no backtracking in parallel systems, it is not required that data having been modified or deleted by the program be retained. During program development and test it is desirable to retain old data, but not during production runs. Consequently, in parallel mode retaining deleted data may be turned off. FLOPS furnishes an "erase ON/OFF" command to control retention of old data. If erase is OFF, old data are indefinitely retained; if erase is ON, data deleted or modified by the program are immediately removed from memory and the space used returned to the operating system. In this way, old data may be made available during program development and test, but may be removed in production runs.

15.6   DEVELOPMENT OF ON-LINE REAL-TIME PROGRAMS

Modularization of on-line real-time programs is even more important than in most other types or programs. Basic modules are data acquisition and output; graphical user interface; and data analysis.

a. **Data acquisition.** The first module to be written should be for data acquisition. Initially, data should be acquired and written to disk in a record format similar to that in which the data will be presented to the analysis module when running on line. This will permit program development and debugging off line.

b. **Data screening.** After the data are input, they should be screened for obvious artifacts. Data smoothing can be incorporated next, to prepare the data for analysis. Further checks for data validity can use the smoothed data, to check for random noise, unreasonable rates of change, and other artifacts.

c. **Processing the data.** After the data screening section, we are ready for processing the data. This is, of course, completely application dependent. Since many if not most on-line real-time run unsupervised by humans, the analysis routines tend to be fairly complex to take care of all reasonable eventualities. If events are to be detected, we can make sure that the event lasts long enough not to be artifactual.

d. **Check for validity of output.** In the analysis phase, further check for validity may be made, together with checks that any serious artifacts are no longer occurring.

e. **Program output.** Finally, the program output is programmed.

We discuss below the structure of an actual deployed real-time on-line fuzzy expert system for event detection and alarm generation for patients in a hospital intensive care unit. Omitted from this discussion are the program blocks for acquiring the data. Output of this program was voice alarm messages sent over the computer's speakers, in addition to hard disk log of events.

Table 15.4 lists the major program blocks for processing the input data stream. Data for this program were obtained via RS232C in one institution and via Ethernet in another; Table 15.4 does not list the program blocks that implement I/O, but only lists the processing blocks. Block 9 detects a single event, but this may be a fluke; initiation of a formal event and issuance of an alarm require more than a single detected event, and are done by blocks 11 and 12. If an event is taking place on an input measurement variable, block 14 suspends updating the exponentially smoothed and delayed baselines.

In Table 15.4, block 9 does initial event detection. However, alarms are not issued as soon as an event is detected on one data input record; it is necessary to verify that an alarm event is indeed taking place. Blocks 10, 11, and 12 perform this verification. Alarms are actually issued by Block 12. While events are taking

TABLE 15.4   Rule Blocks for Processing Input Data in an On-Line Real-Time Program for Event Detection and Alarm Generation

Block 3: Update missing data count, preliminary data calculations
Block 4: Eliminate unreasonably high amplitudes
Block 5: Initialize or update short-term exponential smoothing
Block 6: Get short-term rates of change
Block 7: Eliminate artifacts based on high rate of change
Block 8: Initialize long-term exponentially smoothed baselines once
Block 9: Detect events
Block 10: Mediate conflicts between events
Block 11: Get data for initiation and termination of formal events
Block 12: Initiation and termination of formal events
Block 13: Reset events if data back to normal, get noise
Block 14: Update long-term exponentially smoothed baseline

place, or if it is found that noise in the input data exceeds allowable limits, updating baselines by block 14 is suspended until Block 13 determines that the process has returned to normal.

15.7 SPEEDING UP A PROGRAM

In spite of the tremendous increases in computer processor speeds and the speed advantage of parallel over sequential rule-firing modes, it is still quite possible that the speed demands made by the real world may be too much for a program written in such a language as FLOPS to handle. While production systems are relatively slow compared to procedural languages, their power, flexibility, and debugging features make program development and debugging more convenient than say a C compiler. One way to approach this situation is to develop the program methodology using a production system off-line, and then recode the working production system into a procedural language, replacing fuzzy logic with interval logic. This procedure was followed in the alarm expert system outlined in Section 15.6. The initial program was developed, tested, and debugged in FLOPS. While FLOPS program worked very well to monitor a few patients, the final system would have to monitor perhaps several dozen patients simultaneously. After recoding into C++, the program was capable of handling a large number of patients concurrently. Interestingly, the program was written in the 1980s, when computers were more than an order of magnitude slower than at this writing; the original FLOPS program, without recoding into C++, could well have handled a few dozen patient beds if run on a modern 2.5 or 3-GHz machine.

15.8 DEBUGGING REAL-TIME ONLINE PROGRAMS

It is usually very undesirable to attempt to debug a real-time on-line program while it is directly wired to the source of data, especially so if the program is closed-loop. It is best to collect the input data in a disk file or files, so that the program can be run off line for creation and debugging.

One should seldom attempt to write the whole program before testing it. The program should be developed in modular fashion, beginning with the program section that inputs the data. Next, one proceeds to the sections that check for obvious artifacts in the input data, and compensates for noisy data, perhaps adjusting moving average time constants. When the data are successfully input and screened, we can go on to the sections that perform the appropriate actions.

It is often helpful to write a program that will simulate the process that generates the data. For example, a program that stabilized a patient's blood pressure by controlling injection of sodium nitroprusside used a small analog computer to simulate the heart action and its nitroprusside response in order to debug the expert system. More often, a procedural language program or another expert system can be written to simulate the process.

One important note. A general principle for computer programs is *Always give the user a way out.* It is imperative that there be checks that the program is not malfunctioning, with provision for an orderly shutdown if necessary.

15.9 DISCUSSION

The ability of a complex expert system to run in real-time on-line to a process has strong implications for event detection, especially for fault detection and analysis. While such a system resembles fuzzy control systems insofar as input is concerned, the programming techniques for event detection and analysis are quite different and more complex than for fuzzy control. We have written two such programs, both for hospital intensive care units (ICU). The first and simplest was for suppression of false alarm detections in a neonatal ICU for low blood oxygen saturation. As an infant squirmed around, a simple threshold method detected many more false alarms than true ones. The second was for detection and classification of several alarm conditions from pulmonary artery pressure catheters in a heart transplant ICU and an open-heart surgery ICU. Not only was the detection and classification difficult, but like the first problem there were many measurement artifacts that had to be accounted for. Both projects were successful.

15.10 QUESTIONS

15.1 What are two differences between programs that interact with a human via keyboard or mouse on-line in real-time and a program hard-wired to a process?

15.2 What objectives other than process control can real-time on-line fuzzy expert systems achieve?

15.3 What FLOPS command is used to input and output real-time on-line data?

15.4 How can obvious data artifacts be detected?

15.5 How can data be smoothed?

15.6 What characteristic of exponential smoothing is a possible disadvantage?

15.7 What useful purposes can the time delay introduced by exponential smoothing serve?

15.8 How can relatively high-frequency input noise be quantitated?

15.9 How can rates of change be corrected for the presence of second or third derivatives in the input data?

15.10 Write a typical fuzzy control rule, and define the data types to which the symbols correspond.

15.11 What are the advantages and disadvantages of typical fuzzy control rules?

15.12 What are the advantages and disadvantages of focused fuzzy reasoning rules?

15.13 What are the advantages of using fuzzy numerical comparisons?

15.14 How do data-driven programs that fire their rules sequentially manage memory of data? Why? What disadvantage does this have for real-time on-line work?

15.15 How do data-driven programs that fire their rule in parallel manage memory of data? Why? What advantage does this have for real-time on-line work?

15.16 What are the five major steps in processing on-line data in real-time?

15.17 How can a real-time on-line fuzzy expert system be speeded up?

15.18 What is the procedure for debugging a real-time on-line program?

APPENDIX
List of FLOPS Programs on Wiley Web Site

(May be slightly modified from this list.)

```
:Exercise AndOrNot.fps

message "Compiling AndOrNot.fps";
declare Data p flt q flt

  NotP flt                                    :tv, NOT P
  ZandPQ flt ZorPQ flt    :tv, P and Q, P or Q, Zadehian
                            max-min logic
  PandPQ flt PorPQ flt    :tv, P and Q, P or Q,
                            probabilistic logic
  BandPQ flt BorPQ flt;   :tv, P and Q, P or Q, bounded
                            sum/difference logic
:rule r0
rule (goal Input p and q truth values)
IF (in Data p.cf = 0)
THEN
     write "Input p" ,
     read 1 p,
     write "Input q (negative to quit)",
     read 1 q;

:rule (goal Quit if q negative)
:rule r1
rule
IF (in Data q < 0)
THEN exit;

:rule (goal Calculate NotP, aANDb, aORb by various
```

Fuzzy Expert Systems and Fuzzy Reasoning, By William Siler and James J. Buckley
ISBN 0-471-38859-9   Copyright © 2005 John Wiley & Sons, Inc.

```
 multivalued logics)
:rule r2

rule
IF (in Data p = <P> AND q = <Q> AND NotP.cf = 0 AND q >= 0)
THEN
      in 1 NotP = (1 - <P>),
      in 1 ZandPQ = (min(<P>, <Q>)) ZorPQ = (max(<P>,
      <Q>)),
  in 1 PandPQ = (<P> * <Q>) PorPQ = (<P> + <Q> - <P> * <Q>),
  in 1 BandPQ = (max(0, <P> + <Q> - 1)) BorPQ = (min(<P>
  + <Q>, 1));

:rule r3
rule (goal Print results and try again)
IF (in Data NotP = <NOTA> ZandPQ = <ZAND> ZorPQ = <ZOR>
PandPQ = <PAND> PorPQ = <POR>
          BandPQ = <BAND> BorPQ = <BOR> p = <P> q = <Q>)
THEN
  write "p <P> q <Q>\n",
  write "Max-min Zadehian logic\n",
  write "p AND q <ZAND> p OR q <ZOR> NOT p <NOTA>\n",
  write "Probabilistic logic\n",
  write "p AND q <PAND> p OR q <POR> NOT p <NOTA>\n",
  write "Bounded sum logic\n",
  write "p AND q <BAND> p OR q <BOR> NOT p <NOTA>\n\n",
  delete 1,
      make Data;

make Data;
message "Ready to run";
run;

: ***********************************************************
:program AUTO1.FPS - why doesn't the auto start ?
:all knowledge stored in rules
:total rules = 14 = number of nodes in decision tree + 3
:number of rules goes up as complexity of tree increases
: ***********************************************************

string = "Trouble diagnosis\: auto will not start.\n" ;
string + "Auto1.fps has 14 rules - expert knowledge in
          rules.\n";
string + "compiling program auto1.fps...\n" ;
message "<string>";
```

```
declare Answer
  reply str
  verify str ;

declare Hypothesis
  working str ;


: +++++++++++++++++++++++++++++++++++++++++++++++++++++++++

:tests whether engine turns over
:rule r0
rule rconf 999 (goal Check whether engine turns over)
  IF (Answer)
     (in Hypothesis working.cf = 0)
  THEN
     reset ,
     input "Does the starter turn your engine over
     (y/n) ?\n"
       1 reply lcase y n ,
     in 1 verify = "n" ,
     in 2 working = "engine will not turn over" ;

:tests battery
:rule r1
rule rconf 999 (goal Check if dead battery)
  IF (in Answer reply = <R> AND verify = <R>)
     (in Hypothesis working = "engine will not turn over")
  THEN
     reset ,
     input "Do your lights come on (y/n) ?\n"
       1 reply lcase y n ,
     in 1 verify = "n" ,
     in 2 working = "dead battery" ;

:tests blown fuse
:rule r2
rule rconf 998 (goal Check if blown fuse)
  IF (in Answer reply = <R> AND verify = <R>)
     (in Hypothesis working = "engine will not turn over")
  THEN
     reset ,
     input "Are any of your fuses blown (y/n) ?\n"
       1 reply lcase y n ,
     in 1 verify = "y" ,
     in 2 working = "blown fuse" ;
```

```
:tests battery connectors
:rule r3
rule rconf 997
  (goal Check if loose battery connectors)
  IF (in Answer reply = <R> AND verify = <R>)
    (in Hypothesis working = "engine will not turn over")
  THEN
    reset,
    input "Are your battery connectors loose (y/n) ?\n"
      1 reply lcase y n,
    in 1 verify = "y",
    in 2 working = "loose battery connectors"  ;

: -----------------------------------------------------------
:tests of no fuel
:1st level hypotheses
:rule r4
rule rconf 998 (goal Check if no fuel to engine)
  IF (in Answer reply.cf = 0)
    (in Hypothesis working.cf = 0)
  THEN
    reset ,
    input "Do you smell gas at your carburetor (y/n) ?\n"
      1 reply lcase y n ,
    in 1 verify = "n" ,
    in 2 working = "no fuel to engine" ;

:tests out of gas
:rule r5
rule rconf 999 (goal Check if no gas in tank)
  IF (in Answer reply = <R> AND verify = <R>)
    (in Hypothesis working = "no fuel to engine")
  THEN
    reset ,
    input "Does your gas gauge read empty (y/n) ?\n"
      1 reply lcase y n ,
    in 1 verify = "y" ,
    in 2 working = "out of gas" ;

:tests fuel filter
:rule r6
rule rconf 998 (goal Check if clogged fuel filter)
  IF (in Answer reply = <R> AND verify = <R>)
    (in Hypothesis working = "no fuel to engine")
  THEN
```

```
     reset ,
     input "Is your fuel filter clogged (y/n) ?\n"
        1 reply lcase y n ,
     in 1 verify = "y" ,
     in 2 working = "bad fuel filter" ;


: -----------------------------------------------------
:tests whether any spark
:rule r7
rule rconf 997 (goal Check if no spark)
   IF (in Answer reply.cf = 0)
      (in Hypothesis working.cf = 0)
   THEN
      reset ,
      input "Can you see a spark between plug lead and
        ground (y/n) ?\n" 1 reply lcase y n ,
      in 1 verify = "n" ,
      in 2 working = "no spark" ;

:check if distributor points open.
:rule r8
rule rconf 999 (goal Check if distributer points do not open)
   IF (in Answer reply = <R> AND verify = <R>)
      (in Hypothesis working = "no spark")
   THEN
      reset ,
     input "Do your distributor points open slightly (y/n)\n"
        1 reply lcase y n ,
      in 1 verify = "n" ,
      in 2 working = "distributor points misadjusted" ;

:checks for rainy weather
:rule r9
rule rconf 998 (goal Check if raining)
   IF (in Answer reply = <R> AND verify = <R>)
      (in Hypothesis working = "no spark")
   THEN
      reset ,
      input "Is it raining (y/n) ?\n" 1 reply lcase y n ,
      in 1 verify = "y" ,
      in 2 working = "raining" ;

:checks for wet ignition
:rule r10
rule rconf 999 (goal Check if ignition wiring wet)
```

```
   IF (in Answer reply = <R> AND verify = <R>)
     (in Hypothesis working = "raining")
   THEN
     reset ,
     input "Is your ignition system wet ?\n" 1 reply
     lcase y n ,
     in 1 verify = "y" ,
     in 2 working = "wet ignition" ;


: -----------------------------------------------------

:report trouble if at end of path

:rule r11
rule rconf 0 (goal Terminal hypothesis verified - print
trouble)
   IF (in Answer reply = <R> AND verify = <R>)
     (in Hypothesis working = <H>)
   THEN
     message 'Your trouble is <H>\n' ,
     stop ;

:report failure to find trouble

:can't find the trouble
:rule r12
rule rconf   0   (goal Hypotheses all rejected - can not
find trouble)
   IF (in Answer reply.cf = 0)
     (in Hypothesis working.cf = 0)
   THEN
     message 'Cannot find the trouble. Call a tow truck.
       \n' ,
     exit ;


: -----------------------------------------------------

:backtracks if answer not verified
:rule r13
rule rconf 999 (goal Backtracks if hypothesis rejected)
   IF (in Answer reply = <R> AND verify <> <R>)
     (in Hypothesis working = <X>)
   THEN
     reset ,
     write 'Checked <X> NG and backtracking\n' ,
```

```
    delete 1 ,
    delete 2 ;


: ++++++++++++++++++++++++++++++++++++++++++++++++++++++++


make Answer ;
make Hypothesis ;
message 'AUTO1.FPS ready to run -\n' ;
:run ;
: *********************************************************


: *********************************************************
:program AUTO2.FPS - general tree search program
:expert knowledge in data base
:five rules - number does not increase with depth or
:breadth of search
:includes data for auto problem
: *********************************************************

string = "Trouble diagnosis\: auto will not start.\n" ;
string + "Auto2.fps has 5 rules, expert knowledge in data
         base,\n" ;
string + "Data base in blackboard data file (relational
         data base) format.\n" ;
string + "Compiling auto2.fps...\n" ;
message "<string>";

declare Answer     :element to store user's reply
  reply str ;

declare Node       :library data
  hypo1 str            :preceding hypothesis
  hypo2 str            :current hypothesis
  question str         :hypothesis-verifying question
  verify str ;         :hypothesis-verifying response

declare Messages
  hypo str             :verified hypothesis
  message str;         :message to send

declare Working    :working hypothesis at the moment
  hypo1 str            :preceding hypothesis
  hypo2 str            :hypothesis under test
  verify str;          :hypothesis-verifying yresponse
```

```
: +++++++++++++++++++++++++++++++++++++++++++++++++++++++++

:rule r0
rule (goal Sets up hypotheses, gets user response to
question)
IF (in Answer reply.cf = 0)
   (in Working hypo1 = <H1>)
   (in Node hypo1 = <H1> AND hypo2 = <H2> AND question
   = <Q> AND verify = <V>)
THEN
   reset ,
   input "<Q> (y/n) ?\n" 1 reply lcase y n,
   in 2 hypo1 "<H1>" hypo2 "<H2>" verify "<V>" ,
   delete 3 ;


: ---------------------------------------------------------
:rule r1
rule (goal fires if hypothesis accepted)
IF (in Answer reply = <R>)
   (in Working hypo1 = <H1> AND hypo2 = <H> AND verify
   = <R>)
   (in Node hypo1 = <H> AND hypo2 = <H2>)
THEN
   reset ,
   write "Verified <H>, next hypothesis <H2>\n" ,
   in 1 reply.cf 0 ,
   in 2 hypo1 "<H>" hypo2 "<H2>" ;
:rule r2
rule (goal fires if hypothesis rejected)
IF (in Answer reply = <R>)
   (in Working hypo2 = <H> AND verify <> <R>)
THEN
   write "rejected <H> and backtracking\n" ,
   delete 1 ,
   delete 2 ;


: ---------------------------------------------------------
:diagnosis

:writes out verified hypothesis and quits
:rule r3
rule 0 (goal writes out verified terminal hypothesis and
quits)
IF (in Answer reply <R>)
   (in Answer reply = <R>)
   (in Working hypo2 = <H2> AND verify = <R>)
```

```
   (in Messages hypo = <H2> AND message = <M>)
THEN
  write "Verified hypothesis <H2>\n" ,
  message nocancel "<M>\n" ,
  write "Auto2 finished\n" ,
  exit ;

:rule r4
rule 0 (goal fires if can\'t find the trouble)
IF (in Working hypo2.cf = 0)
THEN
  message "Can\'t verify any hypothesis. Better call a
  mechanic!\n" ,
  exit ;

: +++++++++++++++++++++++++++++++++++++++++++++++++++++++++++++

:knowledge data base - preceding hypothesis, succeeding
 hypotheis,
:hypothesis-verifying question, verifying response
transfer Node from nodes.dat ;
transfer Messages from messages.dat ;

:internal memory elements
make Answer;
make Working hypo1 "TOP" ;
message "AUTO2.FPS ready to run -\n" ;
run ;
exit ;
: *************************************************************

// Function CorrLogic - given a, b and default r,
// returns aANDb and aORb
// 04-17-2004 WS

#include <math.h>

double min(double x, double y);
double max(double x, double y);

bool CorrLogic (double a, double b, double r, double
*aANDb, double *aORb)
{
  double std, ru, r1;

  if (a < 0 || a > 1 || b < 0 || b > 1 || r < -1 || r > 1)
```

```
                return false;
        std = sqrt(a * (1 - a) * b * (1 - b));
   if (std > 0)
   {
      ru = (min(a, b) - a * b) / std;
      rl = (max(a + b - 1, 0) - a * b) / std;
      if (r < rl)
        r = rl;
      else if (r > ru)
        r = ru;
   }
   *aANDb = a * b + r * std;
   *aORb = a + b - a * b - r * std;

        return true;
}

double min(double x, double y)
{
        if (x < y)
                return x;
        else
                return y;
}
double max(double x, double y)
{
          if (x > y)
                return x;
          else
                return y;
}

:program DEFUZZ.PAR

message 'Compiling program DEFUZZ to fuzzify and defuzzify
height of a person\n' ;

thresh 1 ;

declare Data
  height flt
  defuzz flt
  size fzset
    ( Short Medium Tall ) ;
```

```
memfunct Data size linear
  Short -1e6 4 4.5 5.5
  Medium 4.5 5.5 5.5 6.5
  Tall 5.5 6.5 7 1e6 ;

message 'Membership functions for fuzzy set size\:\n' ;
drawmemf Data size ;

:rule r0
rule (goal Enter height data)
IF ( in Data height.cf = 0 )
THEN
  input "Enter person\'s height in feet\, 0 to quit\n" 1 height ;

:rule r1
rule (goal Quit on entry of zero height)
IF ( in Data height 0 )
THEN
  message nocancel 'Terminating program DEFUZZ\n' ,
  exit ;
:rule r2
rule (goal Fuzzify height into fuzzy set size)
IF ( in Data height <H> AND height > 0 )
THEN
  message 'Height before fuzzification: <H>\n' ,
  fuzzify 1 size <H>,
  fire block 0 off ,
  fire block 1 on ;

:enable firing rule with zero cdonfidence in fuzzy set
 members
TestFsetOff;

rule block 1 (goal Print fuzzy set size\, defuzzify into defuzz)
IF ( in Data defuzz.cf = 0 size.Short <S> size.Medium <M>
  size.Tall <T> )
THEN
  message 'Fuzzified height:\nShort <S> Medium <M> Tall
    <T>\n' ,
  defuzzify 1 size maxav 1 defuzz ;

rule block 1 (goal Print defuzzified value\,
re-initialize
  program)
IF ( in Data defuzz <X> )
```

```
THEN
  message 'Defuzzified value <X>\n' ,
  in 1 defuzz.cf = 0 height.cf = 0 ,
  fire block 1 off ,
  fire block 0 on ;

make Data ;
fire all off ;
fire block 0 on ;
message 'Program DEFUZZ ready to run\n' ;
:run ;

: ********************************************************
:DRAWMEMF.FPS - illustrates drawmemf command
: ********************************************************

message "Program DRAWMEMF.FPS to illustrate the drawmemf
command." ;

:Specifications for the individual functions are given
 in the memfunct
:command. The first number is the point where the
 function first begins
:to rise from zero; the second number is the point where
 the function
:reaches 1000. The third number is the point where the
 function begins
:to decline from 1000; the fourth number is the point
 where it reaches zero again.

:If the first number is -1e6, the function starts at 1000
 for all values
:less than the third number, where it begins to decline
 toward zero;
:the only effect of the second number is to tell drawmemf
 where to start its plot.

:Similarly, if the fourth number is 1e6, the function
 never declines
:toward zero after its initial rise to 1000 at the value
 given by the
:second number; the only effect of the third number is to
 tell drawmemf
:where to stop its plot.
```

```
message "First membership functions are linear." ;

declare Data size fzset (SMALL MEDIUM LARGE) ;

memfunct Data size linear
  SMALL -1e6  0 2 4
  MEDIUM 2 4  4 8
  LARGE  4 8 10 1e6 ;

drawmemf Data size ;

message "Next membership functions are s-shape." ;

memfunct Data size s-shape
  SMALL -1e6  0 2 4
  MEDIUM 2 4  4 8
  LARGE  4 8 10 1e6 ;

drawmemf Data size ;

message "Last membership functions are normal." ;

memfunct Data size normal
  SMALL -1e6  0 2 4
  MEDIUM 2 4  4 8
  LARGE  4 8 10 1e6 ;

drawmemf Data size ;
message "DRAWMEMF.FPS finished." ;
:exit ;
: ********************************************************

: ********************************************************
: sample program ECHO.PAR for classification of image
  regions
: resolves contradictions: simplified for demonstration
  purposes
: uses rule-generating rules for preliminary
classifications
: and crisp final classifications.
: ********************************************************

message "Program ECHO.PAR for pattern recognition on
echocardiograms " ;
s-shape ;
```

```
string = "Program ECHO.PAR for pattern recognition
          has 26 " ;
string + "rules, five of which are to display information
          to the " ;
string + "user. Twelve more rules will be generated from
          a ";
string + "blackboard file, for getting preliminary and
          crisp ";
string + "final classifications. Since this is a
          demonstration ";
string + "program, fewer rules are generated than would ";
string + "normally be the case. \n";
string + "ECHO2 starts in parallel mode, but switches to
          serial " ;
string + "mode so that the last printout of region data
          is ordered " ;
string + "sequentially by region numbers.\n";
message "<string>";

string = "Classification and image data are read in
          from ";
string + "blackboard files created by previous programs,
          and ";
string + "final classifications are written to a black-
          board file ";
string + "for succeeding programs.\n";
message "<string>";
message "Compiling program ECHO.PAR\n" ;

: DECLARATIONS

:raw data
declare Data
  frame int
  rnum int
  area flt
  xbar flt
  ybar flt
  border str ;

:region characteristics
declare Region      :global region characteristics - INPUT
  frame int         :frame number
  rnum int          :region number within frame
  area fznum        :global region features
```

```
   size fzset       :word equivalent of area
     ( TINY SMALL MEDIUM LARGE HUGE)
   xbar fznum       :x-centroid
   xpos fzset       :word equivalent of xbar
     ( FAR-LEFT LEFT CENTER RIGHT FAR-RIGHT)
   ybar fznum       :y-centroid
   ypos fzset       :word equivalent of ybar
     ( VERY-HIGH HIGH MIDDLE LOW VERY-LOW)
   border str       :YES or NO
   class fzset      :classifications
     (
     ARTIFACT        :artifact
     LUNG            :lungs
     LA              :left atrium
     LV              :left ventricle
     LA+LV           :merged left atrium and ventricle
     RA              :right atrium
     RV              :right ventricle
     RA+RV           :merged right atrium and ventricle
     LA+LV+RA+RV     :all four chanbers artifactually
                      merged
     )
   final str ;        :final classification

:rule firing control
declare Enable
   block int ;

:printout control
declare Print
   rnum int ;

:definitions for creating classification rules
declare Classdef
   goal str size str x str y str class str borderop str
border str ;

: +++++++++++++++++++++++++++++++++++++++++++++++++++++
:Membership functions

memfunct Region size s-shape
   TINY -1E6 50 100
   SMALL 0 50 200 300
   MEDIUM 100 200 500 1000
   LARGE 300 500 2000 3000
```

```
    HUGE 1000 2000 5000 1e6 ;

memfunct Region xpos s-shape
    FAR-LEFT -1e6 0 144 200
    LEFT 88 144 256 312
    CENTER 144 200 312 368
    RIGHT 200 256 368 424
    FAR-RIGHT 312 368 512 1e6 ;

memfunct Region ypos s-shape
    VERY-HIGH -1e6 0 144 200
    HIGH 88 144 256 312
    MIDDLE 144 200 312 368
    LOW 200 256 368 424
    VERY-LOW 312 368 512 1e6 ;

string = "Membership functions for fuzzy sets\:\n" ;
string + "First fuzzy set is size, equivalent to region
        area.\n" ;
string + "Members of size are TINY, SMALL, MEDIUM, LARGE
        and HUGE.\n";
message "<string>";
drawmemf Region size ;
string = "Next fuzzy set is xpos, equivalent to
        x-centroid position.\n" ;
string + "Members of xpos are FAR-LEFT, LEFT, CENTER,
        RIGHT AND FAR-RIGHT.\n";
message "<string>";
drawmemf Region xpos ;
string = "Last fuzzy set is ypos, equivalent to
        y-centroid position.\n" ;
string + "Members of ypos are VERY-HIGH, HIGH, MIDDLE,
        LOW and VERY-LOW.\n";
message "<string>";
drawmemf Region ypos ;
: ----------------------------------------------------------
: RULES
: ----------------------------------------------------------

:Block 0 - creates preliminary classification rules,
 convert data to fznums

:rule r0
rule block 0 (goal Moves input data to "Region",
  converts to fuzzy numbers)
```

```
IF (in Data frame = <F> AND rnum = <N> AND area = <A> AND
   xbar = <X>
     AND ybar = <Y> border = <B>)
THEN
    make Region frame = <F> rnum = <N> area = <A> 10 0.1
      xbar = <X> 20 0 ybar = <Y> 20 0 border = "<B>" ;

:rule r1
rule block 0 (goal Creates preliminary classification rules)
IF (in Classdef goal = <G> AND size= <S> AND x = <X> AND y = <Y>
     AND class = <CL> AND borderop = <OP> AND border =
     <B>)
THEN
  write 'Creating rule for classification as <CL>\n' ,
  rule block 2 (goal <G>)
  IF (in Region <S> AND <X> AND <Y> AND border <OP> "<B>")
  THEN
    in 1 class is <CL> ;     :fire rule off ;

: ---------------------------------------------------
:Block 1 - fuzzifies data, writes out data converted to
 fuzzy numbers

:rule r2
rule block 1 (goal Fuzzifies area, xbar, ybar into size,
xpos, ypos)
IF (in Region area = <A> AND xbar = <X> AND ybar = <Y>)
THEN
  fuzzify 1 size <A> ,
  fuzzify 1 xpos <X> ,
  fuzzify 1 ypos <Y> ;

:rule r3
rule block 1 (goal Writes out data converted to fuzzy
numbers)
IF (in Region rnum = <N>)
THEN
  write 'Raw data for region <N> (fuzzy numbers) -\n' ,
  prmem 1 rnum area xbar ybar ;

: ---------------------------------------------------
:Block 2 rules write out fuzzy sets, get preliminary
 classifications
:classification rules created by r1
```

```
:rule r4
rule block 2 (goal Writes out fuzzy sets)
IF (in Region rnum = <N>)
THEN
  write 'Fuzzy sets for region <N>:\n' ,
  prmem 1 rnum size xpos ypos ;

: ------------------------------------------------------
:Block 3 - writes preliminary classifications to screen

:rule r5
rule block 3 (goal Writes preliminary classifications to
screen)
IF (in Region frame = <FR> AND rnum = <N>)
THEN
  write 'Preliminary classifications for frame <FR>
region <N>:\n' ,
  prmem 1 rnum class ;

: ------------------------------------------------------
:Block 4 - commences resolution of contradictions

:The following rules reduce confidences, using non-
 monotonic logic.
:Fuzzy set memberships are modified directly. This
 overrides the Fuzzy Truth
:Maintenance System, and permits setting memberships to
 any value.

:rule r6
rule block 4 (goal Rule out LA+LV if both LV and LA+LV
  and also LA)
IF (in Region frame = <FR> AND rnum = <N1> AND class is
LV AND class is LA+LV)
  (in Region frame = <FR> AND rnum = <N2> AND rnum <>
    <N1> AND class is LA)
THEN
  reset,
  write 'Frame <FR> Region <N1> - Ruling out LA+LV in
    favor of LV and LA\n',
  in 1 class is LA+LV = 0 ;

:rule r7
rule block 4 (goal Rule out RA+RV if both RV and RA+RV
and also RA)
```

```
IF (in Region frame = <FR> AND rnum = <N1> AND class is
RV AND class is RA+RV)
  (in Region frame = <FR> AND rnum = <N2> AND rnum <>
  <N1> AND class is RA)
THEN
  reset ,
  write 'Frame <FR> Region <N1> - Ruling out RA+RV in
favor of RV and RA\n' ,
  in 1 class is RA+RV = 0 ;


: -----------------------------------------------------
:Block 5 - more conflict resolution

:rule r8
rule block 5
  (goal Rule out LV if both LV and LA+LV, no LA else
LA+LV would be cleared)
IF (in Region frame <F> rnum <N> class is LV AND class is
LA+LV)
THEN
  reset ,
  write 'Frame <F> rnum <N> - Ruling out LV in favor of
LA+LV\n' ,
  in 1 class is LV = 0 ;

:rule r9
rule block 5
  (goal Rule out RV if both RV and RA+RV, no RA else
RA+RV would be cleared)
IF (in Region frame <F> rnum <N> class is RV AND class is RA+RV)
THEN
  reset ,
  write 'Frame <F> rnum <N> - Ruling out RV in favor of
RA+RV\n' ,
  in 1 class is RV = 0 ;

: -----------------------------------------------------
:Block 6 - more conflict resolution

:rule r10
rule block 6 (goal checks for LA+LV and RV in same
region)
IF (in Region frame <F> rnum <N> class is LA+LV AND class
is RV)
  (in Region frame <F> class is RV AND rnum <> <N>)
```

```
THEN
  write 'Frame <F> rnum <N> - Ruling out RV in favor of
LA+LV\n' ,
  in 1 class is RV = 0 ;

:rule r11
rule block 6 (goal checks for RA+RV and LV in same
region)
IF (in Region frame <F> rnum <N> class is RA+RV AND class
is LV)
   (in Region frame <F> class is LV AND rnum <> <N>)
THEN
  write 'Frame <F> rnum <N> - Ruling out LV in favor of
  RA+RV\n',
  in 1 class is RV = 0 ;

:rule r12
rule block 6
   (goal checks for RA+RV and LA+LV in same region, RA+RV
in another)
IF (in Region frame <F> rnum <N> class is RA+RV AND class
is LA+LV)
   (in Region frame <F> class is RA+RV AND rnum <> <N>)
THEN
  write 'Frame <F> rnum <N> - Ruling out RA+RV in favor
  of LA+LV\n',
  in 1 class is RA+RV = 0 ;

:rule r13
rule block 6
   (goal checks for RA+RV and LA+LV in same region, LA+LV
   in another)
IF (in Region frame <F> rnum <N> class is RA+RV AND class
is LA+LV)
   (in Region frame <F> class is LA+LV AND rnum <> <N>)
THEN
  write 'Frame <F> rnum <N> - Ruling out LA+LV in favor
  of RA+RV\n',
  in 1 class is LA+LV = 0 ;

: -------------------------------------------------------
:Block 7 rules check that all chambers are present,
:store final classification

:rule r14
```

```
rule block 7 (goal Checks for LA, LV, RA, RV in same frame)
IF (in Region frame = <FR> AND class is LA)
   (in Region frame = <FR> AND class is LV)
   (in Region frame = <FR> AND class is RA)
   (in Region frame = <FR> AND class is RV)
THEN
   reset ,
   write 'LA, LV, RA, RV present in frame <FR>\n',
   in 1 final = "LA" ,
   in 2 final = "LV" ,
   in 3 final = "RA" ,
   in 4 final = "RV" ;

:rule r15
rule block 7 (goal Checks for LA, LV, RA+RV in same frame)
IF (in Region frame = <FR> AND class is LA)
   (in Region frame = <FR> AND class is LV)
   (in Region frame = <FR> AND class is RA+RV)
THEN
   reset ,
   write 'LA, LV, RA+RV present in frame <FR>\n' ,
   in 1 final = "LA" ,
   in 2 final = "LV" ,
   in 3 final = "RA+RV" ;

:rule r16
rule block 7 (goal Checks for LA+LV, RA, RV in same frame)
IF (in Region frame = <FR> AND class is LA+LV)
   (in Region frame = <FR> AND class is RA)
   (in Region frame = <FR> AND class is RV)
THEN
   reset ,
   write 'LA+LV, RA, RV present in frame <FR>\n' ,
   in 1 final = "LA+LV" ,
   in 2 final = "RA" ,
   in 3 final = "RV" ;

:rule r17
rule block 7 (goal Checks for LA+LV, RA+RV in same frame)
IF (in Region frame = <FR> AND class is LA+LV)
   (in Region frame = <FR> AND class is RA+RV)
THEN
   reset ,
   write 'LA+LV, RA+RV present in frame <FR>\n' ,
   in 1 final = "LA+LV" ,
```

```
  in 2 final = "RA+RV" ;

:rule r18
rule block 7 (goal Checks for LA+LV+RA+RV)
IF (in Region frame = <FR> AND class is LA+LV+RA+RV)
THEN
  reset ,
  write 'LA+LV+RA+RV present in frame <FR>\n' ,
  in 1 final = "LA+LV+RA+RV" ;

:rule r19
rule block 7 (goal Checks for ARTIFACT)
IF (in Region frame = <FR> AND class is ARTIFACT)
THEN
  reset ,
  write 'ARTIFACT present in frame <FR>\n' ,
  in 1 final = "ARTIFACT" ;

:rule r20
rule block 7 (goal Checks for LUNG)
IF (in Region frame = <FR> AND class is LUNG)
THEN
  reset ,
  write 'LUNG present in frame <FR>\n' ,
  in 1 final = "LUNG" ;

: --------------------------------------------------------
:Block 8 rules write classifications to screen in serial
mode

:rule r21
rule block 8 (goal Writes final classifications to
screen )
IF ( in Region frame <FR> AND rnum <N> AND final <CK> )
  ( in Print rnum = <N> )
THEN
      write 'Final crisp classification for frame <FR>
      region <N>\: <CK>\n', in 2 rnum = (<N> + 1) ;


:rule r22
rule block 8 (goal Checks for regions with no final
classification)
IF ( in Region frame <FR> AND rnum <N> AND final.cf 0 )
  ( in Print rnum = <N> )
```

```
THEN
  in 2 rnum = (<N> + 1) ,
  error 'No final classification for frame <FR> region
  <N>!\n' ;


: -------------------------------------------------------
:Block 20 - block firing control

:rule r23
rule 1 20 (goal Enables blocks sequentially)
:rconf is 1 so rule 30 will fire before rule r31
IF ( in Enable block = <B> AND block < 8 )
THEN
  reset ,
  write 'Turning off rule block <B>, activating next
  block\n' ,
  in 1 block ( <B> + 1 ) ,
  fire block <B> off ,
  fire block (<B> + 1) on ;

:rule r24
rule rconf 0 block 20 (goal Switches to serial mode when
block 6 fires)
:rconf is 0 so this is the last rule to fire in block 20
IF ( in Enable block = 7 )
THEN
  reset ,
  make Print rnum = 1 ,
  message "Switching from parallel to serial mode for
    printout\n",
  serial ;


: ++++++++++++++++++++++++++++++++++++++++++++++++++++++++++

: INPUT DATA

:turn all rules off
fire all off ;
:take in input data
message "Reading run-specific data from
blackboard..\n" ;
transfer -conf Data from echodata.dat;
:transfer data to file with confidences so it can be
viewed with FLEDIT
transfer Data to echoin.dat;
```

```
:enabled rule block control
make Enable block 0 ;
:turn on block 0, block 20
fire block 0 on ;
fire block 20 on ;
:bring in data for classification rule generation
message "Reading data from blackboard to generate
classification rules..\n";
transfer Classdef from classes.dat ;
string = "Ready to create new rules and process input
data -\n" ;
string + "A lot of output will scroll by - you can scroll
up and view" ;
string + "it in detail by selecting Cancel from any
message box\, " ;
string + "then entering 'resume\; 'when ready to proceed.\n" ;
message "<string>";
:run block 0
run 1;
:turn new rules off
fire block 2 off ;
:run blocks 1 and 2
message "Ready to print and fuzzify input data -\n" ;
run 1 ;
message "Input data after fuzzification -\n" ;
run 1 ;
:run blocks 3, 4 and 5
message "Preliminary classifications -\n" ;
run 1 ;
message "Resolving contradictory classifications -\n" ;
run 3 ;
:run block 7
message "Check all heart chambers present -\n" ;
run 1 ;
message "Getting final classifications\n" ;
run ;
message "ECHO.PAR finished.\n" ;
exit ;
:: *************************************************************
: *************************************************************
:program FUZZIFY.PAR - fuzzifies
: *************************************************************

thresh 1 ;
```

```
declare Data x flt size fzset ( small medium large ) ;

memfunct Data size normal
   small -1e6 1 2
   medium 1 2 2 3
   large 2 3 1e6 ;

:rule r0
rule (goal Fuzzifies x into fuzzy set size)
IF (in Data x = <X> AND x <= 3.5)
THEN
   message 'Fuzzifying <X>\n',
   fuzzify 1 size <X>,
   fire block 0 off,
   fire block 1 on;

:Permit firing rules with zero confidence in fuzzy set
member TestFsetOff;

rule block 1 (goal Prints out results of fuzzification)
IF (in Data x = <X> AND size.small = <S> AND size.medium = <M>
   AND size.large = <L>)
THEN
   message '<X> fuzzified: small <S> medium <M> large <L>\n',
   reset,
   in 1 x = (<X> + 0.5),
   fire block 1 off,
   fire block 0 on;

make Data ^x 0.5;

string = "Program fuzzify.PAR\n";
string + "We have only two rules, one to fuzzify, one to
         print results.\n";
string + "Rule r0 will fuzzify several values of an
         input, x, " ;
string + "Into a fuzzy set size with three members\:
         small, medium, large.\n" ;
message "<string>" ;
prule r0 ;
fire block 1 off ;
message 'Here are the membership functions for fuzzy set
size:\n' ;
drawmemf Data size ;
message 'Ready to run\n' ;
```

```
:run ;
:message 'Fuzzification demonstration finished.\n' ;
:exit ;
: ********************************************************
```

Guess.fps: try to guess a number.

```
declare Guess
  x int ;

:rule r0
rule (goal Guess too low)
IF (x < 6)
THEN
  write "Your guess is too low - guess again\n",
  delete 1;
:rule r1
rule (goal Guess too high)
IF (x > 6)
THEN
  write "Your guess is too high guess again\n",
  delete 1;
:rule r2
rule (goal Guess correct - stop)
IF (x = 6)
THEN
  write "Your guess is correct! Thanks for the game\n",
  stop;

:rule r3
rule (goal Input guess)
IF (x = 0)
THEN
  write "What is your guess for the number ?\n",
  read 1 x;

: ********************************************************
:program HANOI.FPS - solves Tower of Hanoi problem
recursively
:uses rule confidences to control rule firing sequence ;
:if rule r2 and rule r4 concurrently fireable, r2 fires first.
:(rule confidences override normal MEA algorithm for
sequencing rules)
: ********************************************************
```

```
message "Loading program hanoi.fps...\n";

declare Spindles
  n int            :number of disks to be moved
  s str            :source spindle
  d str            :destination spindle
  t str            :temporary spindle
  rtn int;         :pointer for rule(s) to be executed next
: ******************************************************

:rule r0
rule rconf 0 ( goal Inputs number of disks to move )
IF ( in Spindles n.cf = 0 )
THEN
  reset,
  input "Tower of Hanoi - how many disks to move (0 to
  quit)?\n" 1 n ,
  make Spindles s = "S1" t = "S2" d = "S3" rtn = 1 ;
:rule r1
rule rconf 1000 (goal Quits on zero numbers of disks to
move )
IF ( in Spindles n = 0 )
THEN
  message nocancel "Thanks for the game.\n" ,
  exit ;

:rule r2
rule rconf 1000 ( goal Fires if only one disk to move )
IF ( in Spindles n = 1 AND s = <S> AND d = <D> )
THEN
  reset ,
  write 12 "*** move <S> to <D> ***\n" ,
  delete 1 ;

:rule r3
rule rconf 999 (goal Fires if NDisk > 1\; makes r2 or r4
fireable)
IF ( in Spindles n > 1 AND n = <N> AND s = <S> AND d = <D>
   AND t = <T>
  AND rtn = 1 )
THEN
  reset ,
  :save Spindles for return to rule 4 later
  in 1 rtn = 2 ,
  :first recursive call
```

```
  make Spindles n = ( <N> - 1 ) s = "<S>" d = "<T>"
    t = "<D>" rtn = 1;

:rule r4
rule rconf 999 ( goal Fires after r3 if NDisk > 1to move
- recursive )
IF ( in Spindles n = <N> AND n > 1 AND s = <S> AND d = <D>
AND t = <T> AND rtn = 2 )
THEN
  reset ,
  write 12 "*** move <S> to <D> ***\n" ,
  :second recursive call
  in 1 n = ( <N> - 1 ) s = "<T>" d = "<D>" t = "<S>" rtn = 1 ;

: ********************************************************
make Spindles s = "S1" t = "S2" d = "S3" rtn = 1 ;
: ********************************************************

string =
  "We have some disks of different diameters with holes ";
string +
  "bored through the center, and three vertical spindles." ;
string +
  "The disks are loaded onto one spindle in order of size, ";
string +
  "with the largest at the bottom. \n" ;
string +
  "The problem is to move the disks from spindle #1 to #3\,";
string +
  "one disk at a time, never placing a larger disk on a
     smaller. \n";
string +
  "HANOI will solve this problem recursively, in that
     rules ";
string +
  "make themselves refireable until a desired state is ";
string +
  "reached. Rule weights ensure that rules fire in the ";
string +
  "proper sequence. HANOI.FPS has one rule for input,";
string +
  " one to quit, and only three to solve the problem. \n" ;
message "<string>" ;
message "Ready to run...\n" ;
:run ;
```

```
:*********************************************************
:program HANOI.PAR - solves Tower of Hanoi problem
recursively
:uses rule confidences to control rule firing sequence ;
:if rule r2 and rule r4 concurrently fireable, r2 fires
first.
:(rule confidences override normal MEA algorithm for
sequencing rules)
:*********************************************************

message "Loading program hanoi.par...\n" ;

declare Spindles
  n int          :number of disks to be moved
  s str          :source spindle
  d str          :destination spindle
  t str          :temporary spindle
  rtn int ;      :pointer for rule(s) to be executed next

declare True;

:*********************************************************
:rule r0
rule (goal Declares itself in parallel mode, enables
block 1, switches to serial mode)
IF (True)
THEN
  message "First rule firing, block 0 - mode parallel.\n
  Switching to serial mode",
  fire block 0 off,
  fire block 1 on,
  serial;

:rule r1
rule rconf 0 block 1 (goal Inputs number of disks to
move)
IF (in Spindles n.cf = 0)

THEN
  reset,
  input "r0 - Tower of Hanoi - how many disks to move (0
  to quit)?\n" 1 n,
  make Spindles s = "S1" t = "S2" d = "S3" rtn = 1,
  debug 4;
```

```
:rule r2
rule block 1 (goal Quits on zero numbers of disks to
move)
IF (in Spindles n = 0)
THEN
  message nocancel "r1 - Thanks for the game.\n",
  fire block 1 off,
  fire block 2 on,
  parallel;

:rule r3
rule block 1 (goal Fires if only one disk to move)
IF (in Spindles n = 1 AND s = <S> AND d = <D>)
THEN
  reset,
  write "r2 - move <S> to <D>\n",
  delete 1;

:rule r4
rule rconf 999 block 1 (goal Fires if NDisk > 1\; makes
r2 or r4 fireable)
IF (in Spindles n > 1 AND n = <N> AND s = <S> AND d = <D>
AND t = <T>
  AND rtn = 1)
THEN
  debug 0,
  reset,
  write "r3 - modifying Spindles\n",
  :save Spindles for return to rule 4 later
  in 1 rtn = 2,
  :first recursive call
  make Spindles n = (<N> - 1) s = "<S>" d = "<T>"
    t = "<D>" rtn = 1;

:rule r5
rule rconf 999 block 1 (goal Fires after r3 if NDisk > 1
  to move - recursive)
IF (in Spindles n = <N> AND n > 1 AND s = <S> AND d = <D>
  AND t = <T> AND rtn = 2)
THEN
  reset,
  write "r4 - move <S> to <D>\n",
  :second recursive call
  in 1 n = (<N> - 1) s = "<T>" d = "<D>" t = "<S>" rtn = 1;
```

```
:rule r6
 rule block 2 (goal Announce return to parallel mode)
 IF (True)
 THEN
   message "Back to parallel mode in block 2";
   halt;


: *********************************************************
make Spindles s = "S1" t = "S2" d = "S3" rtn = 1;
make True;
: *********************************************************


string =
  "We have some disks of different diameters with holes ";
string +
  "bored through the center, and three vertical spindles. ";
string +
  "The disks are loaded onto one spindle in order of
  size, ";
string +
  "with the largest at the bottom. \n";
string +
  "The problem is to move the disks from spindle #1 to #3\, ";
string +
  "one disk at a time, never placing a larger disk on a
  smaller. \n";
string +
  "HANOI will solve this problem recursively, in that
rules ";
string +
  "make themselves refireable until a desired state is ";
string +
  "reached. Rule weights ensure that rules fire in the ";
string +
  "proper sequence. HANOI.FPS has one rule for input,";
string +
  " one to quit, and only three to solve the problem. \n";
message "<string>";
fire all off;
fire block 0 on;
message "Ready to run...\n";
:run;
```

```
:Exercise Imply.fps - calculates truth value of P->Q for
several implication operators.

declare Data P flt Q flt Imply1 flt Imply2 flt Imply3
flt;

:rule r0
rule (goal Input initial truth values)
IF (in Data P.cf = 0)
THEN
        input "Enter truth value of P" 1 P,
        input "Enter truth value of Q, negative to quite" 1 Q;

:rule r1
rule (goal Calculate truth value of P implies Q for P <= Q)
IF (in Data P = <P> AND Q = <Q> AND Q >= 0 AND P <= <Q>
AND Imply1.cf = 0)
THEN
  in 1 Imply1 = 1 Imply2 = (min(1, 1 - <P> + <Q>)) Imply3
= (max(1 - <P>, min(<P>, <Q>))));

:rule r2
rule (goal Calculate truth value of P->Q for P > Q)
IF (in Data P = <P> AND Q = <Q> AND Q >= 0 AND P > <Q> AND
Imply1.cf = 0)
THEN
  in 1 Imply1 = 0 Imply2 = (min(1, 1 - <P> + <Q>)) Imply3
= (max((1 - <P>), min(<P>, <Q>))));

:rule r3
rule (goal Quit on negative Q)
IF (in Data Q < 0) THEN exit;
:rule r4
rule (goal Print results)
IF (in Data P = <P> AND Q = <Q> AND Imply1 = <I1> AND
Imply2 = <I2> AND Imply3 = <I3>)
THEN
        message "P <P> Q <Q> \nP->Q(1) <I1> : P->Q(2)<I2> :
         P->Q(3) <I3>",
        delete 1,
        make Data;

make Data;
string = "Program IMPLY.FPS to evaluate implications is
         ready to run.\n";
```

```
string + "Comparison of different fuzzy implication
        operators:\n";
string + "See Klir and Yuan(1995, p. 309).\n";
string + "1) P->Q = 1 if P <= Q, else = 0 (Gaines-
        Rescher)\n";
string + "2) P->Q = min(1, 1 - P + Q) (Lukasiewicz)\n";
string + "3) P->Q = max(1 - P, min(P, Q)) (Early Zadeh)";
message "<string>";


REM Sample fuzzy control program IRC.bas
REM Intersection rule matrix
REM 9 rules


DECLARE FUNCTION MIN (A, B)
DECLARE FUNCTION MAX (A, B)
DECLARE FUNCTION Process (Y0, Z, dT)
DECLARE FUNCTION Pause ()


REM****************************************************
REM IRC.BAS: Explanatory information


CLS
PRINT "Sample fuzzy control program with non-linear process"
PRINT "Uses conventional IRC method with nine rules"
PRINT
PRINT "System output is Y"
PRINT "inputs: error E, fuzzy set Error (Negative Zero
      Positive)"
PRINT "rate R, fuzzy set Rate (Negative Zero Positive)"
PRINT "Control value is Z"
PRINT "Control increment DZ, fuzzy set Control (Negative,
      Zero, Positive)"
PRINT "Dt is time interval between input sample value"
PRINT "Press any key to continue..."
WHILE INKEY$ = "": WEND


REM****************************************************
PRINT "Default membership functions"


PRINT
PRINT "ERROR:"
PRINT "1.0 n                   z                   p"
PRINT "    - n                 z z                 p"
PRINT "    -  n               z   z                p"
```

```
PRINT "      -       n           z           z             p"
PRINT "      -       n         z           z       p   n = Negative"
PRINT "0.5 +           n     z               z   p   z = Zero"
PRINT "      -           n z               z p     p = Positive"
PRINT "      -             zn               pz"
PRINT "      -           z   n           p   z"
PRINT "      -         z     n         p       z"
PRINT "0.0 +zpzpzpzpz+pppppppppp+nnnnnnnnn+znznznznz+"
PRINT " 2LLEZ         LLEZ        0      ULEZ        2ULEZ"
PRINT " (-10)         (-5)        0       (5) (10) (Defaults)"
PRINT
PRINT "Press any key to continue..."
WHILE INKEY$ = "": WEND

PRINT "RATE:"
PRINT "1.0 +nnnnnnnnn              z              pppppppppp"
PRINT "      -           n           z z           p"
PRINT "      -             n         z z       p"
PRINT "      -             n     z     z   p"
PRINT "      -             n z       z p       n = Negative"
PRINT "0.5 +               n           z     z = Zero"
PRINT "      -           z   n       p z     p = Positive"
PRINT "      -           z   n     p   z"
PRINT "      -         z         z     n p       z"
PRINT "      -         z         n p       z"
PRINT "0.0 +zpzpzpzpz+pppppppppp+nnnnnnnnn+znznznznz+"
PRINT " 2LLRZ         LLRZ        0  ULRZ              2ULRZ"
PRINT " (-20)         (-10)       0   (10) (20) (Defaults)"
PRINT
PRINT "Press any key to continue..."
WHILE INKEY$ = "": WEND

PRINT "CONTROL"
PRINT "1.0 nb     ns        z        ps      pb"
PRINT "    nb     ns        z        ps      pb"
PRINT "    nb     ns        z        ps      pb"
PRINT "    nb     ns        z        ps      pb"
PRINT "    nb     ns        z        ps      pb"
PRINT "0.5 nb     ns        z        ps      pb"
PRINT "    nb     ns        z        ps      pb"
PRINT "    nb     ns        z        ps      pb"
PRINT "    nb     ns        z        ps      pb"
PRINT "    nb     ns        z        ps      pb"
PRINT "0.0 |----|-+-----+----+-|----|"
PRINT "   -100    -60       0      60   100 (Defaults)"
```

```
PRINT
PRINT "Press any key to continue..."
WHILE INKEY$ = "": WEND

REM***************************************************
REM Define fuzzy sets

TYPE OutputError
  E AS SINGLE
  Negative AS SINGLE
  Zero AS SINGLE
  Large AS SINGLE
END TYPE

TYPE Rate
  R AS SINGLE
  Slow AS SINGLE
  Medium AS SINGLE
  Fast AS SINGLE
END TYPE

TYPE Control
  NB AS SINGLE
  NBval AS SINGLE
  NS AS SINGLE
  NSval AS SINGLE
  Z AS SINGLE
  Zval AS SINGLE
  PS AS SINGLE
  PSval AS SINGLE
  pb AS SINGLE
  PBval AS SINGLE
  Dz AS SINGLE
END TYPE
REM***************************************************
REM Input data

PRINT
PRINT "Input parameters"
PRINT "<ENTER> to select default value"
PRINT
INPUT "Lower limit for Error.Zero (-5)"; LLEZ
IF LLEZ = 0 THEN LLEZ = -5
INPUT "Upper limit for Error.Zero (5)"; ULEZ
IF ULEZ = 0 THEN ULEZ = 5
```

```
INPUT "Lower limit for Rate.Zero (-10)"; LLRZ
IF LLRZ = 0 THEN LLRZ = -10
INPUT "Upper limit for Rate.Zero (10)"; ULRZ
IF ULRZ = 0 THEN ULRZ = 10

INPUT "Control value for Negative Big, NB (-100)";
Control.NBval
IF Control.NBval = 0 THEN Control.NBval = -100
INPUT "Control value for Negative Small, NS (-60)";
Control.NSval
IF Control.NSval = 0 THEN Control.NSval = -60
Control.Z = 0
INPUT "Control value for Positive Small, PS (60)";
Control.PSval
IF Control.PSval = 0 THEN Control.PSval = 60
INPUT "Control value for Positive Big, PB (100)";
Control.PBval
IF Control.PBval = 0 THEN Control.PBval = 100

INPUT "Time interval between input samples (1)"; dT
IF dT = 0 THEN dT = 1
T = 0
INPUT "Process setpoint value (15)"; SetPoint
IF SetPoint = 0 THEN SetPoint = 15
INPUT "Initial process output Y (10)"; Y0
IF Y0 = 0 THEN Y0 = 10
REM For dYdT = 0, sqr(Z) = .1 * Y0^1.5, Z = Y0^3 / 100
Z = Y0 ^ 3 / 100
PRINT "Initial control value"; Z

Start:
REM Get input values
REM Get next value of process output
Y = Process(Y0, Z, dT)
OutputError.E = Y - SetPoint
OutputRate.R = (Y - Y0) / dT
Y0 = Y
A$ = "T ###.# Process ##.# Control ##.## Error ##.## Rate
##.##"
PRINT USING A$; T; Y; Z; OutputError.E; OutputRate.R
PRINT "Press any key to continue, Q to quit"

DO
  X$ = UCASE$(INKEY$)
LOOP WHILE X$ = ""
```

```
IF X$ = "Q" THEN
  END
END IF


REM**************************************************
REM Fuzzify inputs
IF OutputError.E < 2 * LLEZ THEN
  OutputError.Negative = 1
  OutputError.Zero = 0
  OutputError.Positive = 0
ELSEIF OutputError.E < LLEZ THEN
  OutputError.Negative = (0 - OutputError.E) / (0 - 2 * LLEZ)
  OutputError.Zero = 0
  OutputError.Positive = 0
ELSEIF OutputError.E < 0 THEN
  OutputError.Negative = (0 - OutputError.E) / (0 - 2 * LLEZ)
  OutputError.Zero = (OutputError.E - LLEZ) / (0 - LLEZ)
  OutputError.Positive = 0
ELSEIF OutputError.E < ULEZ THEN
  OutputError.Negative = 0
  OutputError.Zero = (ULEZ - OutputError.E) / (ULEZ - 0)
  OutputError.Positive = (OutputError.E - 0) / (2 * ULEZ - 0)
ELSEIF OutputError.E < 2 * ULEZ THEN
  OutputError.Negative = 0
  OutputError.Zero = 0
  OutputError.Positive = (OutputError.E - 0) / (2 * ULEZ - 0)
ELSE
  OutputError.Negative = 0
  OutputError.Zero = 0
  OutputError.Positive = 1
END IF

IF OutputRate.R < LLRZ THEN
  OutputRate.Negative = 1
  OutputRate.Zero = 0
  OutputRate.Positive = 0
ELSEIF OutputRate.R < 0 THEN
  OutputRate.Negative = (OutputRate.R - 0) / (LLRZ - 0)
  OutputRate.Zero = (OutputRate.R - LLRZ) / (0 - LLRZ)
  OutputRate.Positive = 0
ELSEIF OutputRate.R < ULRZ THEN
  OutputRate.Negative = 0
  OutputRate.Zero = (ULRZ - OutputRate.R) / (ULRZ - 0)
  OutputRate.Positive = (OutputRate.R - 0) / (ULRZ - 0)
ELSE
```

```
  OutputRate.Negative = 0
  OutputRate.Zero = 0
  OutputRate.Positive = 1
END IF


REM*****************************************************

REM Rules

REM Rule matrices
'Conventional Rules
'Output rate:
'PB = Positive Big
'PS = Positive Small
'NS = Negative Small
'NB = Negative Big
'                       InputRate
'InputError | Neg | Zer | Pos |
'           _____|_____|_____|_____|
'          Neg___|_PB__|_PS__|_Zero|
'          Zer___|_PS__|_Zer_|_NS__|
'          Pos___|_Zer_|_NS__|_NB__|
'
'Combs method rules
'Output rate:
'Pos = Positive
'ZER = Zero
'Neg = Negative
'                   Input Error or Input Rate
'                   | Neg | Zer | Pos |
'                   |_____|_____|_____|
'                   |_Pos_|_Zer_|_Neg_|

'Simplify symbols
IF OutputError.Negative > 0 AND OutputRate.Negative > 0
THEN
  PB1 = MIN(OutputError.Negative, OutputRate.Negative)
ELSE
  PB1 = 0
END IF

IF OutputError.Negative > 0 AND OutputRate.Zero > 0 THEN
  PS1 = MIN(OutputError.Negative, OutputRate.Zero)
ELSE
  PS1 = 0
```

```
END IF

IF OutputError.Negative > 0 AND OutputRate.Positive > 0 THEN
  Z1 = MIN(OutputError.Negative, OutputRate.Positive)
ELSE
  Z1 = 0
END IF

IF OutputError.Zero > 0 AND OutputRate.Negative > 0 THEN
  PS2 = MIN(OutputError.Zero, OutputRate.Negative)
ELSE
  PS2 = 0
END IF

IF OutputError.Zero > 0 AND OutputRate.Zero > 0 THEN
  Z2 = MIN(OutputError.Zero, OutputRate.Zero)
ELSE
  Z2 = 0
END IF

IF OutputError.Zero > 0 AND OutputRate.Positive > 0 THEN
  NS1 = MIN(OutputError.Zero, OutputRate.Positive)
ELSE
  NS1 = 0
END IF

IF OutputError.Positive > 0 AND OutputRate.Negative > 0 THEN
  Z3 = MIN(OutputError.Negative, OutputRate.Negative)
ELSE
  Z3 = 0
END IF

IF OutputError.Positive > 0 AND OutputRate.Zero > 0 THEN
  NS2 = MIN(OutputError.Positive, OutputRate.Zero)
ELSE
  NS2 = 0
END IF

IF OutputError.Positive > 0 AND OutputRate.Positive > 0
THEN
  NB1 = MIN(OutputError.Negative, OutputRate.Positive)
ELSE
  NB1 = 0
END IF
```

```
REM*****************************************************

REM OR rule consequents
REM Here we are effectively firing the rules in parallel,
REM taking max of consequent values

Control.NB = NB1

Control.NS = MAX(NS1, NS2)

Control.Z = MAX(Z1, Z2)
Control.Z = MAX(Control.Z, Z3)
Control.Z = MAX(Control.Z, Z4)

Control.PS = MAX(PS1, PS2)

Control.PB = PB1

REM*****************************************************

REM Defuzzify
REM For simplicity, weighted average of singletons
REM Normalize memberships

sum = Control.NB + Control.NS + Control.Z + Control.PS +
      Control.PB
Dz = Control.NBval * Control.NB + Control.NSval *
      Control.NS
Dz = Dz + Control.PSval * Control.PS + Control.PBval *
      Control.PB

REM Integrate control
T = T + dT
Z = Z + Dz * dT

GOTO Start

FUNCTION MAX (A, B)
IF A > B THEN MAX = A ELSE MAX = B
END FUNCTION

FUNCTION MIN (A, B)
  IF A < B THEN MIN = A ELSE MIN = B
END FUNCTION
```

```
FUNCTION Process (Y0, Z, dT)
dYdT = -.1 * Y0 ^ 1.5 + SGN(Z) * SQR(ABS(Z))
REM For dYdT = 0, sqr(Z) = .1 * Y0^1.5, Z = Y0^3 / 100
Process = Y0 + dYdT * dT

END FUNCTION

:Program IRIS.PAR to classify iris data

thresh 1;
linear;

declare Data N int PL flt PW flt SL flt SW flt orig str;

declare Iris
  N int
  PetalL  fzset (setosa versicolor virginica)
  PetalW  fzset (setosa versicolor virginica)
  SepalL  fzset (setosa versicolor virginica)
  SepalW  fzset (setosa versicolor virginica)
  species fzset (setosa versicolor virginica)
  orig str
  final str;

:memfunctions by mid=(least+most)/2, bottom=2*least -
 mid, top = 2*most-mid
:least = smallest measurement; most = largest measurement
memfunct Iris PetalL linear
  setosa 3.55 5.05 5.05 6.55
  versicolor 3.85 5.95 5.95 8.05
  virginica 3.40 6.40 6.40 9.40;

memfunct Iris PetalW linear
  setosa 1.25 3.35 3.35 5.45
  versicolor 1.30 2.72 2.72 4.15
  virginica 1.40 3.00 3.00 4.60;

memfunct Iris SepalL linear
  setosa 0.55 1.45 1.45 2.35
  versicolor 1.95 4.05 4.05 6.15
  virginica 3.30 5.70 5.70 8.10;

memfunct Iris SepalW linear
  setosa -0.15 0.35 0.35 0.85
  versicolor 0.60 1.40 1.40 2.20
  virginica 0.85 1.95 1.95 3.05;

:rule r0
```

```
rule block 0 (goal Make instances of iris, holds fuzzy
sets)
IF (in Data N = <N> AND orig = <ORIG>)
THEN
    :write "Making instance of specimen <N>\n",
  make Iris N = <N> orig = "<ORIG>";

:rule r1
rule block 0 (goal Fuzzify input data)
IF (in Data N = <N> AND PL = <PL> AND PW = <PW> AND SL =
<SL> AND SW = <SW>)
   (in Iris N = <N>)
THEN
    :write "Fuzzifying specimen <N> data\n",
  fuzzify 2 PetalL <PL>,
  fuzzify 2 PetalW <PW>,
  fuzzify 2 SepalL <SL>,
  fuzzify 2 SepalW <SW>,
  fire block 0 off,
  fire block 1 on;

:rule r2
rule block 1 (goal classify as setosa)
IF (in Iris N = <N> AND PetalL is setosa AND PetalW is setosa
   AND SepalL is setosa AND SepalW is setosa)
THEN
    :write "Classifying specimen <N> as setosa\n",
  in 1 species is setosa,
  in 1 final is "Iris-setosa",
  fire block 1 off,
  fire block 2 on;

:rule r3
rule block 1 (goal classify as versicolor)
IF (in Iris N = <N> AND PetalL is versicolor AND PetalW
is versicolor
        AND SepalL is versicolor AND SepalW is
versicolor)
THEN
    :write "Classifying specimen <N> as versicolor\n",
  in 1 species is versicolor,
  in 1 final is "Iris-versicolor",
  fire block 1 off,
  fire block 2 on;
```

```
:rule r4
rule block 1 (goal classify as virginica)
IF (in Iris N = <N> AND PetalL is virginica AND PetalW is
virginica
        AND SepalL is virginica AND SepalW is virginica)
THEN
    :write "Classifying specimen <N> as virginica\n",
  in 1 species is virginica,
  in 1 final is "Iris-virginica",
  fire block 1 off,
  fire block 2 on;

:rule r5
rule block 2 (goal detect incorrect classifications)
IF (in Iris N = <N> AND final = <FL> AND orig = <ORIG>
AND final <> <ORIG>)
THEN
  prmem 1,
  message "Specimen <N> incorrect\: <FL> should be
<ORIG>\n";

:rule r6
rule block 2 (goal detect unclassified specimens)
IF (in Iris N = <N> AND species.setosa = 0 AND species.
versicolor = 0
        AND species.virginica = 0)
THEN
  message "Specimen <N> unclassified\n";

transfer -conf Data from myiris.dat;

fire all off;
fire block 0 on;
message "IRIS.PAR ready to run and classify 150 specimens";
message "Membership functions for petal length";
drawmemf Iris PetalL;
message "Membership functions for petal width";
drawmemf Iris PetalW;
message "Membership functions for sepal length";
drawmemf Iris SepalL;
message "Membership functions for sepal width";
drawmemf Iris SepalW;

message "Block 0 - creating instances of data\n";
run 1;
```

```
message "Block 0 - fuzzifying data\n";
run 1;
message "Block 1 - classifying data\n";
run 1;
message "Block 2 - detecting errors\n";
run 1;
message "Iris.par finished";
exit;


message "program IrisCombs.PAR to classify iris data by
Combs method";

thresh 1;

declare IrisData N int PL flt PW flt SL flt SW flt orig
str;

declare True;

declare Iris
  N int
  PetalL fzset (setosa versicolor virginica)
  PetalW fzset (setosa versicolor virginica)
  SepalL fzset (setosa versicolor virginica)
  SepalW fzset (setosa versicolor virginica)
  setosaConf int
  versicolorConf int
  virginicaConf int
  species fzset (setosa versicolor virginica)
  orig str
  final str;

:memfunctions are designed to place minimum and maximum
 of training set at 0.5
:memfunctions by mid (1.0) = median, bottom (0.0 for
 linear distribution) = 2*least - mid, top = 2*most-mid
:least = smallest measurement; most = largest measurement
 in training set
memfunct Iris PetalL normal
: Training set even numbers
   setosa 3.60 5.00 5.00 6.40
   versicolor 3.90 5.90 5.90 7.50
   virginica 4.70 6.50 6.50 9.30;
```

```
memfunct Iris PetalW normal
: Training set even numbers
  setosa 1.30 3.30 3.30 5.50
  versicolor 1.80 2.80 2.80 4.00
  virginica 1.40 3.00 3.00 4.60;

memfunct Iris SepalL normal
: Training set even numbers
  setosa 0.70 1.50 1.50 1.90
  versicolor 2.40 4.20 4.20 6.00
  virginica 4.50 5.30 5.30 8.10;

memfunct Iris SepalW normal
: Training set even numbers
  setosa 0.00 0.20 0.20 1.00
  versicolor 0.70 1.30 1.30 2.10
  virginica 1.00 2.00 2.00 3.00;

thresh;
:rule r0
rule block 0 (goal Make instances of iris, holds fuzzy sets)
IF (in IrisData N = <N> AND orig = <ORIG>)
THEN
    make Iris N = <N> orig = "<ORIG>" setosaConf = 0
    versicolorConf = 0 virginicaConf = 0;

:rule r1
rule block 0 (goal Fuzzify input data)
IF (in IrisData N = <N> AND PL = <PL> AND PW = <PW> AND
SL = <SL> AND SW = <SW> AND tt = <TT>)
    (in Iris N = <N>)
THEN
        write "Fuzzifying tt <TT>\n",
    fuzzify 2 PetalL <PL>,
    fuzzify 2 PetalW <PW>,
    fuzzify 2 SepalL <SL>,
    fuzzify 2 SepalW <SW>,
    fire block 0 off,
    fire block 1 on;


: +++++++++++++++++++++++++++++++++++++++++++++++++++++++++++++++

:rule r2
rule block 1 (goal classify as setosa by PL)
IF (in Iris PetalL is setosa
```

```
  AND setosaConf = <SetCf>)
THEN
  write "Classifying as setosa by PL conf $<SetCf> pconf
  <pconf>\n",
  modify 1 setosaConf = ($<SetCf> + <pconf> / 4);

:rule r3
rule block 1 (goal classify as setosa by PW)
IF (in Iris PetalW is setosa
  AND setosaConf = <SetCf>)
THEN
  write "Classifying as setosa by PW conf $<SetCf> pconf
  <pconf>\n",
  modify 1 setosaConf = ($<SetCf> + <pconf> / 4);

:rule r4
rule block 1 (goal classify as setosa by SL)
IF (in Iris SepalL is setosa
  AND setosaConf = <SetCf>)
THEN
  write "Classifying as setosa by SL conf $<SetCf> pconf
  <pconf>\n",
  modify 1 setosaConf = ($<SetCf> + <pconf> / 4);

:rule r5
rule block 1 (goal classify as setosa by SW)
IF (in Iris SepalW is setosa
  AND setosaConf = <SetCf>)
THEN
  write "Classifying as setosa by SW conf $<SetCf> pconf
  <pconf>\n",
  modify 1 setosaConf = ($<SetCf> + <pconf> / 4);

:rule r6
rule block 1 (goal classify as versicolor by PL)
IF (in Iris PetalL is versicolor
  AND versicolorConf = <SetCf>)
THEN
  write "Classifying as versicolor by PL conf $<SetCf>
  pconf <pconf>\n",
  modify 1 versicolorConf = ($<SetCf> + <pconf> / 4);

:rule r7
rule block 1 (goal classify as versicolor by PW)
IF (in Iris PetalW is versicolor
  AND versicolorConf = <SetCf>)
```

```
THEN
  write "Classifying as versicolor by PW conf $<SetCf>
  pconf <pconf>\n",
  modify 1 versicolorConf = ($<SetCf> + <pconf> / 4);

:rule r8
rule block 1 (goal classify as versicolor by SL)
IF (in Iris SepalL is versicolor
  AND versicolorConf = <SetCf>)
THEN
  write "Classifying as versicolor by SL conf $<SetCf>
  pconf <pconf>\n",
  modify 1 versicolorConf = ($<SetCf> + <pconf> / 4);

:rule r9
rule block 1 (goal classify as versicolor by SW)
IF (in Iris SepalW is versicolor
  AND versicolorConf = <SetCf>)
THEN
  write "Classifying as versicolor by SW conf $<SetCf>
  pconf <pconf>\n",
  modify 1 versicolorConf = ($<SetCf> + <pconf> / 4);

:rule r10
rule block 1 (goal classify as virginica by PL)
IF (in Iris PetalL is virginica
  AND virginicaConf = <SetCf>)
THEN
  write "Classifying as virginica by PL conf $<SetCf>
  pconf <pconf>\n",
  modify 1 virginicaConf = ($<SetCf> + <pconf> / 4);

:rule r11
rule block 1 (goal classify as virginica by PW)
IF (in Iris PetalW is virginica
  AND virginicaConf = <SetCf>)
THEN
  write "Classifying as virginica by PW conf $<SetCf>
  pconf <pconf>\n",
  modify 1 virginicaConf = ($<SetCf> + <pconf> / 4);

:rule r12
rule block 1 (goal classify as virginica by SL)
IF (in Iris SepalL is virginica
  AND virginicaConf = <SetCf>)
```

```
THEN
  write "Classifying as virginica by SL conf $<SetCf>
  pconf <pconf>\n",
  modify 1 virginicaConf = ($<SetCf> + <pconf> / 4);

:rule r13
rule block 1 (goal classify as virginica by SW)
IF (in Iris SepalW is virginica
  AND virginicaConf = <SetCf>)
THEN
  write "Classifying as virginica by SW conf $<SetCf>
  pconf <pconf>\n",
  modify 1 virginicaConf = ($<SetCf> + <pconf> / 4);

:rule r14
rule block 1 (goal Activate next block)
IF (True) THEN fire block 1 off, fire block 2 on;


: ++++++++++++++++++++++++++++++++++++++++++++++++++++++++

:rule r15
rule block 2 (goal Select max confidence = average
confidence, Combs OR)
IF (in Iris setosaConf = <SetCF> AND versicolorConf =
<VerCF> AND virginicaConf = <VirCF>)
THEN
  in 1 species.setosa = <SetCF> species.versicolor =
  <VerCF> species.virginica = <VirCF>;

:rule r16
rule block 2 (goal activate next block)
IF (True) THEN
  fire block 2 off,
  fire block 3 on,
  TMSon;


: ++++++++++++++++++++++++++++++++++++++++++++++++++++++++

:rule r17
rule block 3 (goal Set final classification to setosa)
IF (in Iris species is setosa)
THEN in 1 final is "Iris-setosa";

:rule r18
```

```
rule block 3 (goal Set final classification to
versicolor)
IF (in Iris species is versicolor)
THEN in 1 final is "Iris-versicolor";

:rule r19
rule block 3 (goal Set final classification to
virginica)
IF (in Iris species is virginica)
THEN in 1 final is "Iris-virginica";

:rule r20
rule block 3 (goal activate next block)
IF (True) THEN
  fire block 3 off,
  fire block 4 on;

: ++++++++++++++++++++++++++++++++++++++++++++++++++++++++

:rule r21
rule block 4 (goal detect incorrect classifications)
IF (in Iris N = <N> AND final = <FL> AND orig = <ORIG>
AND final <> <ORIG>)
THEN
  prmem 1,
  message "Specimen <N> incorrect\: <FL> should be <ORIG>\n" ;

:rule r22
rule block 4 (goal detect unclassified specimens)
IF (in Iris N = <N> AND final.cf = 0 OR (species.setosa =
0 AND species.versicolor = 0 AND species.virginica = 0))
  (in IrisData N = <N>)
THEN
  prmem 1,
  prmem 2,
  message "Specimen <N> unclassified\n";
: ++++++++++++++++++++++++++++++++++++++++++++++++++++++++

:transfer -conf IrisData from iristest.dat;
transfer -conf IrisData from Iris.dat;
fire all off;
fire block 0 on;
TMSoff;
TestFsetOff;
make True;
```

```
message "Block 0 first creates memory instances of each
specimen";
run 1;
message "Block 0 now fuzzifies the input data";
run 1;
message "Block 1 gets preliminary classifications for
each specimen";
run 1;
message "Block 2 aggregates preliminary
classifications";
run 1;
message "Block 3 gets final classifications";
run 1;
message "Block 42 checks for incorrect classifications
and specimens not classified";
run 1;
message "IRIS.PAR finished";
exit;


: program LOGIST.fps - solves differential equation of
logistic growth.

declare Population
    size flt    :population size
    K flt               :carrying capacity
    r flt               :growth rate of individual
    T flt               :time
    TMax flt    : max time allowed for continued run
    dT flt              :delta time
    dPdT flt    :growth rate of population
    terminate flt;    :minimum population growth rate to
                        continue run

:rule r0
rule (goal Calculate population growth rate dPdT at
time T)
IF (in Population size = <size> AND K = <K> AND r = <r>
AND T = <T> AND dT = <dT> AND dPdT.cf = 0)
THEN
  write "Time <T> population <size>\n",
    in 1 dPdT = (<r> * <size> * <dT> * (1 - <size> / <K>)),
    in 1 T = (<T> + <dT>);


:rule r1
```

```
rule (goal Calculate population size at T+dT from size
at T recursively)
IF (in Population size = <size> AND K = <K> AND r = <r>
AND T = <T> AND dT = <dT> AND dPdT = <dPdT>
        AND terminate < <dPdT> AND TMax > <T>)
THEN
    in 1 size = (<size> + <dPdT> * <dT>),
    in 1 dPdT.cf = 0;


:rule r2
rule (goal Terminate run)
IF (in Population (T = <T> AND TMax < <T>) OR (dPdT =
<dPdT> AND terminate > <dPdT>))
THEN
    write "Termination criterion met - ending run\n",
    halt;

make Population size = 1000 K = 10000 r = 1 T = 0 TMax =
10 dT = 1 terminate = 0.01;

: program LOGIST.par - solves differential equation of
logistic growth.

declare Population
    size flt    :population size
    K flt               :carrying capacity
    r flt               :growth rate of individual
    T flt               :time
    TMax flt    : max time allowed for continued run
    dT flt              :delta time
    dPdT flt    :growth rate of population
    terminate flt;  : minimum population growth rate to
                        continue run

:rule r0
rule (goal Calculate population growth rate dPdT at
time T)
IF (in Population size = <size> AND K = <K> AND r = <r>
AND T = <T> AND dT = <dT> AND dPdT.cf = 0)
THEN
  write "Time <T> population <size>\n",
    in 1 dPdT = (<r> * <size> * <dT> * (1 - <size> / <K>)),
    in 1 T = (<T> + <dT>);

:rule r1
```

```
rule (goal Calculate population size at T+dT from size
at T recursively)
IF (in Population size = <size> AND K = <K> AND r = <r>
AND T = <T> AND dT = <dT> AND dPdT = <dPdT>
        AND terminate < <dPdT> AND TMax > <T>)
THEN
    in 1 size = (<size> + <dPdT> * <dT>),
    in 1 dPdT.cf = 0;

:rule r2
rule (goal Terminate run)
IF (in Population (T = <T> AND TMax < <T>) OR (dPdT =
<dPdT> AND terminate > <dPdT>))
THEN
    write "Termination criterion met - ending run\n",
    exit;

make Population size = 1000 K = 10000 r = 1 T = 0 TMax =
10 dT = 1 terminate = 0.01;

; *******************************************************
;* MC.FPS - missionaries and cannibals
; *******************************************************
; RULES OF GAME:
; -- can never be more cannibals than missionaries in the
     boat or on either shore, except
; -- all cannibals and no missionaries is OK.
; i.e. miss >= cannibals, OR
;       miss = 0.
; -- must be at least two in boat if L to R, or one if
     R to L.
; ------------------------------------------------------
; ALGORITHM - basically a simulation.
;
; DATA ELEMENTS: "boat" holds missionaries, cannibals, total,
; boat state: "L" when docked at left bank, "R" when docked
; at right bank, "LR" when going from left to right, and
; "RL when going from right to left.
;
; "left" holds missionaries, cannibals, total on left bank;
; "right" holds missionaries, cannibals, total on right bank.
;
; "temp" is temporary storage for finding out what bank
totals
; will be after the boat is unloaded, so we can check whether a
```

```
: missionary will get eaten if we unload.
:
: "max" holds input data: total number of missionaries and
: cannibals, and max number allowed in the boat.
:
: PROCEDURE: first input data (rule r0), then put all the
: missionaries and cannibals on the left bank, nobody in
: boat, nobody on right bank (rule r1).
:
: Now load as many as possible up to the boat limit on
: the left bank (rules r2, r3, r4). Check to make sure
: that nobody will get eaten on the left bank or in the
: boat (rules r5,r6). If this test is passed, sail from
: left to right; if not, forget it and backtrack (rules
: r7, r8).
:
: After we have sailed from the left bank, see what the
: right bank totals will be if we unload (rule r19). If
: nobody will get eaten, unload (rule r20); if somebody
: will get eaten, forget it and backtrack (rule r21).
: Check if we have solved the problem (rule r22). If not:
:
: Now load as few as possible up to the boat limit on the
: right bank (rules r9, r10, r11). Check to make sure
: that nobody will get eaten on the right bank or in the
: boat (rules r12, r13). If this test is passed, sail
: from right to left; if not, forget it and backtrack
: (rules r14, r15).
:
: After we have sailed from the right bank, see what the
: left bank totals will be if we unload (rule r16). If
: nobody will get eaten, unload (rule r17); if somebody
: will get eaten, forget it and backtrack (rule r18).
: Continue until problem is solved.
: ********************************************************

message 'loading program MC.FPS...\n' ;

declare Boat
  miss int
  cann int
  total int
  state str;

declare Left
```

```
  miss int
  cann int
  total int ;

declare Right
  miss int
  cann int
  total int ;

declare Temp
  miss int
  cann int
  total int ;

declare Max
  miss int
  cann int
  boat int
  total int ;
: ++++++++++++++++++++++++++++++++++++++++++++++++++++++++
: INITIALIZE

:rule r0
rule (goal Get numbers of missionaries = cannibals, max
boat will hold)
IF (in Max miss.cf = 0)
THEN
  cls ,
  input "Enter number miss (= # cann)" 1 miss ,
  input "Enter max in boat" 1 boat ;

:rule r1
rule 999 (goal Get total number of people, initialize
people on banks, boat)
IF (in Max miss = <M> AND total.cf = 0)
THEN
  reset ,
  write 'rule r1 - initializing\n' ,
  in 1 cann = <M> total = (2 * <M>) ,
  make Boat miss = 0 cann = 0 total = 0 state = "L",
  make Left miss = <M> cann = <M> total = (2 * <M>) ,
  make Right miss = 0 cann = 0 total = 0 ;


: ++++++++++++++++++++++++++++++++++++++++++++++++++++++++
```

```
: LOAD BOAT LEFT

:rule r2
rule 0 (goal Loading boat from left - first load a
missionary)
IF ( in Boat miss = 0 AND cann = 0 AND state = "L")
  ( in Left miss = <LM> AND total = <LT>)
THEN
  reset ,
  write 'rule r2 - loading first missionary on left\n' ,
  in 1 miss = 1 total = 1 ,
  in 2 miss = (<LM> - 1) total = (<LT> - 1) ;

:rule r3
rule 0 (goal Load another missionary on left)
IF (in Max boat <MX>)
  (in Left miss = <LM> AND cann = <LC> AND miss > 0 AND
  total = <LT>)
  (in Boat state = "L" AND miss = <BM> AND cann = <BC>
  AND total = <BT>
    AND miss > 0 total < <MX>)
THEN
  reset ,
  write 'rule r3 - loading missionary on left\n' ,
  in 2 miss = (<LM> - 1) total = (<LT> - 1) ,
  in 3 miss = (<BM> + 1) total = (<BT> + 1) ;

:rule r4
rule (goal Load a cannibal on left)
IF ( in Max boat <MX>)
  ( in Left miss = <LM> AND cann = <LC> AND cann > 0 AND
  total = <LT>)
  ( in Boat state = "L" AND miss = <BM> AND cann = <BC>
  AND total = <BT>
    AND miss > 0 AND total < <MX>)
THEN
  reset ,
  write 'rule r4 - loading cannibal on left\n' ,
  in 2 cann = (<LC> - 1) total = (<LT> - 1) ,
  in 3 cann = (<BC> + 1) total = (<BT> + 1) ;

: ----------------------------------------------------

: CHECK READY TO SAIL FROM LEFT BANK
```

```
:rule r5
rule 999
(goal Missionaries >= cannibals on left\, shore and
boat-ready to sail)
IF ( in Max boat <MX>)
   ( in Boat state = "L" AND miss = <BM> AND cann = <BC>
     AND total = <BT> AND miss >= <BC> AND total >= 2 AND
     total <= <MX>)
   ( in Left miss = <LM> AND cann = <LC> AND total = <LT>
   AND miss >= <LC>)
THEN
   reset ,
   write 'Boat holds miss <BM> cann <BC> total <BT>\n' ,
   write 'leaving miss <LM> cann <LC> total <LT>\n' ,
   message 'rule r5 - ready to sail from left\n' ,
   in 2 state = "LR",
   in 3 total = <LT> ;

:rule r6
rule 999 (goal Miss 0 on shore miss >= cann on boat,
ready to sail from left)
IF ( in Max boat <MX>)
   ( in Boat state = "L" AND miss = <BM> AND cann = <BC>
     AND total = <BT> AND miss >= <BC> AND total >= 2 AND
     total <= <MX>)
   ( in Left miss = 0 AND cann = <LC> AND total = <LT>)
THEN
   reset ,
   write 'Boat holds miss <BM> cann <BC> total <BT>\n' ,
   write 'leaving miss 0 cann <LC> total <LT>\n' ,
   message 'rule r6 - ready to sail from left\n' ,
   in 2 state = "LR";

: SEE IF NEED TO BACKTRACK
: if backtracking is necessary, forget it: delete boat, left

:rule r7
rule (goal Missionaries < cannibals, <> 0 on shore, boat
up to max, backtrack)
IF ( in Max boat <MX>)
   ( in Boat state = "L" AND total = <MX>)
   ( in Left cann = <LC> AND miss < <LC> AND miss > 0)
THEN
   warning 'rule r7 - miss will get eaten on left on
shore\, backtracking\n' ,
```

```
  delete 2 ,
  delete 3 ;

:rule r8
rule (goal Miss < cann, <> 0 in boat, boat up to max,
backtrack)
IF ( in Max boat <MX>)
   ( in Boat state = "L" AND cann = <BC> AND miss < <BC>
   AND total = <MX>)
   ( in Left TT <TT>)
THEN
   warning 'rule r8 - miss will get eaten on left in
   boat\, backtracking\n' ,
   delete 2 ,
   delete 3 ;


: +++++++++++++++++++++++++++++++++++++++++++++++++++++++
: LOAD BOAT RIGHT

:rule r9
rule 999 (goal Loading first missionary on right)
IF ( in Boat miss = 0 AND cann = 0 AND state = "R")
   ( in Right miss = <RM> AND total = <RT>)
THEN
   write 'rule r9 - loading first missionary on right\n' ,
   in 1 miss = 1 total = 1 ,
   in 2 miss = (<RM> - 1) total = (<RT> - 1) ;

:rule r10
rule 999 (goal Load another missionary on right)
IF ( in Max boat <MX>)
   ( in Right miss = <RM> AND cann = <RC> AND miss > 0 AND
   total = <RT>)
   (in Boat state = "R" AND miss = <BM> AND cann = <BC>
   AND total = <BT>
     AND total < <MX>)
THEN
   reset ,
   write 'rule r10 - loading missionary on right\n' ,
   in 2 miss = (<RM> - 1) total = (<RT> - 1) ,
   in 3 miss = (<BM> + 1) total = (<BT> + 1) ;

:rule r11
rule 999 (goal Load a cannibal from right)
IF ( in Max boat <MX>)
```

```
  ( in Right miss = <RM> AND cann = <RC> AND cann > 0 AND
  total = <RT>)
  ( in Boat state = "R" AND miss = <BM> AND cann = <BC>
  AND total = <BT>
    AND miss > 0 AND total < <MX>)
THEN
  reset ,
  write 'rule r11 - loading cannibal on right\n' ,
  in 2 cann = (<RC> - 1) total = (<RT> - 1) ,
  in 3 cann = (<BC> + 1) total = (<BT> + 1) ;


: ------------------------------------------------------------


: CHECK READY TO SAIL FROM RIGHT BANK

:rule r12
rule (goal Everything OK on right, ready to sail)
IF ( in Max boat <MX>)
  ( in Boat state = "R" AND miss = <BM> AND cann = <BC>
    AND total = <BT> AND miss >= <BC> AND total >= 1 AND
total <= <MX>)
  (in Right miss = <RM> AND cann = <RC> AND total = <RT>
  AND miss >= <RC>)
THEN
  write 'Boat holds miss <BM> cann <BC> total <BT>\n' ,
  write 'leaving miss <RM> cann <RC> total <RT>\n' ,
  message 'rule r14 - ready to sail from right\n' ,
  in 2 state = "RL";

:rule r13
rule (goal Miss 0 on shore miss >= cann on boat, ready to
sail from right)
IF ( in Max boat <MX>)
  ( in Boat state = "R" AND miss = <BM> AND cann = <BC>
    total = <BT> AND miss >= <BC> AND total >= 1 AND total
    <= <MX>)
  ( in Right miss = 0 AND cann = <RC> AND total = <RT>)
THEN
  write 'Boat holds miss <BM> cann <BC> total <BT>\n' ,
  write 'leaving miss 0 cann <RC> total <RT>\n' ,
  message'rule r13 - ready to sail from right\n' ,
  in 2 state = "RL" ;

: SEE IF NEED TO BACKTRACK
: if backtracking is necessary, forget it: delete boat, right
```

```
:rule r14
rule (goal Miss will get eaten on right, backtrack)
IF ( in Max boat <MX>)
   ( in Boat state = "R" AND total = <MX>)
   ( in Right cann = <RC> AND miss < <RC> AND miss > 0)
THEN
   warning 'rule r14 - miss will get eaten on right on
   shore\, backtracking\n' ,
   delete 2 ,
   delete 3 ;

:rule r15
rule (goal Miss will get eaten on right in boat, backtrack)
IF ( in Max boat <MX>)
   ( in Boat state = "R" AND cann = <BC> AND miss < <BC>
   AND total = <MX>)
   ( in Right miss = <RM>)
THEN
   warning 'rule r15 - miss will get eaten on right in
   boat\, backtracking\n' ,
   delete 2 ,
   delete 3 ;

: --------------------------------------------------------- -
: UNLOAD ON LEFT BANK

:rule r16
rule (goal Check new left bank totals to see if unloading
is possible)
IF ( in Boat state = "RL"
     miss = <BM> AND cann = <BC> AND total = <BT>)
   ( in Left miss = <LM> AND cann = <LC> AND total = <LT>)
THEN
   write 'rule r16 - checking new bank totals on left\n' ,
   make Temp miss = (<BM> + <LM>)
     cann = (<BC> + <LC>)
     total = (<BT> + <LT>) ;

:rule r17
rule (goal OK, unload on left bank)
IF ( in Temp miss = <TM> AND cann = <TC> AND cann <= <TM>
AND total = <TT>)
   ( in Boat state = "RL")
   ( in Left miss = <LM> AND cann = <LC> AND total = <LT>)
THEN
```

```
write 'rule r17 - unloading on left\n' ,
write 'Trip complete - now miss <TM> cann <TC> on
L bank\n' ,
delete 1 ,
in 2 state = "L" miss = 0 cann = 0 total = 0 ,
in 3 miss = <TM> cann = <TC> total = <TT> ;
```

`:rule r18`
```
rule (goal NG, cannot unload on left bank, backtrack and
forget try)
IF ( in Temp miss = <TM> AND cann > <TM>)
  ( in Boat state = "RL" )
  ( in Right TT <TT>)
THEN
  warning 'rule r18 - cannot unload on left\, backtracking\n' ,
  delete 1 ,
  delete 2 ,
  delete 3 ;
```

```
: ----------------------------------------------------- -
: UNLOAD ON RIGHT BANK
```

`:rule r19`
```
rule (goal Check new right bank totals to see if
unloading is possible)
IF ( in Boat state = "LR" AND miss = <BM> AND cann = <BC>
AND total = <BT>)
  ( in Right miss = <RM> AND cann = <RC> AND total =
<RT>)
THEN
  write 'rule r19 - checking new bank totals on right\n' ,
  make Temp miss = (<BM> + <RM>)
    cann = (<BC> + <RC>)
    total = (<BT> + <RT>) ;
```

`:rule r20`
```
rule (goal OK, unload on right bank)
IF ( in Temp miss = <TM> AND cann = <TC> AND cann <= <TM>
AND total = <TT>)
  ( in Boat state = "LR" )
  ( in Right miss = <RM> AND cann = <RC> AND total =
<RT>)
THEN
  write 'rule r20 - unloading on right\n' ,
```

```
  write 'Trip complete - now miss <TM> cann <TC> on
  R bank\n' ,
  delete 1 ,
  in 2 state = "R" miss = 0 cann = 0 total = 0 ,
  in 3 miss = <TM> cann = <TC> total = <TT> ;

:rule r21
rule (goal NG, can\'t unload on right bank, backtrack)
IF ( in Temp miss = <TM> AND cann > <TM>)
  ( in Boat state = "LR")
  ( in Left total = <LT>)
THEN
  warning 'rule r21 - cannot unload on right\, backtracking\n',
  delete 1 ,
  delete 2 ,
  delete 3 ;

: ++++++++++++++++++++++++++++++++++++++++++++++++++++++++++

: CHECKS

:rule r22
rule (goal Check if boat will hold two or more)
IF ( in Max boat < 2)
THEN
  error 'cannot do it - boat must hold two or more\n' ,
  delete 1 ,
  make Max ;

:rule r23
rule (goal Check if boat holds more than 3 if 3+ cannibals)
IF ( in Max boat <= 3 AND cann >= 3)
  ( Boat)
  ( Left)
  ( Right)
THEN
  error 'cannot do it - boat not big enough\n' ,
  delete 1 ,
  delete 2 ,
  delete 3 ,
  delete 4 ,
  make Max ;

:rule r25
rule ( goal Check if finished)
```

```
IF ( in Boat state = "R")
   ( in Right total = <RT>)
   ( in Max total = <RT>)
THEN
   reset ,
   message nocancel 'Missionaries and Cannibals
   finished\n' ,
   exit ;


: ---------------------------------------------------------
cls ;
string = "Missionaries and Cannibals problem -\n" ;
string + "On one side of a river, we have some missionaries ";
string + "and cannibals. We also have a boat of limited ";
string + "capacity. The problem is to get everybody from the ";
string + "left to the right bank without any missionaries ";
string + "being eaten.\n" ;
message "<string>";
string = "RULES OF GAME -\n" ;
string + "- can never be more cannibals than missionaries
           in the ";
string + "boat or on either shore, except\n" ;
string + "- all cannibals and no missionaries is OK.\n\n";
message "<string>";
string = "MC.FPS. basically a simulation of the problem,
           illustrates ";
string + "the use of backtracking in the a depth-first
           search of a ";
string + "decision tree.\n" ;
string + "When it is time to load a person onto the boat,
           two rules ";
string + "are concurrently fireable. One loads a
           missionary, and ";
string + "one loads a cannibal. One is selected for
           firing, and the ";
string + " other is stacked. If the rule chosen for
           firing turns out ";
string + "to be the wrong one, the other rule is popped
           off the ";
string + "stack and fired.\n" ;
message "<string>";

make Max ;

message "Ready to run\n" ;
```

```
:run ;
: * * * * * * * * * * * * * * * * * * * * * * * * * * * * * * * * * * * * * * * * * * * * * * * * * * * * * *


: * * * * * * * * * * * * * * * * * * * * * * * * * * * * * * * * * * * * * * * * * * * * * * * * * * * * * *
:program NODES.PAR - finds best route between nodes in a
network
: * * * * * * * * * * * * * * * * * * * * * * * * * * * * * * * * * * * * * * * * * * * * * * * * * * * * * *
declare Pair
    node1 str
    node2 str
    dist int ;

declare Howfar
    node1 str
    node2 str ;

declare Thisfar
    node1 str
    node2 str
    path str
    dist int ;

declare Check      :used to indicate bad node entered
    OK str ;

: +++++++++++++++++++++++++++++++++++++++++++++++++++++++++++++
:Block 0 - writes available nodes

:rule r0
rule ( goal Print out nodes for user choices )
IF ( in Pair node1 = <C1> AND node2 = <C2> AND dist = <D> )
THEN
    write 'route <C1> to <C2> <D> miles\n' ,
    fire block 0 off ,
    fire block 1 on ;

: +++++++++++++++++++++++++++++++++++++++++++++++++++++++++++++
:Block 1 - sets up run

:rule r1
rule block 1 (goal Inputs starting and destination nodes)
IF ( in Howfar node1.cf = 0 )
THEN
    input "From node (NULL to quit) ?\n" 1 node1 lcase ,
    input "to node (NULL to quit) ?\n" 1 node2 lcase ;
```

```
:rule r2
rule block 1 ( goal Quits on null entry )
IF ( in Howfar node1 = "" )
THEN
    message nocancel 'Terminating nodes.PAR\n',
    stop ;

:rule r3
rule block 1 ( goal Makes instances of data with nodes
reversed )
IF ( in Pair node1 = <C1> AND node2 = <C2> AND dist = <D> )
THEN
    make Pair node1 "<C2>" node2 "<C1>" dist <D> ,
    fire rule r3 off ;

:rule r4
rule block 1 (goal Sees if direct path from start to destination)
IF ( in Howfar node1 = <C1> AND node2 = <C2> )
   ( in Pair node1 = <C1> AND node2 = <C2> AND dist = <D> )
THEN
    fire block 1 off ,
    fire block 5 on ;

:rule r5
rule block 1 ( goal Gets all direct paths from start to
another node )
IF ( in Howfar node1 = <C1> AND node2 = <C2> )
   ( in Pair node1 = <C1> AND node2 = <C3> AND dist = <D> )
   ( in Pair node1 = <C3> AND node2 = <C1> AND dist = <D> )
THEN
    make Thisfar node1 "<C1>" node2 "<C3>" path
    "<C1>-<C3>" dist <D> ,
    delete 2 ,
    delete 3 ;

:rule r6
rule block 1 (goal Checks both input nodes on list)
IF ( in Howfar node1 = <C1> AND node2 = <C2> AND node1 <>
<C2> )
   ( in Pair node1 = <C1> )
   ( in Pair node1 = <C2> )
   ( in Check )
THEN
    in 4 OK = "y" ;
```

```
:rule r7
rule block 1 ( goal Block firing control )
IF ( in Howfar node1 = <C1> AND node2 = <C2> AND node1 <> "" )
THEN
    fire rule r3 on ,
    fire block 1 off ,
    fire block 2 on ;

: ++++++++++++++++++++++++++++++++++++++++++++++++++++++++
:Block 2 - resets if bad node entry, else proceeds

:rule r8
rule block 2 ( goal Warns of nodes not on list, restarts
program )
IF ( in Check OK = "n" )
    ( Howfar )
THEN
    error 'node not in data base - reenter\n' ,
    in 2 node1.cf = 0 node2.cf = 0 ,
    fire block 2 off ,
    fire block 0 on ,
    transfer -conf all from nodes.inp ;

:rule r9
rule block 2 ( goal Deletes nodes data for rerunnning
program )
IF ( in Check OK = "n" )
    ( Pair )
THEN
    delete 2 ;

:rule r10
rule block 2 ( goal If nodes OK, enables next block )
IF ( in Check OK = "y" )
THEN
    fire block 2 off ,
    fire block 3 on ;

: ++++++++++++++++++++++++++++++++++++++++++++++++++++++++
:Block 3 - starts finding path - goes to block 6 if finished,
:else on to block 4

:rule r11
rule block 3 ( goal Extends paths to one more node )
```

```
IF ( in Thisfar node1 = <C1> AND node2 = <C2> AND path =
    <P> AND dist = <D1> )
    ( in Pair node1 = <C2> AND node2 = <C3> AND node2 <>
    <C1> AND dist = <D2> )
    ( in Pair node1 = <C3> AND node2 = <C2> )
    ( in Howfar node1.cf > 0 )
THEN
    make Thisfar node1 "<C1>" node2 "<C3>" path "<P>-<C3>"
    dist ( <D1> + <D2> ),
    delete 1 ,
    delete 2 ,
    delete 3 ,
    fire block 3 off ,
    fire block 4 on ;

:rule r12
rule block 3 ( goal Fires if finished, enables rule block 5 )
IF ( in Howfar node1.cf = 0 )
THEN
    fire block 3 off ,
    fire block 6 on ;

: ++++++++++++++++++++++++++++++++++++++++++++++++++++++++++++
:Block 4 - second in pathway chain - goes on to block 5
:rule r13
rule block 4 ( goal Gets rid of longer paths start to
destination )
IF ( in Thisfar node1 = <C1> AND node2 = <C2> AND dist =
<D> )
    ( in Thisfar node1 = <C1> AND node2 = <C2> AND path =
    <P> AND dist > <D> )
    ( in Howfar node1 = <C1> AND node2 = <C2> )
THEN
    write 'shorter path than <P>\, deleting...' ,
    delete 2 ;

:rule r14
rule block 4 ( goal Disables block 3, enables block 4
unless finished )
IF ( in Howfar node1.cf > 0 )
THEN
    in 1 ,
    fire block 4 off ,
    fire block 5 on ;
```

```
: ++++++++++++++++++++++++++++++++++++++++++++++++++++++++++++
:Block 5 - last in pathway chain - goes back to block 3

:rule r15
rule block 5 ( goal Fires if destination reached )
IF ( in Thisfar node1 = <C1> AND node2 = <C2> AND path =
<P> AND dist = <D> )
    ( in Howfar node1 = <C1> AND node2 = <C2> )
THEN
    message '<D> miles <C1> to <C2> path <P>\n' ,
    in 2 node1.cf = 0 ;

:rule r16
rule block 5 ( goal Block firing control -
disables block 5, enables block 3 )
IF ( Howfar )
THEN
    fire block 5 off ,
    fire block 3 on ;

: ++++++++++++++++++++++++++++++++++++++++++++++++++++++++++++

:rule r17
rule block 6 ( goal Deletes data element This far when
finished )
    ( Thisfar )
THEN
    delete 1 ;

:rule r18
rule block 6 ( goal Re-reads node data after finishing a
run )
    ( Howfar )
    ( Check )
THEN
    transfer -conf all from cities.inp ,
    in 2 OK "n" ,
    fire block 6 off ,
    fire block 0 on ;

:rule r19
rule block 6 ( goal Deletes modified node data after
finishing one run )
    ( Pair )
THEN
```

```
    delete 1 ;

; +++++++++++++++++++++++++++++++++++++++++++++++++++++++++
transfer -conf all from cities.inp;
make Howfar ;
make Check OK = "n" ;
fire all off ;
fire block 0 on ;
string = "Program nodes to get best route between
        nodes.\n" ;
string + "Best route involves (first) fewest number of
        intermediate nodes,";
string + "Shortest distance to break ties.";
message "<string>";
message "node-to-node routes are\:\n" ;
run ;

; ***********************************************************
:program NUMBERS.FPS for Boolean tests on two scalar numbers
; ***********************************************************
write 'compiling program numbers.fps...\n' ;

:DECLARATIONS

declare Numbers
    num1 flt
    num2 flt ;

; ----------------------------------------------------------

:RULES

:rule r0
rule rconf 0 (goal Inputs numbers to be compared.)
IF (in Numbers num1.cf = 0)
THEN
    message nocancel 'Enter two numbers to be compared\,
    0 0 to quit.' ,
    reset ,
    input "First number?" 1 num1,
    input "Second number?" 1 num2,
    make Numbers ;

:rule r1
rule (goal Tests for zeroes, quits.)
```

```
IF (in Numbers num1 = 0 AND num2 = 0)
THEN
    message nocancel 'Terminating NUMBERS.FPS.' ,
    stop ;

:rule r2
rule (goal Tests for equality.)
IF (in Numbers num1 = <N1> AND num2 = <N2> AND num2 =
<N1> AND num1 > 0)
THEN
    message '<N1> equals <N2>',
    delete 1 ;

:rule r3
rule (goal Tests for N1 < N2.)
IF (in Numbers num1 = <N1> AND num2 = <N2> AND num1 < <N2>)
THEN
    message '<N1> less than <N2>' ,
    delete 1 ;

:rule r4
rule (goal Tests for N1 > N2.)
IF (in Numbers num1 = <N1> AND num2 = <N2> AND num1 > <N2>)
THEN
    message '<N1> greater than <N2>' ,
    delete 1 ;

: ------------------------------------------------------------

:MAKES
make Numbers ;

string = "NUMBERS.FPS does Boolean comparison of two
          numbers, num1 and num2, ";
string + "for num1 = num2, num1 > num2 or num1 < num2.\n\n" ;
string + "Here is an extremely simple program,
          illustrating ";
string + "basic principles of a rule-based data-driven
          system. ";
string + "After you have run the program, look it over in
          the ";
string + "TFLOPSW editor.\n\n";
string + "If you like, comment out the run command by
          placing a colon ";
string + "in front, thus - '\:run'. You can then enter
          'prstack\;' to see ";
```

```
string + "which rules are fireable\; 'prdata\;' to
inspect the data\; and ";
string + "'run 1\;' to execute one rule-firing step.\n\n";
string + "ready to run..." ;
message "<string>";
:run ;


: *******************************************************


: *******************************************************
:program PAVLOV1.PAR - Classical conditioning
:conditions neutral stimulus to aversive stimulus or
:positive reward by adding data to S/R pair database
:learns by adding stimulus-response pairs to database
: *******************************************************


message "Compiling program PAVLOV1.PAR ...\n";


:MEMORY LAYOUT


declare Input            :accepts stimulus from keyboard
   id str;               :stimulus identification


declare Stimulus       :record of stimuli
   id str               :stimulus ID
   time int             :time received
   response str;        :NULL (neutral), WHEE (positive),
                        :   or RUN (aversive)


declare NewStimulus   :record of new stimuli
   id str               :stimulus ID
   time int             :time when stimulus received
   response str;        :NULL (neutral), WHEE (positive),
                        :   or RUN (aversive)


declare Pair             :observed stimulus pair
   id1 str               :earlier stimulus (response "")
   id2 str               :later stimulus (response + or -)
   T1 int                :time of stimulus id1
   T2 int                :time of stimulus id2
   TF int;               :forget pair after this time
```

```
declare Responses        :library of unconditioned stimuli
                         :and response types
   id str                  :stimulus id
   response str;         :stimulus response


declare Time
   time int              :current time
   pairTime int          :pair with stimulus no earlier
                            :than this time
   forget int;           :forget anything earlier than
                            :this time



declare Count
   id1 str
   id2 str
   N int
   time int;



declare Conditioned  :library of conditioned stimuli
   id1 str                 :conditioned stimulus
   id2 str                 :associated stimulus
response str;             :stimulus response


declare Forget
   delPT int             :time interval allowed to pair
                            :incoming stimuli
   delFT int;            :time interval before stimulus &
                            :pairs forgotten



declare Fire             :block firing control
   block int;



: +++++++++++++++++++++++++++++++++++++++++++++++++++++++++
:Block 0 - stimulus input

:Block 1 - recognize stimulus and update data: put in :
:   response if known,
```

```
: put into stimulus record, forget old data,
: print out conditioned response if there is one

:Block 2 - associate new stimulus with wired-in response
:   :if appropriate

:Block 3 - reports response, forgets old data,
: :holds generated stimulus-response rules

:Block 4 - stimulus with known response paired with
: previous neutral stimulus, moves NewStimulus into
: short-term memory

:Block 5 - if latest stimulus paired with more than one
: neutral stimulus, select latest one

:Block 6 - counts recent stimulus pairs

:Block 7 - stops making new rule if one already exists

:Block 8 - generates new rule if ready

:Block 10 - sequences rule blocks




: +++++++++++++++++++++++++++++++++++++++++++++++++++++++++++++
:Block 0 - stimulus input


:rule r0
rule block 0 (goal Inputs stimulus and updates time)
IF (in Input id.cf = 0)
   (in Time time = <T>)
   (in Forget delPT = <PT> AND delFT = <FT>)
THEN
   reset,
   input "Enter any stimulus\, <CR> to quit\n" 1 id lcase,
   in 2 time = (<T> + 1) pairTime = (<T> - <PT>) forget = (<T> - <FT>);

: ---------------------------------------------------------
:Block 1 - recognize stimulus and update data: put in
: response if known,
: put into stimulus record, forget old data,
```

```
: print out conditioned response if there is one


:rule r1
rule block 1 (goal Quits on null stimulus)
IF (in Input id = "")
THEN
  message nocancel "Exiting PAVLOV --\n" ,
  exit ;


:rule r2
rule block 1 (goal Puts input into new stimulus record)
IF (in Input id = <ID>)
  (in Time time = <T>)
THEN
  reset,
  in 1 id.cf = 0 ,
  make NewStimulus id = "<ID>" response = "" time = <T>;



: ---------------------------------------------------------
:Block 2 - associate new stimulus with wired-in response
:   if appropriate


:rule r3
rule block 2 (goal Associate new stimulus with existing
response if appropriate)
IF (in NewStimulus id = <ID>)
  (in Responses id = <ID> AND response = <R>)
THEN
  in 1 response = "<R>";



: ---------------------------------------------------------
:Block 3 - reports response, forgets old data,


:rule r4
rule block 3 (goal Report response to unconditioned
  stimulus)
IF (in Newstimulus id = <ID> AND response = <R> AND
    response <> "")
THEN
  message "<ID> - <R>!\n";
```

```
:rule r5
rule block 3 ( goal Report response to conditioned
stimulus )
IF (in NewStimulus id = <ID> and response = "" )
   (in Conditioned id1 = <ID> AND id2 = <ID2> AND
response = <R>)
THEN
   message "<ID> - LOOK OUT - <ID2> coming\, <R>!\n";


:rule r6
rule block 3 ( goal Forget old stimuli )
IF (in Time forget = <TF>)
   (in Stimulus time < <TF>)
THEN
    delete 2;


:rule r7
rule block 3 ( goal Forget old stimulus pairs )
IF (in Time forget = <TF>)
  (in Pair T2 < <TF>)
THEN
  delete 2;


:rule r8
rule block 3 ( goal Forget how many pairs we had )
IF (in Time forget = <TF>)
  (in Count time < <TF>)
THEN
  delete 2;


: ----------------------------------------------------------
:Block 4 - stimulus with known response paired with
:previous neutral stimulus, moves NewStimulus into
:short-term memory


:rule r9
rule block 4 ( goal If response known, pair with
  previous neutral stimuli )
IF (in Time time = <T> AND pairTime = <TP>)
  (in NewStimulus id = <ID1> AND response = <R> AND
```

```
  response <> "" AND time = <T1>)
  (in Stimulus id = <ID2> AND response = "" AND time =
  <T2> AND time >= <TP>)
THEN
  reset ,
  make Pair id1 = "<ID1>" id2 = "<ID2>" T1 = <T1> T2 = <T2>,
  make Count id1 = "<ID1>" id2 = "<ID2>" N 0 time = <T>;


:rule r10
rule block 4 (goal Moves NewStimulus into short-term memory)
IF (in NewStimulus id = <ID> AND response = <R> AND time = <T>)
THEN
  make Stimulus id = "<ID>" response = "<R>" time = <T>;


: ------------------------------------------------------------
:Block 5 - if latest stimulus paired with more than one
:neutral stimulus, select latest one

:rule r11
rule block 5 (goal Picks latest neutral stimulus paired
              with current one)
IF (in Pair id1 = <ID1> AND id2 = <ID2> AND tt = <TT>)
   (in Pair id1 = <ID1> AND id2 = <ID2> AND tt < <TT>)
THEN
  delete 2;


:rule r12
rule block 5 (goal picks latest instance of count)
IF (in Count tt = <TT>)
   (in Count N = <N> AND tt < <TT>)
THEN
  in 1 N = <N>,
  delete 2;


:rule r13
rule block 5 (goal Erase earlier instances of same
neutral stimulus )
IF (in Stimulus id is <ID> AND tt = <TT> )
   (in Stimulus id is <ID> AND tt > <TT> )
THEN
  delete 1;
```

```
: ---------------------------------------------------------
:Block 6 - counts recent stimulus pairs


:rule r14
rule block 6 ( goal count number of recent stimulus pairs )
IF (in Count id1 = <ID1> AND id2 = <ID2> AND N = <N1>)
   (in Pair id1 = <ID1> AND id2 = <ID2>)
   (in NewStimulus id = <ID2>)
THEN
   in 1 N ( $<N1> + 1 );



: ---------------------------------------------------------
:Block 7 - stops making new data if one already exists


:rule r15
rule block 7 ( goal Stops making new data if one already
made )
IF (in Conditioned id1 = <ID1> AND id2 = <ID2>)
   (in Count id1 = <ID1> AND id2 = <ID2>)
THEN
   delete 2;



: ---------------------------------------------------------
:Block 8 - generates new conditioned response if ready


:rule r16
rule block 8 (goal Adds response to library)
IF (in Count id1 = <ID1> AND id2 = <ID2> AND N > 2)
   (in Responses id = <ID2> AND response = <R>)
THEN
   reset,
   message "New data\: conditioning <ID2> to <ID1>
     response <R>\n",
   delete 1,
   make Conditioned id1 = "<ID1>" id2 = "<ID2>" response "<R>";


:rule r17
rule block 8 (goal delete instance of NewStimulus - no
```

```
  longer needed
IF (NewStimulus)
THEN
  delete 1;


: ------------------------------------------------------
:Block 10 - sequences rule blocks

:rule r18
rule block 10 (goal Sequences rule blocks for firing)
IF (in Fire block = <B> AND block < 8)
THEN
  in 1 block = (<B> + 1),
  fire block <B> off,
  fire block (<B> + 1) on;

:rule r19
rule block 10 (goal Restarts rule firing sequence after
stimulus processed)
IF (in Fire block = 8)
THEN
  in 1 block = 0,
  fire block 8 off,
  fire block 0 on;

:rule r20
rule block 10 (goal Fires once to report stimuli with
wired-in responses)
IF (in Responses id = <ID> AND response = <R>)
THEN
  string + "Stimulus <ID> response <R>\n";


: +++++++++++++++++++++++++++++++++++++++++++++++++++++++++


:library of wired-in stimulus-response responses

make Responses id = "burn" response = "RUN";
make Responses id = "food" response = "WHEE";
make Responses id = "girls" response = "WHEE";
make Time time = 0;

string = "Simulation of pavlovian conditioning.\n\n";
```

```
string + "A stimulus, with no response associated,
          coming just ";
string + "before a second stimulus with known response,
          tends ";
string + "to associate the known response to the first
          stimulus. \n";
:write out stimulus library to screen

message "<string>";
fire all off;
fire block 10 on;
:write out stimuli with given response
string = "Known stimuli with wired-in responses -\n\n";
run;
message "<string>";
string = "There are two basically different approaches";
string + "to this problem. One way is to generate a";
string + "new rule if a new stimulus becomes";
string + "associated with a previous stimulus";
string + "with known response. \nWe could instead";
string + "modify the data base on which the rules ";
string + "operate\; that is what this program does. \n";
string + "Try seeing if the burnt child dreads the fire. ";
string + "For example, enter fire followed by burn three";
string + "or four times in a row, and see what happens. ";
string + "You can enter stimuli not in the library. \n";
message "<string>";

make Input;
make Fire block = 0;
make Forget delPT = 2 delFT = 12;
fire block 0 on;
message "PAVLOV.PAR Ready to run\n";
:run;
:***********************************************************

:***********************************************************
:program PAVLOV2.PAR - Classical conditioning
:conditions neutral stimulus to aversive stimulus or
:positive reward
:learns by ading new rule for repeated stimulus-
:response pair
:***********************************************************

message 'Compiling program PAVLOV2.PAR...\n';
```

```
:MEMORY LAYOUT

declare Input            :accepts stimulus from keyboard
  id str;                :stimulus identification

declare Stimulus         :record of stimuli
  id str                   :stimulus ID
  myTime int               :myTime received
  response str;          :NULL (neutral), WHEE (positive),
or RUN (aversive)

declare NewStimulus      :record of new stimuli
  id str                   :stimulus ID
  myTime int             :myTime when stimulus received
  response str;          :NULL (neutral), WHEE (positive),
or RUN (aversive)

declare Pair             :observed stimulus pair
  id1 str                  :earlier stimulus (response "")
  id2 str                  :later stimulus (response + or -)
  T1 int                   :myTime of stimulus id1
  T2 int                   :myTime of stimulus id2
  TF int;                :forget pair after this myTime

declare Wired-in         :library of unconditioned stimuli
and response types
  id str                   :stimulus id
  response str;          :stimulus response

declare Time             :clock
  myTime int               :current myTime
  pairTime int           :pair with stimulus no earlier
                         :than this time
  forget int;            :forget anything earlier than this
                         :time

declare Count
  id1 str
  id2 str
  N int
  myTime int;

declare Rulemade
  id1 str
  id2 str;
```

```
declare Forget
  delPT int  :Interval allowed to pair incoming stimuli
  delFT int; :myTime interval before stimulus & pairs
             :forgotten
declare Fire :block firing control
  block int;

: +++++++++++++++++++++++++++++++++++++++++++++++++++++++++++
:Block 0 - stimulus input
:Block 1 - recognize stimulus and update data: put in
:  response if known,
:  put into stimulus record, forget old data,
:  print out conditioned response if there is one
:Block 2 - associate new stimulus with wired-in response
if appropriate
:Block 3 - reports response, forgets old data,
:  holds generated stimulus-response rules
:Block 4 - stimulus with known response paired with
:  previous neutral stimulus, moves NewStimulus into
:  short-term memory
:Block 5 - if latest stimulus paired with more than one
:  neutral stimulus, select latest one
:Block 6 - counts recent stimulus pairs
:Block 7 - stops making new rule if one already exists
:Block 8 - generates new rule if ready
:Block 10 - sequences rule blocks
:
: +++++++++++++++++++++++++++++++++++++++++++++++++++++++++++
:Block 0 - stimulus input

:rule r0
rule block 0 (goal Inputs stimulus and updates myTime)
IF (in Input id.cf = 0 )
  (in Time myTime = <T> )
  (in Forget delPT = <PT> AND delFT = <FT> )
THEN
  reset,
  input "Enter any stimulus\, <CR> to quit\n" 1 id
    lcase,
  in 2 myTime = (<T> + 1) pairTime = (<T> - <PT>)
    forget = (<T> - <FT>);
: ----------------------------------------------------------
:Block 1 - recognize stimulus and update data: put in
:  response if known,
:  put into stimulus record, forget old data,
```

```
:   print out conditioned response if there is one

:rule r1
rule block 1 (goal Quits on null stimulus)
IF (in Input id = "" )
THEN
  message nocancel 'Exiting PAVLOV2 --\n',
  keyboard,
  exit;

:rule r2
rule block 1 (goal Puts input into new stimulus record)
IF (in Input id = <ID> )
  (in Time myTime = <T> )
THEN
  reset,
  in 1 id.cf = 0,
  make NewStimulus id = "<ID>" response = "" myTime = <T>;

: ---------------------------------------------------
:Block 2 - associate new stimulus with wired-in response
:   if appropriate

:rule r3
rule block 2 (goal Associate new stimulus with wired-in
response if appropriate)
IF (in NewStimulus id = <ID> )
  (in Wired-in id = <ID> AND response = <R> )
THEN
  in 1 response = "<R>";

: ---------------------------------------------------
:Block 3 - reports response, forgets old data,
:   holds generated stimulus-response rules

:rule r4
:rule block 3 (goal Report response to unconditioned
                stimulus)
IF (in NewStimulus id = <ID> AND response = <R> AND
response <> "" )
THEN
  message '<ID> - <R>! \n';

:rule r5
rule block 3 ( goal Forget old stimuli )
```

```
IF (in Time forget = <TF> )
   (in Stimulus myTime < <TF> )
THEN
   delete 2;

:rule r6
rule block 3 (goal Forget old stimulus pairs)
IF (in Time forget = <TF> )
   (in Pair T2 < <TF> )
THEN
   delete 2;

:rule r7
rule block 3 ( goal Forget how many pairs we had )
IF (in Time forget = <TF> )
   (in Count myTime < <TF> )
THEN
   delete 2;

: --------------------------------------------------------
:Block 4 - stimulus with known response paired with
:   previous neutral stimulus, moves NewStimulus into
:   short-term memory

:rule r8
rule block 4 ( goal If response known, pair with
previous neutral stimuli )
IF (in Time myTime = <T> AND pairTime = <TP> )
   (in NewStimulus id = <ID1> AND response = <R> AND
    response <> "" AND myTime = <T1> )
   (in Stimulus id = <ID2> AND response = "" AND
    myTime = <T2> AND myTime >= <TP> )
THEN
   reset,
   make Pair id1 = "<ID1>" id2 = "<ID2>" T1 = <T1> T2 = <T2>,
   make Count id1 = "<ID1>" id2 = "<ID2>" N 0 myTime = <T>;

:rule r9
:rule block 4 (goal Moves NewStimulus into short-term
                memory)
:IF (in NewStimulus id = <ID> AND response = <R> AND
     myTime = <T> )
THEN
   make Stimulus id = "<ID>" response = "<R>" myTime = <T>,
   delete 1;
```

```
: ---------------------------------------------------------
:Block 5 - if latest stimulus paired with more than one
:   neutral stimulus, select latest one


:rule r10
rule block 5 (goal Picks latest neutral stimulus paired
with current one)
IF (in Time myTime = <T> )
   (in Pair T1 = <T> AND T2 = <T2> )
   (in Pair T1 = <T> AND T2 < <T2> )
THEN
   delete 3;

:rule r11
rule block 5 (goal picks latest instance of count)
IF (in Count tt = <TT>)
   (in Count tt < <TT> )
THEN
   delete 2;


: ---------------------------------------------------------
:Block 6 - counts recent stimulus pairs

:rule r12
rule block 6 ( goal count number of recent stimulus
pairs )
IF (in Count id1 = <ID1> AND id2 = <ID2> AND N = <N1> )
   (in Pair id1 = <ID1> AND id2 = <ID2> )
THEN
   in 1 N ( $<N1> + 1 );

: ---------------------------------------------------------
:Block 7 - stops making new data if one already exists

:rule r13
rule block 7 ( goal Stops making new rule if one already
               made )
IF (in Rulemade id1 = <ID1> AND id2 = <ID2> )
   (in Count id1 = <ID1> AND id2 = <ID2> )
THEN
   delete 2;

: ---------------------------------------------------------
:Block 8 - generates new rule if ready
```

```
:rule r14
rule block 8 (goal Generates rule for response to
  conditioned stimuli)
IF (in Count id1 = <ID1> AND id2 = <ID2> AND N > 2 )
  (in Wired-in id = <ID1> AND response = <R> )
THEN
  reset,
  delete 1,
  message 'New rule\: conditioning <ID1> to <ID2>
    response <R>\n',
  delete 1,
  make Rulemade id1 = "<ID1>" id2 = "<ID2>",
  rule block 2 (goal Conditioned response <R> to
    stimulus <ID2>)
  IF (in NewStimulus id = "<ID2>" )
  Then
    message 12 '<ID2> - LOOK OUT - <ID1> coming\,
      <R>!\n';

:rule r15
rule block 8 (goal delete instance of count - no longer
  needed)
IF ( Count )
THEN
  delete 1;



: -----------------------------------------------------------
:Block 10 - sequences rule blocks
:rule r16
rule block 10 (goal Sequences rule blocks for firing)
IF (in Fire block = <B> AND block < 8 )
THEN
  in 1 block = (<B> + 1),
  fire block <B> off,
  fire block (<B> + 1) on;

:rule r17
rule block 10 (goal Restarts rule firing sequence after
stimulus processed)
IF (in Fire block = 8 )
THEN
  in 1 block = 0,
  fire block 8 off,
  fire block 0 on;
```

```
:rule r18
rule block 10 (goal Fires once to report stimuli with
wired-in responses)
IF (in Wired-in id = <ID> and response = <R> )
THEN
   string + "Stimulus <ID> response <R>\n";


: ++++++++++++++++++++++++++++++++++++++++++++++++++++++++


:MAKES


:library of wired-in stimulus-response responses


make Wired-in id = "burn" response = "RUN";
make Wired-in id = "food" response = "WHEE";
make Wired-in id = "girls" response = "WHEE";
make Time myTime = 0;

string = "Simulation of pavlovian conditioning.\n\n";
string + "A stimulus, with no response associated,
  coming just ";
string + "before a second stimulus with known response,
  tends ";
string + "to associate the known response to the first
stimulus. \n";

:write out stimulus library to screen
message "<string>";
fire all off;
fire block 10 on;

:write out stimuli with given response
string = "Known stimuli with wired-in responses -\n\n";
run;

message "<string>";

string = "There are two basically different approaches
  to this ";
string + "problem. One way is to generate a new rule if
  a new ";
string + "stimulus becomes associated with a previous
  stimulus ";
```

```
string + "with known response: that is what this program
  does. \n";
string + "We could instead modify the data base on which
  the ";
string + "rules operate. \nTry seeing if the the burnt child
  dreads the fire. ";
string + "For example, enter fire followed by burn three
  or ";
string + "four times in a row, and see what happens. ";
string + "You can of course enter stimuli not in the
  library. \n";
message "<string>";

make Input;
make Fire block = 0;
make Forget delPT = 2 delFT = 12;

fire block 0 on;
message "PAVLOV2.PAR Ready to run\n";
:run;
:******************************************************

:******************************************************
:program RULEGEN.FPS - demonstrates generation of a rule
:by another rule
:******************************************************

message "compiling program rulgen.fps..." ;

declare Proto
  element str
  attr str
  type str ;

:rule r0
rule (goal Enter data for new data element)
IF ( in Proto element.cf 0 )
THEN
  input "Enter data element name - " 1 element,
  input "Enter attribute name - " 1 attr,
  input "Enter attribute type: str\, int or flt -" 1
type lcase str int flt ;

:rule r1
rule (goal Rule-generating rule)
```

```
   IF ( in Proto element <EL> attr <AT> type <TY> )
   THEN
     reset ,
     message "rulgen firing" ,
     declare <EL> <AT> <TY> ,
     rule (goal Inputs data for new attribute\, generates
     second new rule)
        IF ( in <EL> <AT>.cf 0 )
        THEN
         message "New rule firing" ,
         input "Enter value of attribute <AT> type <TY>" 1 <AT>,
         rule (goal Prints rules and data)
          IF ( in <EL> <AT> <X> )
          THEN
            message "New rule\'s new rule firing\n",
            message "with antecedent (<EL> <AT> = \<X\>)\n" ,
             : Note: in printing antecedent, \"s must be
               inserted before <
            : and after >, causing <X> to print. If this is
             not done,
            : the current value of <X>, i.e. the value of
              attribute <AT>
            : in data element <EL>, will be printed.
            message "Rules now are\:\n" ,
            prule ,
            message "Data now are\:\n" ,
            prdata ;

:rule r2
rule rconf 999 (goal Makes instance of new data element)
IF ( in Proto element = <EL> )
THEN
  message "\nmaking instance of <EL> -\n" ,
  make <EL> ;

make Proto ;

string = "This short program is for the stronghearted.\n" ;
string + "rulgen will first create a new memory
          descriptor to your specs\n" ;
string + "and a new rule to enter a value for the new
          attribute.\n" ;
string + "The new rule will make still another rule to
          print rules and data.\n";
message "<string>";
```

```
message "Initial rules:";
prule;
string = "To create a new data element,\n" ,
string + "enter name of data element, attribute and data
          type.\n",
string + "Data type should be one of str, int or flt." ;
message "<string>";
run;
message "RULEGEN finished.\n" ;
exit;
: ********************************************************


: ********************************************************
: program SCHIZO.PAR - psychiatric diagnosis
: Jeff Jones, University of Texas at Arlington
: ********************************************************


thresh 1 ;

write 'compiling program schizo.par....\n' ;

declare Fact
  fact str ;

declare Symptoms
  symptom fzset
  (
  has_depressive_symptoms
  has_manic_symptoms
  has_schizophrenic_symptoms
  ) ;

declare Diagnosis
  dx fzset
  (
  major_depression
  manic_depressive_psychosis
  schizophrenia
  schizophrenia_disorganized_type
  schizophrenia_catatonic_type
  schizophrenia_paranoid_type
  paranoid_disorder
  ) ;

declare enable
```

```
   block int ;

: -------------------------------------------------------
:block 0 - gets patient information

:rule r0
rule
  (goal Gets confidence levels in facts)
IF (in Fact fact <FA> )
THEN
  input "<FA> (0 - 1000) ?\n" 1 fact.cf ;

: -------------------------------------------------------
:block 1 - gets rid of unverified facts for housekeeping

:rule r1
rule block 1 (goal Gets rid of fact if fact.cf 0)
IF (in Fact fact.cf 0 )
THEN
  delete 1 ;

: -------------------------------------------------------
:block 2 - gets symptoms

:rule r2
rule rconf 400 block 2
  (goal Finds symptom is has_depressive_symptoms)
IF (in Fact fact "has sad face" )
  (in Fact fact "has depressed mood" )
  ( Symptoms )
THEN
  write 'has depressive symptoms ', pconf ,
  in 3 symptom is has_depressive_symptoms ;

:rule r3
rule rconf 500 block 2
  (goal Finds symptom is has_depressive_symptoms)
IF (in Fact fact "loses interest in usual activities" )
  ( Symptoms )
THEN
  write 'has depressive symptoms ', pconf ,
  in 2 symptom is has_depressive_symptoms ;

:rule r4
rule rconf 900 block 2
```

```
  (goal Finds symptom is has_depressive_symptoms)
IF (in Fact fact "has self deprecatory ideas" )
  (in Fact fact "has thoughts of death or suicide" )
  ( Symptoms )
THEN
  write 'has depressive symptoms ', pconf ,
  in 3 symptom is has_depressive_symptoms ;

:rule r5
rule rconf 600 block 2
  (goal Finds symptom is has_depressive_symptoms)
IF (in Fact fact "has insomnia" )
  (in Fact fact "is restless" )
  ( Symptoms )
THEN
  write 'has depressive symptoms ', pconf ,
  in 3 symptom is has_depressive_symptoms ;

:rule r6
rule rconf 500 block 2
  (goal Finds symptom is has_depressive_symptoms)
IF (in Fact fact "loses weight" )
  (in Fact fact "has low energy" )
  ( Symptoms )
THEN
  write 'has depressive symptoms ', pconf ,
  in 3 symptom is has_depressive_symptoms ;

:rule r7
rule rconf 600 block 2
  (goal Finds symptom is has_manic_symptoms)
IF (in Fact fact "is restless" )
  (in Fact fact "has euphoria" )
  (in Fact fact "is overactive" )
  ( Symptoms )
THEN
  write 'has manic symptoms ', pconf ,
  in 4 symptom is has_manic_symptoms ;

:rule r8
rule rconf 700 block 2
  (goal Finds symptom is has_manic_symptoms)
IF (in Fact fact "has animated appearance" )
  (in Fact fact "has flight of ideas" )
  (in Fact fact "has push of speech" )
```

```
   (in Fact fact "is distractable" )
   ( Symptoms )
THEN
   write 'has manic symptoms ', pconf ,
   in 5 symptom is has_manic_symptoms ;

:rule r9
rule rconf 800 block 2
   (goal Finds symptom is has_manic_symptoms)
IF (in Fact fact "has excess energy" )
   (in Fact fact "has many big plans" )
   (in Fact fact "has hallucinations" )
   ( Symptoms )
THEN
   write 'has manic symptoms ', pconf ,
   in 4 symptom is has_manic_symptoms ;

:rule r10
rule rconf 600 block 2
   (goal Finds symptom is has_schizophrenic_symptoms)
IF (in Fact fact "has persecutory or jealous delusions" )
   (in Fact fact "has hallucinations" )
   ( Symptoms )
THEN
   write 'has schizophrenic symptoms ', pconf ,
   in 3 symptom is has_schizophrenic_symptoms ;

:rule r11
rule rconf 600 block 2
   (goal Finds symptom is has_schizophrenic_symptoms)
IF (in Fact fact "has somatic or religious delusions" )
   ( Symptoms )
THEN
   write 'has schizophrenic symptoms ', pconf ,
   in 2 symptom is has_schizophrenic_symptoms ;

:rule r12
rule rconf 700 block 2
   (goal Finds symptom is has_schizophrenic_symptoms)
IF (in Fact fact "has incoherent thought and speech" )
   (in Fact fact "has markedly illogical thoughts" )
   (in Fact fact "has bizzare delusions" )
   ( Symptoms )
THEN
   write 'has schizophrenic symptoms ', pconf ,
```

```
  in 4 symptom is has_schizophrenic_symptoms ;

:rule r13
rule rconf 800 block 2
  (goal Finds symptom is has_schizophrenic_symptoms)
IF (in Fact fact "has abnormal motor movement or posture" )
  (in Fact fact "has inappropriate affect" )
  ( Symptoms )
THEN
  write 'has schizophrenic symptoms ', pconf ,
  in 3 symptom is has_schizophrenic_symptoms ;


: -------------------------------------------------------
:block 3 - gets diagnosis from symptoms and facts

:rule r14
rule rconf 800 block 3
  (goal Finds dignosis is major_depression)
IF (in Symptoms symptom is has_depressive_symptoms)
  (in Fact fact "symptoms have lasted for at least one
month" )
  ( Diagnosis )
THEN
  write 'diagnosis major depression ', pconf ,
  in 3 dx is major_depression ;

:rule r15
rule rconf 900 block 3
  (goal Finds diagnosis is manic_depressive_psychosis)
IF (in Symptoms symptom is has_manic_symptoms )
  (in Symptoms symptom is has_depressive_symptoms )
  ( Diagnosis )
THEN
  write 'diagnosis manic depressive psychosis ', pconf ,
  in 3 dx is manic_depressive_psychosis ;

:rule r16
rule block 3
  (goal Finds diagnosis is major_depression)
IF (in Symptoms symptom is has_depressive_symptoms )
  (in Fact fact "has persecutory or jealous delusions" )
  (in Fact fact "has hallucinations" )
  ( Diagnosis )
THEN
  write 'diagnosis major depression ', pconf ,
```

```
    in 4 dx is major_depression ;

:rule r17
rule block 3
  (goal Finds diagnosis is schizophrenia)
IF (in Symptoms symptom is has_schizophrenic_symptoms )
  (in Fact fact "symptoms have been continuous for more
  than 6 months" )
  (in Fact fact "the onset of illness is before age 45" )
  ( Diagnosis )
THEN
  write 'diagnosis schizophrenia ', pconf ,
  in 4 dx is schizophrenia ;

:rule r18
rule rconf 800 block 3
  (goal Finds diagnosis is paranoid_disorder)
IF (in Fact fact "has persecutory or jealous delusions" )
  (in Fact fact "has intact thinking and adaptive functioning" )
  ( Diagnosis )
THEN
  write 'diagnosis paranoid disorder ', pconf ,
  in 3 dx is paranoid_disorder ;

:rule r19
rule block 3
  (goal Finds diagnosis is manic_depressive_psychosis)
IF (in Symptoms symptom is has_manic_symptoms )
  (in Symptoms symptom is has_depressive_symptoms )
  (in Fact fact "has persecutory or jealous delusions" )
  (in Fact fact "has hallucinations" )
  ( Diagnosis )
THEN
  write 'diagnosis manic depressive psychosis ', pconf ,
  in 5 dx is manic_depressive_psychosis ;

:rule r20
rule block 3
  (goal Finds diagnosis is paranoid_disorder)
IF (in Symptoms symptom is has_schizophrenic_symptoms )
  (in Fact fact "has persecutory or jealous delusions" )
  (in Fact fact "has intact thinking and adaptive functioning" )
  ( Diagnosis )
THEN
  write 'diagnosis paranoid disorder ', pconf ,
```

```
    in 4 dx is paranoid_disorder ;

: -----------------------------------------------------------
:block 4 - updated diagnoses

:rule r21
rule rconf 800 block 4
  (goal Updates diagnosis to schizophrenia_disorganized_
type)
IF (in Diagnosis dx is schizophrenia )
  (in Fact fact "has incoherent thought and speech" )
  (in Fact fact "has markedly illogical thoughts" )
  (in Fact fact "has inappropriate affect" )
THEN
  write 'diagnosis disorganized schizophrenia ', pconf ,
  in 1 dx is schizophrenia_disorganized_type ;

:rule r22
rule rconf 800 block 4
  (goal Updates diagnosis to schizophrenia_catatonic_
type)
IF (in Diagnosis dx is schizophrenia )
  (in Fact fact "has abnormal motor movement or posture" )
  (in Fact fact "has inappropriate affect" )
THEN
  write 'diagnosis catatonic schizophrenia ', pconf ,
  in 1 dx is schizophrenia_catatonic_type ;

:rule r23
rule rconf 800 block 4
  (goal Updates diagnosis to schizophrenia_paranoid_type)
IF (in Diagnosis dx is schizophrenia )
  (in Fact fact "has persecutory or jealous delusions" )
  (in Fact fact "has hallucinations" )
THEN
  write 'diagnosis paranoid schizophrenia ', pconf ,
  in 1 dx is schizophrenia_paranoid_type ;

: -----------------------------------------------------------
:block 5 - final diagnosis

:rule r24
rule block 5
  (goal Writes fuzzy set of final diagnoses with
confidences)
```

```
IF ( Diagnosis )
THEN
  message "final diagnosis -\n" ,
  prmem 1 ;


: ------------------------------------------------------------
:block 6 - enables and disables rule blocks

:rule r25
rule block 6
  (goal Controls block firing sequence)
IF (in enable block <N> block < 6 )
THEN
  write '\n' ,
  in 1 block ( <N> + 1 ) ,
  fire block <N> del ,
  fire block ( <N> + 1 ) on ;


: +++++++++++++++++++++++++++++++++++++++++++++++++++++++++++++

write 'reading fact.dat...\n' ;
transfer Fact from facts.dat;
write 'read fact.dat\n' ;

make Symptoms ;
make Diagnosis ;

make enable block 0 ;
fire all off ;
fire block 0 on ;
fire block 6 on ;

string = "Program SCHIZO.PAR does a simple psychiatric
         evaluation.\n" ;
string + "You will be asked if certain behavioral
         manifestations " ;
string + "are present. Enter your confidence, anywhere
         from zero ";
string + "to 1000, that they are present.\n" ;
string + "Zero means you are sure that they are not
         present,\n" ;
string + "250 means probably not,\n" ;
string + "500 means you are evenly balanced between yes
         and no,\n" ;
string + "750 means probably yes,\n" ;
```

```
string + "1000, you are sure that they are present.\n\n" ;
string + "SCHIZO.PAR ready to run\n" ;
message "<string>";
run ;
stop ;

: ********************************************************

: ********************************************************
: Program SIMPLE.PAR to read SAO2 data for neonatal infants
: ********************************************************

write 'Program SIMPLE.PAR to alarm on low SAO2 for
neonatal infants\n';

declare Data
  deltaT flt
  T flt
  SAO2 flt
  status str;

declare File
  fileName str
  lines int
  klines int
  status str;
: ++++++++++++++++++++++++++++++++++++++++++++++++++++++++
: Block 0 - initialization
:rule r0
rule block 0 (goal Read data file name)
IF (in File fileName.cf = 0)
THEN
  write 'Enter data file name (try SIMPLE.DAT) ',
  read 1 fileName,
  in 1 status = "";

:rule r1
rule block 0 (goal Open data file)
IF (in File fileName = <F> AND status = "")
THEN
  acquire disk1 INIT 1 <F>,
  in 1 lines = 0 klines = 0;

:rule r2
```

```
rule block 0 (goal Try again to open file if filename fails)
IF (in File status = "NO_FILE")
THEN
  in 1 fileName.cf = 0 status = "";

:rule r3
rule block 0 (goal proceed if file opened OK)
IF (in File status = "OK")
THEN
  fire block 0 off,
  fire block 1 on;

: ++++++++++++++++++++++++++++++++++++++++++++++++++++++
: Block 1 - read data

:rule r4
rule block 1 (goal Read a data item)
IF (Data)
  (in File lines = <L> AND klines = <KL> AND status = "OK")
THEN
  acquire disk1 READ 1 deltaT SAO2 status,
  :in 2 klines = (<KL> + int((<L> + 1) / 1000))
  :lines = (<L> + 1 - int((<L> + 1)/1000) * 1000),
  in 2 lines = (<L> + 1),
  fire block 1 off,
  fire block 2 on;

:rule r5
rule block 1 (goal Acknowledge closure of data file)
IF ( in File fileName = <F> AND status = "CLOSED")
THEN
  write 'Data file <F> closed\n',
  halt;

: ++++++++++++++++++++++++++++++++++++++++++++++++++++++
: Block 2 - print (process) data, terminate if enough
lines read

:rule r6
rule block 2 (goal Print data read)
IF (in Data SAO2 = <SAO2> AND T = <T> AND deltaT = <DT>
AND status = "OK")
  (in File lines = <L> AND lines < 100 AND klines = <KL>
AND status = "OK")
THEN
```

```
    in 1 T = (<T> + <DT>),
    write 'SAO2 <SAO2> T <T> lines read <KL>k + <L>\n',
    fire block 2 off,
    fire block 3 on;

:rule r7
rule block 2 (goal Close input file if enough lines read)
IF (in File lines = 100 AND status = "OK")
THEN
    acquire disk1 END 1 status,
    fire all off,
    fire block 3 on;

: +++++++++++++++++++++++++++++++++++++++++++++++++++++++++++
:block 3 - clear and reinstate memory, read more data or
terminate

:rule r8
rule block 3 (goal Go back and read more data)
IF (in File status = "OK")
THEN
    transfer all to savedata,
    clear data,
    transfer all from savedata,
    fire block 3 off,
    fire block 1 on;

:rule r9
rule block 3 (goal End run)
IF ( in File status <> "OK")
THEN
    write 'Halting run\n',
    halt;

: +++++++++++++++++++++++++++++++++++++++++++++++++++++++++++
make Data T = 0;
make File;
fire all off;
fire block 0 on;

String Rule

declare True;

rule IF (True)
```

```
THEN
  <string>,
  make True;

string = "rule IF (True) THEN write 'OK'";
:make r0 fireable
make True;
:create new rule
run 1;
:make new rule fireable
modify 1;
:fire new rule
run 1;

: * * * * * * * * * * * * * * * * * * * * * * * * * * * * * * * * * * * * * * * * * * * * * * * * * * * * * * *
:program SUM.FPS to illustrate recursive arithmetic in
 serial FLOPS
:10-15-86 WS
:instances of NUMBER are added in one parallel step to
 SUM TOTAL
: * * * * * * * * * * * * * * * * * * * * * * * * * * * * * * * * * * * * * * * * * * * * * * * * * * * * * * *

string = "Program SUM.FPS computes the sum of s recursively";
string + " in several sequential steps, one for each
        number to be added.\n";
string + "Compiling program SUM.FPS";
message "<string>";

declare Number
  num flt;

declare Sum
  total flt;

: ------------------------------------------------------
:block 0 - accumulates sum recursively in many sequential
 steps

:rule r0
rule (goal Accumulates sum recursively in many
sequential steps)
IF (in Number num <N>)
  (in Sum total <T>)
THEN
  delete 1,
```

```
  write "adding <N> to <T> getting \(<N> + <T>\)\n",
  in 2 total (<T> + <N>);

:rule r1
rule rconf 0 (goal Prints out total when no more
instances of r0 are fireable)
IF (in Sum total <T>)
THEN
  message "total of all is <T>\n",
  halt;

make Number num 12.34;
make Number num 23.45;
make Number num 34.56;
make Number num 45.67;
make Number num 56.78;
make Number num 67.89;
make Number num 78.90;
make Number num 89.01;
make Number num 90.12;
make Number num 01.23;
make Number num 32.10;
make Number num 21.09;
make Number num 32.10;
make Number num 43.21;
make Number num 54.32;
make Number num 65.43;
make Sum total 0;
fire block 1 off;
string = "Like SUM.PAR, these FLOPS commands will be
          issued in sequence\:\n";
string + "\'prstack\' will print the list of fireable
          rules.\n";
string + "Next\, \'run 1\' will execute one rule firing
          step.\n";
string + "The \'prstack\' and \'run 1\' sequence will be
          repeated until finished.\n";
string + "Patience is required in running this
          program:";
string + "Please keep pressing keys until it is finished,";
string + "then run SUM.PAR for a startling comparison.\n";
string + "Ready to run SUM.FPS\n";
message "<string>";
run;
```

```
: **********************************************************
:program SUM.PAR to illustrate recursive arithmetic in
 parallel FLOPS
:instances of are added in one parallel step to SUM TOTAL
: **********************************************************

string = "Program SUM.PAR computes the sum of s recursively";
string + " in one parallel step.\n";
string + "Compiling program SUM.PAR";
message "<string>";

declare Number
  num flt;

declare Sum
  total flt;

: --------------------------------------------------------
:block 0 - accumulates sum recursively in one parallel step

:rule r0
rule (goal Adds num to sum recursively)
IF (in Number num = <N> )
  (in Sum total = <T> )
THEN
  message "adding <N> to $<T> getting \(<N>+$<T>\)\n",
  modify 2 total = ( $<T> + <N> ),
  fire block 0 off,
  fire block 1 on;

: --------------------------------------------------------
:block 1 - final answer

:rule r1
rule block 1 (goal Prints final sum)
IF (in Sum total = <T> )
THEN
  message "total of all is <T>\n";

make Number num 12.34;
make Number num 23.45;
make Number num 34.56;
make Number num 45.67;
make Number num 56.78;
make Number num 67.89;
```

```
make Number num 78.90;
make Number num 89.01;
make Number num 90.12;
make Number num 01.23;
make Number num 32.10;
make Number num 21.09;
make Number num 32.10;
make Number num 43.21;
make Number num 54.32;
make Number num 65.43;
make Sum total 0;
fire block 1 off;
message "ready to run SUM.PAR\n";
message "fireable rule stack\:\n";
prstack;
message "Ready to execute \'run 1\'\n";
run 1;
write "fireable rule stack\:\n";
prstack;
write "Ready to execute \'run 1\'\n";
run 1;
string = "SUM.PAR finished.\n";
string + "Compare to program SUM.FPS!\n";
message "<string>";
exit;
; ******************************************************* *
call urc.exe;
```

ANSWERS

1.1 Unlike most languages, FLOPS is non-procedural (data-driven); has fuzzy mathematics thoroughly integrated; and can be run as either a sequential or a parallel language, emulating a parallel computer.

1.2 Procedural languages execute instructions in the order in which they appear in the program, with specific control transfer instructions permitted. A data-driven language determine that instructions are made executable by the data, and executes these if they are enabled. If FLOPS is in command mode, it is procedural; in run mode, when rules are being fired, FLOPS is data-driven and non-procedural.

1.3 Most importantly, FLOPS can handle both ambiguities and contradictions through the use of fuzzy sets. FLOPS also assumes that all data are uncertain but establishing truth values to all data; crisp (certain) data are a special case of uncertain data, with truth value 1. Data whose value is false or unknown have truth value zero.

1.4 When firing rules, a parallel program executes all fireable rules effectively simultaneously. A sequential program selects one fireable rule for firing but some reasonable criterion, puts the rest of the fireable rules on a stack for firing if no rules are newly fireable (backtracking).

1.5 FLOPS programs have the ability to learn from experience in two ways: they can construct new rules from data, and can add to a data base of expert knowledge, both as a result of experience.

1.6 Rule-based expert systems rely considerably on incorporating the skills of an expert in the problem domain, but relatively little on historical data; neural networks rely heavily on an extensive historical data base, and relatively little on a domain expert.

1.7 Fuzzy control systems deal exclusively with numeric output, and employ a special rule format that is quite inflexible but very efficient for its purpose. General-purpose fuzzy reasoning systems require a rule syntax that is much more flexible and more complex than syntax for fuzzy control rules.

Fuzzy Expert Systems and Fuzzy Reasoning, By William Siler and James J. Buckley
ISBN 0-471-38859-9 Copyright © 2005 John Wiley & Sons, Inc.

1.8   A *domain expert*, who is thoroughly familiar with the field of application; and a *knowledge engineer*, who is thoroughly familiar with the expert system language and techniques of knowledge acquisition techniques.

1.9   Fuzzy expert systems should be able to handle both ambiguities and contradictions, to learn from experience by adding new rules or to a database of expert knowledge, and to fire rules either sequentially or in parallel.

1.10   The first problem for the knowledge engineer is to become adept at a different kind of computer language. Next is the problem of acquiring relevant knowledge from the domain expert. Finally, there are the problems of writing, debugging, calibrating, and validating the expert system itself.

1.11   Like other computer languages, the most important tool is the *IDE*, in which programs can be written, edited and debugged, and that provides extensive help files.

2.1   No. For example, the store of visual images we have accumulated and the ability to extract relevant features from these and relate them to each other and to nonvisual knowledge is of great importance to us, but exceedingly difficult to reduce to computer processing.

2.2   Such problems are more efficiently handled by procedural language programs, using the "call" command and communicating via the blackboard.

2.3   The rule antecedent is a fuzzy logical proposition, that determines whether the rule is fireable. The consequent is a set of FLOPS instructions to be executed when the rule is fired.

2.4   At a minimum, data types should include integers, floats, strings, discrete fuzzy sets, and fuzzy numbers. Integers, floats, and strings should be coupled with truth values; the truth values should be accessible as data. Membership functions coupled to discrete fuzzy set members should be optionally furnished.

2.5   Yes. Having a rule that creates new rules is one way in which a program can learn from experience.

2.6   No. A rule consequent can include any legal FLOPS instruction.

2.7   A metarule is a rule that controls the rule-firing process, and specifies which rules and blocks of rules are enabled or disabled for firing.

2.8   Procedural programs execute instructions in the order in which they appear in the program; data-driven programs execute a rule if the data make it fireable, regardless of its position in the program.

2.9   In "command" method, FLOPS reads commands from a disk file or keyboard, and executes these commands procedurally in the order in which they appear. In "run" mode, FLOPS fires rules in data-driven non-procedural fashion.

2.10 Serial rule-firing is indicated if information must be elicited from a user in context-dependent fashion, so that the next question to be asked depends on the answer to the previous question.

2.11 In forward chaining, we reason from data to goals; in backward chaining, we try to establish what data are needed to reach a goal, and then try to obtain those data.

2.12 A blackboard system integrates several programs and data by providing a structured way for programs to call each other and communicate data among themselves to solve complex problems.

2.13 FLOPS represents uncertainties as truth values between 0 and 1000, corresponding to the usual representation as between 0 and 1.

3.1 **a.** Table Answers 3.7-1a

A	B	P = A AND B	Q = A OR B	P AND Q	P OR Q
0	0	0	0	0	0
0	1	0	1	0	1
1	0	0	1	0	1
1	1	1	1	1	1

b. Table Answer 3.7-1b

A	B	R = A IMPLIES B	S = A OR B	R AND S	R OR S
0	0	1	0	0	1
0	1	1	1	1	1
1	0	0	1	0	1
1	1	1	1	1	1

3.2 **a.** Neither.
Table Answer 3.7-2a

p	q	NOT q	p AND NOT q
0	0	1	0
0	1	0	0
1	0	1	1
1	1	0	0

b. Neither. ((not P) or Q)
Table Answer 3.7-2b

p	q	NOT p	NOT p OR q
0	0	1	1
0	1	1	1
1	0	0	0
1	1	0	1

c. Tautology. (P and (P implies Q)) $\to$ Q
Table Answer 3.7-2c

p	q	p $\to$ q	p AND (p $\to$ q)	(p AND (p $\to$ q)) $\to$ q
0	0	1	0	1
0	1	1	0	1
1	0	0	0	1
1	1	1	1	1

d. Neither. ((P $\to$ Q) and (Q $\to$ R)) $\to$ (P $\to$ R)
Table Answer 3.7-2d

p	q	r	p $\to$ q	p $\to$ r	q $\to$ r	(p $\to$ q) $\cap$ (q $\to$ r)	((p $\to$ q) $\cap$ (q $\to$ r)) $\to$ (p $\to$ r)
0	0	0	1	1	1	1	1
0	0	1	1	1	1	1	1
0	1	0	1	1	0	0	1
0	1	1	1	1	1	1	1
1	0	0	0	0	1	1	0
1	0	1	0	1	1	1	1
1	1	0	1	0	0	0	1
1	1	1	1	1	1	1	1

3.3   **a.**

$$P \text{ AND } B = \min(p, q) \tag{3.1}$$

$$P \text{ OR } B = \text{not}(\min(1 - p, 1 - q)$$

$$= \text{not}(1 - \max(p, q)$$

$$= \max(p, q) \tag{3.4}$$

b.

$$P \text{ AND } B = p * q \tag{3.2}$$

$$P \text{ OR } B = \text{not}((\text{not } p) * (\text{not } q))$$

$$= 1 - (1 - p) * (1 - q)$$

$$= 1 - (pq - p - q + 1)$$

$$= p + q - pq \tag{3.5}$$

c.

$$P \text{ AND } B = \max(0, p + q - 1) \tag{3.2}$$

$$P \text{ OR } B = 1 - \max(0, 1 - p + 1 - q + 1)$$

$$= 1 - \max(0, 1 - (p + q))$$

$$= \min(1, p + q) \tag{3.6}$$

3.4   For a $<= x <= (a+b)/2$:

$\mu(x) = k_1 + k_2(x-a)^2$

$k_1 = 0$

if $x = (a+b)/2$, $\mu(x) = 0.5$

$k_2((a+b)/2 - a)^2 = k_2((b-a)/2)^2 = 0.5$

$k_2 = 2/(b-a)^2$

For $(a+b)/2 <= x <= b$:

$\mu(x) = k_1 + k_2(b-x)^2$

if $x = b$, $\mu(x) = 1$,

$k_1 = 1$

if $x = b - (a+b)/2$, $\mu(x) = 0.5$

$1 + k_2(b - (a+b)/2 - a)^2 = 1 + k_2((b-a)/2)^2 = 0.5$

$k_2 = -2/(b-a)^2$

Similarly for $b <= x <= c/$

3.5   Table Answers 3.7-5a-5b

A	B	A and B (3.1) and (3.3)	not (A and B)
0	0	0	1
0	1	0	1
1	0	0	1
1	1	1	0

3.6   **a.** Table Answer 3.5-6a

A	B	A and B (3.1)	A and B (3.2)
0	0	0	0
0.5	0.5	0.5	0.25
1	1	1	1

b. Table Answer 3.5-6b

A	B	A or B (3.4)	A or B (3.5)
0	0	0	0
0.5	0.5	0.5	0.75
1	1	1	1

3.7 Table Answer 3.5-7

P	Q	not P	P->Q	P and not P->Q	not P and P->Q	if P AND P->Q then Q = not(not P and P-<Q) or Q
0	0	1	1	0	1	1
0	0.5	1	1	0	1	1
0	1	1	1	0	1	1
0.5	0	0.5	0.5	0	1	1
0.5	0.5	0.5	1	0.5	0.5	1
0.5	1	0.5	1	0.5	0.5	1
1	0	0	0	0	1	1
1	0.5	0	0.5	0.5	0.5	1
1	1	0	1	1	0	1

3.8 a.

$$A^2 = \begin{pmatrix} 0.2 & 1.0 & 0.3 \\ 0 & 1.0 & 0.4 \\ 0.4 & 0.3 & 1.0 \end{pmatrix} A^3 = \begin{pmatrix} 0.4 & 0.3 & 1.0 \\ 0.4 & 0.4 & 1.0 \\ 0.3 & 1.0 & 0.4 \end{pmatrix} A^4 = \begin{pmatrix} 0.3 & 1.0 & 0.4 \\ 0.4 & 1.0 & 0.4 \\ 0.4 & 0.4 & 1.0 \end{pmatrix}$$

$$A^5 = \begin{pmatrix} 0.4 & 0.4 & 1.0 \\ 0.4 & 0.4 & 1.0 \\ 0.4 & 1.0 & 0.4 \end{pmatrix} A^6 = \begin{pmatrix} 0.4 & 1.0 & 0.4 \\ 0.4 & 1.0 & 0.4 \\ 0.4 & 0.4 & 1.0 \end{pmatrix} A^7 = \begin{pmatrix} 0.4 & 0.4 & 1.0 \\ 0.4 & 0.4 & 1.0 \\ 0.4 & 1.0 & 0.4 \end{pmatrix}$$

b.

$$A^2 = \begin{pmatrix} 1.0 & 0.2 & 0.2 \\ 0.4 & 1.0 & 0.2 \\ 0.3 & 0.3 & 1.0 \end{pmatrix} A^3 = \begin{pmatrix} 1.0 & 0.2 & 0.2 \\ 0.4 & 1.0 & 0.2 \\ 0.3 & 0.3 & 1.0 \end{pmatrix}$$

$$A^4 = \begin{pmatrix} 1.0 & 0.2 & 0.2 \\ 0.4 & 1.0 & 0.2 \\ 0.3 & 0.3 & 1.0 \end{pmatrix}$$

c. The composed matrix will oscillate or stabilize.

3.9 a. T = 25, Temperature = $\left\{ \dfrac{low}{0.5}, \dfrac{medium}{0.5}, \dfrac{high}{0} \right\}$

b. T = 75, Temperature = $\left\{ \dfrac{low}{0}, \dfrac{medium}{0.5}, \dfrac{high}{0.5} \right\}$

c. T = 50, Temperature = $\left\{ \dfrac{low}{0}, \dfrac{medium}{1}, \dfrac{high}{0} \right\}$

3.10
$$T = \frac{0 \cdot 0.42 + 50 \cdot 0.88 + 100 \cdot 0.14}{0.42 + 0.88 + 0.14} = 40.28$$

4.1 $T_m(x_1, \ldots, x_n) = \min(x_1, \ldots, x_n)$

$T_m(x_1, x_2, x_3) = T_m(T_m(x_1, x_2), x_3)$
$= T_m(\min(x_1, x_2), x_3)$
$= \min(\min(x_1, x_2), x_3)$
$= \min(x_1, x_2, x_3)$

$C_m(x_1, \ldots, x_n) = \max(x_1, \ldots, x_n)$

$C_m(x_1, x_2, x_3) = C_m(C_m(x_1, x_2), x_3)$
$= C_m(\max(x_1, x_2), x_3)$
$= \max(\max(x_1, x_2), x_3)$
$= \max(x_1, x_2, x_3)$

$T_L(x_1, \ldots, x_n) = \max\left(0, \sum_{i=1}^{n} x_i - n + 1\right)$

$T_L(x_1, x_2, x_3) = T_L(T_L(x_1, x_2), x_3)$
$= T_L(\max(0, x_1 + x_2 - 2 + 1), x_3)$
$= T_L(\max(0, x_1 + x_2 - 1), x_3)$
$= \max(0, x_1 + x_2 + x_3 - 1 - 2 + 1)$
$= \max(0, x_1 + x_2 + x_3 - 3 + 1)$

$C_L(x_1, \ldots, x_n) = \min\left(1, \sum_{i=1}^{n} x_i\right)$

$C_L(x_1, x_2, x_3) = C_L(C_L(x_1, x_2), x_3)$
$= C_L(\min(1, x_1 + x_2), x_3)$
$= \min(1, x_1 + x_2, x_3)$

$T_p(x_1, \ldots, x_n) = x_1 \cdots x_n$

$T_P(x_1, x_2, x_3) = T_P(T_P(x_1, x_2), x_3)$
$= T_P(x_1, x_2), x_3)$
$= x_1 x_2 x_3$

4.2   Since all t-norms are required to reduce to the classical for crisp values $\{0, 1\}$, we must get Table 3.1, defined for classical two-valued logic.

4.3   Since all t-norms are required to reduce to the classical for crisp values $\{0, 1\}$, we must get Table 3.1, defined for classical two-valued logic.

4.4   Non-contradiction: $A \cap A^c = \varnothing$.

$T_L(x, y) = \max(0, x + y - 1) = \max(0, x + (1 - x) - 1) = \max(0, 0) = 0/$

Excluded middle: $A \cap A^c = 1$

$$T_C(x, 1-x) = \min(1, x+1-x) = \min(1, 1) = 1$$

4.5   Reformulating Q to isolate combining B and NOT B:

Q = B OR (NOT A AND NOT B) = (B OR NOT A) AND (B OR NOT B)

Analytic solution:

P = NOT(A AND NOT B) = NOT A AND B

Q = B OR (NOT A AND NOT B) = (B OR NOT A) AND (B OR NOT B)

$\quad$ = B OR NOT A

By De Morgan's theorem,

B OR NOT A = NOT(NOT B AND NOT(NOT A))

$\qquad\qquad\quad$ = B AND NOT A

Numeric solution:
Table Answer 4.5

Logic	A	¬A	B	¬B	A∩¬B	P = ¬(A∩¬B)	B∪¬A	B∪¬B	Q = B∪(¬A∩¬B) = (B∪¬A)∩(B∪¬B)
min–max	0.25	0.75	0.5	0.5	0.25	0.75	0.75	0.5	0.5 (Not equal P)
Bounded	0.25	0.75	0.5	0.5	0.25	0.75	0.75	1	0.75 (Equals P)

4.6   The computer program APROXIM.BAS is given in the Appendix. The results are

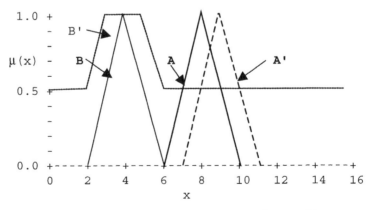

Figure Answer 4.4a   Fuzzy numbers A, A′, B and B′.

4.7 Method a gives good flexibility, and is capable of handling central values at or near zero and cases where the range of the fuzzy number includes both positive and negative numbers. It does, however, result in a less transparent code; it is not immediately obvious what the meaning is of say (20, 2, 0.3).

Method b is less flexible, and assumes that the lower limit is non-zero and of the same sign as the central value; it cannot handle other cases. It is, however, very transparent; it is immediately clear what "roughly x" means.

4.8 **a.** The extension principle.

A is a triangular fuzzy number with lower limit 6, central value 8, and upper limit 12; B is also triangular, with lower limit 7, central value 9, and upper limit 13. a. The extension principle, for addition, is $C(x) = \sup_{x,y}(\min(A(x), B(y))) \mid x + y = z$. If the sum is to be zero for a particular value of z, then $A(x)$ and $B(y = z - x)$ must both be everywhere zero for that value of z. $A(x)$ is zero from $-\infty < x \le 6$, and from $12 \le x < \infty$; $B(y)$ is zero from $-\infty < y \le 7$, and from $12 \le y < \infty$. Accordingly, $C(z)$ will have zero membership from $-\infty < z \le (6 + 7 = 13)$, and from \rm $(12 + 13 = 25) <= z < \infty$. $P(z)$ will have its maximum value of the sum of the central values at only one point, $z = x + y = 8 + 9 = 17$. Our membership function for $A + B$ is then a triangular number rising from 0 at 14 to 1 at 17, declining from there to 0 at 26, and 0 thereafter.

b. Alpha-cuts.

As the alpha-cut level approaches 0, the left-hand termination points for A and B approach $x = 6$ and $x = 7$, respectively; the right-hand termination points are 12 and 13, respectively. Adding these termination values, the $x + y$ values at zero membership range from $-\infty$ to $6 + 7 = 13$, and from $12 + 13 = 25$ to ∞. For the sum to have membership one, both $A(x)$ and $B(y)$ must have membership one. This occurs only at $x = 8$ and $y = 9$; then $C(x)$ has membership one at $8 + 9 = 17$.

   Since the relationships are all linear, the membership for the sum $C(z)$ is 0 from $-\infty$ to 13; from 0 at 13 to 1 at 17; from 1 at 17 to 0 at 25; and 0 thereafter.

c. Interval arithmetic

In interval arithmetic, the membership functions are rectangular, the memberships taking on values of either 0 or 1. The interval of x for which $A(x)$ is non-zero is simply $x = [6, 12]$, and for $B(y)$ [7, 13]. By (4.42), the interval for $C(z)$ has lower limit $6 + 7 = 13$, and upper limit $12 + 13 = 25$. $C(x)$ is then defined by the interval [13, 25].

5.1 Classical logic operators obey the laws of Excluded Middle and Non-Contradiction, However, min–max fuzzy logical operators do not obey these laws.

5.2 The bounded sum and difference operators should be used when combining A and NOT A, since they are maximally negatively associated.

5.3   The min–max operators should be used when combining A and A, since they are maximally positively associated.

5.4   **a.** Fuzzy control techniques are used in shaping membership functions, and are based on many years of experience with current operators; introducing different operators would invalidate much of current working techniques. Further, the precise way of determining the correlation coefficient between two membership functions is not yet agreed upon. However, if the membership functions being combined cross at no greater than 0.5 membership, use of the bounded sum–difference operators produces a much more intuitive smooth result.

     b. Yes. Other operators than the bounded sum–difference produce counterintuitive results, and can make programming difficult. This is especially true when making approximate numerical comparisons such as A less than OR equal to B.

5.5   **a.** Zero. This is a Boolean comparison, and the temperature is 78, not 75. The truth value of Temperature is 0.6; the truth values of the comparison is zero; and the truth value of the literal 78 is 1. The antecedent truth value is min(0.6, 0, 1) = 0.6.

     b. 0.6. The truth value of Temperature is 0.6; the truth value of the comparison is 1; truth value of the literal 78 is 1. Antecedent truth value is min(0.6, 1, 1) = 0.6.

     c. 0.6. Since <X> is a variable, it is assigned the value and truth value of Temperature. Again, the truth value of Temperature is 0.6; truth value of the comparison is 1; the truth value of <X> is 0.6. Antecedent truth value is min(0.6, 1, 0.6) = 0.6.

     d. 0.356. Truth value of the entire fuzzy set is one by default; truth value of the comparison is one; truth value of Large is its grade of membership, 0.356. Antecedent truth value is min(1, 1, 0.356) = 0.356.

     e. One. Truth value of Temperature.cf is one by default; truth value of the comparison is 1; and truth value of the literal 0.5 is also 1. Antecedent truth value is min(1, 1, 1) = 1.0.

5.6   **a.** From the graph in Figure Question 5.6 it appears that the truth value of A ~= B is 0.25.

     b. First, we construct the fuzzy number ~<B, NOT B OR <B. This number is

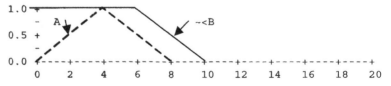

Figure Answer 5.6b   Fuzzy numbers A and ~<B.

Since The highest intersection point of A and $\sim<$B is one, the truth value of the comparison is 1.

c. First we construct the fuzzy number $\sim>=$B, b$>$B OR B

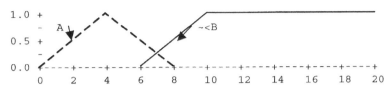

Figure Answer 5.6c   Fuzzy numbers A and $\sim>=$B.

From the graph, it appears that the truth value of A $\sim>=$ B is 0.25.

5.7   At first blush, it might seem that A and B are semantically inconsistent, since they have different names. However, this is not true; A and B have no known prior relation to each other, and therefore they are not semantically inconsistent. Use the default logic.

5.8   Unlike Question 5.7, A and B now have a prior relationship; the both describe the same entity. In this case, the bounded sum–difference operators are appropriate.

5.9   The problem lies in the requirement of prior knowledge of conditional probabilities. If we have such knowledge, Bayesian methods are rock solid; otherwise, they are theoretically shaky.

5.10   Theoretical fuzzy logic deals with two measures of uncertainty: possibility and necessity. Dempster–Shafer methods have two analogous measures: plausibility and credibility. Possibility and plausibility both measure the extent to which the data fail to refute an hypothesis; necessity and credibility both measure the extent to which the data support an hypothesis.

5.11   If we have no knowledge at all, the possibility of a hypothesis is 1, since there are no data to refute it; its necessity is 0, since there are no data to support it.

6.1   Possibility measures the extent to which the data refute a conclusion; necessity measures the extent to which the data support a conclusion.

6.2   In the lack of any evidence, Nec(A) = 0, and Pos(A) = 1.

6.3   a. Zero.

   b. Initializing grades of membership to 0 permits subsequent rules that tend to support a particular classification to increase its grade of membership. If we initialized to 1, we would have to write only rules that refute this classification with non-monotonic reasoning rather than rules that tend to establish it, a much less intuitive task.

6.4   Monotonic reasoning permits truth values to increase, but not decrease; non-monotonic reasoning permits truth values to increase or decrease; and downward monotonic reasoning permits truth values to decrease but not increase.

6.5 Under monotonic reasoning, that instruction would be rejected; the datum's truth value would remain unaltered.

6.6 When we find out that a datum should be wholly or partially invalidated.

6.7 When modifying membership functions prior to defuzzification.

6.8 Monotonic reasoning.

6.9 **a.** Yes.
b. The TMSoff command permits non-monotonic reasoning to be employed; the TMSon command restores monotonic reasoning. In defuzzifying, default inference is downward monotonic.

7.1 **a.**

$$A' = \left\{ \frac{0.25}{a1}, \frac{0.75}{a2}, \frac{0.75}{a3} \right\}, \quad [A_i \text{ AND } B_j] = \begin{bmatrix} 0 & 0 & 0 \\ 0 & 0.5 & 0.5 \\ 0 & 0.5 & 1 \end{bmatrix}$$

$$B' = A' \circ [A_i \cap B_j]$$
$$= \left\{ \begin{array}{l} \max(\min(0.25, 0), \ \min(0.75, 0), \ \min(0.75, 0)), \\ \max(\min(0.25, 0), \ \min(0.75, 0.5), \ \min(0.75, 0.5)), \\ \max(\min(0.25, 0), \ \min(0.75, 0.5), \ \min(0.75, 1)) \end{array} \right\}$$
$$= \{\max(0, 0, 0), \ \max(0, 0.5, 0.5), \ \max(0, 0.5, 0.75)\}$$
$$B' = \{0, 0.5, 0.75\}$$

b.

$$A = \left\{ \frac{0}{a1}, \frac{0.5}{a2}, \frac{1}{a3} \right\}, \quad A' = \left\{ \frac{0.25}{a1}, \frac{0.75}{a2}, \frac{0.75}{a3} \right\}$$
$$p = \max(\min(0, 0.25), \ \min(0.5, 0.75), \ \min(1, 0.75))$$
$$= \max(0, 0.5, 0.75) = 0.75$$
$$B' = \{\min(0.75, B_j'\} = \{0, 0.5, 0.75\}$$

7.2 The advantages of using separate rules for fuzzification and defuzzification is that the discrete fuzzy sets are available for use in later reasoning steps, for output, and for inspection by the programmer during debugging. Most importantly, the consequent fuzzy set may be non-numeric. The only disadvantage is that one or two separate rules are required.

7.3 **a.** Default inference is monotonic.
b. The truth value of Artifact will be 0.7.
c. We assume that both rules, although different, have equal validity, but look at somewhat different kinds of artifact. We would select the rule that best applies to the instance of Region being evaluated.

7.4 Since the consequents of the rules are ORd together, we should set the grade of membership of "deteriorating" to max(0.1, 0.2, 0.5) or 0.5.

7.5 **a.** We will need $4^5 \cdot 6 = 6144$ rules for the conventional IRC.

b. We will need $4 \cdot 5 \cdot 6 = 120$ rules for the Combs URC.

8.1 Necessity is the degree to which the evidence supports a datum. If there is no supporting evidence, then the datum has no support, and its necessity must be 0. If there is no refuting evidence, then there is nothing to refute the datum. Since possibility is the extent to which the data *fail* to support a datum, the evidence fails completely to rfute the datum, and its possibility is 1.

8.2 If we increase Pos(A) to 0.6, leaving Nec(A) unchanged, it will be imposs-ible to correct an error or resolve a contradiction.

8.3 In a dual-truth-value system, this would not be necessary. But in a necessity-based system, we have no way to store possibilities from one step to the next. A calculated Pos(A) and Nec(NOT A) is lost when we go to the next rule-firing step, and we could end up with inflated necessities in later steps unrest-ricted by the possibility calculated in an earlier step. This is a disadvantage of necessity-based systems; fortunately, by reserving consideration of refuting evidence to the last steps, this disadvantage can be overcome.

8.4 In the simple rule IF A THEN B; A and B are indeed nested since if A is true, B must also be true and A $\Rightarrow$ B. However, in more complex rules such as IF A AND B AND C THEN NOT D none of the four individual propositions A, B, C and D need be nested; the complex proposition A AND B AND C is nested with NOT D, but not with D.

8.5 The failure of max$-$min logic to obey the laws of excluded middle (and non-contradiction) means that the use of min$-$max logic to combine A and NOT A is invalid, since min$-$max logic does not obey the law of the excluded middle (A AND NOT A $= 0$).

9.1 An IDE permits the programmer to access all necessary functions—text editor to write the program, language help files, ability to run the program, and view any resulting error messages—within a single program, the integ-rated program development environment.

9.2 A text editor for writing the programs, preferably syntax-oriented; help files covering a broad area, including review of language syntax and explanation of language keywords; ability to run the program being edited, to set break-points, to trace program execution; ability to examine data during the program run; and display of any error messages generated by the program run while editing the program source code are absolute requirements.

9.3 FLOPS is technologically quite advanced compared to such procedural languages as FORTRAN or C. FLOPS operates procedurally in command mode, and non-procedurally in run mode; FLOPS may be run as a parallel language or as a sequential language, and a single program can use both modes. For this reason, some features such as program breakpoints and data inspection, usually built into the IDE for procedural languages, are built into the FLOPS run-time module.

9.4 Important debugging aids built into the FLOPS run-time module include examining data; viewing fireable rule stacks and history of fired rules; viewing or listing data; rules, and data declarations; ability to exit run mode temporarily and accept keyboard debugging commands.

9.5 The complexity of the FLOPS language compared to procedural languages means that it is not feasible to build all debugging aids into the IDE.

9.6 The TFLOPS task bar provides a "check mark" icon that will run a syntax-checking routine.

9.7 TFLOPS provides an option to set trace levels at no trace, trace rules being fired, trace FLOPS commands being executed, and trace of data created or modified during the FLOPS run.

9.8 The FLOPS "Options" menu provides for creating an output file of the FLOPS run, and displaying this file on return from the run to TFLOPS.

10.1 Data declarations; rules; and data creation.

10.2 First, data declarations; next, rules; next, data creation; finally, the run command.

10.3 Symbols must be defined before they are used in the program; the data declarations define the symbols we will use later.

10.4 A rule, when first created, has no reference to any data previously created. Therefore, since FLOPS is data-driven in run mode, a rule when first created will not be fireable.

10.5 `prstack` prints the lists of fireable rules `prdata` prints the data in detail; and `run N` runs N firing steps, then returns to command mode.

10.6 **a.** The LOCAL stack consists of rules found newly fireable since the last rule-firing step.

b. Rules are listed in order of the `pconf` values, from highest to lowest.

c. `pconf` is the value of the combined rule and antecedent confidences,

10.7 The LOCAL stack is a list of rules found fireable after the last rule-firing step; the PERMANENT stack is a list of rules previously found fireable but not yet fired.

10.8 On the local stack, they are listed in order of their `pconf` values. On the Permanent (backtrack), they are listed in the order in which they were pushed onto the stack, latest on top.

10.9 The `prstack` command presents the name of the fireable rule; the identifying time tags of the data that made the rule fireable; and the `pconf` value of that rule instance.

10.10   Serial FLOPS picks one of the newly fireable rules for firing by a rule-conflict algorithm, and adds any fireable but unfired rules to a backtrack stack for possible firing if no rules are found newly fireable. Parallel FLOPS fires all newly fireable rules, and thus cannot add any unfired rules to the backtrack stack.

10.11   If information must be elicited from a user in a context-dependent fashion, so that the next question to be asked depends on the answer to the previous question, serial FLOPS is to be preferred. IF the information is acquired automatically, or is available at the start of the run, parallel FLOPS is to be preferred. If either method can be used, its lower systems overhead makes parallel FLOPS preferable.

11.1   Conventional computer languages operate sequentially, firing one instruction at a time and taking the next instruction in sequence. FLOPS is a much more complex language, that can operate in command mode, in which source language commands are executed sequentially, or in run mode, in which rules are fired; run mode, in turn, can operate either serially, in which one rule is fired at a time, or in parallel, in which all fireable rules are fired concurrently. This flexibility gives FLOPS power, but also makes both writing and debugging programs more difficult.

11.2   A limited number of debugging features are furnished by TFLOPS. These include syntax checking of the FLOPS program being edited, specifiying an output log file that can be returned TFLOPS on completion of the program run, invoking selectable levels of program trace, display of any run-time errors on return to TFLOPS. However, most FLOPS debugging tools are built into FLOPS itself and executed during the program run.

11.3   Debugging a program during a FLOPS run is done by executing a debugging command, either incorporated in the program itself or, more likely, entered through the keyboard when the run has been temporarily interrupted, and FLOPS returned to command mode with keyboard entry of commands.

11.4   There are several ways to interrupt a FLOPS run temporarily for entry of debug commands.

    For simple FLOPS programs with a single `run;` command at the end of the program, the `run` command may be commented out by preceding it with a colon. After FLOPS reads the program it will then revert to command mode with keyboard entry, and debug commands (including `run N`) can be then entered.

    Executing a `run N` command will cause FLOPS to revert to command mode after N rule-firing steps have been executed. However, if there are more commands in the FLOPS program after the `run N;` is executed, FLOPS will take further commands from the program rather than the keyboard.

    Execution of a `keyboard` or `halt` command will place FLOPS in command mode with keyboard command entry.

Setting a breakpoint at a rule by the `breakpoint` command will interrupt program execution just before that rule is fired.

During a FLOPS run, clicking the <Cancel> button in a message box will temporarily revert FLOPS to command mode with keyboard entry.

Debug commands may be placed in the consequent of a rule, to be executed when that rule is fired.

11.5 A FLOPS program run can be resumed after interruption for keyboard command entry by executing a `resume;` command. `halt` or `keyboard` commands must appear last in the consequent clauses.

11.6 The general types of debugging commands are data inspection; rule inspection; and rule-firing inspection and control; and output logging.

11.7 The absolutely indispensable debugging commands are `prdata`, which permits inspection of current data; `prstack`, which permits listing newly fireable rules and the backtrack rule stack, with the time tags of the data that made the rules fireable; and `run N`, to permit executing a specified number of rule-firing steps, then reverting to command mode.

11.8 the first step is *not* to find the offending statement in the program; instead, the first step is to isolate the defect to a relatively small section of the program. After the defect has been so isolated, we can proceed to find what the defect is and fix it.

11.9 The first step is to have a clear understanding of what the overall program or programs are supposed to do. Obviously, in multiprogram projects the first step is to determine which program is malfunctioning. Each FLOPS program consists of modules: data declarations, rules, data created, or externally input. The rules in turn are modularized into rule blocks, with the firing sequence usually controlled by metarules. We now try to determine which module within a program is malfunctioning. Malfunctions can be caused by several defects, which often manifest themselves by incorrect rule-firing sequence or incorrect data transformations. The most important commands are the basic `prdata`, `prstack`, `run N` basic debugging commands. We must determine that the data are correctly input and modified (`prdata`); and whether the rule-firing sequence is correct as each module is fired (`prstack`). After we determine which module is malfunctioning, whether in incorrect data transformations or incorrect metarule functions, we can proceed further to isolate the problem as incorrect input data, incorrect data declarations, or incorrect rules.

11.10 To detect the actual bug, the basic `prdata`, `prstack`, `run N` basic debugging commands are likely to be inadequate and must be supplemented by the other debugging commands in Table 11.1. In addition to the basic commands, we are likely to need `prule` to review what a rule actually is, `fire status` to determine actual firing status, `explain why` and `explain why not` to determine why rules are or are not fireable;

`explain source <TT>` to find out where a data element came from; `prmem <TT>` to read the contents of a data element whose identifying time tag is known; `prdes` to review a data declaration; `outfile <filename>` and `close <filename>` to open and close a text file to which FLOPS output will be routed for later review; and any other of the debugging commands listed in Table 11.1.

12.1 When acquiring data automatically from some process, we do not ordinarily interrogate the process and ask for some specific data after each datum is received. Instead, the process transmits preselected data at preselected intervals automatically. When acquiring data from a human, however, we will ordinarily ask one question and evaluate the reply. We will then ask another question; which question we ask next usually depends on the previous reply.

12.2 The nodes in a decision tree consists of a hypothesis (in a general sense), and a rule or group of rules to determine the validity of the hypothesis.

12.3 If a hypothesis at a node is accepted, we proceed to the node or nodes just beneath that node. If there are more than one nodes at the next level, we must have a scheme for selecting one of them.

12.4 A rule-conflict algorithm is a scheme for deciding which of a number of con-currently fireable rules will be selected for firing. In a depth-first search of a tree, a rule-conflict algorithm may be used to select which of a number of competing nodes will be selected for test.

12.5 Backtracking takes place when a node hypothesis is rejected and when no rules are newly fireable.

12.6 In backtracking, since no rules are newly fireable, a rule is popped off the top of the backtrack stack and fired. If the backtrack stack is empty, FLOPS reverts to command mode.

12.7 We may place our prior knowledge in rules, or may place our prior knowl-edge in a database and write rules to interpret that database.

12.8 If knowledge is placed in rules, the rules are easier for a user to interpret and follow, at the cost of perhaps massive numbers of rules and difficulty of program maintenance. If knowledge is placed in a database and rules are written to interpret that database, we gain great economy in the number of rules required and greatly ease program maintenance, at the cost of having a program that is difficult for a user to comprehend.

12.9 This is sometimes not an easy question to answer. If our program will inter-rogate a human user, when the next question to be asked depends on the answer to the previous question, a depth-first using sequential rule firing will be best. If the information is entered automatically rather than by a human, as in real-time online work or when reading disk files, it is probable that a breadth-first search using parallel rule-firing will be appropriate. Sometimes a depth-first search is easier to visualize, as in MC.FPS. In general, since parallel rule-firing involves less systems overhead than sequential, a breadth-first search is preferred if there is a choice.

13.1 Defuzzification.

13.2 In both cases. Fuzzification converts an input number into its word equivalents, and permits using words in the antecedent of rules fired later on. This is very useful for both numeric or word answers.

13.3 A discrete fuzzy set is a linguistic variable if its member words describe a number, such as {Small, Medium, Large}, and if membership functions defined on the real line are used to map these words onto the real line. It is not a linguistic variable if the words do not describe a number, such as {Ford, Chevrolet, Chrysler}.

13.4 Non-numeric discrete fuzzy sets, where each member corresponds to an answer, such as {Major_depression, Bipolar_disorder, Schizophrenia}. Alternatively, strings may be output together with their truth values.

13.5 An ambiguity occurs when alternate word descriptors both have non-zero grades of membership, and are not mutually exclusive. A contradiction occurs when, in the same situation, the descriptors are mutually exclusive.

13.6 First, data are input and converted if necessary to an appropriate form, such as fuzzification of numbers into words, converting scalars to fuzzy numbers, screening out obvious artifacts, and maintaining moving averages. Next, rules use the input data to arrive at preliminary conclusions. Next, contradictions are detected and resolved. Then, output candidates are checked for reasonableness and completeness. Finally, the checked final conclusions are output.

13.7 Nothing should be done about ambiguities; they lend robustness to a program, and should be held on to. Contradictions, on the other hand, need to be resolved and check before being output.

14.1 New skills and new factual knowledge.

14.2 By adding new rules or by storing new data.

14.3 If the general format of the new rules is known, the rule can be generated by the consequent of a program rule, the previously unknown elements being filled in by variables defined in the rule antecedent.

14.4 A rule from PAVLOV2.FPS, simplified to omit non-essentials, is

```
rule block 8 (goal Generates rule for response to
conditioned stimuli)
IF (in Count id1 = <ID1> AND id2 = <ID2> AND N > 2)
   (in Wired-in id = <ID1> AND response = <R>)
```

```
THEN
  rule block 3
  IF (in NewStimulus id = ''<ID2>'')
  THEN
    message '<ID2> - LOOK OUT - <ID1> coming\,
<R>!\n';
```

14.5 If we are going to learn by generating new rules, the most important command that relates to learning is `rule`, which actually generates the rule itself. We may also require the command `declare`, which declares a new data element, and `make`, that creates an instance of the new data element.

If we are going to learn by adding facts to a library of expert factual knowledge, we will need the `make` command to create the new data. If we have learned that an old datum is incorrect, we will need the `modify` or `in` commands to modify the old datum, or the `delete` command to get rid of it. If the data are completely new, we may need also the `declare` command to create the template for the new data; in that case, we will usually need new rules to deal with the new data format.

14.6 The rules must be written to interpret the database. This can be done simply by using the data from the database for comparison with new data in the rule antecedent as in AUTO2.FPS, or by using the database to generate new rules as in ECHO.PAR.

14.7 Adding expert factual knowledge to a database is to be preferred, for two reasons. First, this gives considerable economy in the number of rules that must be used. Second, program maintainability is greatly eased; often the program itself does not need to be modified, only the database.

14.8 Use of the FLOPS `string` = and `string` + commands gives complete freedom in the format of new rules and new data elements.

15.1 The major difference between human and process interaction programs is that interaction with a human usually have a tolerance of several seconds for time delays between data input and response; hard-wired programs may require response times measured in milliseconds. Also, it is hard for a defective program that interacts with a human to cause undetected catastrophic results; a defective hard-wired program can cause catastrophic results.

15.2 Detection of particular events, such as alarm conditions or fault diagnosis, can be carried out effectively by real-time on-line fuzzy expert systems.

15.3 The acquire command is used to input and output on-line data.

15.4 The easiest artifact to detect is an out-of-range input value. Out-of-range values of the rate of change of input values can also identify artifacts, but the input data will probably need smoothing to calculate a dependable first derivative.

15.5 An exponentially mapped moving average is a very simple way to smooth data.

15.6 Exponential smoothing effectively introduces a time delay equal to the smoothing time constant.

15.7 The time lag introduced by exponential smoothing can furnish a smoothed past reference value for calculation of rates of change or for comparison with present values for event detection.

15.8 High-frequency noise can be quantitated by squaring the difference between current value and an exponential moving average, and taking a relatively short-time-constant moving average of the squared differences.

15.9 Formulas for the rates of change of sampled input data that correct for the presence of second or higher derivatives can be calculated by using a McClauren series to express the input variable for two or more samples ago, and eliminating terms involving the higher derivatives.

15.10 A typical fuzzy control rule might be

```
IF input is Small and rate is Large then control is
Negative;
```

In this rule input, rate, and control are floating-point numbers; Small, Large, and Negative are members of discrete fuzzy sets, linguistic variables, to which membership functions are attached.

15.11 The notation is very compact; fuzzification and defuzzification are automatic. However, the notation is quite inflexible, and does not permit making the discrete fuzzy sets available for use in later rules or for program output.

15.12 Focused rules usually permit a fuzzy reasoning system to be built with a much smaller number of rules than required by unfocused rules following the typical fuzzy control rule pattern. Such rules also usually produce more reliable outputs. The only disadvantage is that the programmer has to think a lot harder; it is difficult to construct such rules by data mining techniques.

15.13 Since many if not most computer programs use the standard array of Boolean numerical comparison operators, it is not surprising that the programs using fuzzy numbers require the fuzzy version of the common Boolean numerical comparison operators.

15.14 Data-driven sequential-rule-firing programs retain all data in memory, in case they are needed during backtracking. This means that if continuously bringing in data on-line, available memory will be exhausted in a finite length of time.

15.15 Data-driven parallel-rule-firing programs do not retain deleted data or data that has been later modified in memory; since there is no backtracking, old data are not again needed. The result is that real-time on-line programs can run indefinitely without overflowing memory.

15.16   The major steps in a real-time on-line program are data acquisition; data screening; data processing; output validity checks; and program output.

15.17   After development off-line using a fuzzy expert system shell, the program can be recoded using a procedural language, possibly replacing fuzzy logic with interval logic.

15.18   The first stage is to acquire data on disk so that the program can be written and debugged off-line. If the program is to be closed-loop, a way of simulating the process should be found so that the dynamics of a program run can be checked. Processes may be simulated by a digital computer program, an analog computer, or some other process model that will accept the expert system output and produce a response that can be input to the expert system.

REFERENCES

Anderson JR (1993). Rules of the Mind. Lawrence Erlbaum, Mahwah, New Jersey.

Baldwin JF, Martin TP, Pilsworth BW (1995). Fril—Fuzzy and Evidential Reasoning in Artificial Intelligence. Research Studies Press, Taunton, Somerset, England.

Brownston L, Farrell R, Martin N (1985). Programming Expert Systems in OPS5. Addison-Wesley, Reading, Massachusetts.

Buchanan BG, Shortliffe EH, eds (1984). Rule-Based Expert Systems. Addison-Wesley, Reading, Massachusetts.

Buckley JJ, Siler W (1998a). Echocardiogram analysis using fuzzy numbers and relations. Fuzzy Sets and Systems 26: 373–380.

Buckley JJ, Siler W (1998b). A new t-norm. Fuzzy Sets and Systems 100: 283–290.

Buckley JJ, Siler W (1999). L-∞ fuzzy logic. Fuzzy Sets and Systems 107: 309–322.

Combs WE, Andrews JE (1998). Combinatorial rule explosion eliminated by a fuzzy rule configuration. IEEE Trans. Fuzzy Systems 6(1): 1–11.

Cox E (1999). The Fuzzy Systems Handbook: A Practitioner's Guide to Building, Using and Maintaining Fuzzy Systems. Morgan Kaufmann, Los Altos, California.

Cox E (2000). Fuzzy Logic for Business and Industry. Charles River Media, Boston.

de Silva CW (1995). Intelligent Control: Fuzzy Logic Applications. CRC Press, Boca Raton, Florida.

Dempster AP (1967). Upper and lower probabilities induced by a multivalued mapping. Annals Mathematical Statistics 38: 325–339.

Dubois D, Prade H (1988). Possibility Theory: An Approach to Computerized Processing of Uncertainty. Plenum Press, New York.

Elkan D (XXX). The paradoxical success of fuzzy logic.

Feigenbaum EA, Buchanan BG (1993). DENDRAL and Meta-DENDRAL: roots of knowledge systems and expert systems applications. Artificial Intelligence 59: 233–240.

Fisher R (1936). The use of multiple measurements in taxonomic problems. Annals of Eugenics 7 (part 2): 179–188.

Forgy C, Rete L (1982). A fast algorithm for the many pattern/many object pattern match problem. Artificial Intelligence 19: 17–37.

Haykin S (1994). Neural Networks: A Comprehensive Foundation. Prentice-Hall, Englewood Cliffs, New Jersey.

Jackson P (1999). Introduction to Expert Systems. Addison-Wesley, Reading, Massachusetts.

Fuzzy Experts Systems: Theory and Practice, by William Siler and James J. Buckley
ISBN 0-471-38859-9 Copyright © 2005 John Wiley & Sons, Inc.

Kandel A, ed (1991). Fuzzy Expert Systems. CRC Press, Boca Raton, Florida.

Kasabov NK (1998). Foundations of Neural Networks, Fuzzy Systems and Knowledge Engineering. MIT Press, Cambridge, Massachusetts.

Kecman V (2001). Learning and Soft Computing: Support Vector Machines, Neural Networks, and Fuzzy Logic Systems (Complex Adaptive Systems). MIT Press, Cambridge, Massachusetts.

Klir GJ, Yuan B (1995). Fuzzy Sets and Fuzzy Logic: Theory and Applications. Prentice-Hall PTR, Upper Saddle River, New Jersey.

Klir GJ, Yuan B, eds (1996). Fuzzy Sets, Fuzzy Logic and Fuzzy Systems: Selected Papers by Lotfi A. Zadeh. World Scientific, Singapore.

Mamdani EH (1976). Advances in the linguistic synthesis of fuzzy controller. International Journal of Man-Machine Studies 8(6): 669–678.

McDermott J (1980). R1: an expert in the computing system domain. In Proceedings of the National Conference on Artificial Intelligence, 269–271.

Minsky M (1975). A framework for representing knowledge. In The Psychology of Computer Vision, Winston PH, ed, McGraw-Hill, New York.

Mitchell TM (1997). Machine Learning. McGraw-Hill, New York.

Newell A, Simon HA (1972). Human Problem Solving. Prentice-Hall, Englewood Cliffs, New Jersey.

Pedrycz W (1995). Fuzzy Sets Engineering. CRC Press, Boca Raton, Florida.

Quillian MR (1968). Semantic Memory. In Semantic Information Processing, Minsky M, ed, 227–270. MIT Press, Cambridge, Massachusetts.

Ruspini EH (1982). Possibility approaches for advanced information systems. Computer 15: 83–91.

Schank RC, Childers PG (1984). The Cognitive Computer: on Language, Learning and Artificial Intelligence. Pearson Addison-Wesley, New York.

Scott AC, Clayton JE, Gibson EL (1991). A Practical Guide to Knowledge Acquisition. Addison-Wesley, New York.

Shortliffe EH (1976). Computer-Based Medical Consultations: MYCIN. Elsevier, New York.

Siler W, Tucker D, Buckley J (1987). A parallel rule firing production system with resolution of memory conflicts by weak fuzzy monotonicity, applied to the classification of multiple objects characterized by multiple uncertain features. International Journal of Man-Machine Studies 26: 321–332.

Thomas SF (1995). Fuzziness and Probability. ACG Press, Wichita, Kansas.

Weinschenk JJ, Marks II RJ, Combs WE (2003). Layered URC fuzzy systems: a novel link between fuzzy systems and neural networks. Proceedings of the IEEE International Joint Conference on Neural Networks, Portland, Oreson: 2995–3000.

Zadeh LA (1965). Fuzzy sets. Information and Control 8: 338–353.

Zadeh LA (1972). A fuzzy-set-theoretic interpretation of linguistic hedges. Journal of Cybernetics 2: 4–34.

Zadeh LA (1974). On the analysis of large-scale systems. In "Fuzzy Sets and their Application to Cognitive and Decision Processes", Academic Press, New York.

FURTHER READING

Adlassnig KP (1986). Fuzzy set theory in medical diagnosis. IEEE Trans. on Systems, Man and Cybernetics 16(2): 260–265.

Altrock CV (1995). Fuzzy Logic and NeuroFuzzy Applications Explained. Prentice Hall PTR, Upper Saddle River, New Jersey.

Aracil J, Gordillo F, eds (2000). Stability Issues in Fuzzy Control. Physica-Verlag, Heidelberg, Germany.

Bardossy A, Duckstein L (1995). Fuzzy Rule-Based Modeling with Applications to Geophysical, Biological and Engineering Systems. CRC Press, Boca Raton, Florida.

Bellman R, Giertz M (1973). On the analytic formalism of the theory of fuzzy sets. Information Sciences 5: 149–156.

Buckley JJ (2003). Fuzzy Probabilities. Physica-Verlag, Heidelberg, Germany.

Buckley JJ, Feuring T (1999). Fuzzy and Neural: Interactions and Applications. Physica-Verlag, Heidelberg, Germany.

Buckley JJ, Siler W (1987) "Managing Uncertainty in a Fuzzy Expert System. Part I: Combining Uncertainties". Proceedings Second International Fuzzy Systems Association Congress, Tokyo: 737–739.

Buckley JJ, Siler W (1988). Fuzzy numbers for expert systems. *In* "Fuzzy Logic in Knowledge-Based Systems, Decision and Control", MM Gupta and T Yamakawa, eds, North-Holland, Elsevier, New York.

Carnap R, Gardner M (1966). An Introduction to the Philosophy of Science. Basic Books, New York.

Deboeck GJ, ed (1994). Trading on the Edge: Neural, Genetic and Fuzzy Systems for Chaotic Financial Markets. John Wiley & Sons, Inc., New York.

Demicco RV, Klir GJ, eds (2004). Fuzzy Logic in Geology. Elsevier Academic Press, New York.

Driankov D, Hellendom H, Reifrank M (1996). An Introduction to Fuzzy Control. Springer-Verlag, New York.

Dubois D, Prade H (1980). Fuzzy Sets and Systems: Theory and Applications. Academic Press, New York.

Englebrecht AP (2002). Computational Intelligence: An Introduction. John Wiley & Sons, Inc., New York.

Fuller R, Carlsson C (2002). Fuzzy Reasoning in Decision Making and Optimization. Physica-Verlag, Heidelberg, Germany.

Hampel R, Wagenknecht M, Chaker N, eds (2000). Fuzzy Control: Theory and Practice. Physica-Verlag, Heidelberg, Germany.

Hirota K, ed (1994). Industrial Applications of Fuzzy Control. Springer-Verlag, New York.

Kacprycz J (1997). Multistage Fuzzy Control. John Wiley & Sons, Inc., New York.

Kandel A, Langholz G (1993). Fuzzy Control Systems. CRC Press, Boca Raton, Florida.

Kosko B (1993). Fuzzy Thinking—the New Science of Fuzzy Logic. Hyperion, New York.

Leonides C (1998). Fuzzy Logic and Expert Systems Applications. Academic Press, New York.

Mamdani EH, Gaines BR, eds (1981). Fuzzy Reasoning and Its Applications. Academic Press, New York.

McNeil D (1994). Fuzzy Logic: the Revolutionary Computer Science Technique That Is Changing Our World. Simon and Schuster, New York.

Mendel JM (2000). Uncertain Rule-Based Fuzzy Logic Systems: Introduction and New Directions. Pretice-Hall PTR, Upper Saddle River, New Jersey.

Mendelson E (1966). Introduction to Mathematical Logic. van Nostrand, Princeton, New Jersey.

Moore RE (1979). Methods and Applications of Interval Analysis. SIAM, Philadelphia.

Nelles O (2000). Nonlinear System Identification: From Classical Approaches to Neural Networks and Fuzzy Models. Springer-Verlag, New York.

Pedrycz W, Gomide F. (1998). An Introduction to Fuzzy Sets: Analysis and Design of Complex Adaptive Systems. MIT Press, Cambridge, Massachusetts.

Ragin CC (2000). Fuzzy-Set Social Science. University of Chicago Press, Chicago, Illinois.

Siler W (1995). Fuzzy Reasoning. PCAI 9: 22.

Siler W (2001). "Building Fuzzy Expert Systems." http://users.aol.com/wsiler/

Siler W, Buckley JJ (1987). "Managing Uncertainty in a Fuzzy Expert System. Part II: Truth Maintenance System". Proceedings Second International Fuzzy Systems Association Congress, Tokyo: pp. 744–746.

Siler W, Martens J (2001). Hemodynamic Alarm System for Pulmonary Artery Catheters. Proceedings of International Fuzzy Systems Association, Vancouver, BC Canada: 1967–1972. IEEE Press.

Siler W, Ying H (1987). Signal processing using a general-purpose fuzzy expert system. Conference Record, Twenty-first Asilomar Conference on Signals, Systems and Computers Vol. 2, 715–718. IEEE Computer Society, Los Alamitos, California.

Slowinski R, ed (1998). Fuzzy Sets in Decision Analysis, Operations Research and Statistics. Kluwer, New York.

Terano T, Asai K, Sugeno M (1992). A Complete Introduction to the Field: Fuzzy Systems Theory and its Applications. Academic Press, New York.

Terano T, Asi K, Sugeno M, eds (1995). Applied Fuzzy Systems. AP Professional, New York.

Verbruggen HK, Babuska R, eds (1999). Fuzzy Logic Control: Advances in Applications. World Scientific, Singapore.

Weinschenk JJ, Combs WE, Marks II RJ (2003). Avoidance of rule explosion by mapping fuzzy systems to a disjunctive rule configuration. Proc IEEE Int'l Conference on Fuzzy Systems, St. Louis, Missouri: 43–48.

INDEX

Fuzzy Expert Systems and Fuzzy Reasoning, By William Siler and James J. Buckley
ISBN 0-471-38859-9 Copyright © 2005 John Wiley & Sons, Inc.

Printed and bound by CPI Group (UK) Ltd, Croydon, CR0 4YY

27/10/2024

14580330-0003